China Turns to Multilat

China's recent rapid economic growth has drawn global attention to its foreign policy, which increasingly has had an impact on world politics. In contrast with China's long-standing preference for bilateralism or unilateralism in foreign policy, recent decades have seen changes in the PRC's attitude and in its declaratory and operational policies, with a trend toward the accepting and advocating of multilateralism in international affairs. Whilst China's involvement has been primarily in the economic arena, for example, participation in the World Trade Organization and ASEAN+3, it has more recently expanded into international security institutions, such as the Shanghai Cooperation Organization.

This book records, analyses, and attempts to conceptualize this phenomenal development in Chinese foreign policy and its impact on international relations, with the emphasis on China's active participation in multilaterally oriented regional security regimes. Written by an impressive team of international scholars, this book is the first collective effort in the field of China studies and international relations to look at China's recent turn to multilateralism in foreign affairs. It will appeal to students and scholars of Chinese politics and foreign policy, security studies, and international relations.

Guoguang Wu holds Chair in China and Asia-Pacific Relations at the University of Victoria, where he is also Associate Professor of Political Science and History. **Helen Lansdowne** is Assistant Director at the Centre for Asia-Pacific Initiatives, and also lectures at the University of Victoria and at Camosun College.

Routledge contemporary China series

1 **Nationalism, Democracy and National Integration in China**
   Leong Liew and Wang Shaoguang

2 **Hong Kong's Tortuous Democratization**
   A comparative analysis
   Ming Sing

3 **China's Business Reforms**
   Institutional challenges in a globalised economy
   Edited by Russell Smyth and Cherrie Zhu

4 **Challenges for China's Development**
   An enterprise perspective
   Edited by David H. Brown and Alasdair MacBean

5 **New Crime in China**
   Public order and human rights
   Ron Keith and Zhiqiu Lin

6 **Non-Governmental Organizations in Contemporary China**
   Paving the way to civil society?
   Qiusha Ma

7 **Globalization and the Chinese City**
   Fulong Wu

8 **The Politics of China's Accession to the World Trade Organization**
   The dragon goes global
   Hui Feng

9 **Narrating China**
   Jia Pingwa and his fictional world
   Yiyan Wang

10 **Sex, Science and Morality in China**
   Joanne McMillan

11 **Politics in China Since 1949**
   Legitimizing authoritarian rule
   Robert Weatherley

12 **International Human Resource Management in Chinese Multinationals**
   Jie Shen and Vincent Edwards

13 **Unemployment in China**
   Economy, human resources and labour markets
   Edited by Grace Lee and Malcolm Warner

14 **China and Africa**
   Engagement and compromise
   Ian Taylor

15 **Gender and Education in China**
   Gender discourses and women's schooling in the early twentieth century
   Paul J. Bailey

16 **SARS**
   Reception and interpretation in three Chinese cities
   Edited by Deborah Davis and Helen Siu

17 **Human Security and the Chinese State**
   Historical transformations and the modern quest for sovereignty
   Robert E. Bedeski

18 **Gender and Work in Urban China**
   Women workers of the unlucky generation
   Liu Jieyu

19 **China's State Enterprise Reform**
   From Marx to the market
   John Hassard, Jackie Sheehan, Meixiang Zhou, Jane Terpstra-Tong and Jonathan Morris

20 **Cultural Heritage Management in China**
   Preserving the cities of the Pearl River Delta
   Edited by Hilary du Cros and Yok-shiu F. Lee

21 **Paying for Progress**
   Public finance, human welfare and inequality in China
   Edited by Vivienne Shue and Christine Wong

22 **China's Foreign Trade Policy**
   The new constituencies
   Edited by Ka Zeng

23 **Hong Kong, China**
   Learning to belong to a nation
   Gordon Mathews, Tai-lok Lui, and Eric Kit-wai Ma

24 **China Turns to Multilateralism**
   Foreign policy and regional security
   Edited by Guoguang Wu and Helen Lansdowne

China Turns to Multilateralism

Foreign policy and regional security

**Edited by Guoguang Wu and
Helen Lansdowne**

LONDON AND NEW YORK

First published 2008
by Routledge
2 Park Square, Milton Park, Abingdon, Oxon, OX14 4RN

Simultaneously published in the USA and Canada
by Routledge
711 Third Avenue, New York, NY 10017

Routledge is an imprint of the Taylor & Francis Group, an informa business

First issued in paperback 2011

© 2008 Selection and editorial matter Guoguang Wu and Helen Lansdowne; individual chapters, the contributors

Typeset in Times by Wearset Ltd, Boldon, Tyne and Wear

All rights reserved. No part of this book may be reprinted or reproduced or utilized in any form or by any electronic, mechanical, or other means, now known or hereafter invented, including photocopying and recording, or in any information storage or retrieval system, without permission in writing from the publishers.

British Library Cataloguing in Publication Data
A catalogue record for this book is available from the British Library

Library of Congress Cataloging in Publication Data
A catalog record for this book has been requested

ISBN10: 0-415-42571-9 (hbk)
ISBN10: 0-415-66646-5 (pbk)
ISBN10: 0-203-94632-4 (ebk)

ISBN13: 978-0-415-42571-1 (hbk)
ISBN13: 978-0-415-66646-6 (pbk)
ISBN13: 978-0-203-94632-9 (ebk)

Contents

List of illustrations x
Contributors xi
Acknowledgements xiv

PART I
Introduction 1

1 **International multilateralism with Chinese characteristics: attitude changes, policy imperatives, and regional impacts** 3
  GUOGUANG WU AND HELEN LANSDOWNE

PART II
Global concerns 19

2 **China's new internationalism** 21
  LOWELL DITTMER

3 **Racing to integrate, or cooperating to compete? Liberal and realist interpretations of China's new multilateralism** 35
  THOMAS G. MOORE

4 **The new player in the game: China, arms control, and multilateralism** 51
  JING-DONG YUAN

Contents

PART III
Regional security   73

5   China's multilateralism and regional order   75
MICHAEL YAHUDA

6   China and the North Korean nuclear problem: diplomatic initiative, strategic complexities, and relevance of security multilateralism   90
SHI YINHONG

7   China and SCO: towards a new type of interstate relations   104
JIANWEI WANG

8   Chinese and ASEAN responses to the US Regional Maritime Security Initiative   127
GAYE CHRISTOFFERSEN

9   Maritime security and multilateral interactions between China and its neighbours   147
KEYUAN ZOU

PART IV
Peaceful rise?   173

10   Intentions on trial: "peaceful rise" and Sino-ASEAN relations   175
YONGNIAN ZHENG AND SOW KEAT TOK

11   Peaceful rise? Soft power? Human rights in China's new multilateralism   198
JEREMY PALTIEL

12   China's petroleum diplomacy: Hu Jintao's biggest challenge in foreign and security policy   222
WILLY WO-LAP LAM

13   China's multilateralism and its impact on cross-strait relations: a view from Taipei   241
DONG-CHING DAY

14   **An exception to the growing emphasis on multilateralism: the case of China's policy towards Hong Kong**   253
JEAN-PHILIPPE BÉJA

PART V
Conclusion   265

15   **Multiple levels of multilateralism: the rising China in the turbulent world**   267
GUCGUANG WU

Index   290

Illustrations

Figure

13.1 Changes in the Taiwanese/Chinese identity as tracked in
surveys by the Election Study Centre, NCCU   248

Tables

4.1 China and international/multilateral nonproliferation treaties/
regimes   59
4.2 Evolution of China's export control system since the 1990s 63
9.1 Selected marine laws of the people's republic of China   150
9.2 Contracting parties to the LOS convention in East Asia   151

Contributors

Jean-Philippe Béja Senior Researcher at the Centre of International Research in Paris and at the Centre National de la Recherche Scientifique, he is a member of the Editorial Board of *China Perspectives*, Perspectives Chinoises and Chinese Cross-Currents (Macau). He supervises PhD dissertations at IEP and at Ecole des Hautes Etudes en Sciences Sociales, Paris. Areas of research are: Chinese politics, the changing nature of the Chinese political system, the emergence of new social categories, floating labour (mingong) and entrepreneurs, the intellectuals and the Party: 1949–97, the history and politics of Hong Kong, and the Wenzhou communities in Europe.

Gaye Christoffersen Associate Professor of Political Science at Soka University of America, Aliso Viejo, California. She has previously taught at the Naval Postgraduate School, Chinese Foreign Affairs University, and Far Eastern National University in Vladivostok (the latter two as a Fulbright Lecturer). Her teaching and research interests include Chinese studies, Asia-Pacific international relations, Asian multilateralism and Northeast Asian oil politics. In her teaching and research, she has tried to foster a wider dialogue about US–China relations among her colleagues and Chinese government officials.

Dong-ching Day Adjunct Assistant Professor at Chihlee College of Technology and Research Fellow at the Foundation on International and Cross-Strait Studies (FICS).

Lowell Dittmer Professor of Political Science at the University of California at Berkeley and editor of *Asian Survey*. He has written or edited *Sino-Soviet Normalization and its International Implications* (1992), *China's Quest for National Identity* (with Samuel Kim, 1993), *China Under Reform* (1994), *Liu Shaoqi and the Chinese Cultural Revolution* (rev. edn, 1997), (with Haruhiro Fukui and Peter N.S. Lee), *Informal Politics in East Asia* (Cambridge, 2000), and many scholarly articles. His most recent book is *South Asia's Nuclear Security Dilemma: India, Pakistan, and China* (Armonk: M.E. Sharpe, 2005).

Willy Wo-Lap Lam is Professor of China and Global Studies, Akita International University, Japan, and a Senior Fellow at Jamestown Foundation, a foreign-policy think tank in Washington, DC. He is the author of *The Era of Jiang Zemin*; his book on the Hu Jintao administration will be appearing soon.

Helen Lansdowne has a BA and MA in Pacific and Asian Studies, University of Victoria and has been with CAPI since 1998. Ms Lansdowne's area of expertise is rural China state–society relations. Her most recent area of study includes mainland Southeast Asia, particularly development and gender related issues. Her work at CAPI includes assisting with the Centre's CIDA funded Projects, Cambodia–Canada Legislative Support Project and Vietnam Legislative Assistance Support Project. In addition, she oversees the publications at the Centre and is in charge of overall administration of CAPI's various programs. Ms Lansdowne also teaches courses on Southeast Asia and Developmental Theory in the Department of Pacific and Asian Studies at UVic and in the Department of Social Sciences at Camosun College

Thomas G. Moore Associate Professor, Department of Political Science, University of Cincinnati. Areas of teaching and research specialization include international political economy, US foreign policy, and Asian politics. Among other publications, he is the author of *China in the World Market: International Sources of Reform and Modernization in the Post-Mao Era* (Cambridge University Press, 2002).

Jeremy Paltiel Associate Professor, Department of Political Science, Carleton University. He specializes in comparative politics, Chinese politics and society, government and foreign policies of Asia (China and Japan), and development politics.

Shi Yinhong Professor of International Relations, Director of American Studies, Renmin University, Beijing. He is a leading scholar in China on the history of international politics, strategic studies, and foreign policies of China and the United States.

Sow Keat Tok A research associate in the China Policy Institute, University of Nottingham, UK. Previously, he worked as a research officer in the East Asian Institute, National University of Singapore between January 2004 and December 2005, where he co-authored many in-house publications on China's foreign policy, including China–ASEAN, China–Japan, and China–Hong Kong relations. He had also produced several works analysing Chinese foreign-policy thinking.

Jianwei Wang Professor and Eugene Katz Letters and Science Distinguished Faculty Member, Department of Political Science, University of Wisconsin-Stevens Point; Guest Professor, School of International and Public Affairs, Fudan University. US–China relations expert, a prolific scholar whose areas of interest also include East Asian international relations, Chinese foreign policy, and Sino-Japanese relations.

Guoguang Wu China Chair in Asia-Pacific Relations, Centre for Asia-Pacific Initiatives, and Associate Professor of Department of Political Science and

Department of History, University of Victoria. Research interests include comparative politics (developing, authoritarian, and communist countries), liberalization and democratization, East Asian politics, China, Hong Kong, Taiwan, Asia-Pacific international relations, and Chinese political thought.

Michael Yahuda Professor Emeritus of International Relations, the London School of Economics and Political Science, currently a Fellow at the Woodrow Wilson International Center for Scholars, Washington, DC. Areas of interest are politics and foreign relations of China, Hong Kong, Taiwan, and international relations of Asia and the Pacific.

Jing-dong Yuan is Director of the education program for East Asia Nonproliferation Program at the Center for Nonproliferation Studies, and an Associate Professor of International Policy Studies at the Monterey Institute of International Studies where he teaches Chinese Politics, Northeast Asian Security and Arms Control, Chinese Nonproliferation and Security Policy, Comparative National Security Policy Making, US Asia Policy, Export Controls, and the multi-lingual Current Issues in Nonproliferation. A graduate of the Xi'an Foreign Language University, People's Republic of China (1982), he received his PhD in Political Science from Queen's University in 1995 and has had research and teaching appointments at Queen's University, York University, the University of Toronto, and the University of British Columbia, where he was a recipient of the prestigious Iaazk Killam Postdoctoral Research Fellowship. He is the co-author of *China and India: Cooperation or Conflict?* (Lynne Rienner, 2003).

Yongnian Zheng Professor and Head of Research, China Policy Institute, University of Nottingham, UK. Research and teaching interests include nationalism and international relations, international and regional security in East Asia, China's foreign policy, globalization, state transformation and social justice, social movements and democratization, comparative central–local relations, and Chinese politics.

Keyuan Zou is Senior Research Fellow at the East Asian Institute (EAI), National University of Singapore. His speciality is international law and Chinese law. He obtained LLD (JSD) in 1989 from Peking University in China. Before joining EAI in 1998, he taught and conducted researches at Dalhousie University (Canada), Peking University (China), and University of Hannover (Germany). He has published *Law of the Sea in East Asia* (London/New York: Routledge, 2005), *China's Marine Legal System and the Law of the Sea* (Leiden/Boston: Martinus Nijhoff, 2005), and over 40 articles in international refereed journals. He is member of the editorial boards of the *International Journal of Marine and Coastal Law*, *Ocean Development and International Law*, the *Chinese Journal of International Law*, and the *China Ocean Law Review*. He has been appointed as Academic Advisor to the China National Institute for the South China Sea Studies since 2000.

Acknowledgements

The editors would like to acknowledge, first of all, the generous support provided by the Foundation on International and Cross-Strait Studies (FICS), which enabled a conference on 'China's Diplomacy of Multilateralism' in December 2004. This volume is the fruit of that conference. In particularly, we thank our friends at the FICS, especially Jonathan Chen, for their help in applying for the conference grant.

The Centre for Asia-Pacific Initiatives at the University of Victoria, with which we are affiliated, organized the conference and facilitated the editing of this publication. Our colleagues at CAPI, including Richard King, Director; Heidi Tyedmers, Program Officer; Joseph Kess, Chair in Japan and Asia-Pacific Relations; and Andrew Harding, Chair in Asia-Pacific Legal Relations, provided great personal, intellectual, and administrative support. Our special thanks go to Stella Chan, CAPI Secretary, who undertook the hard work from conference organizing to volume editing with constant enthusiasm and efficiency.

We are grateful to all the contributors to this volume, and to other participants in the 2004 conference, including those who served as discussants and chairs. Their input made this volume possible.

Stephanie Rogers, our editor at Routledge, has shown her confidence in the volume and has demonstrated her outstanding professionalism since the beginning. She and her colleagues, Helen Baker and Hayley Norton, have been very supportive throughout the process, turning the original drafts of chapters into a book. The anonymous review was helpful for improving the manuscript.

Thanks also go to our families: for Helen Lansdowne to Fenwick, Tristram and Emma, for Guoguang Wu to Xiaoying, Sandy and Felix. They understand perfectly how a collective endeavour often occupies a great amount of the editors' time that would otherwise belong to them.

Finally, we are happy to dedicate this volume to William (Bill) Neilson, our former colleague and Director at the Centre for Asia-Pacific Initiatives and Chair in Asia-Pacific Legal Relations, as a small appreciation of his leadership, mentorship, and friendship.

Guoguang Wu and Helen Lansdowne

Part I
Introduction

1 International multilateralism with Chinese characteristics
Attitude changes, policy imperatives, and regional impacts

Guoguang Wu and Helen Lansdowne

China's turn to multilateral diplomacy: phenomenon and questions

China's recent turn to multilateralism in its foreign policy, as evidenced in both its declaratory and operational polices,[1] has been both apparent and demonstrated in China's increasing involvement in global and regional multilateral organizations. First and foremost, this involvement has been in the economic arena,[2] but now, in the new century, it has remarkably advanced into international security institutions. This volume records, analyses, and attempts to conceptualize this phenomenal development in Chinese foreign policy and its impact on international relations, with the emphasis on China's active participation in multilaterally oriented regional security regimes.

Notoriously, China has for a long time clung to bilateralism or unilateralism in its handling of regional disputes and managing of its foreign relations. Yet, also notoriously, China has constantly, over the decades since 1949, changed its ways and styles of dealing with the outside world in responding to various shifting internal and external factors. This recent multilateralistic adjustment, however, is nevertheless phenomenal enough to call serious attention to it. More than ever before, this adjustment brings the People's Republic of China (PRC) much closer to the evolving Western mentality in the way of viewing world affairs, as, concurrently, multilateralism rises as a principle in the guidance of governmental foreign-policy making in major advanced industrialized countries. This is true except in the case of the United States, but even there multilateralism is equally as powerful as everywhere else in intellectual thought, even though not so in the governmental mentality of constructing the new world since the September 11 tragedy. These two intellectual disparities, namely, that between the United States administration and other democratic countries, and that between the administration and others within the United States, help situate the multilateralistic China in the "mainstream" of international mentality of post-Cold War world politics. Partially due to such closeness between Beijing's declaration of multilateralism and the intellectual trend of international politics, China's multilateralist turn is widely applauded in Western public opinion, praised as China's "new diplomacy."[3] This welcome is extended to China not totally from real-politik considerations as it once emerged during the period of Cold-War strategic tripolarity. Rather, it is based on a perceived share by China of the principles prevailing in international societies of knowledge and, with some limits, of policy, to conduct post-Cold War world politics.

Some questions arise concerning the Chinese concept of "multilateralism," however, as one notices that the phrase is repeated in almost every foreign-policy statement issued by Beijing. What is the Chinese notion of "multilateralism" as it is reflected in both rhetoric and practice of Chinese foreign policy? Has Beijing heartily embraced this principle as it is understood in international society, or has China redefined it with its own understanding? Or has it "correctly" comprehended the concept but intentionally practised it with "Chinese characteristics," to use an infamous phrase affiliated with the new "socialism" in reform China that reflects the Chinese leaders' skill in holding onto Communist dogmatism while practising revisionism? If they are embracing international multilateralism, why are they doing so? If they have their own "multilateralism," what is it? What is the difference between international multilateralism and the Chinese understanding of it? Why did the PRC leaders choose a revisionist version of multilateralism rather than inventing their own doctrine of foreign policy? How does China incorporate multilateralism into its deep-rooted real-politik perception and practice of international politics?

Whatever the answers to these questions, the phenomenon requires further explanations. In other words, in whatever sense China embraces multilateralism, why has this new policy orientation occurred? What, among those elements explaining policy adjustment, such as interest calculation, policy learning, structural transformation, domestic politics, and the like, better accounts for the Chinese multilateralistic turn? How did the leaders in Beijing balance those different factors shaping their foreign-policy choice? What does this Chinese policy change reveal for our knowledge of international politics, foreign policy, and, in particular, of the Chinese logic in the playing of both?

Equally important are the questions of the policy practice and its impact on China's multilateralist adjustment. Needless to say, the policy implications of such an embracing by China of multilateralism and, therefore, the embracing by Western societies of China's multilateral adjustment are profound yet complicated. As China emerges as a great power in economic, military, and diplomatic terms, particularly in East, Southeast, and Central Asia, a policy and behaviour change of China in dealing with regional and global issues inevitably affects, first and foremost, regional stability and, generally, international security. The problems regarding the implications of China's diplomacy of multilateralism in a wider sense are as significant as those concerning the concept and mechanism of the policy. What implications does the Chinese multilateralistic turn of diplomacy have, first of all, on China's role in Asia and the Pacific? How do regional systems of international relations interplay with China's adjustment of foreign engagement? Are those volatile regions neighbouring China, namely, the Taiwan Strait, the Korean Peninsula, and South China Sea, safer and more stable than before with a multilateral China? And, how does China's multilateralism contribute to, or influence, security on those hot points?

Addressing the global level, is the multilateralist China now a responsible player in international relations? As international security is the arena in which cooperation and multilateralism are arguably difficult to achieve, how could China realize its multilateralism in regional and global security affairs?

In both the theoretical and practical senses, the shaping of multilateral regimes in the East, Southeast and Central Asian regions and the dynamic involvement of China therein have formed a front-line territory to which students of international politics and Chinese foreign policy should pay much attention. This volume, based on the papers presented to the conference "China's Diplomacy of Multilateralism," organized in December 2004 by Centre for Asia-Pacific Initiatives, University of Victoria, is a scholarly effort to venture collectively into that territory. Although many previous studies have already noticed the significant change in Chinese foreign policy, this volume is the first systematic examination of the phenomenon. Since the beginning of the twenty-first century, China has broadened its multilateral participation beyond economics to the security realm, moving in the direction of cooperative security. This is the central concern of this volume. For sketching the arguments presented in this collection, this introductory chapter will be organized according to the discussions of the three groups of questions, namely, those concerning the concept, motivations, and implications of Chinese multilateralism.

Multilateralism and multipolarism: combining concept with reality

Scholars of international politics agree that multilateralism can be defined as the "practice of coordinating national policies in groups of three or more states, through ad hoc arrangements or by means of institutions."[4] This concept highlights two dimensions of international multilateralism, namely, that of multilateral institutional involvement and that of policy practice substantively affected by such involvement.

In the first regard, involvement and participation in international organizations, governmental and non-governmental, regional and global, are, of course, an important way to practise multilateralism. By this standard, China is increasingly practising multilateralism, as many chapters in this volume as well as some previous publications indicate. This practice of China can actually be traced back to the 1980s, when China opened its doors through economic liberalization reforms. Since then, China has developed an expanding involvement in regional and global interstate politics and various international, multilateral organizations, and has benefited much from such participation in terms of technology transfer, trade development, foreign-investment inflow, and cultural and educational exchanges.[5] Such active participation in international organizations has been recently extended to the spheres beyond those such as the economy, culture, science and technology, and one primary feature of the development lies in its increasing role in, and contributing to, regional and global multilateral institutions in areas such as arms control, regional security, environment protection, intellectual property rights, and even human rights.[6] To Beijing, "it no longer necessarily views such institutions as a potential means of punishing or coercing China."[7] Rather, they are perceived as effective channels through which China is adapting itself to wider international society.

China's multilateral institutional involvement is highly selective, however. So is that of every nation, and meaningful exploration should ask the question: what is the criterion behind China's selection of multilateral involvement? This volume suggests the following answers.

First, so as to increase its multilateral involvement, China manages to strengthen its status as a regional, and even a world, power that is not strictly bound to multilateral coordination. It sounds contradictory to say that multilateral participation is used to ensure, or enlarge, space in which the participant seeks release from the binding of multilateral coordination, but this is seen to be true as one looks closely at China's selection of such participation. One typical example is shown in China's different attitudes toward the United Nations and the Group 8. In the UN, China enjoys the privilege of veto power through its permanent membership in the Security Council, ranking it as an equal to the other four world powers, France, Russia, the United Kingdom, and the United States. In particular, China is the single one, among the five, which is featured with its economic status as a developing nation, its political characteristics as undemocratic (Russia can be at least viewed as a proto-democracy), and culturally with a non-European heritage. The combination of UN Security Council procedures and China's uniqueness does not hurt China. Rather, it forcefully strengthens China's special position in this multilateral international institution. Further, most of the UN member countries are developing rather than developed, undemocratic or quasi-/proto-democratic rather than democratic, and are non-European. Among these, China can easily find its supporters who together can help get rid of constraints imposed on their policies by their institutional participation of the UN. In other words, China's "minority" identity in the UN Security Council highlights its importance rather than its weakness in world politics, and this strength, in turn, through the institutional guarantee of the bottom line that China can veto what it dislikes, empowers China's bargaining position in policy coordination. This means an intricate situation in which China can compromise less, in comparison with some other members and with its own position in some other international organizations, in policy coordination while activating its organizational involvement. This is conceptually paradoxical, but practically ideal to China's interest.

Imagine that China joins the G8 to make it the G9. China would still be a "minority" combining all developing, undemocratic, and non-European identities (non-European Japan does not have the other two features and Russia's status in all three respects is fuzzy), but this identity loses both procedural and organizational strengths because the decision-making process of the G9 is around consensus-building without veto power of any member, and there is nothing similar to that in the UN Security Council. Despite the fact that China's economic size has been rapidly increasing and is reported to be already ranked the fifth or even fourth largest economy in the world, this cannot guarantee China a position within the G9 as the fourth greatest power, assuming that there are ranks among the members. Rather, China would feel uneasy among the industrialized, democratic, European–American powers, particularly following the result of the G9's coordination, even though China takes part in the coordination process. This is to say, the dimension of policy coordination is less important than institutional involvement to the concept of Chinese multilateralism, as it is reflected in its multilateral practice.

The second clue to comprehend the hidden criterion of China's selection of multilateral involvement also points to China's self-perception as a power and its perception of other powers. It is no doubt that China takes extremely active roles, often leading roles, in regional rather than global multilateralism, to the degree that China initiated the shaping of some ad hoc regional multilateral institutions, as in the cases of the Shanghai Cooperation Organization (SCO), the ASEAN Plus One, and, very recently, the East Asian Summit. The absence of industrialized democratic powers, in particular the United States, from the organizations and mechanisms is quite natural due to the institutions' regional nature. Some of such organizations, however, have gradually revealed China's deep intention against, or, at least deep suspicion of, the United States' involvement in regional affairs. As China constantly makes its effort to warm up Sino-US relations, a convincing interpretation of the China-led-de-Americanization of regional affairs is that China attempts to practise regional multilateralism to develop a collective strength against the sole hegemony of the United States in today's world.

This practical concept of multilateralism is consistent with China's emphasis on "multipolarism," which indicates a diversified international power structure preferred by China in the post-Cold War world. Scholars agree that a multipolar system of world politics could accord China greater leverage and influence.[8] And, to our analysis, multilateralism is a convenient way for a weaker power like China to build up its position as one "pole" among other powers, as it may enable such a nation as China to utilize regional international organizational power to expand its sphere of influence and increase at least its bargaining position in balancing other stronger powers. In particular, many interpret the reality of post-Cold War world power structure "unipolarity" rather than multipolarity, which means to China that there is a gap between the real map and its preferred picture, and the efforts to overcome the gap must include multilateral involvement selected for China's benefit while balancing the sole super power. Multilateralism, as practised, can curb power politics, being an organizational tool of power politics, and is indeed different from scholars' idealistic concept of international coordination.

The new Chinese multilateralism, therefore, has to be understood with its combination with multipolarism, the two being used together as a double-track strategy to deal with the United States, the single super power (the reality of which China is fully, though perhaps painfully, aware), and to shape China's desired future structure of world politics. This combination is Chinese and political in practice, as Beijing modifies the international notion of multilateralism with its diplomacy of "Chinese characteristics." It is also scholarly, however, as it reveals that one cannot simply embrace the Western concept of multilateralism to comprehend China's multilateral conducts of foreign relations. The sophistication embedded in China's subtle "new" diplomacy excludes a single-line observation of the relevant developments. China, on the one hand, makes much effort to cultivate strong working relations with the United States for economic, trade, and technology benefits. China's recognition, acceptance, and even appraisal of American strategic presence in the regions neighbouring China highlights the fact that China is not yet powerful enough to replace the United States in the regions, and that those states, in particular the ASEAN countries, also worry to some degree about China's threat. If the game is zero-sum between China and the United States, China's access into, say, Southeast Asia is potentially greatly limited. China thus turns to "co-existence" with the United States in the regions, while developing close, if not closer in the comparison with the United States' relations with the region, connections with the region via regional multilateral conducts. On the other hand, the recent development in Central Asia indicates that as China becomes powerful enough and the cooperation between China and a neighbouring nation ripe enough, China would be happy to see the withdrawal, or at least shrinking, either forced or voluntary, of the United States' presence there. Optimists can find something positive in China's cooperation with and contribution to the regional order, as stated by Yahuda's chapter in this volume, for instance, in which the United States is a vital player for regional security, but sceptics may see, as Yahuda's sophisticated analysis to some degree at the same time suggests, the marginalization of the United States in the region and, as some recent developments indicate, the "squeezing-out" of American military dominance there.

Selective multilateralism means that there are areas in which China does not want to be bound by multilateral diplomacy, and where it likes to continue to employ a bilateralist and even a unilateralist approach. As it selects multilateral involvements, formal participation in international organizations (IOs), after all, does not necessarily mean "multilateralism," nor does it necessarily mean that the more IOs a country participates in, the more multilateral is the country's foreign policy. In Dittmer's chapter, we can find that as the United States is ranked ninth in the world in the number of IOs it takes part in, the Bush Administration is often criticized for its unilateralism. China is no exception to this intricate phenomenon: as the academia may be progressive enough to seize every new element of international politics that helps coordination, cooperation, and eventually peace, power politics can still be behind all those embracing of politicians of new concepts and even new ways of practice. Multilateralism does occur in China's foreign policy, but it is not something of brand-new thinking. At best, it blends Chinese flavour of multipolarism in power politics with multilateral practice; at worst, it offers a fancy way to encapsulate, or even make manifest, the ideal of power politics.

Why multilateralism? Interpreting the Chinese imperatives

Why this blending or encapsulating? The answer must be that multilateralism provides something valuable that other ways of diplomatic conduct are not able to offer, if we follow the trend of thinking that emphasizes purpose and meaning to explain international relations and foreign policy.[9] In the chapters collected in this volume, the contributors emphasize different yet complementary imperatives that stimulate China to incline to multilateral participation and even, to a less degree, multilateral coordination. Here the summary of those imperatives follows.

Multilateralism as a strategy of economic development in the era of globalization Since the beginning of the economic reform in the late 1970s through the decades after, China has constantly sought material and technological benefits through its participation in international organizations, "attaining asymmetric gains whenever possible."[10] This volume finds further evidence to support the observation that China intentionally and eagerly seeks multilateral channels as effective venues for gaining economic benefits under the new background of globalization, and provides a new observation that China's participation in regional security multilateral mechanisms is also often economics-oriented for serving China's ambitious plan to economically "rise."

Previously, scholars have found that multilateral organizations are treated as a kind of global collective good, and China struggles to be a free rider. "The more free rides China takes the better," as "functional IGOs are treated as the most cost-effective "delivery boys" for global information, science, and technology."[11] This volume contributes further understanding of such behaviour of China with some more characteristics. First of all, China welcomes globalization, and the economic globalization promotes China's learning to take multilateralism for advancing national economic and security interests. Yahuda asserts that multilateralism is part of China's active foreign policy in which new political approaches "have been harnessed to serve China's immediate and longer-term economic interest," while Dittmer finds a reciprocal process in China's foreign-policy leaning and the nation's economic interest, as the former is not only caused by the latter but also has changed China's interpretation of the latter.

Second, this is also consistent with multipolarism, as multipolarity is better for economic expansion.[12] Economic imperatives are thus also applicable to China's recent active involvement in multilateral security regimes, which also has positive implications to Chinese economic development in terms of promoting regional stability and peaceful surroundings for China's concentration on economic development, as well as being beneficial for resource drawing to China.

Multilateralism as a convenient balance against the hegemonic power
Traditionally, the forming of an alliance has been widely practised as an effective way to construct the balance of world power.[13] This situation is not easy and

convenient to apply to post-Cold War China, partially due to the following facts: first, ideology often has impact on alliance formation,[14] which the communist China, even though being revisionist to many degrees, does not share with other major countries in the Asian regions and the world. Second, with the collapse of the Soviet Union, China has had to seek security in a world of unchallenged US military might and in which no major power rivals, perhaps except China per se, exist in Asia.[15]

These two factors, on the other hand, offer China some powerful imperatives to advocate multilateralism. In terms of ideology or guiding principles in international politics, through the advocating of multilateralism China finds common ground with many other countries, some of them being world and regional powers discontented with US unilateralism, and shares some values in world politics that work to curb hegemony. This international mentality greatly narrows China's ideological gap with the rest of the post-Cold War democratic capitalist world. Moreover, the supremacy of the United States in world politics and the absence of major potential full-edge powers in Asia, to which region China's influence is mostly limited, have shaped an environment in Asia friendly to the building-up of China-led regional arrangements through multilateralism. As Dittmer cautiously concludes that "China's positions in world organizations have tended to be anti-American, while in regional organizations China has taken an 'East Asia for the East Asians' line precluding US participation," he is making a telling point.

Multilateralism is here directly merged with China's effort on the promotion of multipolarity of world politics. In China most civilian and military analysts see the rise of multipolarity as the "greatest check on the US quest for hegemony,"[16] so, too, with multilateralism. Bilaterally, China's position within multilateral arrangements has also enhanced its bargaining power with other individual powers, particularly with the United States. Overall, we may say that, at the level of norms, China turns to multilateralism against the increasing trend of US unilateralism; at the level of practical conduct, Beijing's participation in regional multilateral institutions helps China to prevent the emergence of a US-led, multilateral security structure in Asia directed at Beijing, if not yet at this stage to shape a China-led structure against the US.

Multilateralism as an image-improving measure in international society The ideological and political uniqueness in post-Cold War world politics costs China much in international relations. Beijing, therefore, makes much effort to improve its international image, particularly as a "responsible" member of international society, as it has become fully aware of the point that such an image can be crucial in this world of growing globalization to attract foreign resources, material and beyond, to serve both the survival of the authoritarian regime and the economic development of the Chinese nation. Multilateralism is powerful to promote, for the sake of public relations, the multiple identities that the current China seeks in comparison with its past single, frigid identity as a communist state. Almost no other way is more convenient and effective than multilateral involvement to send out this message: in international society China is playing by rules.

The other side of this token is: China also plays with the rules. Quite a few contributors to this volume emphasize foreign-policy learning approach in reading China's change to multilateralism, while most of them agree that China's learning is instrumental. China has thus also learnt, often successfully, how to manipulate the rules for its benefit, often breaking the principles of multilateral coordination. In such cases, international organizations adjusted their rules and requirements vis-à-vis China, and even, as in the case of the International Labour Organization, cited by Dittmer, granted a special exception in the area of labour standards to pave the way for China's entering.

Multilateralism as an effective venue to address security issues, particularly regional Security issues as will be discussed in the section of "regional impacts" that follows.

Combining "nature and nurture," heredity and environment, China's engagement in multilateral mechanisms and, to a less degree, multilateralist practice of foreign relations have its multi-facet purposes. The suggestions made above to read this engagement is, of course, not exhausting all the Chinese purposes. For example, Chinese multilateralism works also as a resource for domestic political legitimacy, both to the regime and to individual leaders. In any case, the linkage between domestic politics and international multilateral behaviour deserves exploration, but one volume cannot cover everything of the subject, though many chapters included here have touched on the Chinese interpretation of its national interest that undermines its foreign-policy claim of multilateralism. In particular, Jean-Philippe Beja's chapter discusses how the Chinese authoritarian regime's political consideration, as reflected in the case of Hong Kong democratization, weakens Chinese multilateralism. This volume does attempt to offer a comprehensive look at China's engagement in multilateral diplomacy, particularly with respect to the complexities of the pressures placed on China, particularly in the realm of security.

Regional impacts and global implications

To a great extent, Chinese multilateralism is more regional than global, as many of the contributors to this volume have found. It is so for several reasons, which are consistent with our understanding of the features of Chinese multilateralism discussed above and, in fact, remarkably reflect those features. It also has rich implications for the understanding of Chinese conduct of multilateral diplomacy. This regional nature of China's multilateral engagement, however, does not deny the profound implications it brings to global politics.

First of all, China's multilateral diplomatic exercise of its newly obtained economic power has to be limited, mostly, to the regional level. This implies that the scale of China's multilateral engagement coincides with its sphere of influence. This phenomenon of the mutual coverage of the intensities of Chinese power and of Chinese multilateralism reveals that China doesn't like to be engaged in multilateral arrangements when its power or influence is thin. In other words, Chinese multilateralism is conducted with the support of its own material power. Multilateralism is, therefore, a tool to influence those peripheral locales where China's power reaches, rather than a mechanism by which China simply prefers to be bound. More exactly, China is keen to develop "China-dominated multilateral arrangements," rather than a multilateralism that emphasizes equal coordination among the involved parts, although China has had to compromise with other members in the China-dominated multilateral regional mechanisms.

The impact of such "China-dominated multilateralism" is the growing influence of China in the regions on the Chinese periphery, not only through its economic ascendance but also because of its sophisticated combination of economic power and skillful diplomacy. To promote this trend, the Chinese emphasis on the regional scale in harnessing multilateralism is also shaping a dynamic of new regionalism in East, Southeast, and Central Asia, with China as the major engine. This is the second facet of the regional impact of Chinese multilateralism. Yet this regionalism is still under the process of development, and the political difficulties implicit in regional economic integration in East and Southeast Asia, let alone in regional security mechanisms, are, of course, greater than those experienced in the integrating of Europe and North America, respectively. Doubtless, however, along with the growth of Chinese influence in the regions and China's increasing involvements in regional multilateral arrangements in economic matters and security, the trend will continue, and will re-shape the geopolitics and geo-economics of the regions involved and of the whole world.

One of the difficulties of China-dominated regional integration of East and Southeast Asia lies in China's "unique" political system, which, with low transparency and weak accountability, arouses foreign neighbours' suspicions of the rise of China as a regional power though they welcome the economic opportunities emerging with this rise. Regional international multilateralism is one method that China employs to reduce such suspicions. This is perhaps the most convincing way and with the lowest cost. Multilateral mechanisms provide China's neighbours with a comfortable venue to sit together with their peers in front of gigantic China, which is believed to be bound by such mechanisms giving these smaller nations more confidence than they otherwise would have to deal with the large regional power. China, for its part, encounters no political harassment under these conditions, such as it often faces in global international organizations where the influence of Western democratic powers often looms large. Despite their suspicions, these Asian neighbours choose not to question, let alone criticize, China's authoritarianism, and, with China, they also share many values – so-called 'Asian values' – in dealing with human-rights issues. This political convenience makes China feel at ease in regional cooperation, though in the long term it doesn't help to reduce the obstacle rooted in China's political system for regional integration.

China, on the contrary, becomes active to promote its own ideas for international norms and regimes in the regional scale. It was agreed among the Chinese leaders that China should become more active in shaping its regional environment. It takes the lead in creating regional multilateral institutions on both security and the economy, such as in the cases of the initiation of the Shanghai Cooperation Organization and the ASEAN+1. Basically, it is helpful to resolve, or at least to relax, the tensions between China and its neighbours on land disputes and, it is hoped, on maritime territories, such as in the South China Sea, through China's active participation in regional multilateral arrangements. Some new tensions concerning regional security, however, also arise from China's domination of regional economic and security multilateralism.

The most obvious tension, partially stimulated by China's aggressive pursuing of regional involvement, lies in Sino-Japanese relations. Historical and other issues on the agenda of the two nations' quarrels aside, observers of the relationship believe that the competition between them for the regional leadership is a major concern behind their problems. Taiwan is another case in this regard: China's growing involvement in multilateralism doesn't provide any leeway for the relationship across the Taiwan Strait. Rather, the China that gains more of an international reputation becomes less ready to compromise than before, as reflected in its "anti-succession law," its implacable stance in regarding Taiwan as a renegade province and threatening the use of coercive force to take it "back" as necessity is unilaterally perceived to occur. Taiwan is constantly excluded from international organizations where China requests so, which forms an irony even to the Chinese: as China as a whole is more and more included in international and regional activities, Taiwan, claimed as part of China, is more isolated from multilateral arrangements.

China is not yet powerful enough to exclude the United Stated from the region where it is becoming dominant. It rather takes, as Yongnian Zheng and Tok Sow Keat suggest, a "non-confrontational," multilateralist approach to undermine American influence in Asia. This will certainly cause a profound change of the Asian, as well as global, security landscapes, even if one includes the possibility of Sino-US security cooperation in the region in the future picture. Multilateralism indeed provides a tool for China to curb and, at the same time, tap the US in regional affairs, as reflected in China's sponsorship of "Six-Party Talks" on the North Korean nuclear problem. In many degrees, this involvement of China in the Korea crisis, often regarded a major evidence of China's "new diplomacy," epitomizes the regional impacts and global implications of Chinese multilateralism: it has prolonged the breakout of the crisis but not made substantive progress, at least so far, to resolve the problem; it is a Chinese accomplishment of diplomacy without an achievement in regional security. It is, of course, multilateralistic in form but by nature is bilateral (the six parties are often divided into two camps) or even unilateral (has the mechanism changed any preference of the White House, or of Pyongyang?); and it is a venue where the United States has to invite Beijing's intervention in regional affairs while Beijing strengthens its bargaining position through the multilateral conduct vis-à-vis the United States and China's Asian neighbours.

Organization of the volume

The structure of the chapters that follow reflects two features of this volume: first, it addresses China's multilateralism conduct on regional security issues and its ramifications with regard to global politics; second, it presents a balanced treatment of the rise of Chinese multilateralism with both optimism and caution.

Part II, "Global Concerns," focuses on the general question of why China has taken a multilateral approach to some global issues. We begin with Lowell Dittmer's "China's new internationalism," which examines China's new role as a member of various intergovernmental organizations (IGOs), such as the United Nations and the WTO, as well as of regional bodies such as ASEAN+3 and the APEC. The author argues that while China's long-term nationalist interests have not changed since its participation in IGOs, the way in which China chooses to uphold its domestic interests has shifted, allowing space for full IGO membership. Dittmer points out that this new role has allowed China to claim a place in the international arena while at the same time has contributed to its national identity.

Thomas Moore's chapter continues the examination of China's shifting foreign policies, offering both a liberal internationalist and realist analysis of China's increasing engagement in multilateral relations. He suggests that China's approach is a strategic one, with long-term goals dictating which relationships China will enter into and which ones it will avoid. Its membership in large, institutionalized groups, such as the WTO, can be viewed as safer trade liberalization mechanisms than membership in the APEC where US dominance creates political hurdles. However, the selectivity of China's approach to multilateralism does not preclude complementary results. China's move might be strategic but the results might be liberal internationalist gains.

Chapter 4, entitled "New Player in the Game: China, Arms Control, and Multilateralism," by Jing-dong Yuan supports the above findings with the evidence from the security issue-areas, particularly China's guarded approach to multilateral arms-control negotiations. The author argues that China engages, though reluctantly, because, viewed pragmatically, at some level, multilateral diplomacy works and is useful for meeting one's own needs. China is, therefore, able to cast itself in a more favourable light in the international community by engaging in multilateral arms-control negotiations, thereby enhancing its overall image.

The volume turns to Part III "Regional Security," which draws evidence from China's new role as a multilateralist in those prominent regional security issues in Asia and the Pacific to further confirm the common thread of how China shines as a new world power within the community of its neighbours without having to give up its internal political interests. Michael Yahuda's chapter, "China's Multilateralism and Regional Order," points to China's participation in ASEAN as being conducive to good relations with China's Southeast Asian neighbours. However, as Yahuda points out, the participation in ASEAN is not particularly threatening to China's domestic political interests, as the nature of

ASEAN (its rules of diplomacy–consensus, lack of interference in domestic relations and absence of rules of conduct) enables China to participate in its negotiations without compromising over its sovereignty.

The new role as a regional multilateralist does not come without a price, argues Yinhong Shi in his contribution on "China and the North Korean Nuclear Problem." As an arbiter in the Six-Party Talks, Shi maintains, China has placed itself in a precarious position, as what will be deemed a successful conclusion will be up for interpretation by the various nations at the table. China is, undoubtedly, in the best position to orchestrate negotiations between the US and the DPRK in its quest for peace in the region. However, to successfully bring about a satisfactory end to the nuclear dispute with North Korea for all involved is a tall order. China prefers partial settlement, but it is unlikely that the DPRK would agree to or comply with complete denuclearization and yet China will find it tough to convince the US that "partial settlement is better than a protracted stalemate of non-settlement."

On a more optimistic note, Jianwei Wang offers an examination of China's successful participation in the Shanghai Cooperation Organization. He emphasizes the importance of norms such as mutual trust, mutual advantages, equality, joint consultation, respect for cultural diversity, and the desire for common development in China's attempts at multilateral negotiations, and suggests that there are successes to be found in this new model of multilateral diplomacy. Unlike other institutional relationships in which China is involved, the SCO, at the outset, focused on security issues rather than economics, engaging the members in negotiations that reflected the urgency of addressing one of the longest shared borders in the world. It is, however, evolving into a mechanism for member countries to address a range of issues outside the realm of security.

One of the most pressing areas of multilateral engagement is that of maritime security. In her chapter "Chinese and ASEAN Responses to the US Regional Maritime Security Initiative," Gaye Christoffersen offers an analysis of how the US proposal for the Regional Maritime Security Initiative has challenged the emerging East Asian security order that China and ASEAN are busy constructing, a security order that is multi-layered. The author argues that China's participation in Asian multilateralism cannot be viewed in isolation, focusing only on China's actions. Instead, "China's approach to multilateralism is interactive, and cannot be understood separately from the approaches of the US, Japan and ASEAN to security multilateralism." China's involvement in the security of the Malacca Straits is a case in point. In this situation, ASEAN's opposition to the US proposal of the Regional Maritime Security Initiative illustrates its favouring of a multilateral approach that would involve the immediately surrounding littoral states as well as the users of the Straits in the region, namely, China and Japan. In this regard, China was drawn into the multilateral approach to security dictated by ARF terms.

Keyuan Zou continues with the question of maritime security, but turns to the many laws and treaties that have been signed by China and other nations surrounding the South China Sea, and highlights that, although China has in the past taken a bilateral approach to maritime negotiations, it has engaged more recently in multilateral arrangements. However, the author does argue that the multilateral approach of which China has chosen to be part, is aligned with China's Five Principles of Co-Existence, thereby ensuring that its sovereignty will not be jeopardized in multilateral negotiations.

Part IV of this volume focuses on China's "peaceful rise" as a new world power, an approach that corresponds with its multilateral diplomacy. In the chapter contributed by Yongnian Zheng and Sow Keat Tok, "Intentions on Trial: 'Peaceful Rise' and Sino-ASEAN Relations," we turn to an examination of China's relationship with ASEAN as a test case with respect to its foreign policy commitment of a "peaceful rise" as a new world power. Rather than dealing directly with the US in its new foreign policy, China has taken a back route through ASEAN, argues the authors. They further suggest that China's reality as a player in the international arena demands that it takes such a non-confrontational approach. China is not equal to the task of challenging the US directly and its internal problems of trying to economically develop for the benefit of everyone preclude international posturing. China's efforts to be friendly to its Southeast Asian neighbours, efforts such as engaging in favourable trading relations (in favour of ASEAN), have demonstrated China's commitment to being a benign player. The authors are cautious in making their conclusion, however, as they also think that China's relationship with Taiwan speaks volumes about selective peaceful means.

The "peaceful rise" theme of China's participation in multilateral diplomacy is a complex issue, particularly if extended to include the issue of human rights. Jeremy Paltiel's chapter, "Peaceful Rise? Soft Power? Human Rights in China's New Multilateralism," examines China's multilateral engagement in the area of human rights within the overall context of Chinese foreign policy. The author argues that China is caught between a rock and a hard place with respect to human rights. On the one hand, China wishes to use the sovereignty card against the finger-pointing by the international community over human-rights issues. By playing this card, however, China runs the risk of appearing to contradict, vis-à-vis the Universal Declaration of Human Rights, the platform of the UN, a multilateral institution in which the Chinese wishes to become more involved.

Another pressing area of foreign engagement that sorely tests the idea of "peaceful rise" is the issue of energy resources. Willy Lam focuses on this issue in his chapter, examining China's diplomacy relating to securing a steady supply of oil and gas. The author argues that "the CCP leadership's multidimensional efforts to attain 'energy security' has exacerbated the country's already fragile and problematic ties with other countries, including the US and Japan." The race for resources, with Japan and India after the same resources in the same region, has led to China's engaging in energy negotiations with "pariah" states such as Myanmar, Sudan, and Venezuela, damning its own reputation as a good citizen of the global community, and that the race for oil has led to the opting for bilateral negotiations with respect to disputes in the South China Sea.

The issue of Taiwan, which continues to run through all chapters of the volume, is widely regarded the toughest test of China's self-claimed "peaceful rise." In "China's Multilateralism and its Impacts on Cross-Strait Relations," Dong-Ching Day offers a perspective from Taiwan to look at China's entry into the WTO and its ramifications over Taiwan. He suggests that China's participation in multilateral diplomacy is dictated by a cost/benefit analysis. When China has moved toward greater multilateral positions, the moves have come from external pressure such as ASEAN–American relations. When focusing on Taiwan, however, China has not yet moved toward multilateralism in any significant way.

Jean-Philippe Béja echoes this pessimist conclusion, but with the case of Hong Kong. His chapter, "An Exception to the Growing Emphasis on Multilateralism: the Case of China's Policy toward Hong Kong," aptly points out that China's new multilateral approach to international affairs in the case of Hong Kong is two-dimensional. Economically, the CCP is willing to reach beyond its sovereign borders and engage the international community with Hong Kong as a "World City." On a political level, however, a multilateral approach is sorely tested even though the "One Country, Two Systems" formula continues to be implemented. With little patience for including the international community in discussions about democratization of Hong Kong, the CCP clings tightly to political manoeuvres that belie its true position with respect to foreign policy.

Notes

1 Peter Van Ness suggests this distinction useful to observe Chinese foreign policy. See Peter Van Ness, "China and the Third World: Patterns of Engagement and Indifference," in Samuel S. Kim (ed.) *China and the World: Chinese Foreign Policy Faces the New Millennium,* 4th edition, Boulder: Westview Press, 1998, p. 151.
2 Numerous publications have been devoted to China's multilateral participation in the economic areas. See, for example, Harold K. Jacobson and Michel Oksenberg, *China's Participation in the IMF, the World Bank, and GATT: Toward a Global Economic Order*, Ann Arbor: University of Michigan Press, 1990; *China Joins the World: Progress and Prospects*, Elizabeth Economy and Michel Oksenberg (eds), New York: Council on Foreign Relations Press, 1999; Nicholas R. Lardy, *Integrating China into the Global Economy*, Washington, DC: Brookings Institution Press, 2002.
3 As termed in Evan S. Medeiros and M. Taylor Fravel, "China's New Diplomacy," *Foreign Affairs*, vol. 82, no. 6, November/December 2003.
4 Robert O. Keohane, "Multilateralism: An Agenda for Research," *International Journal* XLV, Autumn 1990, p. 731.
5 Samuel S. Kim, "China's International Organizational Behaviour," in Thomas W. Robinson and David Shambaugh (eds) *Chinese Foreign Policy: Theory and Practice*, Oxford: Clarendon Press, 1994, pp. 401–34.
6 For an incomplete list of previous studies in these areas, see, Alastair Iain Johnston and Paul Evans, "China's Engagement with Multilateral Security Institutions," in Alastair Iain Johnston and Robert S. Ross (eds) *Engaging China: The Management of an Emerging Power*, London: Routledge, 1999, pp. 235–72; Michael D. Swaine and Alastair Iain Johnston, "China and Arms Control Institutions," and Andrew J. Nathan, "China and the International Human Rights Regime," both in Economy and Oksenberg (eds) *China Joins the World*, pp. 90–135 and pp. 136–60.
7 Michael D. Swaine, "China: Exploiting a Strategic Opening," in Ashley J. Tellis and

Michael Wills (eds) *Strategic Asia 2004–05: Confronting Terrorism in the Pursuit of Power*, Seattle: The National Bureau of Asian Research, 2004, p. 72.
8 Ibid., p. 69.
9 For a review of international relations studies in this regard to emphasis purposes, see Kjell Goldmann, "International Relations: An Overview," in Robert E. Goodin and Hans-Dieter Klingemann (eds) *A New Handbook of Political Science*, Oxford: Oxford University Press, 1996, pp. 401–27.
10 Kim, "China's International Organizational Behaviour," Michael D. Swaine and Ashley J. Tellis, *Interpreting China's Grand Strategy: Past, Present, and Future*, Santa Monica: RAND, 2000. The quotation is from Swaine and Tellis, p. 113.
11 Kim, "China's International Organizational Behaviour," p. 427.
12 Jack Snyder, *Myths of Empire: Domestic Politics and International Ambition*, Ithaca: Cornell University Press, 1991, p. 26.
13 Stephen M. Walt, *The Origins of Alliances*, Ithaca: Cornell University Press, 1987.
14 Ibid.
15 Michel Oksenberg, "China: A Tortuous Path onto the World Stage," in Robert A. Pastor (ed.) *A Century's Journey: How the Great Powers Shape the World*, New York: Basic Books, 1999, p. 310.
16 David Shambaugh, *Modernizing China's Military: Progress, Problems, and Prospects*, Berkeley: University of California Press, 2002, p. 298.

Part II
Global concerns

2 China's new internationalism

Lowell Dittmer

The People's Republic of China's (PRC) involvement in international organizations was in effect precluded during the first 22 years of its existence, as the previous Nationalist regime, though defeated and driven from the mainland, survived on the island of Taiwan and, with America's powerful support, continued to occupy one of the five permanent seats of the United Nations Security Council and to represent China in most other international organizations as well. During its first decade, the PRC participated in the full repertoire of socialist international organizations, but as the Sino-Soviet split escalated in the early 1960s these became increasingly polarized and Beijing stopped attending. Estranged from both superpowers in a bipolar world, China thus became something of a radical redoubt in the 1960s. Upon its admission to the United Nations in late 1971 as an unintended byproduct of Washington's triangular diplomacy, China's membership in IGOs expanded gradually from 1–21 in 1971–77. With the launching of Deng Xiaoping's reform and opening policy in 1977–89, IGO membership rose from 21–37. After the end of the Cold War, China affiliated with an increasing range of IGOs (from 37 to 52 in 1989–97), now going beyond the UN framework to include Asian regional organizations. Although membership in nongovernmental international organizations, or INGOs, is worth a separate study (and will not be analysed here), as the universe of INGOs exploded upon the collapse of the Cold War framework, China's affiliation expanded very rapidly, rising from 58–71 in 1966–77, from 71–677 in 1977–89, and from 677–1,136 in 1989–97. In sum, the policy of reform and opening to the outside world has had an important impact on China's involvement in international organizations, as measured in relative as well as absolute terms. In 1989, China belonged to 12 per cent of all IGOs (300), and by 1997 this had increased to 20 per cent of the new total; in 1989, China belonged to 15 per cent of all INGOs, and by 1997 this had increased to 20 per cent (of a new total of 5,585). By the latter date China belonged to the 11th most IGOs in the world (tied with Russia and Indonesia), that is, 45. By way of comparison, the United States ranked ninth (with 47).

In international-relations theory there are roughly two ways of interpreting China's more active involvement in IGOs: realism and liberalism. According to realism the nation-state finds itself in an anarchic and dangerous world in which its primary goal is survival, meaning that security considerations will always have highest foreign-policy priority. If a given state perceives itself to be threatened by the power of another state it may either invest to upgrade its defense capabilities or form an alliance with another state or states to counterbalance the threat. International organizations do not have an independent impact on state behaviour, according to realists, who argue that institutions are not independent power centres but simply arrangements that formalize the involved states' relative power positions at the time of the institution's creation.[1] According to liberalism, on the other hand, specifically the variant of that approach known as neoliberal institutionalism, trade, investment, and other forms of international intercourse (e.g. tourism, postal communications, diplomacy, electronic media) are ways of persuading people to recognize their common interests, thereby fostering mutual identification and mitigating the prospect of war. Because trade can, however, also exacerbate friction in the case of imbalanced relative gains, institutions, or "regimes," which stipulate a set of rules guiding such intercourse, are extremely useful in lowering the transaction costs of cooperation, deterring free-riding or cheating, and hence building trust among nations. Institutions may also link together interactions in different issue areas, thereby deterring cheating in one issue area for fear the offended party may retaliate in another. According to this perspective, international organizations, as a relatively resourceful and potentially powerful form of institution, may play an important independent role in enhancing cooperation, enforcing rules, and reducing the risk of conflict.[2]

The approach adopted here is a foreign-policy learning perspective, according to which China's perspective has shifted over time from realism to a form of self-interested idealism not inconsistent with realist premises. Learning has sometimes been led by ideological or rhetorical change, while sometimes behavioural modification has preceded doctrinal adjustments. The political science literature on learning sometimes distinguishes between instrumental and cognitive learning, and if we adopt that distinction, the Chinese case would probably be deemed instrumental, for it has consistently been informed by, and oriented to, a sense of the national interest, even at the liberal end of the learning curve. Yet the argument here is that motive is not a meaningful criterion, first because motives cannot easily be verified scientifically and second because China's prioritization of national interest is hardly unique. By behavioural criteria, learning has clearly taken place over time, and national behaviour has been modified. This learning curve may be explained by two factors. The first is China's growing enmeshment in the international economic arena, which has in effect changed China's interpretation of its national interest. Economic reform and opening to the outside world has increased China's economic interdependence, including growing reliance on foreign investments, technological transfers, and access to foreign markets to fuel economic growth.[3] China's GDP has increased about ten times over the past thirty years, from $147 billion in 1978 to $1.4 trillion in 2004, while its trade volume rose from $21 billion to $1.15 trillion; trade as a proportion of GDP more than doubled each decade, from 5.2 per cent in

1970 to 70 per cent by 2004, ranking China the world's third largest trading state (and biggest recipient of FDI).[4]

The second factor is that China's position within the IGOs has enhanced its bargaining power, making it possible to negotiate the adjustment of policies deemed inimical to China's interests and to introduce new policies more amenable to them. Membership in an IGO may in any case be viewed as a mutual, dialectical, learning experience, not solely a matter of membership socialization to organizational norms. Thus it is hardly surprising that both China and the host IGOs have modified their expectations and behaviour over time. A decisive watershed in this process was the 4 June 1989 Tiananmen "incident": in the two previous decades, China was welcomed into various IGOs with open arms as that rara avis, a successfully reforming communist command economy, and Beijing in turn took full advantage of its privileged status. In the decade thereafter, China was viewed as an oppressive and autocratic human-rights violator, and placed under greater constraint to comply with IGO norms. Whether it complied or fought back depended of course on the priority Beijing attributed to the specific national interests at stake in that particular case. Still under Deng Xiaoping's stewardship, Beijing played its hand calmly and shrewdly, however, and as China's economy robustly bounced back following Deng's 1992 "voyage to the south," its relative power to withstand adverse IGO pressures and shape its IGO environment revived commensurately.

The objective of this chapter is to analyse the mutual learning involved in China's reconciliation of its national interests with the international norms and rules prescribed and enforced by the IGOs in which it has elected to participate. China's entrée into IGOs came in two clusters. The first cluster consisted of joining the UN and its affiliate agencies, which began in the 1970s and accelerated in the 1980s. The second cluster consisted of joining various regional IGOs, the most important of which were ASEAN and APEC. Phase II took place in the 1990s, as China turned to the Asian region it had previously ignored to fill the vacuum left by the simultaneous collapse of the Communist bloc and the strategic triangle, and to escape from value-based ostracism by the West. (Curiously, China has never sought formal membership in any of the IGOs specifically representing Third World interests: the Group of 77, the Nonaligned Movement, or OPEC.) Based on a more detailed examination of these examples, we shall argue that while China's long-term national interests have remained constant, its strategy for realizing these interests has undergone a progressive modification from an early focus on exploiting IGO resources without seeking to alter IGO policies to a more active attempt to comply with, legislate, and even help to enforce, IGO rules and norms. For their part, the IGOs have been able to exert varying amounts of pressure to modify China's relevant policies, depending on the strength and unity of the organization. Depending on China's interpretation of how its interests are affected in a given case, it would comply or manoeuvre for a more favourable interpretation of the rules or fight to change them, usually within the bounds of officially permissible behaviour.

China and the United Nations

China's involvement in the UN may be subdivided into two phases. During the late Maoist period (1971–77), China participated only cautiously and selectively, staying away from the UN functional committees and subsidiary bodies, opting to enter into only eight of the specialized agencies. In the immediate post-Mao period (i.e. in the 1980s), Beijing's interest in the UN intensified considerably, with China joining most UN-affiliated agencies, including the World Bank and the International Monetary Fund in 1980. In 1986 it renewed its application to regain its seat as one of the founding members of the General Agreement on Tariffs and Trade, later renamed the World Trade Organization. By the end of the 1990s, China had joined several hundred groups, including the International Atomic Energy Agency, the Conference on Disarmament (1980), and the Human Rights Commission (1982). In 1984 China gained a seat on the International Court of Justice. China also signed and acceded to a great variety of multilateral treaties and agreements, including the Non Proliferation Treaty (1992), the United Nations Convention on the Law of the Sea (UNCLOS) in 1996, and both major human rights conventions – the International Covenant on Economic, Social and Cultural Rights, and the International Covenant on Civil and Political Rights – although only the first of these has thus far been ratified by the National People's Congress. China was represented by Prime Minister Li Peng in the first Security Council summit in January 1992, the first Earth summit at Rio in 1994, and the first World Summit on Social Development at Copenhagen in 1995; President Jiang Zemin attended the 50th anniversary of the founding of the UN in New York in October 1995. The UN and its activities have consistently received positive media coverage in China.[5]

As Samuel Kim has noted, China's more active involvement in the full panoply of UN IGOs at the end of the 1970s coincided with a revised self-identification as a needy supplicant of all international aid available and no longer a proud model of Maoist self-reliance. China in late 1978 asked the UN General Assembly to decrease its assessment rate, and the rate was accordingly reduced from 5.5 per cent to 0.79 per cent; it has since been boosted to slightly more than 2 per cent. This reduces China's participatory dues across the board, as all specialized agencies follow the scales of assessment determined by the General Assembly. Among Security Council permanent members, China pays the lowest assessment rate. China argues that this is justified by its less developed status, as is China's status as largest recipient of World Bank multilateral aid (about $3 billion per year) and the most frequent borrower of subsidized loans from the International Bank of Reconstruction and Development and the soft-loan window of the IMF. In fact, China has now progressed to the ambiguous status of a system in transformation, with a very large economy in absolute terms (fourth largest in nominal terms, second largest if PPP estimates are used) but still developing in terms of per capita income ($1,290 in 2004 in nominal terms, or $5,530 on a PPP basis). Thus, though still a leading recipient of foreign aid, China has begun to donate aid to selected recipients (who are often gratified by the lack of preconditions). Moreover, though not a big contributor, China has played by the rules. In contrast to the US, which now owes a total of c. $1.3 billion in back dues (some withheld for political reasons), China has no outstanding debt at all (to be sure, the US assessment is 25 per cent of the total budget whereas China's is a fraction of 1 per cent). Playing by the rules has also entailed a promise to comply with conditionality, such as the requirement by the Multilateral Investment Guarantee Agency to subordinate Chinese law to international law and international arbitration.

Samuel Kim has argued that China's opportunistic free-riding has depleted its moral capital in the UN, but there seems to be little evidence of this. China has built a political base in the UN as the champion of the Third World and the only developing country with a permanent seat on the Security Council and one of the world's five acknowledged nuclear powers, an economic growth prodigy and future superpower. China's voting record in the General Assembly has consistently favoured policies and causes deemed vital to the community of developing nations, at least on symbolic issues – meaning it has also quite consistently voted against the United States: the coincidence figures on all recorded votes in the General Assembly in 1994–96 place China in the category of those states (with Cuba, North Korea, Iraq, and Vietnam) whose votes least frequently coincide with those of the US.[6] China in the Security Council has also frequently taken issue with American policy initiatives (such as the 1999 Kosovo intervention), though China has expressed its "principled opposition" not through the veto (an act it deems hegemonial) but through abstentions. China has used the veto only four times during its tenure on the UNSC, while it has abstained quite frequently. China's opposition to US-led sanctions for human rights violations has been articulate and predictable – also highly popular among developing countries. This is both an effective constituency-building strategy and serves China's broader strategy of counterbalancing unilateral tendencies in world politics.

China endured its most difficult period in the UN in the wake of the June 1989 suppression of the democracy protests. Beijing was shocked when the UN Human Rights Commission in 1990 voted sanctions on China for the sanguinary Tiananmen crackdown, opting, however, to fight this and every such sanction. Resorting to rules of parliamentary procedure, Beijing prevented any draft resolution critical of China's record from ever emerging from the group of experts to be presented to the Commission floor by calling a "no action motion." No other state under UN human-rights scrutiny has resorted to this parliamentary stratagem. In order to ensure positive votes in these no action motions, China lobbied other developing countries with great intensity, promising to withhold commercial contracts from resistors and offering aid projects and other emoluments to sympathizers. In 1995 China also proposed to reform the commission by increasing still further representation by less developed countries and in effect cutting its budget. Though this attempt failed, in 2001 China ultimately succeeded in having the United States voted off the commission, thereby eliminating the strongest and most consistent sponsor of critical draft resolutions.[7]

Meanwhile, China has also become much more articulate in defending its own position on human rights, setting up scholarly commissions and journals and publishing a series of white papers. By 1997 the PRC had signed the International Covenant on Economic, Social and Cultural Rights (ICESCR) and accepted the principle of universality of human rights. Also its shift from opposition to support of (in 1981) and eventual (1990) participation in UN peacekeeping operations (PKOs) signified approval of the principle of IGO humanitarian intervention (not viewed as an infringement of sovereignty because UN peacekeeping missions do not intervene without an invitation from the host state). Thus China played significant roles in the PKOs in Cambodia and East Timor and in August 2006 agreed to send 1,000 troops to help monitor the border after the Israeli incursion into south Lebanon.

China's hitherto amicable working relationship with the International Labour Organization was also adversely affected by Tiananmen. The ILO in 1983 had taken the unusual step, at China's request, of cancelling the accrued debt representing China's statutory contribution due since November 1971. Since 1983, China had occupied one of the ten non-elective governing body seats and since February 1984, the ILO had a Chinese assistant director-general. When China entered the organization, the ILO also granted a special exception in the area of labour standards, as China claimed (using the "Asian values" arguments it used in human rights) that Western standards were not appropriate to China. To protect itself from possible imposition of ILO norms, China also avoided ratifying most of the ILO conventions (by 1994, it had ratified only 17 of 175 ILO conventions). The Chinese participated avidly in the ILO's technical assistance programme (directed from a branch office in Beijing), which was highly valued. But the ILO was clearly disturbed by the killing of large numbers of protesting workers in connection with Tiananmen, as a result of which its focus shifted from technical assistance (which was temporarily suspended) to labour standards. After the crackdown, the International Confederation of Free Trade Unions brought complaints against China, as a result of which the ILO required the Chinese government to supply detailed information on alleged violations of human rights. China was initially indignant, thinking it had exempted itself by failing to ratify the conventions, only to find that the complaints were based on the ILO constitution. Although China initially protested these requests for interference in internal affairs, the government was, by 1993, persuaded to report information concerning trials and imprisonment of protesters and even to release a few of them. The new Labour Law that came into effect in January 1995 did not restore the right to strike (which had been rescinded in 1981), but it did give the union the right to "organize its activities autonomously and independently in accordance with the law." Han Dongfang, a labour activist imprisoned for his activities in 1989, was also released at this time under the proviso that he leave the country.[8]

A final example is China's long and bitter struggle to enter into the World Trade Organization. China was actually one of the contracting parties to the General Agreement of Tariffs and Trade (GATT), which was founded in 1948, as the Republic of China, whose status was downgraded to that of a GATT observer in 1965. The PRC formally applied for restoration of its contracting party status in GATT in 1986, and a working committee on China's application was set up by GATT in 1987 to oversee the case. In 1994, China put forward a proposal for admission and began negotiations, but these were unsuccessful. When GATT became the WTO in January 1995, China became an observer, and a new working committee was set up at the end of that year, which convened a series of eight meetings in 1997–98. China insisted on entering the organization before Taiwan could be admitted as a separate customs territory, and also sought permission to enter as a developing country, with more time to lower tariffs and trade barriers. In a series of intensive and protracted negotiations, China resolved its bilateral differences with its leading trade partners, including the United States, Japan, and the European Union, and finally succeeded in entering the organization on 31 December 2001 (with Taiwan entering the following day). The price of admission has been some very major concessions on China's part, including tariff reductions on both agricultural and manufacturing products (China agreed to reduce its average tariff from 16.7 per cent to 10 per cent in five years and to reduce the number of items under import licence and quota from c.300 to zero), all imports are to receive national treatment within three years, and foreign banks will get full market access within five years (later extended to January 2007). These concessions entail major economic risks, accelerating the bankruptcy of inefficient state-owned enterprises and thereby exacerbating urban unemployment, and aggravating the problem of rural migration to urban areas by undercutting Chinese agricultural prices. This does not necessarily mean a sacrifice of national interest but rather a calculated gamble, the major anticipated benefits being elimination of the threat of losing most-favoured nation treatment in the American market, acceleration of GDP growth through the doubling of external trade and an increase in the influx of FDI, and a major stimulus to legal reform (e.g. intellectual property laws) to conform with WTO legal regimes.[9] The gamble so far seems to have paid off, both in terms of benefits to China's economy and in exemplary compliance to WTO norms, but it has involved unprecedented curtailment of Chinese sovereignty.

Regional organizations

China's interest in regional organizations coincided with the greater interest in the region that came in the wake of the collapse of the strategic triangle at the end of the Cold War, which reduced China's global leverage – isolated by the West, China launched its "good neighbour policy" (*mulin zhengce*). In 1986, China became a full member of the Asian Development Bank, for the first time not expelling Taiwan (a founding member of the ADB in 1966), but permitting its continued membership under a name change to "Taipei, China." Beijing lost no time taking advantage of membership: by the end of September 1999 loans approved by the ADB to China totaled $8.276 billion, together with $37.3 million in capital stock investment, $145 million in technical assistance and

$540 million of co-financing consisting mainly of infrastructure projects in the fields of energy, transportation and environmental protection. China joined the Asian Pacific Economic Cooperation (APEC) forum in its founding year, 1989, agreeing to permit Taiwan's admission under the same formula. While APEC grew from its dozen founding members to embrace 21 countries on the Pacific Rim accounting for nearly half of the world's merchandise trade, half the global GNP, and approximately half of the world's population, it has remained consistently limited to economic issues (particularly the liberalization of trade and investment, such as the landmark 1994 Bogor resolution to eliminate all trade barriers between industrialized country members by 2010 and among developing countries by 2020), though its anaemic response to the 1997–99 Asian financial crisis has weakened its credibility. China's consistent emphasis (Jiang Zemin personally attended each annual leaders' summit since Clinton introduced these in 1993, exploiting the forum for side meetings with Clinton and other world leaders) has been on the diversity of the region, the need for mutual opening without exclusion, and noninterference in internal affairs. China participated in several rounds of tariff reductions and took a leading role in the establishment of scientific and technological exchange programmes, in 1998 donating $10 million to set up a "China APEC Fund on Scientific and Industrial Cooperation."

China initially viewed the launching by the Association of Southeast Asian Nations (ASEAN) of its expanded ASEAN Regional Forum (ARF) in 1994 with some reservations, but by 1997 China had become an active participant both in ARF and in the 'track II" unofficial dialogue process that complements official deliberations (in addition to ARF, the Council for Security Cooperation in the Asian Pacific, or CSCAP). When ASEAN launched the Asian European Meetings (ASEM) in March 1996 in Bangkok, Premier Li Peng attended the inaugural meeting and China has been represented at all subsequent meetings, donated $500,000 to the ASEM Trust Fund and asked to host the Foreign Ministers meeting in Beijing in 2001. In 1998 China initiated an annual political dialogue with the EU, and in 2002 approached NATO to begin a similar series of conversations. In 1997, China helped initiate the ASEAN+3 forum, a series of annual meetings between China, Japan, South Korea, and the ten members of ASEAN, and in 2000 China initiated ASEAN+1, culminating in a 2002 agreement (finally formalized at the Bangkok summit in November 2004) to form the world's largest free trade agreement, the Chinese–ASEAN Free Trade Agreement, or CAFTA, comprising some 1.7 billion people in China and Southeast Asia. Whether this visionary proposal contains the answer to ASEAN's economic quandary remains to be seen. Since the Asian Financial Crisis, foreign direct investment has shifted from Southeast Asia to China: in 1999, China received three-fifths of developing Asia's FDI, while ASEAN economies got just 17 per cent – reversing the ratio of the early 1990s. As for portfolio investment, the Hong Kong stock market has enabled PRC firms to more or less corner capital markets. China's exports, exploiting the advantage of an apparently inexhaustible supply of cheap labour, grew by some 30 per cent annually, enjoying very large positive trade imbalances as ASEAN export industries (at least initially) stagnated.[10] Beijing also helped organize the first East Asian Summit (EAS) in December 2005 (and has offered to host the next one in 2007), which now also included Australia, New Zealand, and India, but like the APT, excluded the US.

The most important of the regional IGOs, and the only one to tackle difficult political issues so far, is the ARF. Indeed, one of the putative reasons for its founding was ASEAN's perceived need to engage China in a dialogue about issues China was not eager to discuss multilaterally (Beijing had preferred to negotiate these issues bilaterally), and China was initially suspicious that the forum would become part of an American scheme to mobilize pressure on issues sensitive to China. Thus ARF officials presented an early "concept paper" on the broad outlines for the ARF, stating that the ARF meetings would have no formal agenda and would approach sensitive security issues in a non-confrontational manner, as in the "ASEAN way" used to reconcile intra-ASEAN disputes, moving forward only at a pace "comfortable" to all participants. This assuaged the Chinese, who have consistently opposed any move to enhance the decision-making powers of the forum beyond "dialogue" (*duihua luntan*). Among ASEAN members, China has had friendly relations with Thailand dating back to its role in resolving the Indochina turmoil at the end of the 1980s, and during the Asian financial crisis China offered $1 billion to Thailand to overcome its difficulties, did not devalue its currency when others (e.g. Japan) did, and pledged $4–6 billion to the IMF's bailout package for Southeast Asia. Trade between ASEAN and China has increased from $14.29 billion in 1994 to $130 billion by 2005 (vs. $148 billion between ASEAN-US) and has been growing 20 per cent per year. With its economically potent overseas Chinese population, ASEAN has also become an increasingly significant investor in the PRC, FDI rising from $1.21 billion in 1993 to $3.62 billion in 1997. China's repudiation of Western human-rights meddling parallels the "Asian values" position that originated in Malaysia and Singapore, and Beijing supported the Malaysian proposal for an East Asian Economic Caucus excluding the US, eventually realized as the APT. Surely, this belongs with the following pair. But ASEAN has nonetheless consistently been apprehensive about two things:

One has been the accelerated pace of Chinese arms spending since the Tiananmen incident, and the lack of transparency about that build-up. Although official arms-budget figures are widely believed to understate actual spending by at least half, even if we accept official figures and control for inflation, Chinese arms spending increased very rapidly throughout the 1990s, considerably outpacing the rapid growth of GDP. Thanks to the purchase of new military hardware from Russia, including supersonic SU-27 fighters, modern diesel submarines and high-tech destroyers, China has been closing the military technology gap with its Asian neighbours and developing its power projection capability. During their high-speed growth phase in the early 1990s several ASEAN countries were able to keep pace with Chinese arms spending, but upon being stricken by the Asian financial crisis, ASEAN military budgets were cut.

The ASEAN proposal to deal with the situation was to call for more adequate information concerning China's budgetary process, hitherto highly confidential. In 1995, Qian Qichen promised that at an appropriate time China would publish a defence white paper as one of its contributions to confidence-building. In November of that year Beijing did produce what it called a white paper on arms control and disarmament, and in early 2001 it published a white paper on defence. While both of these documents have been criticized as relatively unrevealing, they represent progress. China has since issued over 30 of these documents on a variety of sensitive issues, including national defence, Taiwan, Tibet, and human rights.

ASEAN anxieties about the Chinese air and naval build-up is closely connected to China's territorial claim to the c.50 scattered islets and atolls in the South China Sea, known as the Spratlys. The confrontation between China and the various other claimants to these tiny but potentially rich and strategically pivotal islands has already been analysed elsewhere, so our discussion here will be focused exclusively on the mobilization of ARF to arbitrate the issue. ASEAN did not respond to the 1988 Sino-Vietnamese clash, probably because Vietnam did not join until 1995. After China passed its "Law on Territorial Waters and Adjacent Areas" in February 1992, claiming the entire chain, the ASEAN Ministerial Meeting issued its first formal statement, subsequently referred to as the Manila Declaration, calling on claimant states to settle the issue by peaceful means. But in early 1995, Philippine fishermen were detained by Chinese sailors, leading to the discovery that China had begun to fortify Mischief Reef, also claimed by Manila. In response, ASEAN foreign ministers in March issued a statement expressing "serious concern" over the incident, and to Beijing's surprise, ASEAN raised the issue in discussions attending the second ARF conference in Hangzhou the following month. Qian Qichen responded that the matter should be resolved according to the 1982 Law of the Sea (UNCLOS), to considerable ASEAN relief. But there were continuing small skirmishes around Mischief Reef, and in 1996 China amended its "baseline" for UNCLOS to be in the Paracels, vastly extending its claims. In May 1997 there was an additional fracas at Scarborough Shoal, prompting another ASEAN call to settle the matter by arbitration.[11] China has not relinquished its claims, but after four years of negotiation, ASEAN and China signed a declaration agreeing on a Code of Conduct for such matters in 2002, and the following year China became the first non-ASEAN country to sign the association's Treaty of Amity and Cooperation. Without relinquishing its sovereignty claims, Beijing seems to have assuaged ASEAN concerns with promises of peaceful resolution and joint development of the islets.

Besides taking an increasingly visible role in ASEAN-led forums (where ASEAN reserves leadership to its own members), China's movement to a leadership position has been visible in two instances: the Shanghai Cooperation Organization (SCO) and the six-party talks. The SCO was formally inaugurated in July 2001 as an outgrowth of the Sino-Soviet border negotiations, which became talks with four independent countries (Russia, Kyrgyzstan, Kazakhstan, and Tajikistan) when the USSR disintegrated in 1991 to be replaced by the Commonwealth of Independent Countries. These four negotiating counterparts remained together in a team by mutual consent, meeting in Shanghai in 1996 and 1997 to ratify agreements involving border security and confidence-building measures reached bilaterally, but China took the initiative to expand the forum (now also including Uzbekistan) into the SCO, the world's first security forum not involving the US, in June 2001. The agenda has also broadened to include counter-terrorism efforts, plans for a common market, and annual joint military exercises. In 2006 the group included four observers: India, Pakistan, Iran, and Outer Mongolia, now scheduled to become permanent members at the next summit. China's second important initiative is the six-party talks (including China, Russia, Japan, the US, the ROK, and the DPRK), initiated and hosted by Beijing in the wake of the collapse of the 1994 Agreed Framework, following the apparent discovery that North Korea had been secretly conducting nuclear weapons research with highly enriched uranium. Although three sessions have been held, success has remained elusive, due to the DPRK's reluctance to forfeit its incipient nuclear deterrent and the American reluctance to offer concessions for that forfeiture without solid assurances it will be kept. Yet the talks, which seemed to offer agreement in August 2005, only to collapse in mutual bickering about timing and sequence, provide the only contact between the two principals and demonstrate Beijing's strategic leverage in this fragile region.

In view of the well-known predilection of Chinese leaders and strategic thinkers for a realist approach (or "parabellum strategic culture," in Johnston's language), the evidence we have adduced of a shift to a more multilateral approach is sometimes discounted. The usual argument is that China's liberalism conceals an underlying realism. Thus it is pointed out that China's increased participation in IGOs has been predominantly in the economic area, corresponding to the country's rational interest in fostering cooperation to promote GDP growth. This was clearly true of China's participation in the IMF, the World Bank Group (WBG), or the Asian Developmental Bank, where grants, loans, and other financial concessions were at stake. It also fits the cases of the WTO and CAFTA, though it should be noted that accession entailed substantial Chinese concessions, including the dismantling of infant industry tariff protection, opening to foreign investors, and a pledge to honour intellectual property rights and other international laws and conventions at the expense of Chinese sovereignty claims. China's clearest departure from this model, expanding IGO participation beyond economics and moving toward cooperative security, are the SCO and the six-party talks, the first of which seems to have been more successful, though both signal a new trend. Whereas before the mid-1990s Beijing (like Washington) preferred bilateral agreements, it has now ratified the Treaty on Nonproliferation of Nuclear Weapons (NPT) and the Chemical Weapons Convention, and agreed to adhere to the basic tenets of the Missile Technology Control Regime (MTCR). At the 2003 ASEAN summit, China proposed an ARF Security Policy Conference (ASPC) among military leaders of the APT countries, which has also been successfully instituted.

Conclusions

We have argued that China's foreign policy has made a transformation to a more multilateral orientation, in accord with the regime's "new security concept" (*xin anquan guan*) and in order to enhance China's "comprehensive national power." We have supported this argument with evidence of a much more active involvement in IGOs, first and foremost in the international economic arena, but now increasingly in multilateral security organizations, as well, particularly at (but not limited to) the regional arena, and preferably, it would appear, in the absence of direct US involvement. Although China's IGO involvement has not been oblivious to its national interests, taking full advantage of the resources contingent on membership in the IGOs it has joined, China's participation has adhered to the rules of the organization in question and Beijing has accordingly played increasingly prominent roles in the organizations to which it belongs (for example, the current chief justice of the World Court is a PRC legal official). And so far, IGO participation has had a substantial pay-off for China at relatively negligible cost, accelerating domestic economic development by vouchsafing China's credibility as a team player in the international community.

At the same time China has sought to make clear that its shift in orientation is a result of cognitive, rather than simply instrumental, learning, in the sense that its more idealistic and multilateral international persona has been thoroughly inculcated into China's national identity. This is why its occasional concessions of once closely guarded sovereignty issues (as in the accession negotiations for WTO membership) have been useful, to demonstrate the principled quality of its new national identity. China is now posing as a new "model" of good citizenship in the international arena, a "responsible great power" committed to a "peaceful rise" (*heping jueqi*). In this role, China's financial officials have thus resisted American pressure to revalue their currency with adjurations to reduce US budgetary and current account deficits before lecturing other countries, and repeatedly admonished the Japanese prime minister not to visit the Yasukuni shrine where Japanese war dead (including some class A war criminals) are buried. Yet on the whole, Beijing has played its new role as model with unusual sensitivity, dropping "anti-hegemonism" from its rhetorical vocabulary since the late 1990s and priding itself on good relations with the US. The implication is to be sure that China exemplifies a new, more multilateral model of international leadership in stark contrast to the pre-emptive unilateralism of the US, but this remains implicit, as China has learned its lesson from Germany and Japan: a rising great power must not overtly offend stake-holders in the international status quo.

China's adoption of its new, more idealistic, and multilateral, national identity has, of course, not proceeded without snags. Interestingly enough, the two most conspicuous flaws in China's national image of responsible and multilateral power have been two new members of "Greater China," Hong Kong and Taiwan. In Hong Kong, Deng's "one country, two systems" model has had too much emphasis on "one country" and too little on "two systems" for many Hong Kong citizens' tastes, fostering a rather demoralized instance of what was to have been a showcase of Chinese magnanimity. Meanwhile, Taiwan's democratization has propelled that island towards an increasingly bold claim to its right to national self-determination, provoking China's reassertion of its right to repress violently any such assertion. In neither case has China shown the multilateral tolerance it has displayed in its IGO diplomacy. In both cases, successful, extensive, integration with the mainland economy has not given rise to political identification with the Chinese communist regime, confounding Marxist expectations of a functional co-determination of politics and economics. Neither Hong Kong nor Taiwan have much purchase on China's new foreign-policy profile because they are not, by Chinese definition (nor by the definition of those who have official relations with China, by the terms of their recognition), "foreign," but are legally part of "one China" – though China's troubles with these two anomalous outliers can have an adverse demonstration effect on the image of open-minded, enlightened, multilateralism that China has so energetically striven to project (e.g. the unsuccessful effort to induce the EU to drop arms sanctions in the wake of the Anti-Secession Law).

Johnston et al. to the contrary notwithstanding,[12] this is not China's maiden voyage on the seas of international liberalism. It should not be forgotten that during the Maoist era China was an outspoken and principled adherent to the Marxist-Leninist variant of internationalism, in defence of which it made many clear sacrifices of its national interest, including war with the most powerful country in the world in Korea (and thereafter, protracted risk of war), extensive strategic and developmental aid to fraternal parties and movements in pursuit of world revolution at the expense of its own people's livelihood, and so on. The host IGO coordinating these efforts was, of course, the Moscow-centred "international communist movement," in which the PRC participated as one of the two leading, most honoured members. And yet this experience ended badly. After scarcely a decade, the IGO fractionalized, as China and its supporters either seceded or were evicted, depending on one's perspective, and the CCP attempted to form its own, more purist, IGO with this rump grouping. Having emerged from its quest for ideological utopia in the late 1970s with a renewed appreciation of the importance of national interests, Beijing under Deng Xiaoping made *Realpolitik* such a decisive criterion in its post-Mao foreign policy-making that it has been easy to forget its previous commitment to internationalism. Yet by the end of the 1990s the perils of excessive nationalism had also become clear, leading to dangerously antagonistic relations with China's leading trade partners, Japan, and the US. Now China has, at the dawn of the new century, renewed its interest in multilateral diplomacy.

The situation is so different now that it is hard to say whether any lessons from the previous experience with idealism might still apply. The IGOs in which China is currently invested are for the most part far less ideologically oriented and less clearly dominated by a single hegemon than the erstwhile international communist movement. Contemporary IGOs are so fluid, multi-purpose, pluralistic, and market-driven, it is hard to see any massive cleavage arising of the sort that led to the Sino-Soviet schism. But to the extent that China's earlier troubles with IGO membership arose from the (perhaps inadvertent) smuggling of nationalist ambitions into internationalist auspices, China will wish to be particularly sensitive to the possibility of that recurring.

Notes

1. Shaun Narine, "Institutional Theory and Southeast Asia: The Case of ASEAN," *World Affairs*, 161, Summer 1998, pp. 33–47.
2. See Robert Keohane, *Neorealism and Its Critics*, New York: Columbia University Press, 1986; Robert Keohane and Lisa Martin, "The Promise of Institutionalist Theory," *International Security* 20, Summer 1995, pp. 39–51.
3. Robinson, "Interdependence in China's Foreign Relations," in Samuel S. Kim, *China and the World*, 1998, pp. 191–4; Denny Roy, "Hegemon on the Horizon? China's Threat to East Asian Security," in Michael E. Brown, Sean M. Lynn-Jones, and Steven E. Miller (eds), *East Asian Security*, Cambridge, Massachusetts: MIT Press, 1996, pp. 121–2; and William R. Feeney, "China and the Multi-Lateral Economic Institutions," in Samuel S. Kim, *China and the World*, Boulder: Westview Press, 1998, pp. 245–7.
4. See Samuel Kim, "Chinese Foreign Policy Faces Globalization Challenges," in Alastair Iain Johnston and Robert S. Ross (eds) *The Study of China's Foreign Policy*, Stanford: Stanford University Press, 2006, pp. 276–306.
5. Kim, "China and the UN," p. 44.
6. Kim, "China and the UN," p. 65.
7. See Ann Kent, *China, the United Nations and Human Rights: Compliance, Learning and Effectiveness*, Philadelphia: University of Pennsylvania Press, 2000.
8. Ann Kent, "China, International Organizations and Regimes: The ILO as a Case Study in Organizational Learning," *Pacific Affairs*, 70, 4, Winter 1997, pp. 517–23.
9. James C. Hsiung, "The Aftermath of China's Accession to the World Trade Organization," *Independent Review*, 8, 1, Summer 2003, pp. 87–110; Penelope Prime, "China Joins the WTO," *Business Economics*, 37, 2, April 2002, pp. 26–34.
10. According to a 2006 UNDP Report, Cambodia had $452 million in imports from the PRC and sold only $30 million exports in 2004, and Bangladesh had $1.9 billion in imports and only $57 million in exports. Yet the picture is mixed, with more advanced economies like Thailand and the Philippines seeing rising exports (e.g. Thai exports to China increased by a third in 2005). Tyler Marshall, "Southeast Asia's New Best Friend," *Los Angeles Times*, 17 June 2006.
11. See Rosemary Foot, "China and the ASEAN Regional Forum," *Asian Survey*, 38, 5, May 1998, pp. 425–41; David Denoon and Wendy Freeman, "China's Security Strategy: The View from Beijing, ASEAN, and Washington," *Asian Survey*, 36, 4, April 1996, pp. 422–40; and Ian James Storey, "Creeping Assertiveness: China, The Philippines and The South China Sea Dispute," *Contemporary Southeast Asia* 21, 1, April 1999, pp. 95–116.
12. Alastair Iain Johnston, *Cultural Realism: Strategic Culture and Grand Strategy in Chinese History*, Princeton: Princeton University Press, 1995.

3 Racing to integrate, or cooperating to compete?
Liberal and realist interpretations of China's new multilateralism

Thomas G. Moore

Defined by Robert Keohane as the "practice of co-ordinating national policies in groups of three or more states, through ad hoc arrangements or by means of institutions," multilateralism enjoys an increasingly high profile in Chinese foreign policy.[1] In a recent assessment of the prospects for security regionalism in Asia, with a focus on the Association of Southeast Asian Nations (ASEAN), Sheldon Simon observed that "in many ways, China appears to be more willing to support multilateral institutions in Southeast Asia than the United States – a remarkable reversal from only a few years ago."[2] After beginning as a consultative partner in 1991, China participated in the establishment of the ASEAN Regional Forum (ARF) in 1994, and became a full ASEAN dialogue partner in 1996. Subsequent highlights of ASEAN–China cooperation include the 2002 signings of the Declaration on the Conduct of the Parties in the South China Sea and the Joint Declaration on Cooperation in the Field of Nontraditional Security Issues. Even more notable was China's 2003 accession to ASEAN's Treaty of Amity and Cooperation, as well as the simultaneous signing of a Joint Declaration on Strategic Partnership for Peace and Prosperity. Among other things, the latter called for a security dialogue to be established between China and the ten members of ASEAN. Beijing's separate proposal for, and subsequent hosting of, a first-ever ARF Security Policy Conference in 2004 broadened this initiative even further. Additional evidence of China's unprecedented activism includes two events it hosted in 2005: the Second Greater Mekong Subregion (GMS) Summit and an ARF seminar exploring cooperation on non-traditional security threats. As documented elsewhere in this volume, China's participation in security regionalism extends beyond ASEAN to initiatives such as the Shanghai Cooperation Organization (SCO) and the six-party talks on North Korea's nuclear-weapons programme.

A similar, and indeed even stronger, assessment would apply to economic regionalism, where Beijing has taken an especially active leadership role. Overall, China's integration into multilateral institutions (global as well as regional) seems to have proceeded even more quickly than many proponents of engagement policies had projected during the intense political debates in the United States (US) and elsewhere during the 1990s. Today, Beijing holds membership in every significant global and regional economic forum for which it qualifies, including the World Trade Organization (WTO), International Monetary Fund, World Bank, Asia Pacific Economic Cooperation (APEC) forum, Asian Development Bank, Asia–Europe Meeting (ASEM) dialogue, East Asia Summit (EAS), and ASEAN Plus Three (APT) process. (APT consists of the ten members of ASEAN plus China, Japan, and South Korea.)

At a global level, the most significant development in China's economic multilateralism over the past decade is surely Beijing's long-sought WTO accession in 2001. At a regional level, there have been several noteworthy developments, perhaps highlighted by China's pursuit of numerous free trade agreements (FTAs) – most notably, an ASEAN–China Free Trade Agreement (ACFTA) – and its participation in various efforts at enhanced financial and monetary cooperation within APT. In the latter issue area, Beijing has been an active participant in the Chiang Mai Initiative, which was created to provide emergency liquidity during regional currency crises, and the Asian Bond Market Initiative, which seeks to enhance the development of regional bond markets.[3]

In the area of FTAs, ACFTA has received the most attention, but China has in fact pursued FTAs with 28 countries or regions since 2001. All told, ten FTAs covering one quarter of China's total trade are currently under formal study, in negotiation, or have been concluded. Although China's FTA partners represent a wide geographic range (e.g. Iceland, Chile, Gulf Cooperation Council, Southern African Customs Union, Mercosur, Pakistan), much of China's focus has been in East Asia. Among its 15 EAS partners, for example, only South Korea and Japan are not currently pursuing FTAs with China. Discussions with ASEAN, Australia, New Zealand, and India are at various stages of progress, and China is lobbying South Korea hard to begin a formal FTA process. Beijing has periodically broached the idea of an FTA within APT, although this idea has not been pursued seriously by the group. Similarly, China proposed in 2003 that the six members of the SCO consider establishing an FTA. Although no feasibility study has yet been authorized, Beijing remains ready to pursue an FTA in Central Asia if its SCO partners agree to proceed.

Although China has often been cited in the past as a bastion of realpolitik, Beijing's recent turn toward multilateralism raises the question of whether Chinese foreign policy is moving in a more liberal direction.[4] From this perspective, China's pursuit of institutionalized cooperation signifies a growing commitment to a rules-based, norm-driven, international order. Responding to incentives for cooperation provided by international institutions and challenges associated with multidimensional globalization, so the liberal argument would contend, China's leaders have made a strategic choice to pursue an order based more on rules than power.

By all accounts, multilateralism has recently enjoyed an unprecedentedly high profile in China's foreign-policy discourse. In one of his annual statements to the United Nations (UN) General Assembly, Foreign Minister Li Zhaoxing declared that "multilateral cooperation ... should become the principal vehicle in the handling of international affairs," identifying multilateralism as central to the "future well-being of mankind."[5] On another occasion, Li opined that;

multilateralism is an effective way to deal with the common challenges of humanity. It is an important means to resolve international disputes. It is a forceful promotion and guarantee for the benign development of globalization. It is also the best way to promote democratic and law-based international relationships.[6]

In keeping with this growing rhetorical emphasis on multilateralism, terms such as common security, interdependence, and cooperative development have become commonplace in China's foreign-policy lexicon. Security and prosperity are increasingly identified as positive-sum objectives that cannot be achieved at the expense of other countries. From this perspective, the successful management of inter-state relations through multilateralism is presented as a win–win proposition. Accordingly, as David Shambaugh notes, even China's perception of security institutions in East Asia has evolved over the past decade "from suspicion, to uncertainty, to supportiveness."[7]

The bulk of this chapter is structured as a thought experiment in which liberal and realist interpretations of China's growing use of multilateralism in East Asia are considered. The next section explores in detail the view that China is moving towards liberal internationalism. According to this view, Beijing has become – seemingly against all odds – a catalyst for East Asian regionalism. Indeed, this position argues that China should be characterized as "racing to integrate" (or, alternatively, "competing to cooperate") given its propensity for trying to stay a step ahead in the promotion of FTAs, security dialogues, and other regional initiatives. From this perspective, China is driving the process of regional cooperation by inducing similar initiatives from Japan, the US, and India, especially among others, in their relations with ASEAN.

The subsequent section tries to reconcile China's new emphasis on multilateral diplomacy with realist thinking. From this perspective, the pattern of China's participation in regional multilateralism reveals that Beijing is actually "cooperating to compete" (or, alternatively, "integrating to compete") with the likes of Japan, the US, and India. For example, China is seen as using FTAs and other regional initiatives primarily to compete for political influence in East Asia. This analysis suggests a zero-sum dynamic, rooted in a struggle for relative power, in which countries vie over the strength of ties with various partners. Seen in this light, FTAs are instruments of economic statecraft as China pursues a regional sphere of influence. For example, what Beijing seeks through ACFTA is not the development of a rules-based order or greater interdependence for its own sake, as the liberal interpretation would contend, but institutionalized cooperation with ASEAN as a means to advance the interests of the Chinese state, interests still best understood primarily in terms of coercive power, political influence, and national security. The concluding sections of the chapter discuss various implications of this analysis for the larger study of Chinese foreign policy.

Cultivating rules-based, norm-driven, interdependence: Chinese multilateralism as liberal internationalism

In general terms, China's increased emphasis on multilateralism would seem to violate the basic realist expectation that countries prefer to preserve flexibility in their foreign relations by pursuing relatively informal, ad hoc, non-binding, commitments that carry low exit costs in the event that intergovernmental agreements prove to be disadvantageous.[8] From this perspective, Beijing's active pursuit of WTO membership, FTAs such as ACFTA, and enhanced financial and monetary cooperation in APT – not to mention its promotion of various economic and security initiatives in multilateral groupings such as SCO, ARF, ASEM, EAS, and APEC – represents an analytical puzzle, in considerable measure because China consistently evinced strong scepticism of multilateralism until less than a decade ago.

Whereas realism generally expects states to regard the collective management of shared problems with suspicion because they wish to maximize independence, from the liberal perspective China's recent behaviour indicates that Beijing is willing to tolerate – and may even be trying to cultivate – mutual dependence on certain issues.[9] Simply put, China seems to be consciously increasing levels of interdependence rather than avoiding deeper ties. In its relations with ASEAN and as a member of the SCO, for example, Beijing no longer insists upon the compartmentalization of economic and security dialogues. In fact, China has begun to link the economic and security arenas in ways that seemingly challenge the realist expectation that countries will seek to preserve their autonomy as a top priority.

Especially noteworthy is China's unprecedented embrace of institutionalized forms of cooperation. Consider ACFTA. In the words of Zha Daojiong, ACFTA "will bind China to work with ASEAN under a set of negotiated rules."[10] Furthermore, the fact that China's leaders have pursued ACFTA, despite numerous studies predicting that ASEAN's material benefit from trade liberalization will outstrip China's, would seem to contradict realist expectations about the importance of relative gains.[11] In this respect, the favourable terms China granted ASEAN in their 2002 Framework Agreement on Comprehensive Economic Cooperation, to say nothing of subsequent concessions such as the "early harvest" provisions in the FTA process, also require further explanation.

In keeping with this analysis, Justin Hempson-Jones argues that China has become, "strikingly liberal in its emphasis on the cooperative nature of state interaction," especially in its "interactions with economic, political, and security intergovernmental organizations..."[12] More generally, Hempson-Jones observes that "liberal patterns in the PRC's foreign policy are embodied in a more relaxed attitude toward interdependence."[13] While Hempson-Jones acknowledges that China's liberal turn has been most pronounced in the economic realm, he also argues that "liberal trends exist in Chinese foreign policy even in the fundamentally important area of state security – the stronghold of prudent realpolitik," citing China's multifaceted engagement of ASEAN and its participation in ARF as evidence.[14]

Indeed, authors writing in this vein often focus on China's relations with ASEAN in arguing that China's recent behaviour represents a significant change in foreign policy orientation rather than simple pragmatism. To cite another example, Shambaugh argues that "China's efforts to improve its ties with ASEAN are not merely part of a larger 'charm offensive.' They represent, in some cases, fundamental compromises that China has chosen to make in limiting its own sovereign interests for the sake of engagement in multilateral frameworks and pursuit of greater regional interdependence."[15] Along similar lines, Hempson-Jones contends that by joining the WTO and otherwise increasing its participation in various multilateral economic, political, and security forums, China has "embarked on a course that has substantially compromised its autonomy." Specifically, he cites Beijing's "acceptance of conditionality" in interstate relations and its "adherence to WTO requirements" as evidence that China's approach to international relations has undergone fundamental change.[16]

Not surprisingly, Shambaugh and Hempson-Jones both regard realism as a degraded tool for understanding Chinese foreign policy. Although Shambaugh recognizes the limitations of any single theoretical perspective for understanding China's engagement of Asia and the resulting transformation of regional order, he argues that, "realist theory seems particularly incapable of explaining such a complex and dynamic environment ..."[17] Hempson-Jones agrees, concluding that Chinese behaviour is more consistent with neo-liberal institutionalism than realism. From its "sovereignty-bending admission" to the WTO to its "more pragmatic stance (on UN peacekeeping) that sanctions a certain level of interference into other states' affairs," Hempson-Jones argues that, "constraints on Chinese behaviour have been accepted in exchange for gains for the state."[18] Whatever China's original intentions were in interacting more extensively with the outside world, the benefits accrued have reinforced China's cooperative orientation by continually pushing "Chinese behaviour in a more liberal direction."[19] According to this interpretation, a neoliberal institutionalist dynamic has been plainly evident as Beijing has accepted weakened sovereignty and greater compromises in policy autonomy over time.

One interpretation of China's increased emphasis on multilateralism is that Beijing now believes its quest for development, security, and status is best served by deeper engagement in world affairs generally and greater participation in institutionalized forms of cooperation specifically. At a minimum, this perspective suggests that China's leaders regard growing interdependence as a fundamental condition of international relations that cannot be resisted in conducting state-to-state relations. More provocatively, Beijing can be seen as actually embracing liberal internationalism as a strategic choice in an era defined by globalization. According to this second position, interdependence has become an end as well as a means in the conduct of Chinese foreign policy.

As a strategic context, globalization is seen as introducing – or at least accelerating the emergence of – new sources of economic and security vulnerability such as unregulated capital flows, weapons proliferation, drug trafficking, transnational terrorist networks, cyber crime, and the spread of infectious diseases.

The fact that mainstream leaders, bureaucrats, and scholars in China view such a wide range of issues in terms of globalization underscores the phenomenon's importance as a lens through which elites view the challenges facing the country. Indeed, globalization figures more and more prominently in China's strategic thinking.[20] From the rising threat of non-state terrorism and the regional economic weaknesses highlighted by the Asian Financial Crisis, to the outbreak of Severe Acute Respiratory Syndrome (SARS) and the transnational diffusion of lethal military technologies, forces associated with globalization are seen as providing significant challenges to Chinese interests. As a result, the liberal interpretation contends, Beijing now wishes for the world's great powers to move away from a traditional, zero-sum, unilateralist struggle for security and prosperity – which is increasingly self-defeating – in favour of positive-sum, multilateral, efforts, what Chinese officials have called "common security" and "globalized cooperation."[21]

Indeed, China's leaders have repeatedly acknowledged that globalization encourages broad participation in multilateral institutions at both the regional and global levels.[22] Although Beijing remains cautious about the implications of multilateralism for national autonomy, institutionalized forms of cooperation are now seen as instruments by which China can pursue its interests both effectively and with international legitimacy. Notably, multilateralism allows China to assert a leadership role – especially in Central and East Asia – without unnecessarily exacerbating fears that Beijing harbours revisionist intentions. According to a liberal interpretation of Chinese behaviour, Beijing increasingly subscribes to notions such as win–win economic competition and collective security. Whereas interdependence used to be accepted rather narrowly as an economic means to China's developmental ends, in the new millennium Beijing appears to assign independent weight to interdependence as a broader political goal of Chinese foreign policy. From this perspective, China is a status-quo power that seeks to advance its interests through the existing international system.

In one variant of this position, the emerging Chinese colossus can be seen as pursuing what John Ikenberry calls an "institutional bargain." In this bargain, the leading state "agrees to tie itself to the commitments and obligations of an interstate institution" so long as those "institutional agreements ... lock in other countries into a relatively congenial and stable order" conducive to the leading state's long-term interests.[23] In this way, multilateral agreements can enhance the exercise of what Joseph Nye calls "co-optive behavioural power – getting others to want what you want."[24] In what Ikenberry calls a "free-floating" (i.e. uninstitutionalized) order, the leading state must resort to the "constant and costly exercise of power to get its way."[25] In this way, institutionalized cooperation can be seen as a mechanism of political control. Even though China must accept some measure of reduced policy autonomy as a demonstration of self-restraint, this trade-off is more efficient than repeated reliance on coercive power. Especially as power resources become "less fungible, less coercive, and less tangible" over time, institutionalized cooperation becomes an increasingly attractive tool for rising powers such as China.[26]

Integrating or competing? 41

Finally, the liberal trend in Chinese thinking is also arguably reflected in the increasing emphasis Beijing places on multilateralism over multipolarity. Whereas the promotion of multipolarity suggests that China seeks explicitly to balance against US power, Beijing's increasing diplomatic emphasis on multilateralism "reflects a preference for a more democratic world order that emphasizes proper management of state-to-state relations over the redistribution of power."[27] According to a liberal interpretation, China is increasingly eschewing realist great-power struggle, as characterized by internal military mobilization and hostile external alliances, in favour of a more cooperative, multilateral approach to development and security.

Cooperating to compete: Chinese multilateralism as realist internationalism

Although Chinese behaviour seems to be at odds with certain general realist expectations, many of Beijing's actions can also be reconciled quite satisfactorily with specific lines of realist thought. For example, China's engagement of ASEAN countries fits well with the classic realist explanation of Germany's trading relations with its smaller European neighbours between the First and Second World Wars, as set forth by Albert Hirschman in his landmark book *National Power and the Structure of Foreign Trade*.[28] In Hirschman's account, Germany sought to increase its political leverage by offering favourable trade arrangements to its smaller neighbours. Rather than try to dominate by extracting economic concessions from weaker parties, Germany sought to increase its political influence by purposely accepting asymmetric economic relations. From this perspective, contemporary China would be seen as cultivating interdependence with smaller countries such as its ASEAN partners, not as a separate end or primarily for economic purposes, but as a means of enhancing its political power. If analogous arguments are made about China's participation in the SCO, or even its ongoing, multifaceted, bilateral engagement of countries such as South Korea, Australia, New Zealand, and Pakistan, one could identify a realist-oriented strategy in which Beijing is trying to increase its regional political influence through economic statecraft.

It remains to be seen whether ASEAN or China will benefit more from ACFTA in the long run. Many of the initial feasibility studies forecast that ASEAN would enjoy greater welfare gains. Subsequently, China has made "early harvest" concessions in the negotiation process that would seem to make that outcome even more likely. Even if ASEAN countries enjoy higher rates of economic growth from ACFTA, China will still accrue critical benefits such as newly expanded export markets and improved access to raw materials and other inputs vital to its economic well-being. In this way, ACFTA could enhance China's long-term autonomy in world economic affairs vis-à-vis dominant players such as the US, the European Union (EU), and Japan, thereby enhancing its security.

Similarly, for all the wealth creation that ASEAN countries might enjoy as a result of ACFTA, this would come at the expense of greater dependence on

China. As the importance of trade with China grows for ASEAN countries, so too does Beijing's political leverage. In this way, Hirschman argued that "commerce can become an alternative to war ... by providing a method of coercion of its own in the relations between sovereign nations," namely, through the potential disruption of economic ties.[29] To be sure, any interruption in commerce can be expected to hurt both sides, but the adjustment costs are likely to be far greater for the smaller partner. It is in this respect that Hirschman's analysis was quintessentially realist: he focused on the use of foreign trade to create "relationships of dependence and influence between nations" that increased coercive power.[30]

In fact, China may not even need to twist arms or threaten punitive action to ensure that ASEAN acts in accord with Beijing's interests. As the International Political Economy literature has repeatedly noted, small states often perceive their interests as converging with those of larger neighbours as the result of FTAs and other agreements that institutionalize cooperation. More broadly, domestic politics has long been understood as being significantly shaped by the structure of a country's international economic relations.[31] Specifically, the beneficiaries of trade liberalization in the smaller countries (e.g. ASEAN) have an interest in defending and even advancing relations with the larger partner (e.g. China). From this perspective, economic restructuring associated with ACFTA should strengthen those sectors, firms, and factors of production in ASEAN that are advantaged by trade liberalization with China. Indeed, new political interests and coalitions could be expected to emerge that favour the articulation of domestic and foreign policies beneficial to China.[32]

From this perspective, China's more active participation in multilateralism signifies not a commitment to liberal internationalism but a realist-oriented willingness to use institutionalized cooperation in managing relations with certain countries. Consistent with Hegemonic Stability Theory, a leading realist explanation of US behaviour in the post-Cold War era, China can be seen as a large power trying to "build long-term security, political, and economic commitments that are difficult to retract," often by providing public goods or other benefits to smaller countries on favourable terms through multilateral institutions.[33] Indeed, China seems focused on calculating the opportunity cost of institutionalized cooperation (as expressed in reduced policy autonomy) compared with the gains available by "locking other states into enduring policy positions."[34] To this point, it should be noted, China's multilateral agreements with partners such as ASEAN and SCO have not been very costly in terms of reduced policy autonomy.

While Beijing's longstanding aversion to institutionalized cooperation has weakened substantially, China's leaders remain cautious about the obligations they accept, often still preferring codes of conduct and statements of principle in favour of legalized agreements with robust enforcement mechanisms. For example, Beijing maintains a preference for pacts, such as ASEAN's Treaty of Amity and Cooperation, which reinforce principles of sovereignty, territorial integrity, non-interference in domestic affairs, peaceful settlement of disputes, and renunciation of the threat or use of force.[35]

Indeed, a point often missed by observers who emphasize a liberal trend in Chinese foreign policy is that the regional groups in which China holds membership have largely eschewed any movement toward supranationality. For its part, China has sought to promote (or at least reinforce) the norm of sovereignty. For example, Beijing has skilfully used East Asian regionalism to further ostracize Taiwan. Not only is Taiwan excluded from the likes of APT, ARF, and EAS, but China has used these groups and other forums to socialize its neighbours – especially ASEAN – to accept Beijing's views on matters such as Taiwan's status. This example shows that socialization is a two-way street. For analysts who see China's participation in multilateralism as pushing Chinese foreign policy in a liberal direction, discussion is too often restricted to how China will become socialized by its interlocutors rather than the other way around.

Similarly, Beijing is most enthusiastic about agreements that emphasize consultation and consensus on key issues such as dispute management. The SCO is defined by the so-called Shanghai Spirit, just as China's expanding relations with ASEAN extend and strengthen the much-ballyhooed ASEAN Way. Although the SCO is a formal organization, it is based on voluntary principles that reinforce Westphalian notions of sovereignty.

In many respects, China seems to be engaged in a balancing act. On the one hand, growing economic and security interdependence in world affairs has increased China's interest in the kind of stable, rule-governed, environment associated with deepening multilateralism. At the same time, Beijing's traditional resistance to shared sovereignty and the constrained policy autonomy that accompanies collective decision-making militate against greater acceptance of formal institutionalization. To this point, Beijing has coped with these conflicting pressures by pursuing institutionalized cooperation on a selective basis. Specifically, Chinese leaders have pursued institutionalized cooperation most enthusiastically either in global multilateral settings (e.g. WTO and UN) or regionally with weaker partners (e.g. ASEAN and SCO).

In recognition that small numbers can be a source of vulnerability, Beijing seems to prefer larger groups except when China is the most powerful participant. Consistent with realist concerns about the danger of entering into agreements with stronger partners who might find their leverage further enhanced, China favours trade liberalization in the WTO over APEC. Although its membership draws on 21 economies from both sides of the Pacific, APEC still lends itself to dominance by the US (and its allies such as Japan). As a result, there has long been concern in Beijing that institutionalized cooperation in APEC would likely reflect US interests at China's expense. Whatever the risks of WTO entry, China's participation in a group with 149 members offers a more attractive alternative because its agenda is less easily dominated by the US. To the extent that growing interdependence advances a Chinese interest in a stable, rule-oriented, environment, the pursuit of institutionalized cooperation in large groups such as the WTO represents a more desirable choice.

China's differentiated approach to trade liberalization – favouring WTO negotiations and FTAs with weaker actors such as ASEAN, all while demonstrating less enthusiasm for similar agreements in APEC – undermines not only the notion that China opposes institutionalized cooperation altogether but also the notion that Beijing uniformly supports institutionalized cooperation. As such, a realist interpretation would emphasize the selective, partial, and generally uneven, nature of China's turn toward multilateralism. In this sense, it is not so much institutionalized cooperation that China resists as the prospect that certain venues for institutionalized cooperation might produce outcomes adverse to Chinese interests.[36]

The fact that Beijing has pursued trade liberalization more actively within East Asia rather than on a trans-Pacific basis, when the latter would yield greater economic benefits for China, supports the realist view that the goal of initiatives such as ACFTA has been more political than economic. If economic gain were valued most, Chinese policy would likely follow one of two paths. First, Beijing could try to force its smaller partners to accept disadvantageous trade deals. Second, Beijing could pursue broader trade liberalization, as studies have shown that China stands to enjoy the greatest welfare gains – both absolutely and relative to its partners – through trade liberalization in the WTO, APEC, and APT, respectively.[37] In this respect, initiatives such as ACFTA are economically suboptimal.

China's new-found support for FTAs also reflects the powerful opportunity that FTAs provide to establish new rules, standards, and procedures consistent with Chinese interests. As discussed earlier, FTAs such as ACFTA also stand to create regional trade structures that would make China's partners more dependent economically. This in turn would confer power on Beijing. As numerous studies have shown, China's deepening participation in the world economy – as symbolized and accelerated by Beijing's WTO accession – is already having a profound re-structuring effect on global trade patterns.[38] ACFTA and China's other FTA initiatives represent a regional intensification of this trend. Indeed, changing trade patterns have profound security externalities. Consistent with Hirschman's analysis of interwar Germany, the strategic use of economic multilateralism by contemporary China seems designed to cultivate interdependence with smaller countries as a means of enhancing its political power.

Consistent with this interpretation, another purpose of China's efforts at regionalism may be to balance against US power. In the absence of formal military alliances, it could be argued that China's approach is one of soft balancing or, at least, hedging. Indeed, realists would argue that Beijing's promotion of "partnerships without alliance" – an application of China's New Security Concept – in its relations with ASEAN and SCO countries is a thinly veiled effort to counter Washington's dominance. Whereas the liberal interpretation would emphasize how Beijing's growing commitment to multilateral processes reflects its preference for a rules-based order, albeit, one that arguably restrains the exercise of US power, the realist interpretation would be that Chinese multilateralism – pursued selectively and opportunistically rather than uniformly – is actually designed to enhance Chinese power at the expense of the US by weakening the bilateral alliances that serve as the core of Washington's grand strategy in East Asia. In the long run, moreover, China seeks to position itself as the hub of a new network of regional relationships. While multilateralism may be a useful foreign-policy tool, the realist view would argue, institutional constraints are no substitute for coercive power in international politics.[39]

Multilateralism as China's strategic choice in an era of globalization and regionalism

By exploring liberal and realist interpretations of China's turn towards multilateralism, this chapter has essentially presented a thought experiment. As such, it simplifies the subject in ways that must be acknowledged. First, the analysis far from exhausts the universe of specific liberal and realist interpretations, to say nothing of constructivist interpretations and other perspectives. Second, the chapter downplays both the role of domestic politics and how the choices China makes are conditioned by the international environment with which it interacts.

Presented in this form, the chapter paints a somewhat static picture of Chinese decision-making. Domestic impulses, such as the political imperative of maintaining robust economic growth, are largely absent. Similarly, international stimuli are not examined at length. On the one hand, space does not allow detailed analysis of how China's evolving policies on multilateralism have been shaped by interaction with its external environment. That said, it should be acknowledged that Chinese initiatives in the area of economic cooperation are, at least in part, a response to factors such as the lessons of the Asian Financial Crisis and the spread of FTA fever that has gripped the international political economy in recent years. At a global level, China's epochal choice to join the WTO cannot be understood in isolation from the long-term commitment displayed by the advanced industrial democracies – and the US, in particular – to the commercial engagement of China. At a regional level, ASEAN's receptivity to Chinese initiatives such as ACFTA has, of course, also been critical in shaping Beijing's evolving position on multilateralism.

In contrast to the liberal and realist interpretations presented in this chapter, a structuralist interpretation emphasizing the nature of the contemporary global capitalist system might address some of the limitations identified above. For example, one aspect of China's integration into the world economy not explored in this chapter is the growing role of global commodity chains (also known as production chains or value chains) in shaping Chinese behaviour. Given the ongoing transnationalization of production and distribution, global political economy approaches that focus on non-state actors such as multinational corporations and multi-level, network, forms of governance have increasing salience. From this perspective, the Chinese state exercises a much reduced and altogether different type of "strategic choice" (i.e. agency) than that suggested by the liberal and realist interpretations presented in this chapter. Indeed, in many structuralist approaches the conception of the state as a political actor would be fundamentally different from that found in the particular international relations literature on multilateralism that informs this collaborative volume.

The point, therefore, is to acknowledge that the analysis presented in this chapter is state-centric (as per the liberal and realist interpretations provided) and underestimates the dynamic, interactive, nature of China's relations with the outside world. Chinese decision-makers do, of course, operate in a world characterized by features such as unipolarity, interdependence, globalization, and regionalism. With respect to the last feature, for example, it is legitimate to ask whether it is China that is turning to regional multilateralism or whether it is East Asia more broadly that is actually turning to regional multilateralism, with China primarily following this trend. This point relates to the larger issue of whether China has a grand strategy that calls for the greater use of multilateralism as a means of pursuing specific objectives in its foreign policy. In different ways, the liberal and realist interpretations presented in this chapter concur that China's more active participation in multilateralism reflects strategic choice rather than serendipity or simple pragmatism.

While a case can be made that Beijing has "crossed the river by feeling for stones" (*mozhe shitou guohe*) in its foreign policy as well as in its domestic economic reform, it would seem that China's increased use of multilateralism reflects more than a trial-and-error unfolding of events or the simple weakening over time of Beijing's principled opposition to the practice. Specifically, China's turn toward multilateralism seems to have coincided with high-level political decisions about the country's proper course domestically and internationally. Taken together, a series of major policy moves taken at the end of the 1990s and early in the new millennium suggest that China's turn towards multilateralism reflected the crystallization of a grand strategy, or at least a de facto grand strategy. For example, by the late 1990s Chinese leaders had come to the realization that unipolarity was likely to persist indefinitely. Indeed, it was also around this time that China lessened its official opposition to US alliances in East Asia, tacitly recognizing that American presence in the region benefits Chinese interests in certain respects. By electing not to openly oppose the US, Beijing made it easier for neighbours such as ASEAN and South Korea to develop closer relations with China because they were not, in essence, forced to choose between Beijing and Washington. As discussed earlier, the timing of China's decision to join the WTO, followed by its comprehensive engagement of SCO, ASEAN, and other countries on its periphery, further suggests that the rapid erosion of China's longstanding scepticism of multilateralism reflected strategic choice.

Even if there was no master plan with a blueprint detailing exactly what initiatives to take and how precisely these steps would fit into a formal grand strategy for making China rich and strong, the intensity and depth of China's forays into multilateralism – from FTAs to security dialogues – seems hard to square with an argument that these developments were largely serendipitous and unconnected. Even if China's much-ballyhooed pragmatism played a role, it is difficult to see how, for example, the SCO evolved in unintended fashion as quickly as it did from a loose forum for the inter-state coordination of border issues to a formal organization embodying aspects of a quasi-military alliance. Indeed, Beijing's active leadership role in the establishment of SCO further undermines the notion that little or no element of conscious strategy was involved. As Jianwei Wang's chapter documents, China pushed to expand the SCO's agenda from security cooperation to economic cooperation in a self-conscious effort to maintain what Beijing regarded as the group's flagging momentum. Similarly, the broadening of China's engagement of ASEAN since the late 1990s seems far too comprehensive to have unfolded in the absence of some strategic direction. All told, it is hard to fathom that China has unwittingly allowed its participation in multilateral cooperation to grow in ways that it actively resisted in the past.

Is China learning?

This chapter focuses on why China pursues multilateralism. Some observers, particularly liberal thinkers, might argue that the question of whether Chinese policy is informed by liberal internationalism or realist internationalism is much less important than the fact that China has become more active multilaterally. According to this position, China's interests are likely to be fundamentally transformed by its participation in multilateralism – regardless of Beijing's initial intentions. From this perspective, participation in multilateralism is a slippery slope. What may begin as instrumental participation (adaptation) often leads to enmeshment (adaptive learning) as national interests are transformed over time through the experience of participating in multilateral cooperation. The point, in short, is that norms often follow behaviour. Cooperative behaviour socializes the participants, creates incentives to conform to multilateral principles, and otherwise contributes to the genuine (i.e. cognitive) learning in which value change takes place.

The realist interpretation would caution, however, that this process is neither as seamless nor as irreversible as described here. From this perspective, China's current commitment to multilateralism is too opportunistic, conditional, and selective to dismiss the question of motivations so easily. As much as China's views of, and policies toward, multilateralism have evolved, the permanence of Beijing's commitment to institutionalized cooperation on the basis of generalized principles of conduct is by no means assured. Particularly given China's traditional scepticism of multilateralism, realists would caution that Beijing's recognition that multilateralism has utility in advancing Chinese interests should not be mistaken for value change.

While the liberal and realist interpretations differ markedly on a wide variety of issues, perhaps the most significant issue is whether Beijing is likely to continue down the "multilateral path" in the future, and, if so, how far. According to the liberal view, China can be expected to broaden and deepen its participation in multilateral groups, especially as the process of globalization continues to unfold. As such, growing interdependence in world affairs is likely to serve as an important stimulus in China's foreign-policy learning. By contrast, the realist view would expect China's commitment to multilateralism to remain decidedly uneven, particularly in terms of acquiring new partners or expanding China's current participation to new institutions. Moreover, realist analysis would anticipate a possible re-evaluation of current multilateral arrangements as the costs of constrained autonomy rise. As China becomes more powerful relative to its partners, the opportunity cost of constrained autonomy will grow, even if neither the scope nor the depth of existing cooperative arrangements increases. Consequently, it is unclear – and even doubtful – from a realist perspective whether Beijing will be willing to take the next step in regionalism by sharing governance in any meaningful way. More generally, realists would caution against any assumption that a more "multilateral" China will necessarily be more altruistic or civic-minded, as multilateral institutions have proved to be tools of domination in the past.

Concluding thoughts

By exploring liberal and realist interpretations of China's more active participation in multilateralism, this chapter raises but does not resolve a central question: what is Beijing's ultimate goal – integration or domination? This dichotomy portrays the alternatives too starkly, to be sure, but the liberal interpretation does see China's increased pursuit of institutionalized cooperation as signifying a growing commitment to a rules-based, norm-driven, international order. By contrast, the realist interpretation sees China's growing participation in multilateralism as little more than a mechanism by which Beijing can increase its coercive power and political influence, with regional (or even global) primacy as the ultimate objective. In other words, China is "cooperating to compete" rather than "racing to integrate."

For all of Beijing's increased emphasis on multilateralism, there is also evidence of resurgent bilateralism (e.g. strategic economic dialogue with the US, new FTA discussions with individual countries) as well as persistent unilateralism (e.g. Chinese policy on Hong Kong and Taiwan). As this suggests, China's foreign relations remain multifaceted. In this respect, the biggest story may not be Beijing's increased use of multilateralism as much as the larger, more active, role China is playing in international affairs more generally. Contrary to Deng Xiaoping's belief that China should avoid a leading role in world affairs (*bu chu tou*), choosing instead to bide its time while building up capabilities (*taoguang yanghui*), Beijing has pursued a more activist foreign policy over the past decade under both the Jiang Zemin/Zhu Rongji leadership and the Hu Jintao/Wen Jiabao leadership. For reasons that the liberal and realist positions interpret differently, China has expanded its use of multilateralism in recent years. Especially for the realist interpretation, but also for the liberal interpretation, this increasing reliance on multilateralism is only one aspect of a broader, even more significant, phenomenon.

Notes

1 Robert O. Keohane, "Multilateralism: An Agenda for Research," *International Journal* XLV, Autumn 1990, p. 731. In a slight variation, John Ruggie defines multi-

lateralism as "an institutional form that coordinates relations among three or more states on the basis of generalized principles of conduct." See John Ruggie, "Multilateralism: The Anatomy of an Institution," in John Ruggie (ed.) *Multilateralism Matters*, New York: Columbia University Press, 1993, p. 11.
2 Sheldon W. Simon, "Southeast Asia: Wither Security Regionalism?" in Richard J. Ellings and Aaron L. Friedberg (eds) *Strategic Asia 2003–04,* Seattle: National Bureau of Asian Research, 2003, p. 282.
3 For a recent overview of these initiatives, see William W. Grimes, "East Asian Financial Regionalism in Support of the Global Financial Architecture? The Political Economy of Regional Nesting," *Journal of East Asian Studies* 6, 2006, pp. 353–80.
4 This issue is the subject of Justin S. Hempson-Jones, "The Evolution of China's Engagement with Intergovernmental Organizations: Toward a Liberal Foreign Policy?" *Asian Survey* 45:5, September/October 2005, pp. 702–21. For additional background, see Evan S. Medeiros and M. Taylor Fravel, "China's New Diplomacy," *Foreign Affairs* 82:6, November/December 2003, pp. 22–35, Jianwei Wang, "China Multilateral Diplomacy in the New Millennium," in Yong Deng and Fei-Ling Wang (eds) *China Rising: Power and Motivation in Chinese Foreign Policy,* Lanham, Md: Rowman and Littlefield, 2005, pp. 159–200; and Yong Deng and Thomas G. Moore, "China Views Globalization: Toward a New Great-Power Politics?" *The Washington Quarterly* 27:3, Summer 2004, pp. 117–36.
5 Li Zhaoxing, speech to UN General Assembly, 24 September 2003. Online. Available: www.un.org/webcast/ga/58/statements/chinaeng030924.htm (accessed 9 October 2003).
6 "Full Text of Chinese FM's Press Conference," 6 March 2004. Online. Available: www.english1.peopledaily.com.cn:80/200403/07/print20040307_136794.html (accessed 7 February 2005).
7 David Shambaugh, "China Engages Asia: Reshaping the Regional Order," *International Security* 29:3, Winter 2004–05, 64–99, quote on p. 69.
8 For an excellent primer on the different expectations of realism and liberalism as applied to comparative regionalism, see Steve Chan, "Liberalism, Realism, and Regional Trade: Differentiating APEC from E.U. and NAFTA," *Pacific Focus* 16:1, Spring 2001, pp. 5–34. On the preference for flexibility, see p. 10.
9 For a classic realist statement on interdependence, see Kenneth N. Waltz, *Theory of International Politics*, Reading, MA: Addison-Wesley, 1979, chapter 7.
10 Daojiong Zha, "The Politics of China–ASEAN Economic Relations: Assessing the Move Toward A Free Trade Area," *Asian Perspective* 26:4, 2002, pp. 53–82, quote on p. 55.
11 See, for example, *Forging Closer ASEAN–China Economic Relations in the Twenty-first Century*, October 2001. Online. Available: www.aseansec.org/newdata/asean_chi.pdf. This is the report submitted by the ASEAN–China Expert Group on Economic Cooperation in October 2001.
12 Hempson-Jones 2005, quotations on p. 711 and p. 703 respectively.
13 Ibid., 703.
14 Ibid., 704.
15 Shambaugh 2004–05, p. 76.
16 Hempson-Jones 2005, p. 711.
17 Shambaugh 2004–05, p. 99.
18 Hempson-Jones 2005, p. 704.
19 Ibid., 711.
20 For a detailed argument that goes well beyond the analysis provided in this section of the chapter, see Deng and Moore 2004.
21 China State Council, Information Office, "China's National Defense, 2002," *Renmin Ribao,* overseas edition, 10 December 2002, pp. 1–4. For more on common security, see Wu Bangguo, "Create a Hundred Years of Peace in Asia, Jointly Build Sustained

Development of Asia," 1 September 2003, in *Foreign Broadcast Information Service*, CPP2003–0901000066. For more on globalized cooperation, see Li Zhaoxing, Speech to UN General Assembly, New York, 24 September 2003. Online. Available: www.un.org/webcast/ga/58/statements/chinaeng030924.htm (accessed 9 October 2003).

22 On economic affairs, see Jiang Zemin, speech at the Eighth APEC Informal Leadership Meeting, 16 November 2000. Online. Available: www.fmprc.gov/cn/eng/6004. html. On security affairs, see Tang Jiaxuan's speech at the Ninth ASEAN Regional Forum Foreign Ministers' Meeting, Brunei, 31 July 2002. Online. Available: www.fmprc.gov. cn/eng/33228.html (accessed on 11 March 2003).
23 G. John Ikenberry, "Multilateralism and US Grand Strategy," in Stewart Patrick and Shepard Forman (eds) *Multilateralism and US Foreign Policy*, Boulder, CO: Lynne Rienner, 2002, pp. 121–40, at 124.
24 Joseph S. Nye, Jr., *Bound to Lead*, New York: Basic Books, 1990, p. 188.
25 Ikenberry 2002, p. 124.
26 Nye 1990 p. 188.
27 Deng and Moore 2004, p. 122.
28 Albert O. Hirschman, *National Power and the Structure of Foreign Trade*, Berkeley: University of California Press, 1945.
29 Ibid., 15.
30 Ibid.
31 Drawing on Hirschman, Jonathan Kirshner presents an excellent analysis of these dynamics. See Kirshner, "States, Markets, and Great Power Relations in the Pacific," in G. John Ikenberry and Michael Mastanduno (eds) *International Relations Theory and the Asia-Pacific*, New York: Columbia University Press, 2003, p. 277. Other relevant literature on the subject includes Robert O. Keohane and Helen V. Milner (eds) *Internationalization and Domestic Politics*, Cambridge: Cambridge University Press, 1996; Suzanne Berger and Ronald Dore (ed.) *National Diversity and Global Capitalism*, Ithaca: Cornell University Press, 1996; and Ronald L. Rogowski, *Commerce and Coalitions*, Princeton: Princeton University Press, 1989.
32 For a more general argument along these lines, see Kirshner 2003, p. 277.
33 G. John Ikenberry, *After Victory*, Princeton: Princeton University Press, 2001, p. 41.
34 Ikenberry 2002, p. 127.
35 For the text of the *Treaty of Amity and Cooperation*. Online. Available: www.aseansec.org/1217.htm (accessed 22 November 2004).
36 The China-specific argument presented here is consistent with the more general analysis of Asia-Pacific institutionalization provided in Miles Kahler, "Legalization as Strategy: The Asia-Pacific Case," *International Organization* 54:3, Summer 2000, pp. 549–71.
37 See, for example, Robert Scollay and John P. Gilbert, *New Regional Trading Arrangements in the Asia Pacific?* Washington, DC: Institute for International Economics, 2001.
38 See, for example, Zhi Wang, "The Impact of China's WTO Accession on Patterns of World Trade," *Journal of Policy Modeling* 25, 2003, pp. 1–41; Thomas Rumbaugh and Nicholas Blancher, "China: International Trade and WTO Accession," *IMF Working Paper*, WP/04/36, March 2004; and Yongzheng Yang, "China's Integration into the World Economy: Implications for Developing Countries," *IMF Working Paper*, WP/03/245, December 2003.
39 I am indebted to an anonymous reviewer for Routledge for emphasizing this point.

4 The new player in the game
China, arms control, and multilateralism

Jing-dong Yuan

Introduction

Over the last 25 years, and in particular since the early 1990s, China has become increasingly receptive to multilateralism and cooperative security and more actively engaged in regional security dialogues and global arms control and non-proliferation negotiations. Beijing's growing involvement in these multilateral processes is a reflection of its changing perspectives on the role of international and regional institutions in maintaining peace and security. When set against its traditional strategic culture, which places a high premium on sovereignty and independence, China's changing attitudes and approaches towards arms control and nonproliferation over the past two decades seem a welcome departure from its past behaviour and practices. This is major progress.

This chapter takes stock of Chinese participation in multilateral arms control and nonproliferation and discusses the factors that have influenced Beijing's perspectives and policies. In particular, I examine the evolution of Chinese approaches to multilateral arms control and nonproliferation and explain how and why Beijing's interests, preferences, and policies, have changed over time as a result of its participation in, and interactions with, multilateral institutions and processes in these areas. I argue that China's approaches to multilateral arms control and nonproliferation institutions and processes remain tentative, cautious, and selective. While it is more active and participatory in most international and multilateral institutions and processes, Beijing has yet to fully embrace the principles of multilateralism even as it becomes more active in both regional and global arenas.

The next section briefly introduces the concepts of cooperative security and multilateralism and discusses their relevance in the areas of multilateral arms control and nonproliferation. This is followed by an account of the evolution of China's arms control and nonproliferation policies and the impact of multilateralism on its behaviour and practices. The chapter concludes with some preliminary assessments.

Cooperative security and multilateralism

In an anarchical international system where states seek survival and pursue security through self-help and/or alliances, armament, deterrence, and the threat or use of forces have long defined state behaviours and the competitive nature of inter-state relations (Waltz 1979; Mearsheimer 2001). During the Cold War, the United States and the Soviet Union maintained huge conventional and nuclear arsenals, with each side seeking to dominate the game by building up higher levels of armament in both quantitative and qualitative terms. Arms races ensued, as did the deepening of security dilemmas (Bundy 1988; Freedman 2003). The recognition of the futility of pursuing security through armament, brinkmanship, and threat or use of forces and the failure of increased armament to provide lasting security led competing rivals to introduce, accept, and develop, the concepts of arms control (Schelling and Halperin 1961; Schelling 1966) and cooperative security (Carter *et al.* 1992; Nolan 1994; Steinbruner 2000). The former focuses on the need to regulate armament, promote crisis stability and reduce the costs of peace-time arms build-up while the latter essentially argues that the reliance on the preparation and use of military force should be replaced with "agreed-upon measures to prevent war and to do so primarily by preventing the means for successful aggression from being assembled." This represents "in essence, a commitment to regulate the size, technical composition, investment patterns, and operation practices of all military forces by mutual consent for mutual benefits" (Carter *et al.* 1992: 6).

Closely related to the concept of cooperative security is the idea (or ideal) of multilateralism, which is often referred to as "the practice of coordinating national policies in groups of three or more states" (Keohane 1990: 731). However, this definition merely describes the processes and formats in which states interact, not the prescription as to what states should do. In contrast to this *nominal* version of multilateralism is what scholars have referred to as the *qualitative* multilateralism:

> an institutional form which coordinates behaviour among three or more states on the basis of 'generalized' principles of conduct – that is, principles which specify appropriate conduct for a class of actions, without regard to the particularistic interests of the parties or the strategic exigencies that may exist in any specific occurrence.
>
> (Ruggie 1992)

In an influential edited volume, John Ruggie stipulates the three key principles of multilateralism: nondiscrimination, indivisibility, and diffuse reciprocity (Ruggie 1993). What is critical here is that subscribers to multilateralism are expected to forsake short-terms gains, accept a certain level of constraint on flexibility of action, in the expectations that long-term benefits can be achieved (Martin 1992).

Multilateralism has long been credited with its unique role in facilitating and promoting international cooperation in the areas of trade and investment through such institutions as the General Agreement on Tariffs and Trade (GATT) and later the World Trade Organization (WTO) (Goldstein 1993). The concept has also attracted considerable attention from policy-makers and academia alike as a useful approach to dealing with both traditional and emerging security and non-traditional security issues, which may defy unilateral or bilateral solutions. The growing interest in multilateralism reflects a genuine belief that through regularized dialogues and institution building, existing (and potential) global and regional security issues can be more effectively and equitably addressed without recourse to threat, coercion, or use of force (Acharya 2003; Smith et al. 2004).

Multilateralism remains a process and an approach to managing security. The extent to which it can replace, rather than merely complement, traditional security arrangements such as balance of power and military alliances will largely depend on whether and how it can affect states in re-evaluating and redefining their threat perceptions and security interests in fundamental ways. Short of this transformational effect, multilateralism will continue to serve as one of the means through which states pursue and protect their security interests (Mearsheimer 1994/95). The intellectual and policy contribution that cooperative security and multilateralism make is that the pursuit of absolute security based on an understanding of international relations as a zero-sum game has by and large failed to realize the objective of achieving security in a cost-effective way. The preoccupation with achieving security against, rather than with, either real or potential adversaries, only leads to greater security dilemmas and hence, less security, as countries strive to maximize relative capabilities and military power that fuel arms races and intensify distrust. This has already been amply demonstrated by the experiences of the superpowers during the Cold War. Clearly, cooperative security through multilateralism geared toward reassurance rather than deterrence, a greater and more broadly based participation than rigid bilateral alliances, and the promotion of both military and non-military security, offers a better chance for long-lasting stability (Weiss 1993; Nolan 1994).

However, there are certain conditions that must be present for cooperative security/multilateralism to work. The realistic suspicion, and worse, dismissal, of the role of institutions notwithstanding, it should be obvious that whether or not, and in what form, cooperative security arrangements will be established may, to a large extent, depend on the "interrelationship of structural, cognitive and (resulting) behavioural factors." While structural variables such as the distribution of power, geography, state resources, etc., may offer opportunities for, or impose constraints on, concerned or prospective players, it is the cognitive features of the environment that would determine the particular form of security arrangements (Job 1997; Krause 2004). In other words, the "non-like-minded" must convert to the "like-minded" within a defined group of states or in a specified geographic region before a particular security arrangement can take shape and be adopted. The evolution of the Conference on Security and Cooperation in Europe (CSCE) would be a case in point. People tend to forget that prior to 1985, when Gorbachev assumed the Soviet leadership, any attempt at cooperative security (or common security, as it was better known in the European context), and multilateralism was overshadowed by superpower competition (Smith *et al.* 2004).

Another obstacle to multilateralism is the fact that its acceptance requires states to eschew a certain degree of independence in making policy choices, in particular in resisting the temptation for short-term gains, all for the purpose of obtaining collective common policy decisions. This can be seen as immediate cost versus long-term but uncertain benefits that may or may not obtain. This being the case, self-interested states will turn to multilateralism only if they see this route serves their interests better than alternatives in a given situation. Their degree of willingness to embrace multilateralism as a cooperation mechanism will also depend on the type of cooperation problems they face, and the ease or difficulty of implementation (Martin 1993).

Indeed, the realist understanding of international relations suggests that international cooperation would be difficult but possible to some degree under certain circumstances. In this regard, realism would explain states' willingness to behave cooperatively and their participation in multilateral arrangements, be they international organizations and acceptance of certain norms and principles concerning behaviour, as largely utility-oriented (Glaser 1995). In other words, states choose cooperation out of rational choice (Lake and Powell 1999). Two points immediately come to mind: one, that states, and, in particular, great powers, may be less than forthcoming if they see multilateral arrangements as potentially constraining; and two, they may be prepared to endorse multilateral arrangements if the latter do not impose significant constraints or if nonparticipation per se accrues no absolute gains but relative losses (in terms of opportunities created through collective actions or simply the tarnishing of image). The premises here are that multilateralism itself cannot be a criterion in evaluating a state's behaviour; rather, emphasis should be put on when, and under what conditions, states are more forthcoming in accepting the value of multilateralism, and to the extent they would actually endorse and promote its wider acceptance and application.

There is a huge literature on cooperative security and multilateralism with regard to the European experiences, especially the CSCE/OSCE processes and, to a growing extent, the Asia-Pacific processes (Tow 2001; Gurtov 2002; Acharya 2003; Tan and Acharya 2004; Thakur and Newman 2004). In the areas of arms control and nonproliferation, however, discussions focus either on the superpower (i.e. the United States and the Soviet Union/Russia) negotiation or on the issues concerned (e.g. nuclear, chemical, and biological, and conventional weapons, and ballistic missiles) (Larsen 2002; Smith and Hall 2002). Postwar multilateral arms control and nonproliferation processes could be traced to the 1963 Partial Test Ban Treaty (PTBT) and have become more developed since the end of the Cold War. The current treaties, conventions, and multilateral regimes cover the entire gamut of nuclear, chemical, and biological weapons (the so-called weapons of mass destruction, or WMD), conventional arms, and ballistic missiles, both at the global level, and in multilateral formats (Center for Nonproliferation Studies, updated 2006). States participate in multilateral negotiation in limiting, reducing, and dismantling these weapons and pledge either to forsake or not to possess them in exchange for non-acquisitions by others. They also negotiate and agree upon accepted procedures for inspections and verification to ensure that that WMD proliferation will not take place. In important ways, states forsake the options of WMD acquisitions and accept constraints on the levels of their conventional armament, and instead, choose the cooperative security arrangements of greater transparency, confidence building, and assurance, to ensure their security (Levi and O'Hanlon 2004).

A new player in the game: China and multilateral arms control

In analysing and understanding China's approaches to multilateral diplomacy in arms control and nonproliferation, it is important to note three important facts. The first is China's traditional way of handling and interacting with foreign powers. For an extended period in its history, China occupied an unchallenged position in East Asian international relations and, as the centre of that system, did not feel the need to engage in multilateral diplomacy. Indeed, successive Chinese dynasties did not even consider bilateral exchanges as a necessary component of inter-state relations. If anything, China treated other countries either as fit to be sinicized and therefore entitled to receive the Middle Kingdom's blessings for status and materials, or as of little consequence (Fairbank 1968; Mancall 1984).

Second, its experiences with multilateralism since the Opium War of the 1840s for the most part did not endear this particular format of international relations to China. It was forced to open up to the outside world and the subsequent one hundred years of debilitating and humiliating experience convinced the Chinese rulers that multilateral diplomacy did not benefit China. Being a weak player in a game of power politics, its limited interaction with the international community left much to be desired. Only when China finally "stood up" was it able to really participate in multilateral diplomacy with dignity and respect from other members of the international community (Zhang 1991).

Finally, as a latecomer to the international community, China's understanding of, and approaches to, multilateralism are invariably cautious and selective as it is still undergoing a process of socialization. That process involves a readiness to redefine one's national interests; a preparedness to re-negotiate and even accept limitation on one's sovereignty; and a willingness to tolerate short-term loss for long-term benefits (Kent 2002; Johnston 2003). In fact, Chinese understanding and discussions suggest that when they refer to multilateralism, they are most likely talking about multilateral diplomacy, as differentiated from bilateral interactions. There is a strong emphasis on the number of players and the processes rather than on the structural implications of multilateralism – nondiscrimination, indivisibility, and diffuse reciprocity. Indeed, complete endorsement of multilateralism would work against the traditions of Chinese diplomacy and strategic culture, which place a high premium on flexibility and sovereignty.

The foreign policy of the People's Republic of China (PRC) has undergone significant changes in both contents and approach since 1949 (Van Ness 1971; Robinson and Shambaugh 1994; Hunt 1996; Kim 1998; Swaine and Tellis 2000; Lampton 2001; Zhao 2004). Until the early 1970s, China stayed out of most international organizations and its participation in various international/ multilateral forums therefore has been of relatively recent experience (Kim 1979). Since its triumphant re-instatement as a permanent member in the United Nations Security Council in 1971, Chinese participation in, and membership of, both international organizations and non-government organizations have registered significant growth. In 1966, these were one and 58, respectively; by 2000, however, the numbers had expanded to 50 and 1,275 (Kent 2002: 344–5). It is in those forums that Beijing's diplomats have been exposed not only to issues of transnational nature but also the very concept and practice of multilateralism, including the issue areas of arms control and nonproliferation. (Kim 1981; Chan 1989).

Despite its growing participation in international organizations, both Chinese analyses and practices remain limited in conceptualization and execution. Chinese scholars and policy-makers rarely refer to multilateralism per se but more to multilateral institutions or processes, or simply multilateral diplomacy to differentiate it from bilateral interactions (Hongying Wang 2000: 74–5; Yizhou Wang 2001a, 2001b). The former would require the acceptance of constraints in coordinating policies with others; the latter merely refers to the fact that more than two players are involved. Indeed, many Chinese analyses would use the term of multilateral diplomacy without accepting the principles of multilateralism. And the point on the continuum between *nominal* and *qualitative* multilateralism that best characterizes China's degree of acceptance will also depend on the types of issues. Beijing is more willing to accept *qualitative* multilateralism in international trade and investment but less so in international and regional security arrangements (Feeney 1998; Economy and Oksenberg 1999).

China's positions on arms control and disarmament have changed since the late 1970s when it first participated in the United Nations Special Session on Disarmament and, later on, the UN's Disarmament Committee, and the Conference on Disarmament (Johnston 1986; Wu 1996; Frieman 2004). During the 1960s and 1970s, Beijing was highly critical of US/Soviet arms control activities, regarding them as nothing more than schemes of superpower collusion designed to seal in permanency their nuclear monopoly. Consequently, Beijing categorically rejected superpower arms control proposals and refused to accept any constraint on its own weapons development programmes. For instance, China argued that the 1963 Partial Test Ban Treaty (PTBT) was meant to freeze the monopoly of nuclear weapons by a few powers, while condemning others to nuclear threat, as the treaty would still allow nuclear weapons states (NWS) to use nuclear weapons, conduct underground tests, continue to produce, store, and even transfer, nuclear weapons, and technology to their respective allies. In this regard, the PTBT was highly discriminatory and could not be accepted (Zhou 1990: 335–9). Beijing maintained that genuine arms control measures should include the establishment of nuclear-weapon-free zones (NWFZs), complete prohibition and thorough destruction of nuclear weapons, withdrawal of all troops and nuclear weapons from foreign soils, prohibition of nuclear exports and imports in any form, and a complete halt of all nuclear tests, including underground tests (Zhou 1990: 330–4, 338).

In the early 1980s, Chinese position shifted from outright rejection of arms control measures to partial and guarded endorsement of selected arms control that would constrain superpower arms races. To quote a China scholar, the Chinese position underwent a change, "from complete refusal to join in any multilateral arms control processes in the Maoist period to tentative involvement in institutions like the Conference on Disarmament" (Johnston 1996: 34). During most of the 1980s, China's arms control agenda focused on issues important to its security interests: chemical weapons, space weapons, and superpower nuclear disarmament (Johnston 1986, 1990: 176). China also began to participate in the international arms-control process, primarily with its presence at the Conference on Disarmament (CD), beginning in February 1980, and membership in the International Atomic Energy Agency (IAEA) in 1984. However, the pace of China's participation remained slow and its scope narrow during this period; it continued to remain outside of major international nonproliferation regimes and negotiations (Kim 1981; Garrett and Glaser 1995/96; Johnston 1996).

While the UN's Disarmament Committee and the Conference on Disarmament, as well as other international and regional official meetings, provided the venues for China to engage in multilateral diplomacy, the positions that Beijing took during these early years of its participation initially focused mostly on superpowers' obligations in nuclear disarmament and embodied several key principles (Johnston 1986). First and foremost, Beijing argued that since the United States and the Soviet Union possessed the largest nuclear and conventional arsenals in the world, they bore a primary responsibility in disarmament. In addition, China emphasized the ultimate goal should be toward the complete prohibition and thorough destruction of all nuclear weapons, with nuclear nonproliferation, nuclear test ban, fissile material production cut-off, etc. as the specific interim measures and steps. Furthermore, Beijing called for greater participation by all concerned countries since the danger of nuclear war threatens the entire human race. Finally, the Chinese government insisted that arms control would not succeed unless the root causes of global/regional conflicts were addressed. This would involve economic, political, as well as military and arms-control measures. Not surprisingly, China's definition of arms control at that time was a very narrow one, with an almost exclusive focus on nuclear weapons and the superpowers.

Chinese arms-control and nonproliferation policy underwent the most significant changes in the 1990s (Yuan 2003; Frieman 2004). These include Beijing's accession to major international arms-control and nonproliferation treaties and the introduction of domestic regulations governing exports of nuclear, chemical, and dual-use materials and technologies. These developments were prompted by Beijing's growing recognition of proliferation threats; an acute concern over its international image; its assessment of how progress in nonproliferation could promote better Sino-US bilateral relations; and by US nonproliferation initiatives aimed at influencing Chinese behaviour (Gill and Medeiros 2000; Medeiros forthcoming).

An important indicator of China's acceptance of international nonproliferation norms can be found in its participation in major international treaties and conventions (see Table 4.1). Since the early 1990s China has joined the NPT (1992), signed (1993) and ratified (1997) the CWC, and signed the CTBT (1996). Beijing has on various occasions enunciated in clear terms the three principles governing its nuclear exports: (1) IAEA safeguards; (2) peaceful use; and (3) no re-transfers to a third country without China's prior consent. In May 1996, the Chinese government further pledged not to provide assistance to unsafeguarded nuclear facilities. In October 1997, China formally joined the Zangger Committee. In May 2004, China joined the NSG. Beijing is engaged in consultation with the other multilateral export control regimes – the Missile Technology Control Regime (MTCR), the Australia Group (AG), and the Wassenaar Arrangement (WA) (Kerr and Boese 2004: 37, 39). In a significant way, China's participation in these arms-control and nonproliferation arrangements indicates a level of acceptance of the norms and rules, as well as the very principles of multilateralism, since the latter would also constrain the behaviour of other great powers, including the United States and Russia.

Clearly, Beijing has become more active and participatory in multilateral arms-control and nonproliferation forums, which range from the CD to the UN First Committee, to the IAEA. At the non-governmental level, Chinese academics and analysts are also increasingly involved in a multitude of activities that include international and regional conferences, exchange programmes, and joint research projects. As a result, the Chinese accumulate additional expertise and experiences in multilateral diplomacy and develop a better appreciation of both the benefits and the obligations – and even the costs and constraints – that are involved.

Indeed, Beijing is now even applying elements of multilateralism and seeking active multilateral diplomacy to protect and advance its national security interests. Chinese efforts in opposing US missile defence are a case in point (Yuan 2003; *Urayama 2004*). From the late 1990s to 2002, Chinese officials launched intense diplomatic offensives at various international forums to warn against the adverse consequences for global arms-control and nonproliferation efforts should US missile-defence plans be implemented and to emphasize the importance of keeping outer space out of a potential arms race. At the United Nations, China, in collaboration with Russia and other countries opposing US missile defense, pushed through a non-binding resolution in its First Committee on sustaining the 1972 Anti-Ballistic Missile Treaty and preventing weaponization in outer space. At the CD, Beijing has been active in pushing for the negotiation of an international treaty to ban weaponization in outer space at the Conference on Disarmament adopting PAROS (Prevention of an Arms Race in

Table 4.1 China and international/multilateral nonproliferation treaties/regimes

International treaties and negotiations	Multilateral export control regimes
Acceded to the Non-Proliferation Treaty (NPT), March 1992 Supported the indefinite extension of the NPT, May 1995 Signed the Comprehensive Test Ban Treaty (CTBT), September 1996 Signed and ratified the IAEA Additional Protocol in 2002 (the only nuclear-weapons state to do so) Signed on to the Latin American Nuclear Weapons-Free Zone (1973); South Pacific Nuclear Weapons-Free Zone (1987); Africa Nuclear Weapons-Free Zone (1996); Southeast Asian Nuclear Weapons-Free Zone (1999) Signed the Geneva Protocols in 1952 Signed the Biological Weapons Convention in 1984 Signed the Chemical Weapons Convention (CWC), January 1993 Ratified the CWC and joined the Organization for the Prohibition of Chemical Weapons (OPCW) as a founding member, April 1997 Participated in but later withdrew from the P-5 talks on Middle East Arms control, 1991–92 Participated in the United Nations Register of Conventional Arms from 1993 to 1997 Signed the Inhumane Weapons Convention in 1981 Signed the Outer Space Treaty in 1983 Participated in the negotiation of but did not sign on to the Hague Code of Conduct against the Proliferation of Ballistic Missiles	Joined the International Atomic Energy Agency (IAEA) in 1984 Joined the Zangger Committee in October 1997 Applied for membership in the Nuclear Suppliers Group (NSG) in January 2004 and was accepted into the NSG in May 2004 Issued domestic regulations on exports of chemical, biological and dual-use items with control list similar to that maintained by the Australia Group (1995–2002) Consultation with the Australia Group Consultation with the Wassenaar Arrangement Pledged to abide by the original 1987 Missile Technology Control Regime (MTCR) guidelines in February 1992 Agreed in the October 1994 US–China joint statement to adhere to the MTCR and agreed to apply the concept of "inherent capability" to its missile exports US–China official talks during 1997–98 on China's possible membership in the MTCR Chinese statement on missile nonproliferation, November 2000 Consultation with the MTCR on membership; bid not successful at the October 2004 plenary meeting

Sources: Adapted from Center for Nonproliferation Studies, Inventory of International Nonproliferation Organizations and Regimes (Monterey, CA: Center for Nonproliferation Studies, updated 2006). Online. Available: www.cns.miis.edu/pubs/inven/index.htm; database compiled by the East Asia Nonproliferation Program, Center for Nonproliferation Studies. Online. Available: www.nti.org.db.china/.

Outer Space). In his statement at the 2000 NPT Review Conference in New York on 24 April 2000, Sha Zukang, head of the Chinese delegation, argued that PAROS "is of a more urgent nature at CD given some country's determination to develop and deploy missile defenses." At the minimum, there should be a reasonable balance between PAROS, FMCT, and nuclear disarmament. A Chinese working paper submitted to the conference echoed this stand (China 2000; Sha 2000).

Finally, China is also playing an active role in seeking to defuse and find a solution to the North Korean nuclear issue. Beijing has been instrumental and, indeed, has taken the lead in initiating first the trilateral meeting between China, North Korea, and the United States, in early 2003, and, later, the Six-Party Talks that also include Japan, South Korea, and Russia. This suggests not only China's acceptance (albeit selective, given the importance of a peaceful and stable Korean Peninsula to Chinese security interests) but also its practice of multilateral diplomacy at its finest. To a significant extent, Beijing's more active mediation in the North Korean nuclear crisis also reflects its recognition of the serious threat that WMD proliferation could pose to its security interests. The potential East Asian nuclear chain reactions as a result of Pyongyang's nuclear programs and the A. Q. Khan network of international nuclear smuggling drive home the importance of strengthened international coordination in meeting the proliferation challenge (Gill 2004: 216–18).

The logic of Chinese arms-control policies: does multilateralism make a difference?

Alastair Iain Johnston once observed that "China's arms control behaviour appears to be influenced by two basic concerns – the degree to which arms control threatens or benefits Chinese conceptions of military security, and the degree to which arms control affects China's international image" (Johnston 1990: 175). Security concerns remain the guiding principle for Chinese arms-control policies. At the same time, image consideration influences the degree and extent of Chinese participation in international nonproliferation arrangements. Given past experience, the Chinese have continued to regard sufficient defence capabilities as the only reliable guarantee of their security (Cheung 1993: 113). This means that Chinese arms-control policies of necessity must be selective, conditional, cautious, and remain subordinate to security considerations.

Security concerns would explain why China has been wary of the process of arms control in certain areas. With the least sophisticated nuclear arsenal among the five *de jure* nuclear-weapons states, Beijing for a long time insisted that the superpowers had greater responsibilities and should take the lead in nuclear disarmament. In this context, it has set certain conditions for its own participation in multilateral nuclear-disarmament negotiations. Beijing also displayed some hesitation in those multilateral arms control and disbarment negotiations that could impose serious constraints on its nuclear weapons systems and hence on its ability to maintain minimum deterrence. For instance, both a CTBT and a fissile materials production cut-off treaty could seriously affect China's current and future nuclear weapons modernization programmes. As China conducted the least number of nuclear tests among the NWS, it has a greater need for the kinds of data derived from testing with regard to the preparedness, survivability, and penetrating capability of its limited nuclear force. A CTBT "will probably freeze the gap of nuclear warhead design and testing between China and the other nuclear weapon states" (Shen 1995: 26).

China has been averse to regional arms-control processes that may place undue constraints on its defence-modernization programmes. While a weaker power compared with the US, in the Asia-Pacific context, China likely will be the focus of any multilateral arms-control process. Its image as a weaker, militarily inferior, and largely defensive, country would not play well in a regional context; instead, China will be seen as a strong, superior, and sometimes aggressive, power. Electing to be constrained by regional arms-control measures may harm its military and security interests (it prefers to think globally in calculating the forces it needs to maintain a strategic balance); on the other hand, refusing to participate in the regional arms-control processes will tarnish China's image as a major force for global/regional peace and stability (Johnston 1990: 184–5). This latter consideration may explain its more receptive attitudes in recent years toward regional initiatives, such as the ASEAN Regional Forum. In certain areas where China feels both its security interests and image can be boosted by multilateral diplomacy, it has taken the initiative in promoting multilateralism and institutionalization of security cooperation, such as its role in the establishment of the Shanghai Cooperation Organization (SCO) (Chung 2004; Gill 2004: 213–6).

Image consideration has been an important factor in Beijing's formulation and proclamation of arms control and nonproliferation policies. It explains why, for a long time, China refused to accede to the NPT but was willing to sign on to regional NWFZs. The former demonstrates that China was not part of "them" (nuclear monopolists) but a representative of the "have nots," despite the fact that China had by then become a nuclear-weapon state. The latter would reinforce the former in that it shows that China did not exploit its "have" position but rather acted as a more responsible power by indicating its support of the concerns of the "have nots" (Johnston 1990: 176).

Image concerns also make Chinese opposition to certain arms-control initiatives difficult, if these are supported by a large number of Non-Aligned Movement (NAM) countries. Recognizing that voting against or being an uncompromising hold-out can do serious damage to its preferred image of a responsible power, China occasionally drops its original positions; at other times, China simply chooses not to vote. China's unexplained absence in two important votes may be largely because of such considerations: one for setting up the UNCAR and the other for approving the UN expert group study on verification (Interviews 1996). Consideration of itself as a peace-loving country sympathetic to non-nuclear weapons states can also lead China to advocate policies that downplay the importance of nuclear weapons and objective nuclear threats, and call for the states that have nuclear weapons to make greater efforts in nuclear disarmament (Li 2005).

However, while Chinese arms-control policies continue to be driven by security consideration (and most countries would base their policies on similar rationales), Beijing's participation in multilateral arms control and nonproliferation processes has had an indelible impact on its behaviour. As Elizabeth Economy (2001: 231) suggests, an analysis of such an impact could, "illuminate the ways in which international regimes may influence the evolution of foreign policy-making in China through the establishment of new institutions, the emergence of new foreign-policy actors (or the enhancement of others), and the development of new ideas, values, or orientations among Chinese decision-makers." In other words, "Does China's engagement in international security institutions affect how it defines the relationship between multilateralism and security?" (Johnston and Evans 1999: 236).

Clearly one significant development in China's changing perspectives on international arms control and nonproliferation over the last decade has been the introduction of domestic export control regulations (see Table 4.2). Beginning with the May 1994 Foreign Trade Law, the Chinese government has issued a series of regulations, decrees, and circulars. Taken together, they constitute a nascent export control system (Yuan *et al.* 2002; Cupitt 2003; Bulkeley 2004; Davis 2005; Medeiros 2005). In addition, there has been institutional development indicating clearly that arms control and nonproliferation is increasingly assuming a higher profile in the making of China's national-security policy. In 1985, an Ambassador for Disarmament Affairs was created. In April 1997, a new Department of Arms Control and Disarmament was established within the Ministry of Foreign Affairs (MFA). There has been increasing coordination among MFA, MOFCOM/MOFTEC (Ministry of Commerce/Ministry of Foreign Trade and Economic Cooperation), COSTIND/CAEA (Commission on Science and Technology, and Industry for National Defence/China Atomic Energy Agency), and the PLA's General Armament Department officials in implementing export control regulations (Gill and Evans 2000; author's private correspondence 2004). Non-governmental research and outreach organizations have also emerged as China's participation in global, multilateral, and regional arms-control grows and the demands for expertise increase. The China Arms Control and Disarmament Association (CACDA), established in 2001, has become a lead organization (although with strong government endorsement and partial funding) that coordinates China's emerging NGO arms-control research programmes.

China's acceptance of greater military transparency and the signing of the CTBT also demonstrate that its participation in multilateral security and arms control affects how it defines its interests, including how it wants to be perceived. This is significant given the PLA's traditional views on these issues. Indeed, one could argue that broader considerations of China's overall national security and arms-control objectives have prevailed over the military's more narrowly defined interests even as the civilian leadership has been careful in assuaging its concerns. China began to participate and contribute to the United Nations Register of Conventional Arms (UNROCA) in the early 1990s and submitted annual reports between 1992 and 1996 (Gill 1996). While China's record of participation in the UNROCA remains mixed, one has to take account of the fact that the PLA and the Chinese foreign-policy community had not been enthusiastic about military transparency, worrying that China's weakness could be revealed in the process, hence undermining its limited deterrence (Shirk

Table 4.2 Evolution of China's export control system since the 1990s

Sectors	Laws and regulations
General	Foreign Trade Law, 1994
Chemical, biological and dual-use	Regulations on Chemical Export Controls, December 1995 Supplement to the December 1995 regulations, March 1997 A ministerial circular (executive decree) on strengthening chemical export controls, August 1997 Decree No. 1 of the State Petroleum and Chemical Industry Administration (regarding chemical export controls), June 1998 (Note: These regulations have expanded the coverage of China's chemical export controls to include dual-use chemicals covered by the Australia Group) Measures on Export Control of Certain Chemicals and Related Equipment and Technologies and Certain Chemicals and Related Equipment and Technologies Export Control List, October 2002 Regulations of the People's Republic of China on Export Control of Dual-Use Biological Agents and Related Equipment and Technologies and Dual-Use Biological Agents and Related Equipment and Technologies Export Control List, October 2002 (amended in July 2006)
Nuclear and dual-use	Circular on Strict Implementation of China's Nuclear Export Policy, May 1997 Regulations on Nuclear Export Control, September 1997 (Note: The control list included in the 1997 regulations is identical to that used by the Nuclear Suppliers Group, of which China is not a member) Regulations on Export Control of Dual-Use Nuclear Goods and Related Technologies, June 1998 Amended Nuclear Export Control List, June 2001
Military and dual-use	Regulations on Control of Military Products Export, October 1997 The Procedures for the Management of Restricted Technology Export, November 1998 (Note: The new regulations cover 183 dual-use technologies, including some on the Wassenaar Arrangement's "core-list" of dual-use technologies) China's Ministry of Foreign Trade and Economics Cooperation (MOFTEC) released a Catalogue of Technologies which are Restricted or Banned in China, presumably also in late 1998 Decision of the State Council and the Central Military Commission on amending the PRC Regulations on Control of Military Product Exports, October 2002
Ballistic missiles	Regulations of People's Republic of China on Export Control of Missiles and Missile-related Items and Technologies and the Missiles and Missile-related Items and Technologies Export Control List, August 2002

Sources: Adapted from database compiled by the East Asia Nonproliferation Program, Centre for Nonproliferation Studies. Online. Available: www.nti.org/db/china/.

1994: 11). Indeed, only a few years ago, the top Chinese arms-control official, Ambassador Sha Zukang, argued that it is "impossible to have absolute military transparency" and that China "opposes the pursuit of military transparency that disregards a nation's real conditions" (Sha 1996: 4). In the post-Cold War era, as military transparency has become an accepted multilateral security norm, Beijing finds it difficult not to follow along.

Perhaps the international agreement that Beijing signed on to and one that would have the most constraining effect on its future nuclear modernization program is the CTBT (Johnston 1997). China, among the five nuclear-weapons countries, conducted the least number of tests (same as the United Kingdom), with 45 in all over a period of over three decades (1964–96), compared to 1,050 tests by the United States and about 700 by the former Soviet Union. One of the rationales behind Chinese tests was to improve the safety and reliability of its nuclear weapons, i.e. to prevent nuclear accident. Chinese analysts also pointed out that the reasons why the United States and Russia were more willing and pushing the test-ban and fissile-materials cut-off were because the two superpowers had already conducted a large number of nuclear tests from which they had accumulated sufficient data and experience. Furthermore, the two countries possessed sophisticated simulation technology so they were in a position to continue their nuclear weapons modernization programmes without nuclear tests (Wang 1991; Shen 1994).

During the CTBT negotiations, China pressed for the inclusion of three provisions at the CD in Geneva: that the treaty not ban peaceful nuclear explosions (PNEs); that all nuclear weapons states make no-first-use (NFU) and negative security assurance (NSA) commitments; and that an international monitoring system (IMS), rather than the use of national technical means (NTMs) of individual states, should be the means of verification (Garrett and Glaser 1996: 54–5). Chinese insistence on including PNEs in the CTBT continued until the final days of the second session of the 1996 CD. China eventually dropped its demand for the PNE exemption clause on the condition that the treaty would undergo review after ten years and after it had conducted six more nuclear tests in 1994–96 and signed the CTBT on 24 September 1996 (Karnoil 1996: 25; Gill 2001: 258–61).

That China was willing to accept significant constraint on its nuclear-weapons capabilities despite deep reservations within the military-scientific community clearly says something about the image factor in its arms-control policy formulation. Senior Colonel Zou Yunhua, a seasoned PLA arms-control analyst and a senior research fellow in the Foreign Affairs Bureau at the General Armament Department, argues that by signing the CTBT, China made great sacrifices as the treaty "will impose severe limitations on any further modernization of the Chinese nuclear arsenal" (Sun 1997; Zou 1998: 26). In overall terms, the need to project an image as a responsible power in support of international arms-control endeavours and in particular to fulfil its earlier pledge to an international test-ban treaty by 1996 convinced the leadership that Chinese interests would be served by signing the treaty. However, it was also recognized that the PLA's concerns over its own nuclear-weapons capabilities, specifically in the context of possible US ballistic missile defences, must be addressed. The insistence on including the PNE provisions in a way bought time for an enhanced test schedule despite international outcries and protests against Chinese testing (Zou 1998). But in overall terms, the multilateral pressure played a significant part in inducing China to sign on to the treaty.

Western analysts have observed that "there is growing support in China for the view that multilateral agreements to reduce mutual threats can provide meaningful complements to self-help measures to enhance Chinese security as well as be politically useful in deflecting criticism of China's nuclear weapons policies" (Garrett and Glaser 1995–96: 49). This change in thinking about security and about the utility of arms control in serving both security and image objectives may over time lead to changes in Beijing's current attitudes toward regional arms control in an Asia-Pacific context. While it is still cautious about Asia-Pacific arms control, shifts in threat perceptions may eventually lead China to appreciate the benefits of such endeavour. Certainly, some mechanisms to place Japan and, for that matter, India, and DPRK, under some regional arms control framework also would seem to serve China's security interests (Johnston 1990: 195–8).

Conclusions

The records of Chinese multilateralist behaviour on the international stage are certainly mixed. From the above discussions one can detect at least three important revelations. One is that China has gradually moved from earlier suspicion and passivity in multilateral interactions to a qualified acceptance (ARF), and even active promotion in selected cases such as the establishment of the SCO. The explanation of this shift could be, on one hand, that Beijing has come to realize that diplomatic interactions in forums such as the United Nations are by design multilateral, at least in process if not in binding outcome. On the other hand, it may be that China has recognized the value of applying multilateral principles to advance its own interests. Negotiations at CD could be an example, where multilateralist practice would mitigate superpower dominance in agenda-setting and hence making it possible for China to voice its own concerns in arms-control and disarmament issues. China's effort to mobilize international opposition to US missile defence by resorting to multilateral diplomacy is another possible explanation.

A second revelation is that China's earlier differentiation between international treaties and conventions that are more inclusive and universal in terms of membership and equality in status – NPT, CWC (at least in nominal terms) on the one hand, and those multilateral arrangements that it considered to be in essence exclusive, discriminatory, and predominantly Western on the other – has gradually been erased as Beijing's participation in multilateral arms-control processes expands and its perspectives change. China has now found it more comfortable to participate in both types of arrangements even as it continues to have some reservations on the latter. However, Chinese participation in, and acceptance of, multilateralism remain in the realm of *nominal* processes and institutions rather than being an indication of complete embrace of *qualitative* multilateralism. Indeed, multilateralism to the Chinese remains tantamount to multilateral diplomacy, as differentiated from China's traditional approach and emphasis on bilateral interactions. The unwillingness to be constrained by the norms and rules would immediately come to mind; more so when considering that China played no part in designing these rules and norms. But more important, China has never believed that multilateralism can be truly effective; indeed, Beijing has established and maintained regular bilateral arms-control and non-proliferation consultation and dialogue with a host of countries. From China's perspective, because of the complexity of issues, interests, and policy priorities of member states, generality can seldom be achieved, not to mention that certain powers will always dominate these settings and co-opt others into submission. Therefore, giving too much due to the role multilateralism can play would be self-deceiving, at best. Multilateralism must be put into proper perspective and treated as one among a multitude of approaches to security issues.

The third revelation is that, even though China today may pay lip service to multilateralism, there are certain fundamental issues about which a trade-off cannot be made without serious consequences. In a significant way, power comes with responsibility. China's rising status in the international community provides it with greater influence and benefits; at the same time, it demands greater responsibility, including demonstration that it complies with international rules and practices that, in turn, may impose constraint and costs (Foot 2001). Chinese arms-control policies constantly have to reconcile these two considerations: how to protect and promote fundamental national security interests, and how to maintain an image as a responsible, peace-loving country. Security imperatives require that China avoid certain arms-control commitments that may place constraints on its current and future defence modernization programmes and the continuance of certain controversial activities, such as nuclear tests; at the same time, image consideration would preclude Beijing from acting in open defiance of existing arms-control norms and generally accepted practices, and sometimes oblige China to make high-profile, if token, gestures toward meeting Third World countries' demands.

However, while China's desired image as a peace-loving, responsible power remains constant, the policy considerations for maintaining such an image untarnished have changed over the years as China has become more involved in, and comfortable with, multilateral diplomacy, if not with multilateralism per se. Rather than passivity and shunning of controversial issues to avoid alienating NAM and Third World countries, Chinese diplomacy today has become more confident and active, in part to support its carefully projected image of a rising power. Beijing's role in the Six-Party Talks, its recent announcement of dispatching 1,000 peacekeeping troops to Lebanon, and its call for diplomacy in dealing with both the Iranian and North Korean nuclear issues, represent a distinct departure from past approaches. At the same time, China increasingly recognizes that its national-security interests could be better served through active diplomacy conducted through multilateral forums and in a more high-profile fashion. China's "New Diplomacy" and its use of "soft power" to extend its influence and promote its interests have already been noted in areas from regional security to global issues, including arms control and nonproliferation (Medeiros and Fravel 2003; Gill and Huang, 2006). If the degree of socialization could be used as a measure to size up China's level of acceptance of *qualitative* multilateralism, China could be described as being still in the process of "learning," in the sense that its perspectives on security can undergo fundamental transformation, even though it has made sufficient "adaptation" as a new player in the multilateral game (Johnston 1996, 2003).

References

Acharya, Amitav, *Regionalism and Multilateralism: Essays on Cooperative Security in the Asia-Pacific*, Singapore: Eastern Universities Press, 2003. Author's private correspondence with Chinese export control officials, October–November 2004.

Bitzinger, Richard, "Arms to Go: Chinese Arms Sales to the Third World," *International Security*, Fall 1992.

Bulkeley, Jennifer C., "Making the System Work: Challenges for China's Export Control System." *The Nonproliferation Review* 11:1, Spring 2004, pp. 145–69.

Bundy, McGeorge, *Danger and Survival: Choices about the Bomb in the First Fifty Years*, New York: Random House, 1988.

Byman, Daniel and Roger Cliff, *China's Arms Sales: Motivations and Implications*, Santa Monica: RAND, 1999.

Carter, Ashton B., William J. Perry, and John D. Steinbruner, *A New Concept of Cooperative Security,* Brookings Occasional Papers, Washington, DC: The Brookings Institution, 1992.

Center for Nonproliferation Studies, *Inventory of International Nonproliferation Organizations and Regimes,* Monterey, Calif.: Center for Nonproliferation Studies, 2006. Online. Available: www.cns.miis.edu/pubs/inven/index.htm.

Chan, Gerald, *China and International Organizations*, Hong Kong: Oxford University Press, 1989.

Cheung, Tai Ming, "Emerging Chinese Perspectives on Naval Arms Control and Confidence-building Measures," in Andrew Mack (ed.) *A Peaceful Ocean? Maritime Security in the Pacific in the Post-Cold War Era*, Canberra: Allen and Unwin in association with the Department of International Relations, Research School of Pacific Studies, Australia National University, 1993.

China, "Working Paper submitted to Main Committee I, the 2000 NPT Review Conference," 1 May 2000, New York.

Chung, Chien-peng, "The Shanghai Co-operation Organization: China's Changing Influence in Central Asia," *The China Quarterly* 180, December 2004, pp. 989–1009.

Cupitt, Richard T., "Nonproliferation Export Controls in the People's Republic of China," in Michael D. Beck, Richard T. Cupitt, Seema Gahlaut, and Scott A. Jones, *To Supply or To Deny: Comparing Nonproliferation Export Controls in Five Key Countries*, The Hague: Kluwer Law International, 2003, pp. 117–42.

Davis, Jonathan E., *Export Controls in the People's Republic of China 2005*, Athens, GA: Center for International Trade and Security, University of Georgia, 2005.

Economy, Elizabeth, "The Impact of International Regimes on Chinese Foreign Policy-Making: Broadening Perspectives and Policies ... But Only to a Point," in David M. Lampton (ed.) *The Making of Chinese Foreign and Security Policy in the Era of Reform,* Stanford, CA: Stanford University Press, 2001, pp. 230–53.

Economy, Elizabeth and Michel Oksenberg, *China Joins the World: Progress and Prospectis,* New York: Council on Foreign Relations Press, 1999.

Fairbank, John K., "A Preliminary Framework," in Fairbank (ed.) *The Chinese World Order: Traditional China's Foreign Relations,* Cambridge, Mass.: Harvard University Press, 1968, pp. 1–19.

Feeney, William R., "China and the Multilateral Economic Institutions," in Kim, *China and the World,* 1998, pp. 239–63.

Foot, Rosemary, "Chinese Power and the Idea of A Responsible State," *The China Journal* 45, January 2001, pp. 1–19.

Freedman, Lawrence, *The Evolution of Nuclear Strategy* (3rd edn), New York: Palgrave Macmillan, 2003.

Frieman, Wendy, *China, Arms Control, and Nonproliferation,* London and New York: Routledge, 2004.

—— "New Members of the Club: Chinese Participation in Arms Control Regimes, 1980–1995," *The Nonproliferation Review,* Spring–Summer 1996, pp. 15–30.

Garrett, Banning N. and Bonnie S. Glaser, "Chinese Perspectives on Nuclear Arms control," *International Security* 20:3, Winter 1995–96, pp. 43–78.

—— *Chinese Arms Transfers: Purposes, Patterns and Prospects in the New World Order,* Westport, CT: Praeger Publishers, 1992.

—— "Asia-Pacific Participation in the United Nations Register of Conventional Arms: Prospects for Regionalization," in *Workshop on the United Nations Register of Conventional Arms: The Experience of the Asia-Pacific Regime,* United Nations Center for Disarmament Affairs, New York: United Nations, 1996, pp. 21–31.

—— "Two Steps Forward, One Step Back: The Dynamics of Chinese Nonproliferation and Arms control Policy-Making in an Era of Reform," in David M. Lampton (ed.) *The Making of Chinese Foreign and Security Policy in the Era of Reform,* Stanford: Stanford University Press, 2001, pp. 257–88.

Gill, Bates, "China's New Security Multilateralism and Its Implications for the Asia-Pacific Region," *SIPRI Yearbook 2004: Armaments, Disarmament and International Security,* Oxford: Oxford University Press for SIPRI, 2004, pp. 207–31.

Gill, Bates and Evan S. Medeiros, "Foreign and Domestic Influences on China's Arms Control and Nonproliferation Policies," *The China Quarterly* 161, March 2000, pp. 66–94.

Gill, Bates and Yanzhong Huang, "Sources and Limits of Chinese 'Soft Power,'" *Survival* 48:2, June 2006, pp. 17–36.

Glaser, Charles L., "Realists as Optimists: Cooperation as Self-Help," in Michael E. Brown, Sean M. Lynn-Jones, and Steven E. Miller (eds) *The Perils of Anarchy: Contemporary Realism and International Security,* Cambridge, Mass.: MIT Press, 1995, pp. 377–417.

Goldstein, Judith, "Creating the GATT Rules: Politics, Institutions, and American Policy," in John Gerard Ruggie (ed.) *Multilateralism Matters: The Theory and Praxis of An Institutional Form,* New York: Columbia University Press, 1993, pp. 201–32.

Gurtov, Mel, *Pacific Asia? Prospects for Security and Cooperation in East Asia,* Lanham: Rowman and Littlefield Publishers, Inc., 2002.

Hopmann, P. Terrence, "Managing Conflict in Post-Cold War Eurasia: The Role of the

OSCE in Europe's Security 'Architecture,'" *International Politics* 40, 2003, pp. 75–100.

Hunt, Michael H., *The Genesis of Chinese Communist Foreign Policy*, New York: Columbia University Press, 1996.

Interviews with Chinese diplomat and DFAIT officials, March and June 1996.

Job, Brian L., "Matters of Multilateralism: Implications for Regional Conflict Management." in David A. Lake and Patrick M. Morgan (eds) *Regional Orders: Building Security in a New World*, University Park, PA: Pennsylvania State University Press, 1997, pp. 165–91.

Johnston, Alastair I. *China and Arms Control: Emerging Issues and Interests in the 1980s*, Aurora Papers 3, Ottawa: The Canadian Centre for Arms control and Disarmament, 1986.

—— "China and Arms Control in the Asia-Pacific Region," in Frank C. Langdon and Douglas A. Ross (eds) *Superpower Maritime Strategy in the Pacific*, London and New York: Routledge, 1990, pp. 173–204.

—— *Cultural Realism: Strategic Culture and Grand Strategy in Chinese History*, Princeton: Princeton University Press, 1995.

—— "Learning Versus Adaptation: Explaining Change in Chinese Arms Control Policy in the 1980s and 1990s," *The China Journal* 35, January 1996, pp. 27–61.

—— "Prospects for Chinese Nuclear Force Modernization: Limited Deterrence Versus Multilateral Arms Control," in David Shambaugh and Richard H. Yang (eds) *China's Military in Transition*, Oxford: Clarendon Press, 1997, pp. 284–312.

—— "Socialization in International Institutions: The ASEAN Way and International Relations Theory," in G. John Ikenberry and Michael Mastanduno (eds) *International Relations Theory and the Asia-Pacific*, New York: Columbia University Press, 2003, pp. 107–62.

Johnston, Alastair I. and Paul Evans, "China's Engagement with Multilateral Security Institutions," in Alastair Iain Johnston and Robert S. Ross (eds) *Engaging China: The Management of An Emerging Power*, London and New York: Routledge, 1999, pp. 235–72.

Kan, Shirley A., *China and Proliferation of Weapons of Mass Destruction and Missiles: Policy Issues*, CRS Report for Congress, Washington, DC: Congressional Research Service, 2003.

Karnoil, Robert, "China to Sign Pact after One More Nuclear Test," *Jane's Defence Weekly*, 19 June 1996, p. 25.

Kent, Ann, "China's International Socialization: The Role of International Organizations," *Global Governance* 8:3, July–September 2002, pp. 343–64.

Keohane, Robert, "Multilateralism: An Agenda for Research," *International Journal*, Autumn 1990, p. 731.

Kerr, Paul and Wade Boese, "China Seeks to Join Nuclear, Missile Control Groups," *Arms Control Today* 34:2, March 2004, pp. 37, 39.

Kim, Samuel S., *China, the United Nations, and World Order*, Princeton: Princeton University Press, 1979.

—— "Whither Post-Mao Chinese Global Policy?" *International Organization* 35:3, Summer 1981, pp. 433–65.

—— (ed.) *China and the World* (4th edn) Boulder, Colo.: Westview, 1998.

Krause, Joachim. "Multilateralism: Behind European Views," *The Washington Quarterly* 27:2 (Spring 2004), 43–59.

Lake, David A. and Robert Powell (eds) *Strategic Choice and International Relations*, Princeton: Princeton University Press, 1999.

Lampton, David M. (ed.), *The Making of Chinese Foreign and Security Policy in the Era of Reform*, Stanford: Stanford University Press, 2001.

Larsen, Jeffrey A. (ed.) *Arms Control: Cooperative Security in a Changing Environment*, Boulder and London: Lynne Rienner Publishers, 2002.

Levi, Michael A. and Michael E. O'Hanlon, *The Future of Arms Control*, Washington, DC: The Brookings Institution Press, 2004.

Lewis, John W., Hua Di, and Xue Litai, "Beijing's Defense Establishment: Solving the Arms-Export Enigma," *International Security* 15:4, Spring 1991, pp. 87–109.

Li, Bin, "China: A Crucial Bridge for the 2005 NPT Review Conference," *Arms Control Today* 35:1, January/February 2005, pp. 22–4.

Mancall, Mark, *China at the Center: 300 Years of Foreign Policy*, New York: Free Press, 1984.

Martin, Lisa L., "The Rational State Choice of Multilateralism," in Ruggie (ed.) *Multilateralism Matters*, 1993, pp. 91–121.

—— "Interests, Power, and Multilateralism," *International Organization* 46:4, Autumn 1992, pp. 765–92.

John J. Mearsheimer, "The False Promise of International Institutions," *International Security* 19:3, Winter 1994/95, pp. 5–49.

—— *The Tragedy of Great Power Politics*, New York: W.W. Norton, 2001.

Medeiros, Evan S., *Chasing the Dragon: Assessing China's System of Export Controls for WMD-Related Goods and Technologies*, Santa Monica, CA: RAND, 2005.

—— *Shaping Chinese Foreign Policy: The Evolution of Chinese Policies on WMD Nonproliferation and the Role of US Policy, 1980–2004*, Stanford: Stanford University Press (forthcoming).

Medeiros, Evan S. and M. Taylor Fravel, "China's New Diplomacy," *Foreign Affairs* 82:6, November/December 2003, pp. 22–35.

Nolan, Janne, *Global Engagement: Security and Cooperation in the 21st Century*, Washington, DC: The Brookings Institution Press, 1994.

Robinson, Thomas W. and David Shambaugh (eds) *Chinese Foreign Policy: Theory and Practice*, Oxford: Clarendon Press, 1994.

Ruggie, John Gerard (ed.) "Multilateralism: The Anatomy of an Institution," *International Organization* 46:3, Summer 1992, pp. 561–98.

—— *Multilateralism Matters*, New York: Columbia University Press, 1993.

Schelling, Thomas, *Arms and Influence*, New Haven: Yale University Press, 1966.

Schelling, Thomas and Morton Halperin, *Strategy and Arms Control*, New York: Twentieth Century Fund, 1961.

Sha, Zukang, quoted in the *Jiefangjun Bao* (*Liberation Army Daily*) 16 November 1996, p. 4.

—— "Statement at the 2000 Review Conference of the Parties to the Treaty on the Non-Proliferation of Nuclear Weapons," 24 April 2000, New York, FBIS-CPP20000429000026.

Shen, Dingli, "Toward A Nuclear-Weapon-Free World: A Chinese Perspective," *The Bulletin of the Atomic Scientists*, March/April 1994, pp. 51–3.

—— "China," in Eric Arnett (ed.) *After the Comprehensive Test Ban Treaty*, Oxford: Oxford University Press for SIPRI, 1995, p. 26.

Shirk, Susan L., "Chinese Views on Asia-Pacific Regional Security Cooperation," *NBR Analysis* 5:5, December 1994, p. 11.

Smith, James M. and Gwendolyn Hall, *Milestones in Strategic Arms Control, 1945–2000*, Maxwell AFB, AL: Air University Press, 2002.

Smith, Michael E. *et al.* (eds) *Europe's Foreign and Security Policy: The Institutionalization of Cooperation*, Cambridge: Cambridge University Press, 2004.
Steinbruner, John D. *Principles of Global Security*, Washington, DC: The Brookings Institution Press, 2000.
Sun, Xiangli, *Implications of a Comprehensive Test Ban for China's Security Policy*, Palo Alto, Cal.: Center for International Security and Arms Control, Stanford University, June 1997.
Swaine, Michael D. and Alastair Iain Johnston, "China and Arms Control Institutions," in Elizabeth Economy and Michel Oksenberg (eds) *China Joins the World: Progress and Prospects*, New York: Council on Foreign Relations Press, 1999, pp. 90–135.
Swaine, Michael D. and Ashley J. Tellis, *Interpreting China's Grand Strategy: Past, Present, and Future*, Santa Monica: RAND, 2000.
Tan, See Seng and Amitav Acharya (eds) *Asia-Pacific Security Cooperation: National Interests and Regional Order*, Armonk, New York: M.E. Sharpe, 2004.
Thakur, Ramesh and Edward Newman (eds) *Broadening Asia's Security Discourse and Agenda: Political, Social, and Environmental Perspectives*, Tokyo: United Nations University Press, 2004.
Tow, William T., *Asia-Pacific Strategic Relations: Seeking Convergent Security*, Cambridge: Cambridge University Press, 2001.
Urayama, Kori, "China Debates Missile Defence," *Survival* 46:2, Summer 2004, pp. 123–42.
Van Ness, Peter, *Revolution and Chinese Foreign Policy: Peking's Support of Wars of National Liberation*, Berkeley: University of California Press, 1971.
Hongying Wang, "Multilateralism in Chinese Foreign Policy: The Limits of Socialization?" in Weixing Hu, Gerald Chan, and Daojiong Zha (eds) *China's International Relations in the 21st Century: Dynamics of Paradigm Shifts*, Lanham and New York: University Press of America, Inc., 2000, pp. 74–5.
Wang, Ling, "Why Is the U.S. Active in Banning Nuclear Tests?" *Beijing Review*, 13–19 September 1991, p. 8.
Wang, Yizhou, *China and International Organizations*, Ford Foundation Project Working Paper No.1, Beijing: Institute of World Economics and Politics, Chinese Academy of Social Sciences, 2001.
—— "China and Multilateral Diplomacy," Beijing: Institute of World Economics and Politics, Chinese Academy of Social Sciences, 2001.
Weiss, Thomas G., *Collective Security in a Changing World*, Boulder and London: Lynne Rienner, 1993.
Wu, Yun, "China's Policies towards Arms Control and Disarmament: From Passive Responding to Active Leading," *The Pacific Review* 9:4, 1996, pp. 577–606.
Yuan, Jing-dong, "China's Pragmatic Approach to Nonproliferation Policy in the Post-Cold War Era," in Suisheng Zhao (ed.) *Chinese Foreign Policy: Pragmatism and Strategic Behavior*, Armonk, NY: M.E. Sharpe, Inc., 2003, pp. 151–76.
—— "Chinese Responses to U.S. Missile Defenses: Implications for Arms Control and Regional Security," *The Nonproliferation Review* 10:1, Spring 2003, pp. 75–96.
Yuan, Jing-dong, Phillip C. Saunders, and Stephanie Lieggi, "New Developments in China's Export Controls: New Regulations and New Challenges," *The Nonproliferation Review* 9:3, Fall–Winter 2002, pp. 153–67.
Zhang, Yongjin, *China in the International System, 1918–20: The Middle Kingdom at the Periphery*, New York: St. Martin's Press, 1991.

Zhao, Suisheng (ed.) *Chinese Foreign Policy: Pragmatism and Strategic Behavior*, Armonk, New York: M.E. Sharpe, 2004.

Zhou, Enlai, *Zhou Enlai Waijiao Wenxuan* (*Selected Works of Zhou Enlai on Diplomacy*) Beijing: Zhongyang Wenxian Chubanshe (Government Document Press), 1990.

Zou, Yunhua, *China and the CTBT Negotiation,* Palo Alto, CA: Center for International Security and Arms Control, Stanford University, December 1998.

Part III
Regional security

5 China's multilateralism and regional order

Michael Yahuda

China's multilateralism and regional order

The continuing rise of China and its energetic diplomacy in Asia, which has been taking an increasingly multilateral form, is changing the character of the international politics of the region. Although the United States and its alliances still provide the main underpinnings of military security in the region, the emergence of China as the principal economic dynamo of the region on which much of the economic growth of resident states in the region depends has begun to challenge the broader balance of power. Hitherto, the economies of East Asia relied principally on open access to the American market and on investment from Japan and the United States. Since the beginning of the twenty-first century even Japan has come to rely on economic relations with China to generate growth in its economy after ten years of relative stagnation.

China's strategy of economic growth and development depends very much on openness to the international economy and since the end of the Cold War China's leaders have developed foreign policies to support its economy strategy. In seeking a tranquil international environment, China has cultivated better relations with the great powers, but it first developed closer relations with its neighbours. However, China has traditionally preferred bilateral relationships for the conduct of its diplomacy, as it feared that multilateral institutions tended to be controlled by their most powerful members.

It was the experience of cultivating better relations with neighbouring states that led China towards the embracing of multilateral associations of states as vehicles within which to work with others on cooperative endeavours and within which it could also enhance its own interests. In the process, China has not only changed fundamentally the character of its relations with neighbouring countries, but it has also begun to challenge, and perhaps change, the character of international order within its region.

The purpose of this chapter is to examine the development and the characteristics of Chinese new-found multilateralism and to ask in what ways it may have changed the regional order, in addition to furthering Chinese interests. Based on the so called "English School," order may be understood as denoting the patterns of state behaviour and the norms that underpin them in the context of a particular distribution of power (Bull 1977; Buzan 2004). At issue, therefore, is whether China's growing power and influence in its region, as expressed through multilateral associations, can be accommodated within the framework of the existing order.

In particular, this raises questions as to what form China's multilateral diplomacy takes. Does it provide a framework within which the very different states of the region can address common challenges and mitigate or solve the various kinds of disputes and potential conflicts, of which there are many in the region? Finally, what kind of a challenge does China's rise pose to the pre-eminence of the United States and to the significance of Japan as the other major regional power?

The evolution of China's new multilateralism

It should be noted at the outset that, unlike Western multilateral institutions, which are characterized by rule-making and procedures for rule enforcement, such institutions in Asia tend to be defined by voluntarism and consensual decision-making. Compare, for example, the European Union (EU) and the Association of Southeast Asian Nations (ASEAN). The former demands as a condition of membership that states should be democracies which practise the rule of law and that they should be bound by EU laws and answerable to supranational bodies such as the EU Commission and the European Court of Human Rights. Further, EU institutions are characterized by defined rules of procedure, whose decisions are legally binding on member states. ASEAN, by contrast, does not allow interference in the internal affairs of member states, its procedures are opaque, agreements are reached by consensus and they lack any enforcement mechanism (Haacke 2003). Not surprisingly, perhaps, China has not found membership of regional associations in Asia unduly demanding (Yahuda).

However, it should also be recognized that in the same period that China's leaders embraced Asian multilateralism they also accepted the more stringent obligations of international institutions of the Western type. These include, for example, arms-control regimes and, most notably, the World Trade Organization (Medeiros and Travel 2003). If the former required the Chinese government to override objections from sections of the military, who saw some of their options curtailed, the latter required of the government to change domestic laws, financial regulations and business procedures, to conform to obligations demanded by an external authority. In previous times both might well have been considered to have infringed on China's independence and sovereignty.

Yet even the less binding multilateralism of the Asian kind did not come easily to the Chinese. The first early steps were the development of confidence-building measures (CBMs) taken in the course of border negotiations with the Soviet Union and with its successor states on the borders of China, namely Russia, Kazakhstan, Kyrgyzstan, and Tajikistan. Beginning with unilateral moves that were then reciprocated by the other side, Beijing and Moscow first withdrew troops from along their border, then reduced vigorous patrolling, until they had built sufficient mutual confidence to coordinate further measures through meetings of military personnel at local and regional levels as accompanied by negotiations in their respective capitals over their disputed borders. Following the collapse of the Soviet Union these negotiations were continued, but on a multilateral basis in Moscow with representatives of the three new Central Asian Republics taking part. That was a product of necessity because Moscow, as the capital of the Soviet Union which had been conducting the negotiations, had all the relevant documentation and the Central Asian negotiating teams had been diplomats of the former Soviet Union. The incremental steps taken to reach agreements about demarcating the borders with China provided the Chinese leaders with sufficient confidence in the value of conducting diplomacy on a multilateral basis. They recognized that, far from the four former members of the Soviet Union combining against China, all five could work together in accommodating their core interests. By the mid-1990s the border talks led to the creation in 1996 of what was called the Shanghai Five, who signed the "Agreement on Confidence-Building in the Military Field along the Border Areas," that was soon followed by the 1997 "Agreement on Reducing Each Other's Military Forces along the Border Regions."

By this time the Chinese Ministry of Foreign Affairs and China's leaders had gained extensive experience of multilateral diplomacy of the ASEAN kind. Both the Asia Pacific Economic Cooperation forum (APEC – which China joined in 1989) and the ASEAN Regional Forum (ARF – in whose first meeting China participated in 1994) have operated on the basis of consensus, voluntarism, and non-interference in domestic affairs. APEC, which is the only economic organization covering the region as a whole, had its voluntary character confirmed when, largely at Japanese insistence, the American attempts of 1993 and 1994 to obtain mandatory agreement for the establishment of free trade by particular dates were rebuffed in 1995 (Ravenhill). The ARF, which is the only pan-Asian-Pacific security institution, has procedures that are explicitly modelled on those of ASEAN, and from the outset the security it sought to establish was of the less demanding, cooperative, kind. Cooperative security may be best understood as appropriate for arrangements between states, which are neither allies nor enemies. It involves no military commitments by member states to come to the assistance of others in the event of their being attacked. Instead, it seeks to mitigate or resolve potential conflicts among member states by diplomatic means (Leifer 1966; Acharya 2001).

Interestingly, the Chinese indicated a degree of discomfort with the initial drafting of the 1995 ARF concept paper that was designed to provide it with operational guidelines. This depicted cooperative security as a process that would unfold in three stages, beginning with confidence-building measures, going on to preventive diplomacy (by which potential conflicts would be identified and perhaps minimized), and concluding with conflict resolution. The Chinese side openly objected to the term "conflict resolution" and that was amended to emphasize a more consultative and a less prescriptive approach. At that stage, the Chinese still entertained the suspicion that the ARF was driven principally by American interests.

Later that year, however, Chinese views of the ARF began to change when it found that one way of avoiding diplomatic isolation over the crisis with Taiwan and the US was to respond positively to overtures from the ASEAN states, who wanted to be addressed on South China Sea issues collectively, rather than separately. By agreeing to do so, the Chinese side found that it was able to assuage much of their concerns arising from China's unilateralist actions of the previous year regarding Mischief Reef (one of the Spratly group, located near the Philippines). The readiness to address the issue on a multilateral basis was in one sense a matter of form only, as it did not touch on the question of disputes about sovereignty over the Spratlys themselves, but in another sense it significantly raised mutual confidence. Meanwhile, the Chinese found that they could control the pace of the development of the agenda of the ARF and that they could use the Forum to pursue their own ends. On the one hand, the Chinese effectively prevented the ARF from proceeding towards the stage of preventive diplomacy, which could have led to exposing its territorial disputes with others in the South China Sea to external multilateral scrutiny, rather than leaving the disputes to be settled with different disputants individually at a later stage. On the other hand, the Chinese were instrumental in expanding CBMs into new areas; and that suited the Chinese interest of presenting themselves as cooperative and solicitous to the concerns of the Southeast Asian neighbours, in particular.

The next stage in the evolution of China's embrace of multilateralism involved its acceptance of the American security presence in Asia as positive factor. In 1996 the Chinese Foreign Minister, Chen Qichen, presented to the ARF what he called a "New Security Concept" (NSC) that was more fully developed by President Jiang Zemin at a UN Disarmament conference in 1999. The NSC may be seen as a Chinese version of cooperative security. Building on the Five Principles of Peaceful Co-existence from the 1950s,[1] the NSC declared that it sought "to conduct dialogue, consultation, and negotiation on an equal footing ... to solve disputes and safeguard peace" (Information Department, the State Council). Bland as the NSC was, China's leaders in the late 1990s sought to promote it in Southeast Asia as an alternative to the American alliances, which were said to be relics of the Cold War (Chi Haotian 1998). That was not well received in Southeast Asian capitals and, following a thorough debate in China in late 1999 (i.e. after the bombing of the embassy in Belgrade by "US-led NATO"), the Chinese concluded, first, that the United States was going to continue to be the world's pre-eminent power for some time to come, and that China had better stabilize and improve its relationship with America. Second, it was also agreed that China should become more active in shaping its regional environment (Finkelstein 2000; Shambaugh 2004: 23–4).

Having determined that China had better cultivate working relations with the United States, China's leaders immediately renewed their bid to enter the World Trade Organization, even though they knew that it would require the Chinese government to alter many of its laws and change both its system of administration and the running of economic institutions. In earlier years this would have been regarded as interference in China's domestic affairs, but Jiang Zemin successfully removed the political dimension from open debate by defining international relations as encompassing "economic globalization and political multipolarity." Indeed, economic reformers welcomed entry into the WTO as a means of effecting further economic change within China. In other countries, of course, globalization was seen very much as a constraint upon government's capacity to determine domestic economic and social priorities. Interestingly, about this time a so-called "New Left" emerged in China that criticized the social and environmental consequences of what they saw as unbridled globalization (Fewsmith 2001: 214–17; Chaohua Wang 2003).

A second consequence of the new approach was the undertaking of several new regional multilateral initiatives. This time, China did not explicitly challenge the system of American alliances and that made its approaches to the ASEAN countries more attractive. The latter had looked askance at China's previous attempt to separate them from America, seeing it as an attempt to bring the region under its aegis. But now that they did not have to choose between China and America and could continue to rely upon the American strategic presence in the region, it enabled the ASEAN states in particular to respond positively to the new Chinese regional initiatives. These now came thick and fast as China built on its growing economic significance to its neighbours.

In 2001, at the instigation of China's Premier, Zhu Rongji, an agreement was reached to establish a China–ASEAN Free Trade Agreement within ten years. This involved a long process of continual dialogues and sets of negotiations, hence the enterprise has been dubbed ASEAN+1. China also took the initiative in building upon a longstanding proposal of the Malaysian Premier, Mahathir Mohammed, to develop an ASEAN+3 (ASEAN, China, Korea, and Japan). China also took the initiative to sign a wide range of agreements with ASEAN, covering human-resource management, public health, information and communication, the environment, cultural and educational exchanges. In 2002 China and ASEAN signed the much-debated Declaration on Conduct in the South China Sea, the Joint Declaration on cooperation in the Field of Nontraditional Security Issues and other agreements to intensify their economic cooperation. The following year China became the first non-ASEAN state to accede to its Treaty of Amity and Cooperation of 1976, which formalized the ground rules for the conduct of peaceable relations between the signatories. China has also become much more active within the framework of the ARF and has taken the lead in hosting a meeting of the defense ministers of member states. In 2004 China took the lead in proposing the establishment of an East Asian community, to be based, presumably, on the ASEAN+3 (Shambaugh 2005), but it had to give way to pressure from Japan and Singapore to expand membership to include Australia, New Zealand, and India. The expanded membership, it was thought, would prevent China from dominating proceedings.

Meanwhile, in 2001 China upgraded the Shanghai Five meetings into the Shanghai Cooperative Organization (SCO) and gradually extended its agenda from security, anti-separatist, and anti-terrorist concerns, to embrace economic exchanges, as well. The SCO certainly went beyond the CBMs typical of China's relations with the Southeast Asia states to include joint-border military exercises, the establishment of an anti-terrorism centre in Bishkek, Kyrgyzstan, and the development of both bilateral and multilateral approaches to combating threats aimed at both the Central Asian regimes and Beijing's rule in Xinjiang. Meanwhile, China's attempts to boost economic relations with the Central Asian states through investments, joint ventures, and, above all, by attempts to build highways and railroads have been augmented by China's rapidly growing need for energy and gas. In this regard, China is in competition with the Europeans, the Americans and the Japanese (with their huge multinational oil companies), but it is making some gains, both in terms of agreements to construct pipelines, accompanying railroads, and in gaining access to sources of oil and gas in Kazakhstan, especially (Gill and Oresman 2003: 22–30). In the longer term, the land routes for China's oil supplies will be greatly valued as they are less vulnerable to interdiction than those reliant on sea passage.

The Chinese contribution to order in the region

Any assessment of the role of multilateralism in China's contribution to regional order must take account of China's general policies in the region of which multilateralism is only a part – albeit, a novel and important part. The Tiananmen massacre was a huge turning-point in China's foreign policy, as well as in its domestic policies. It marked the point at which China's foreign policy stopped considering the region through the lens of its strategic triangle with the USSR and the US and began to treat it as a place to be cultivated in its own right. Indeed, the Chinese soon came to appreciate its new significance as its Asian neighbours took a more forbearing attitude to the Tiananmen disaster and as Beijing came to see how important the region was becoming to the growth and development of the Chinese economy. For example, the lion's share of foreign direct investment in China came from the region and that share has not significantly diminished down the years. After the disintegration of the USSR, and especially after the renewed emphasis on rapid economic growth following Deng Xiaoping's famous 'journey to the south' in 1993 (*nanxun*), the region became even more significant economically. But that was paralleled by a deliberate Chinese policy to secure a "tranquil environment" in which it could focus on its economic development without having to divert excessive resources to the military. By this stage, China had been a member of APEC for several years and it was on the point of becoming a founding member of the ARF.

China's growing economic weight in the region was seen as contributing to overall regional political stability. This was not only because China was seen to have an increasing stake in the stability of the region, but it was also because of the political significance attached to economic growth and development. That was seen throughout the region as the key to the consolidation of statehood and to the enhancement of the authority of governments (Yahuda 2006). The agreement in 1995 with the ASEAN states to discuss issues of the South China Sea collectively served the interests of both sides. First, it provided a degree of reassurance to the ASEAN states that China was alert to their concerns about having to address the huge Chinese state separately, with the attendant anxiety that their divisions would be exploited to enable China to exert its preponderance. Second, coming as it did at a time of a Sino-American confrontation over Taiwan, the agreement showed the Chinese that the cultivation of neighbours could be used to counter the United States and to prevent it from isolating their country.

Another dimension of China's search for peaceable relations in the region was its pursuit of settlements of its long-standing border disputes with its continental neighbours. By the end of 2004 virtually all of the border problems with Russia had been settled and, with the exception of India, practically all the remaining land-border issues had been settled, too. Even though India and China had been unable to reach agreement about disputed territories, they carried out a raft of CBMs along their lines of control as relations among the two Asian giants began to improve significantly. Their trade grew substantially, exchanges of visits between leaders took place and they even carried out a joint naval exercise in 2004 (Mohan 2004).

But even as late as 1998, the question of whether China was genuinely committed to the existing pattern of order still remained unanswered as Chinese leaders continued to press their Southeast Asian neighbours to turn away from the American alliance system. The problem was that there was still a degree of lingering distrust of China in the region. In the not-too-distant past China had supported communist insurgencies in the region and it had sought to use Overseas Chinese to serve Chinese interests against those of the established governments. The openly expressed desire by China's leaders and by senior diplomats to remove the American strategic presence from the area was seen in several regional capitals as indicative of a Chinese aim to establish primacy in the region (Chi Haotian 1998).

It was not until the beginning of the twenty-first century that the Chinese approach changed and its leaders began to acknowledge that they too benefited from the American presence. Foreign Minister Tang Jiaxuan explicitly told Secretary of State Colin Powell on 29 July 2001, "China welcomes the American presence in the Asia-Pacific as a stabilizing factor." The change of heart had the effect of assuring the resident states of Southeast Asia, in particular, that they could rely upon the American strategic presence in the region and simultaneously establish closer relations with China. Indeed, they were reassured that the Chinese were not seeking regional hegemony – at least for the immediate future. As a consequence, they felt greater confidence in responding positively to overtures from China. From the perspective of the ASEAN states, their relations with the US and China were mutually reinforcing and, even as China's weight in the region was rapidly increasing, it was paying attention to their concerns.

The new Chinese approach was particularly important at a time when China's economic influence in the region was growing rapidly and the local economies were becoming increasingly dependent on their relations with China. The

Chinese proposal to establish an FTA with ASEAN within ten years and the attendant detailed negotiations that followed helped to mitigate fears that China's economic rise would be at the expense of the Southeast Asians. Indeed, several Southeast Asian leaders argued that their best economic strategy was to link their economies more closely with China (Vatikiotis and Heibert 2003). The closer economic ties found expression in further multilateral (and bilateral) agreements. They were augmented also by important steps taken by the Chinese side on security matters to indicate the depth of their commitment to orderly relations with their Southeast Asian neighbours, including the signing of a Declaration on Conduct in the South China Sea, and a year later, in 2003, ASEAN's Treaty of Amity and Cooperation. Both agreements committed China, albeit, on a largely voluntary basis, to observe the norms of conduct that underpinned peaceable relations between ASEAN members. However, Chinese claims to be interested in the stability of the region were enhanced by a variety of other activities, including military and social, in addition to the economic and the political. Thus, tourism and educational exchanges were greatly expanded. Hundreds of thousands of Chinese tourists began to visit Southeast Asia every year and tens of thousands of Asian students were attracted to study in China (Shambaugh 2005). China also became the main driving force in promoting the ASEAN+3 framework which linked the ten Southeast Asian states with China, South Korea, and Japan.

The acceptance of the American presence was also evident in China's revitalized approach to Central Asia. As we have seen, the Shanghai Cooperation Organization was established in June 2001 on a more formal basis than its predecessor. Its founding documents made no mention of the allegedly "common struggle against hegemony" (as featured sometimes in key documents issued by the Shanghai Five). Unlike the different groupings in Southeast Asia, the SCO openly asserted that it "assigns priority to regional security" and that it would coordinate action to combat terrorism, separatism and a number of transnational problems such as illicit trafficking in weapons and narcotics, illegal migration, and other criminal activities. It also focused on efforts to step up economic cooperation among SCO members (Gill and Oresman 2003: 8).

Even though the strategic situation in Central Asia was suddenly transformed by the insertion of American forces after 9/11, the Chinese approach did not change. Notwithstanding the views expressed in some Chinese strategic journals that China faced a renewed danger of encirclement by the United States, the Chinese government made no objections to the physical presence of American power for the first time near its vulnerable Western region of Xinjiang and, in fact, it lent its support to the American defeat of the Taliban in Afghanistan and the American attempt to establish a democratic government there. Beijing sent a lone police officer to serve with UN peace-keepers in Afghanistan. He may not have been able to contribute much personally to the UN mission there, but his presence spoke volumes about China's official approval of the American-led venture, with all its intimations of being precisely the sort of armed intervention to effect regime change that Beijing generally opposed.

Since then, the SCO has acquired organizational weight with a budget to fund a secretariat based in Beijing and mechanisms to facilitate annual summits and a host of other activities. From a Chinese perspective, the SCO provides a framework for working with Russia in Central Asia, rather than in undeclared rivalry. In addition to contributing to the settling of contested borders and coordinating the management of border security in the context of combating terrorist, separatists, and Muslim extremists, the SCO also contributes to the maintenance of the territorial integrity of the new states of Central Asia and to the consolidation of their regimes. As we have seen, the Chinese are also active in gaining access to the region's energy and other resources and that, too, is seen as in the interests of the new states who are eager to avoid dependency on the West or Russia. However, American support for democratic movements in Central Asia, especially through the financial aid given to NGOs, was perceived by the Russians and the Chinese to threaten the tacit endorsement of existing regimes that had underpinned the SCO and, as a result, they issued a statement in the name of the SCO urging Uzbekistan to close down the American military base there. It should be noted that the Chinese response arose from a change in American conduct rather than from a fundamental reorientation to a regionalism that had tolerated an American presence.

Thus, China's active approach to regionalism may be seen to embody a much more sophisticated and nuanced diplomacy, which has succeeded in advancing China's broad foreign-policy goals, while making China's growing weight in the region more acceptable to the resident states. Moreover, by ceasing to oppose the American alliances in the region, which were regarded by most states within the region as important for their security and as hedges against potential Chinese hegemony, the Chinese were seen to be contributing to regional order, rather than to be challenging it. Finally, China's approach to regionalism broadly followed the norms of ASEAN that stressed consultative procedures based on consensus, voluntarism, and non-interference. These may have lacked the firmer base of Western-style regional institutions that had rule-making and rule enforcement at their core, but they served the interests of new and often fragile states with developing economies, who could not take their independence and territorial integrity for granted. One of the abiding achievements of ASEAN was that its members had succeeded in avoiding military conflict with each other since the founding of the Association in 1967 (Leifer 1989, 1996). China's embrace of the ASEAN operating procedures was therefore seen in positive terms.

One distinctive feature of China's new regionalism was an emphasis on Asia as a principal organizing geographic theme. China has called for the development of an Asian security community and most of the institutions in which it has taken new initiatives have focused on Southeast, Northeast, and Central Asia. The United States has not been deliberately excluded, as it has been invited, as a member of the ARF, to participate in a proposed meeting of ministers of defence and Americans have also taken part in the annual deliberations of China's Bo'an conference (China's equivalent to Davos) targeted at Asian affairs. Yet America fits in only at the margins of China's new regionalism. Indeed, many take the view that America has been pushed to the periphery of Asian regionalism and its associated diplomacy (Pan 2003; Perlez 2003). That may be the consequence of a relative neglect of regional concerns by the Bush Administration after 9/11, as it has focused almost single-mindedly on its global war against terror (which, of course, has had a regional dimension), the war in Iraq, and, to a lesser extent, on North Korea and Taiwan.

Some limitations and problems of China's contribution to regional order

The difficulties that China's new regionalism pose to regional order stem less from concern that China is somehow displacing American influence in the region than from the particular dimensions of the Chinese approach. Some of these are inherent in the consensual voluntaristic regionalism that China has adopted from the intramural practices of ASEAN. Others arise from the effects of China's militaristic focus on Taiwan and from the failure to develop good relations with Japan beyond those of economics. Both the latter may be said to flow from the strength of nationalist sentiments in China. Finally, the relatively closed character of politics and policy-making of the Chinese Communist Party also constrains the depth of cooperation and coordination that is critical to the further development of the kind of regionalism which so far has been promoted by China's leaders.

China's multilateralism suffers from at least four structural problems as far as most regional participants are concerned:

1   The injunction against non-interference in the domestic affairs of member states may enable the Chinese government to deal with all kinds of governments that others, including some ASEAN members, may find beyond the pale (e.g. Myanmar), but, by the same token, the injunction also acts against the prospect of cooperation and coordination in certain fields that Beijing is keen to promote. Take, for example, the goal of creating some kind of Asian monetary mechanism such as the currency swap arrangement that was agreed by the ASEAN+3 in Chiangmai in May 2000. Although it has facilitated some relatively small bilateral swap agreements, it faces formidable problems in being extended multilaterally to prevent repeats of the 1997 Asian financial crisis, especially because of the sovereignty question (Soesastro 2002). Interestingly, the Japanese proposal to establish an Asian monetary fund to the value of up to $100 billion, which was turned down in 1997 largely because of US pressure, has not been revived. In order to be operable, it, too, would require IMF type conditionality that necessarily would constitute "interference" in domestic affairs. Thus, the IMF remains the only institution that could be effective in the event of a recurrence of a crisis of the magnitude of 1997. The presumption must be, therefore, that governments in the region would prefer the intrusion to be done by an inter-

national body subject to definite rules, than by a regional body and its attendant uncertainties.
2 The ASEAN Way has proved to be a method of conflict avoidance (rather than a process that has led on to preventive diplomacy, let alone to conflict resolution). That has served the member states well over the years. But in some of the capitals in the region it is suggested that, by following the ASEAN Way, China is simply putting off disputes about sovereignty over the Spratlys in the South China Sea until some time in the future, when, not coincidentally, its relative strength and bargaining power will have improved by leaps and bounds. It has not gone unnoticed in the region that China claims that its sovereignty over the Spratlys is "indisputable."
3 The non-binding character of China's regional multilateralism will place a great onus on peer pressure to ensure implementation. But the pressure of the Chinese "elephant" will always be greater than that of its smaller neighbours (India and Japan excepted). The smaller "minnows" will have no option, but to rely on balance-of-power type considerations as could be provided principally by the US, and, to a lesser extent, by Japan. They will not have recourse to legally binding regulations to protect them.
4 So far, the Chinese have effectively prevented those areas where they have incipient conflicts with neighbours from being subject to multilateral scrutiny. In the cultivation of cooperative security the Chinese have yet to go beyond the stage of developing and refining confidence-building measures in the ARF to exploring preventive diplomacy, let alone to suggesting how the third stage of some kind of conflict resolution might be addressed.

Perhaps the most serious problem in China's approach to multilateralism in the region is the way it tackles the Taiwan problem. Its readiness to use force and to demonstrate that its threat is credible not only against the island's defences, but also against the US Seventh Fleet that might come to its aid, means that the Taiwan issue is a threat to the peace and stability of the region as a whole. Although it is evident that none of the parties seeks a military conflict, there is concern throughout the region that a conflict could nevertheless break out, with dire consequences for all the other states in the region. Meanwhile, the Chinese government adamantly defines the problem as a domestic issue and will not allow the conflict to be addressed in the inter-state regional institutions. It has also demanded of regional states ever-stricter compliance with its insistence upon the avoidance of contacts with Taiwanese political leaders. Thus, Singapore, which long had a special relationship with Taiwan, in which Lee Kuan Yew had been able to pay visits to both Taipei and Beijing, found itself in trouble when the Prime-Minister-to-be, Lee Hsien Loong, visited Taipei in 2004, only to raise the ire of Beijing. Relations with Beijing were improved only once Singapore gave assurances that such a visit would not recur (Lee Hsien Loong 2004).

The result is that the United States is increasingly isolated in its support of Taiwan, even though its stated objective of allowing only a peaceful resolution of the problem in accordance with the wishes of the people of the island in itself is not controversial in the region. Moreover, few of the resident states would wish to see the United States simply abandon its support for the island as that would weaken the credibility of the US as an ally and as a guarantor of strategic stability in the region as a whole. Yet the one issue on which regional order may be totally destroyed is left to be determined by the difficult relationships between Beijing, Taipei, and Washington.

The Taiwan issue is perhaps only rivaled in importance as an obstacle to the development of a multilateral regional order by the problematic Sino-Japanese relationship. The two great powers of East Asia have not been able to establish political or security relations commensurate with the significance of their economic relations. It is only since the end of the Cold War that the two have experienced a relationship in which neither is clearly inferior to the other. Yet neither has found the means of reaching an understanding of what might be termed the legitimate national-security interests of the other. In the absence of what is deemed a proper acknowledgement of Japan's terrible acts of aggression against China in the Pacific War, the Chinese side continually claims to see continuing signs that portend the possible revival of militarism in Japan and it complains that Japan's widening military relationship with the United States is leading Japan to deepen its interests in its former colony of Taiwan. The mutual distrust extends to their conduct of relations in the region where an evident competitiveness, if not down right rivalry, underlies their professed adherence to multilateralism. However, now that Hu Jintao and Shinzo Abe, the relatively new leaders of China and Japan were able to hold a summit meeting and agree to a forward-looking agenda in their Joint Press Statement of 8 October 2006, a change for the better seems likely. Interestingly, it is their membership of the various regional associations that will enable them to meet fairly frequently in order to address their outstanding problems and to move forward. Meeting at these venues should contribute to the enhancing of regional cooperation as that has been threatened of late by the rivalry between these two great regional powers.

Nevertheless, improvements in Sino-Japanese relations are likely to continue to be constrained by the rise of nationalistic sentiments in both countries since the end of the Cold War. In China, this was stimulated by a deliberate campaign of patriotic education that was carried out by the communist leadership in 1993–95, in which the ideological basis on which the regime appealed for legitimacy shifted from socialism to that of nationalism. Central to the new patriotism was the message that it was the Chinese Communist Party (CCP) that had saved the Chinese nation from its century of humiliation by defeating the last and worst of the invaders, the Japanese, leading to the establishment of the new Chinese state. Thus, it is among the younger, educated, generation in China that the most virulent form of anti-Japanese nationalism is found (Zhao 2004). Since the articulation of patriotic sentiments, especially on the internet, is the one form of overt political expression allowed by the CCP, anti-Japanese patriotism has become a severe constraint on the central government's capacity to conduct more accommodating diplomacy towards Japan (Gries 2004). Since a growing hostility towards China is also evident in Japan, the prospects for a significant improvement in their relationship do not look good.

Finally, it may be argued that the CCP itself is an obstacle to effecting the kind of intensive cooperation and coordination that China's leaders claim to seek in the region. The communist political system is still closed (albeit, not as closed as before) by comparison with its more open regional partners. It is not too difficult to ascertain the different personal predilections of leaders and the various kinds of pressures, groups, and ideas that seek to influence them among China's partners in Asia. The same cannot be said about China. That in itself imposes limitations on the scale and the scope of the cooperation and accommodation that may be possible. Thus, it is much easier for the Chinese side to seek constituencies and to cultivate "friends" within the countries of its regional partners than vice versa.

Conclusions

China's embrace of multilateralism in the Asian region gathered pace at the beginning of the twenty-first century and it must be seen as part of a much more confident and active foreign policy in which new political approaches have been harnessed to serve China's immediate and longer-term economic interest. With China now having become a major economic player in the region, and even in the world as a whole, Chinese diplomacy has gone beyond trying to secure a peaceful international and regional environment to serve its economic needs. Within its region China is trying to fashion sets of relationships that tie neighbours in multiple networks that bind them together in what China's leaders hope will be a new kind of Asian community. Beyond that, China's foreign policy is being geared to support the country's quest for ever-greater supplies of commodities – especially oil and gas.

Its new regional policies reflect a new awareness that China must pay heed to the interests and perspectives of neighbouring governments. To that end, Beijing appreciates that the multilateral approach is the best way to allay lingering suspicions about possible threats that China's rise may pose to the independence of its neighbours and fears about potential Chinese hegemonism. The conduct of relations with smaller powers on a bilateral basis necessarily puts them at a disadvantage and raises suspicions that Beijing might seek to exploit divisions among them. The multilateral approach not only helps to dispel such fears, but it also provides a mechanism with which China can actively contribute to shaping regional developments.

The multilateralism of the ASEAN kind has found favour with China precisely because it abjures interference in domestic affairs and because it does not impose rules of conduct. Unlike the multilateralism of Western institutions, such as those concerned with arms control or trade, the regional institutions do not tie China down, nor do they demand changes in China's domestic arrangements that require the central government to overcome powerful vested interests. In particular, the lack of transparency that is characteristic of CCP politics is not at all challenged by this. The consultative and consensual procedures that lie at the core of the ASEAN Way suit the Chinese admirably as they are able to control the pace of institutional development as is evident by their delaying of the evolution of cooperative security guidelines in the ARF from the stage of confidence-building to that of preventative diplomacy.

Nevertheless, there can be no doubt that through its multilateralism China is becoming increasingly enmeshed in the practices and networks in the region. That doubtless constrains China from pursuing its own narrow interests as the political costs of reversing the multilateral approach must be high and are rising continuously. More positively, China is acquiring a growing stake in the region and in its institutions. In that respect, regional order is considerably enhanced. The fact that China's leaders regard the promotion of economic growth and stability at home as directly linked to growth and stability in the region means that China's attachment to regional institutions has acquired depth and continuity. Hence, China may be said to have become a status quo power in the sense of the way that is understood by the "English School." China has internalized the norms of inter-state regional order.

The current regional order is best thought of as multi-tiered as well as multilateral. It consists, in the first instance, of the American alliances and the American strategic presence, which are the bedrock of the region's security and the provider of most of its public goods. A second tier may be said to consist of the peculiar shifting patterns of competitive and cooperative relations among the great regional powers, including China, Japan, India, and Russia, with a rising China at the centre of the region. The third tier is composed of a complex network of overlapping multilateral regional institutions. China's role is critical in all three tiers. It is the only potential challenger to American predominance in the first tier and it is perhaps the key player in the second. Finally, it is China's new-found activity in multilateral regional institutions that has made it their main driver.

Note

1 Mutual respect for territorial integrity and sovereignty, non-aggression, non-interference in each other's internal affairs, equality and mutual benefit, and peaceful co-existence.

References

Acharya, Amitav, *Constructing a Security Community in Southeast Asia*, London and New York: Routledge, 2001.
Bull, Hedley, *The Anarchical Society: A Study of Order in International Society*, London and Basingstoke: Macmillan, 1977.
Buzan, Barry, *From International to World Society? English School Theory and the Social Structure of Globalization*, Cambridge University Press, 2004.
Wang, Chaohua (ed.), *One China, Many Paths*, London and New York: Verso, 2003.

Haotien, Chi, Minister of Defence, speech in Singapore summarized in *International Herald Tribune*, 28 November 1998.
Fewsmith, Joseph, *China Since Tiananmen*, Cambridge University Press, 2001.
Finkelstein, David, *China Reconsiders its National Security: The Great Peace and Development Debate of 1999*, Alexandria, Va.: CNA Corporation, 2000.
Gill, Bates and Matthew Oresman, *China's New Journey to the West*, Washington, DC: CSIS, August 2003.
Gries, Peter Hays, *China's New Nationalism: Pride Politics and Diplomacy*, Berkeley: University of California Press, 2004.
Haacke, Jurgen, *ASEAN's Diplomatic and Security Culture: Origins, Development and Prospects*, London: RoutledgeCurzon, 2003.
Information Office, the State Council, *China's National Defense, 2000*, Beijing: Information Office of the State Council, 2000.
Loong, Lee Hsien, "National Day Address," *Straits Times*, 23 August 2004.
Leifer, Michael, *ASEAN and the Security of South-East Asia*, London: Routledge, 1989.
—— *The ASEAN Regional Forum: Extending ASEAN's Model of Regional Security*, Adelphi Paper 302, Oxford University Press for IISS, 1996.
Medeiros, Evan and Fravel Taylor, "China's New Diplomacy," *Foreign Affairs*, vol. 82, no. 6, November/December 2003, pp. 22–35.
Mohan, C. Raja, "India and China a Shifting Paradigm," *The Hindu*, Delhi, 29 July 2004.
Pan, Philip, "China's Improving Image Challenges U.S. in Asia," *Washington Post*, 15 November 2003.
Perlez, Jane, "Asian Leaders Find China a More Congenial Neighbour: Beijing's Soaring Economy Weakens U.S. Sway," *New York Times*, 18 October 2003.
Shambaugh, David, "New Stability in U.S.–China Relations: Causes and Consequences," in Jonathan D. Pollack (ed.) *Strategic Surprise? U.S.–China Relations in Early Twenty-First Century*, Newport, RI: US Naval War College, 2004.
—— "China Engages Asia: Reshaping the Regional Order," *International Security*, vol. 29, no. 3, Winter 2004/05, pp. 64–99.
Soesastro, Hadi, "Strategies Towards the Development of New Regional; Trading Arrangements in East Asia," paper presented to PECC Trade Forum, Pacific Economic Cooperation Council, Vancouver, Canada, 11–12 November 2002.
Suisheng, Zhao, *Nation-State by Construction: Dynamics of Modern Chinese Nationalism*, Stanford University Press, 2004.
Vatikiotis, Michael and Murray Hiebert, "How China is Building an Empire," *Far Eastern Economic Review*, 20 November 2003, pp. 30–3.
Yahuda, Michael, "The Evolving Asia Order, Adjusting to China's Rise," in Shambaugh David (ed.) *Power Shift: China and Asia's New Dynamics*, Berkeley: University of California Press, January 2006.

6 China and the North Korean nuclear problem

Diplomatic initiative, strategic complexities, and relevance of security multilateralism

Shi Yinhong

This chapter will describe, interpret, and, implicitly or explicitly, to some extent predict China's policy behaviour on the North Korean nuclear problem. This is a major security problem which has especially tormented the four most concerned and involved powers, China, the United States, the Democratic People's Republic of Korea (DPRK), and the Republic of Korea (ROK), since the crisis began in October 2002. The chapter will also discuss the significant but ambiguous topic of creating and building up East Asian or North East Asian multilateral security regimes, focusing on China in general, with a particular discussion of the relevance and significance of China's experience of multilateralism on the North Korea nuclear problem.

An overall analysis of the strategic complexities will be the critical part (Sections I and II) of the whole observation, exhibiting the most fundamental determinants of China's behaviour toward the North Korea nuclear problem, and reducing them to three categories: the perceived national interests, the dynamic situation, and the available policy means or instruments, all of them including some "conventional" or well-known contents, but some oft-ignored or undervalued ones as well. Following this general picture is a brief survey of China's engagement in the effort to solve the crisis at its height (i.e. the widely talked-about diplomatic initiative and deepening involvement of China in both bilateral and multilateral frameworks), and the aftermath of these efforts up to the present. It includes an observation of China's changed (largely implicitly changed) policy posture and the probable underlying major causes, after the "crisis" had passed and the de-nuclearization of DPRK recognized as being extremely difficult (Sections III and IV). The strategic complexities will be revisited in a further analysis of limitations on what China wants to do in pressing North Korea for de-nuclearization (Section V). Combined with an understanding of the positions on North Korea and the United States, respectively, and with some reference to that of ROK, a general prediction of the future development of the North Korea nuclear problem can be made, providing a cautiously optimistic/pessimistic picture (Section VI). Finally, a discussion and speculation on the issue of the relevance of security multilateralism and the meaning of China's experience of the North Korean nuclear problem thereon will conclude the chapter.

I

The history of the North Korean nuclear problem, from October 2002 to the present, is full of puzzles, among them the puzzle of China's related behaviour. No one, even policy-makers themselves, can obtain the full answer before all the related data are available, or even after that. However, careful observation, "historical" perspective, sophisticated, empathetic understanding, and strategic sense can help. If the primary task is to produce and develop some minimum "equation" for interpreting or predicting China's policy, then the most fundamental parameters can be revealed in a rather logical way with the help of the above-mentioned cognitive attributes, and be reduced to three categories: the perceived national interests, the dynamic situation, and the available policy means or instruments.

The most "conventional," or well-known, factor is Beijing's definition of the vital interests of China over the issue. They are: (1) general peace in the Peninsula and between North Korea and the United States and its allies, in the sense of at least a cold peace, even if a very cold one, and absolute peace between China and the United States relating to the peninsular, not letting the North Korean nuclear problem involve these two great and increasingly interdependent powers in any direct or indirect military confrontation or high tension; to prevent the North Korean nuclear problem deteriorating to such a degree that China would have to face a great policy-making dilemma, a choice impossible to make without sacrificing this or that most valued national interest; (2) *de-nuclearization* of North Korea, preventing the DPRK nuclear arms programme from causing dangerous strategic chain-reactions, including an always present possibility of an American military strike or full-scale war against a North Korea that has been "primitively" armed with offensive nuclear capability. This would be a near-nightmare, with Japan and the ROK (and maybe even Taiwan) "going nuclear," stimulated or facilitated by the nuclear "break-through" of North Korea. There is also the apprehension that a too-self-confident and provocative North Korea might be inclined to blackmail other countries in the region, thereby bringing great diplomatic and strategic trouble to China; (3) to keep a historically and geographically shaped *"strategic special relationship"* with DPRK (or this most "entangled alliance") in a dynamic and generally far-from-benign regional security environment, leaving it at a minimum as a "strategic buffer-zone" and an "automatic diversionary force," and at maximum as a more positive strategic partner, never letting the process of de-nuclearizing North Korea damage China–DPRK relations so seriously that China would lose this strategic asset. So, roughly speaking, on the North Korean nuclear problem China's national interest as perceived in Beijing, is peaceful de-nuclearization without the loss of DPRK.

It is not too difficult to find the above three vital national interests of China, even to define them in detail. What is critical and easy to lose sight of is the frequent inner tension between them. Therefore, setting a priority between them is a number one strategic necessity. This task is obviously not an easy one because the dynamic nature of the situation China faces in both the North Korea nuclear problem and in the much broader strategic environment. Strictly speaking, peace, because of the high stakes and the great decision-making difficulties China would have to face in failing to maintain it, is always a priority. However, setting the first does not help greatly in deciding the order of priority for the second and third above-mentioned interests, because of the dynamic situation and changing requirements. Moreover, although peace or the lack of war (and the lack of any grave crisis that may lead to war) is an absolute demand perceived by Beijing in relating to the peninsular, and therefore not permitting any reservation. The de-nuclearization and maintenance of the "strategic special relationship" with DPRK have more room for interpretation, with different possible "bottom lines" according to the always complex and changeable relationship between ends and means, or between desirability and feasibility.

The process of China's search for a peaceful solution of the North Korea nuclear problem, especially since her active approach, a result of her developing sense of urgency to prevent the deterioration of the situation (as emphasized later in this article), led her to sponsor the Six-Party Talks in Beijing, from which an added important interest has emerged and developed. That resulting interest is to enhance China's international prestige, diplomatic role, and strategic importance, through promoting a peaceful resolution of the nuclear problem by both multilateral and bilateral means, as a leader and indispensable middle-man between the United States and DPRK, the two main antagonists in the dispute. This lately emerged interest and the very positive feedback resulting from its pursuit were so stimulating, and even exciting, to Chinese foreign-policy opinion, that during the latter half of 2003 and the early months of 2004, China's critical role as the organizer and main promoter of the Beijing Six-Party Talks received warm international appreciation, and was taken as a manifestation of China's new, positive, foreign-policy style and her increasingly constructive role in regional security affairs and world politics. However, especially in retrospect, two points should be emphasized: first, this perceived interest is a by-product of China's active pursuit of a peaceful solution, which, in turn, originated from the more fundamental objective of preventing danger, rather than of obtaining benefits; secondly, the Six-Party Talks still have not produced any major breakthrough in their main task, i.e. to solve the North Korean nuclear problem. It is still too early to assess what will be its overall effect upon China's international prestige and other diplomatic/strategic interests.

Strictly speaking, the contemporary phrase, "national interests" in most cases refers to perceived and defined objectives. Among them, the most prominent and significant, or only, in state practice are often government-set policy objectives. All we know fully indicates that the Chinese government has always been taking, and will continue to take, the above three vital interests as its fundamental objectives in dealing with the North Korean nuclear problem. So, without any mistake, the term "policy objective" can be used in place of "national interest," as exhibited and elaborated above, with all that has just been said kept intact, whether about peace, de-nuclearization, "Strategic Special Relationship," and the rather complex matter of priority, "bottom line," and the implied determinants of the two latter matters.

II

It is obvious from the above that the perceived "situation" is an extremely important category of the fundamental determinants deciding China's policy, and even more important, in almost any practical observation and analysis of the North Korean nuclear problem, than the general vital interests or major objectives. The latter are relatively simple, constant, or, as it were, "static." The former, on the contrary, is much more complex, changing, and dynamic, especially during the period of "crisis." For practical statesmen, what is desirable in principle is, in most cases, less important than what is necessary and feasible in practice, and, by and large, they take major action more often due to the urgent pressure of situation than because of some innovative desire to "create" a favourable fresh environment, especially on unusually difficult matters such as the North Korea nuclear problem. This is especially true of the Chinese leaders after Deng Xiaoping, who have been characterized by a very prudent and even by a somewhat conservative political culture of policy-making, with "taking a low profile" being among the most important foreign-policy doctrines.

On the North Korean nuclear problem, the factors first of all are the perception or assessment on the part of China or her leaders of the dangers in the changing situation of the problem, and the accompanying degree of urgency. Primarily, there are "double dangers": (1) the danger of a military solution by the United States, including a military strike against DPRK or some grave and escalating military "squeeze," easily resulting in military conflict and war; (2) the danger of North Korea's developing or even accelerating its nuclear arms programme, even to the extent of creating and building up its usable nuclear arsenal. The former will destroy peace as China's number one interest or objective, probably together with destroying number three, i.e. the existence of the DPRK regime as a strategically valued partner of China, while the latter will bring about all or most of the dangerous consequences to China's security and diplomatic interests. If these "double dangers" were to develop and become prominent, the Chinese government would feel the need to take urgent action or a major "initiative" to mitigate them, to prevent their becoming "disasters." If these dangers were to subside, the need to act quickly and determinedly would lose much of its momentum and China's behaviour would enter a relatively "relaxed" period, with some "passivity" or, if you will, more patience. Because peace is the number one interest or objective, China would be most active in her diplomatic efforts for a peaceful resolution when the danger of a US military attack were greatest. But, if the danger of North Korea's developing or accelerating its nuclear arms programme became real, as the only danger for the predictable future, China's diplomatic activity would be less. The reason is that to deal with this danger effectively means exerting more pressure (together with usually far-from-effective persuasion) on North Korea, thereby risking the strategic special relationship, which is perceived in Beijing as an important, long-term, asset for China's security.

It is easy to imagine that the strategic values of DPRK would be more often remembered and more keenly perceived by the Chinese leaders when the picture of the overall security environment of China is dark. When the danger of *de jure* independence of Taiwan becomes more urgent, China–US relations in strategic areas more tense, because of the Taiwan issue, or the assertiveness of Japanese militant nationalism and the deterioration of Sino-Japanese relations more acute, it would be natural for the Chinese strategists to attend more to the possible strategic value of DPRK to China. The perceived or potential dangers could develop to such a degree that the North Korea nuclear problem would be "de-escalated" in the order of priority of China's national security and diplomatic affairs, together with a decrease or increase of pressure upon DPRK to abandon its nuclear arms programme. In this kind of darker strategic situation, only one "scenario" could make a difference, i.e. if North Korea's action in nuclear-arms development were so bad and risky that it would bring about a grave danger of a US military strike against DPRK, thereby threatening China's overall vital interests. The strategic connection between the North Korean nuclear problem and the much broader security needs of China is profound and indispensable to a penetrating understanding of China's behaviour toward the problem. The expectation that China would focus "whole-heartedly" on it and dramatically use her "last resort" of withdrawing as the main supplier of DPRK's foreign aid in forcing it to de-nuclearize is, generally speaking, quite naïve.

China's policy has also been shaped by Beijing's perception of the means available to use in pursuing a peaceful solution to the North Korean nuclear problem. There have been five means or instruments, four of them having been "conventional wisdom" for a long time to every experienced observer of the problem. They are: (1) bilateral diplomatic persuasion to influence North Korea and the United States, respectively, for a peaceful de-nuclearization, which China's special relationship with the former and her importance to the latter have facilitated; (2) multilateral talks between all the major concerned parties, with Beijing Six-Party Talks as the institutional framework, to which China's prestige, quite reasonable policy position, and almost uniquely effective working relations with the other five powers have critically contributed; (3) potential background strength as the most important aid supplier of North Korea, as a major diplomatic partner of the United States, and, as the most important and almost uniquely available bridge (aside from the much under-mobilized Russian one) between the two main antagonists; (4) extremely rare and very limitedly used leverage, with massive economic pressure to be applied only as a last resort. This has not been used so far and will certainly not be used in any predictable future.

Besides these four well-known available means of pursuing a peaceful settlement, a fifth one emerged, mainly in 2004 (perhaps since the end of the second round of the Beijing Six-Party Talks). About this means, and its profound influence upon China's general policy toward the North Korea nuclear problem, many observers still lack a keen sense and understanding. This one could be termed, "reformist approach," with increased economic aid as a main stimulant, to encourage, assist, and very tactfully, push, some slow, and slowly accumulating, economic reform in North Korea. This would be in the hope that DPRK would gradually change its domestic and foreign-policy outlook and voluntarily end its nuclear arms programme, or become a "rational and responsible" possessor of (suspected) nuclear weapons, if it cannot be assuredly de-nuclearized.

A characteristic of any good strategy is its ability (1) to define its ends in accordance with the available means; (2) to fully mobilize and employ the available means in serving its ends. To many observers (especially those outside China), what has been most lacking in Beijing's policy towards the North Korean nuclear problem is the latter. This we shall discuss more fully later, in addition to what already has been pointed out briefly at the end of the second paragraph of Section II. Up to now, the Chinese government seems to have kept quite a strong sense of the limitations of available means, leading it almost never to push both DPRK and US strongly, except, as we shall mention later, during a short period in mid-2003 when a US-launched military strike against that country seemed a real possibility. Moreover, what is not sensed sufficiently by many observers is that this perceived limitation of available means is inclined, sooner or later, to limit the definition of China's actual objective in the issue of de-nuclearizing North Korea.

III

Now China's diplomatic initiative and deepening involvement in both bilateral and multilateral frameworks in a two-year span should be surveyed, keeping firmly in mind the above elaboration of the most fundamental determinants of her behaviour. These respectively relate to the perceived national interests, the dynamic situation, and the available policy means or instruments in connection with the North Korean nuclear problem.

Undoubtedly, the North Korean nuclear problem has been the greatest and most critical diplomatic test confronting China for a long time. Since the beginning of the crisis, toward the end of 2002, the principal strategic objective of China over the North Korean nuclear problem has been the de-nuclearization of the DPRK by peaceful means. For China, this problem can have only one solution: North Korea must be given some form of guarantee for its security as well as some political/economic concessions from the United States so that it accepts an international inspection of de-nuclearization via a peaceful way. This correct and "complicated" objective, *together with* its necessarily changing assessment or estimation of the two fundamental situations – the state of North Korea's nuclear arms development and the degree of danger of the crisis' escalating to military conflict or even war – have determined the trajectory of China's diplomacy on the North Korean nuclear issue, at least up to the weeks and months around the third round of the Beijing Six-Party Talks.

Primarily through China's efforts, the North Korean nuclear crisis has undergone two breakthroughs, though only in a procedural nature. The Three-Party Talks held in Beijing in late April 2003 were the first of these, indicating, by an accomplished fact, the possibility of such diplomatic dialogue between two participating antagonists extremely hostile toward each other, the United States and DPRK. However, due to the respective attitudes and policies of these two countries, the three-side talks in Beijing did not mitigate the crisis to any degree. Following that, the United States immediately launched a series of intensive diplomatic activities to very energetically construct a narrower "core coalition" on the North Korean nuclear problem, consisting of only the United States, the Republic of Korea, and Japan, the three allied powers, and taking military *compellance* and deterrence as its dominant approach, even though the Republic of Korea, disagreeing with the US, still insisted on a peaceful solution. At the same time, North Korea declared that it already had nuclear weapons and would resolutely further accelerate its nuclear arms programme. In this context, probably together with the stimulation of rapidly achieved military success in the Iraq War, the United States greatly strengthened its planning and preparations for military *compellance* and even a possible military strike against Kim Jong-il's regime. In particular, the Proliferation Security Initiative (PSI), a kind of partial and selective naval blockade, proposed formally by the Bush Administration for the first time last May, was being prepared with great publicity and intensity. Generally speaking, the "double dangers" inherent in the nuclear crisis, the danger of crisis escalation into some major military conflict or that of a substantial North Korean nuclear arsenal's being developed, remarkably increased since the end of the Three-Party Talks in Beijing.

In such a situation, the last two primary elements in determining China's diplomacy on the North Korean nuclear issue, mentioned at the beginning of this chapter, suddenly came into play with unprecedented force. It may be said that at last China had a really strong sense of urgency which, relatively speaking, had been largely absent since last October, when the crisis began. Hence the round of China's extraordinarily broad and intensive diplomatic activity for a peaceful solution, especially the successive visits to Moscow, Pyongyang, and Washington, from July 3 to 19, 2003 by the Chief Deputy Minister for Foreign Affairs, Dai Bingguo. On one hand, China repeatedly pointed out to the United States that DPRK's legitimate or reasonable security demands should be met, and empathized with the absolute requirement of peaceful achievement of non-nuclearization of the peninsular as the only feasible one for the vital interests of all concerned parties. On the other hand, even the Chinese government, and on one critical occasion, President Hu Jingtao himself, insistently attempted, with patience but with unmistakable determination, to persuade North Korea's leaders, focusing upon the enormous dangers to the Pyongyang regime itself of developing a nuclear-arms programme, together with the necessity and feasibility of multilateral talks on its nuclear problem, and treating it as a legitimate multilateral concern of the regional international society. Moreover, during the whole process, China, from her vital concern for maintaining peace and keeping the survival and the basic security of DPRK as China's geo-strategic asset in the long term, firmly opposed any intention of the United States for "regime change." Primarily due to China's critical efforts, in addition to respective contributions made by all other concerned parties, there finally came the second and more significant procedural breakthrough of the North Korea nuclear problem: the Six-Party talks in Beijing toward the end of last August.

In February 2004 there was the second round of Beijing Six-Party Talks. The general environment of this round was characterized by a notable decrease of the above-mentioned double danger, due to the remarkable difficulties both the US and the DPRK have faced. For the former, the quagmire of Iraq and its domestic and international consequences have been the most prominent and serious of these, depriving, to a great extent, the Bush Administration of both the capability and the will solve the North Korean nuclear problem by chiefly military means. For the latter, the serious economic and diplomatic difficulties, together with the strategic/tactical calculation to broaden and utilize differences between US and other major concerned parties, especially the ROK and China. certainly played a strong part in revising its policy posture. In this way, the North Korean nuclear crisis largely passed over. There was some minor progress through the second round of the Talks, but the general stalemate remained. What is more important from the perspective of observing China's behaviour was the reduced momentum of China's efforts, due to the relaxation of tension.

IV

The third round of Beijing Six-Party Talks was held in June 2004. The general context remained largely the same as four months previously, with US incapacitation caused by the chaotic situation of Iraq even more aggravated. Moreover, there emerged a new political need on the part of the Bush Administration to mitigate tensions a little further over the North Korean nuclear problem and even to try to make some progress to show domestically in consideration of the coming US presidential election. Therefore, the US position on the problem changed a little in its appearance, moving in the direction of moderation shortly before and during the third round of the Six-Party Talks, while Pyongyang raised a more concrete "freeze" proposal, winning more sympathy, and even support, from Beijing and Seoul.

The fourth round of the Beijing Six-Party talks was originally scheduled to be held toward the end of September 2004, against the background of the previously emerged partial progress. But the mutual distrust of the DPRK and US towards each other has been so deep, the positions, strategic calculations, and political priorities, of these two antagonists so mismatched, and a real, broad, "coalition" for the de-nuclearization of North Korea so far from existing, that the fourth round of talks remains still-born, with the present stalemate showing

98 *Shi Yinhong*

no indication of being broken in the predictable future. The basic confrontation between the positions of DPRK and US, respectively, has already been set: the re-elected Bush Administration insists that North Korea must definitely promise to a "complete verifiable, and irreversible de-nuclearization" (C.V.I.D.), in exchange for the US promise for some security assurance and political/economic concessions, North Korea refuses to make such a promise, only indicating its willingness to a "partial settlement" on the condition of assured security, normalization of diplomatic relations with the US, and various kinds of substantial economic and energy assistance. The predictable result of US insistence on "all or nothing" is that the North Korean nuclear problem remains in a protracted stalemate of "non-settlement," in effect, letting Pyongyang have time, publicly, or secretly, to develop nuclear weapons. Moreover, the Bush Administration may remain in this state for a long time, thereby "de-escalating" to a remarkable degree the North Korean nuclear problem in the order of priority of American foreign policy.

China has already done the same, together with every major concerned party on the North Korean nuclear problem. It is not only the extreme difficulty of the problem but also the changed security environment and focus of attention that has led to this state of affairs. Since Taiwan's presidential election on 20 March 2004, the danger of Taiwanese *de jure* independence has become extraordinarily grave, raising for the first time the very concrete probability of China's using force to stop that independence and the absolute necessity of building up with seriousness the creditable military deterrence to prevent it. Because of the Taiwan issue, China–US relations have been in partial tension, only improving recently by the repeated, very clear, statements from the highest level of the US government in opposition to Taiwanese independence. China has begun to prepare seriously for the possibility of fighting with the intervening US armed forces, if it is absolutely necessary for crushing the *de jure* independence of Taiwan.

Furthermore, in the context of further deterioration of Sino-Japanese political relations and the increasing concern in Japan over the "security" of Taiwan, China looks with deep worry at the steady development of Japanese militant nationalism and its manifestations in pursuing one and then another "extra" military right and increasing military build-up. Adding to all these anxieties are the strengthening and "rationalization" of the American military presence in the region and constant "optimization" of the US–Japan military alliance, with its increasing nature of, among other major purposes, guarding against China. In such situations, the factual and potential strategic values of DPRK naturally demand more attention than in the recent past, reminding the Chinese strategists more frequently of the related facts of history, geo-strategy, and priorities, of the peninsula in a broader context. The effects of these circumstances upon China's policy towards North Korea and its nuclear problem are not difficult to imagine.

In fact, there already seem to have been some changes in China's related policy since the third round of Beijing Six-Party Talks: (1) China has committed to support North Korea's "freeze" proposal, and to refuse implicitly the American C.I.V.D. position; (2) it has publicly expressed serious doubts on North Korea's possession of any enriched uranium programme; (3) it has directed its persuasion and pressure mainly toward the US, and largely ended the previous "neutral" position between the US and North Korea; (4) it has seemed to begin to endorse North Korea's "right" to have "nuclear devices for peaceful purpose," thereby implying a great discounting of the importance of the de-nuclearization of North Korea.

V

All the above being said, the strategic complexities should be revisited in a further brief elaboration of limitations on what China wants to do to put pressure on North Korea for de-nuclearization.

Is China able and willing to change North Korea's behaviour? This has been the single most frequently asked question by government officials, journalists, and professional researchers, in the western world and the East Asian neighbouring countries since October 2002, when the North Korea nuclear crisis began. The answer is yes and no. China, of course, has been the main external supplier of North Korea. The massive amounts of food, oil, and other goods sent year by year from China to that country have been very significant, and even indispensable, to its so-hard, but still "normal," economic survival, and also for the minimum vitality of its armed forces and party apparatus. Moreover, China's diplomatic connection with DPRK and her not-so-rhetorical public expression at times of "brotherly friendship" towards it provides certain political, diplomatic, and strategic assets, which have been generally important to that semi-isolationist country. So there is great potential for China to tactfully use the influence and "leverage" embedded in its North Korean policy, which led to China's success in assuring North Korea's attending the Beijing Three-Party Talk and the three rounds of the Six-Party Talks, together with the emerging indications of embryonic economic reform in the DPRK, which, especially in China's eyes, is indirectly helpful to the cause of de-nuclearization. Because of this great potential, the criticism that China has not fully done what she could without hurting greatly her other strategic interest in the Peninsula may be correct.

But still, there are limitations. The power of being DPRK's main external supplier is strong and effective in supporting diplomatic persuasion. Threatened or actual economic pressure in any substantial degree is so repugnant to the extremely sensitive nationalism of the North Koreans and their regime's nationalistic ideology that it would certainly meet fierce resistance, including "strategic retaliation," i.e. the threat to break the "strategic special relationship." This would be a case of the weak employing "interdependence" against the strong, or of the former compensating for its economic weakness with a perceived strategic value to the latter.

Most important, to be really effective on an issue which is vital to the target country, economic pressure has to be exerted on a large scale and with a great intensity, but this kind of economic pressure, by its own nature, is a last resort for China in its relations with countries like North Korea. Because it is the last resort, it cannot be used in most circumstances. The United States "theoretically" has war as its last resort in dealing with Pyongyang, but can the US Administration use it? Or even, does it dare to use it? The rational answer is obvious. Even suppose that to use the last resort would enable you to achieve your objective on the issue in question (often a dubious supposition), it could, at the same time, destroy or greatly damage another objective, which may be of equal or greater importance. Were China willing to drastically reduce or even stop economic assistance to DPRK, and this action forced Pyongyang to "surrender" its nuclear-arms programme, everyone in the West and other East Asian neighbouring countries would applaud and say thank you to China. However, a nuclear-free North Korea would certainly hate China forever (and most South Koreans, for obvious reasons, would also hate China, though to a lesser degree). The strategic "special relationship" would be broken in fact or in name, an important perceived strategic asset of China would be lost, and no one in that corner of the world would help China in any way if changes in the broader strategic environment made China really require help.

The strategic common sense should be repeated again: the North Korea nuclear problem is not China's only concern about the Peninsula and Northeast Asia. Other concerns also exist and play roles in determining China's policy toward the problem; concern with the US, with Taiwan, with South Korea, with Japan, and the meaning of North Korea as an important, though troubling, partner. China's priority of interests or objectives perceived in Beijing consciously or unconsciously has always been: peace, de-nuclearization, *and* keeping North Korea at least as a minimum partner or ally in terms of a security buffer zone, which means, first of all, opposition to "regime change" and the exclusion of almost any options that would eliminate China's influence as a partner of North Korea. This *also* means that, depending upon the degree of difficulty in achieving the de-nuclearization of North Korea, together with China's assessment of her overall security and the actual or potential threat from the US and its military allies over the Taiwan issue, the order of priority between the above no. 2 and no. 3 interests can be changed. Complete de-nuclearization could be treated, though reluctantly, by China and by other closely related powers, as a largely rhetorical objective.

VI

The roughly predictable prospect of the North Korean nuclear problem during the year 2005 or beyond could be divided into two aspects. First, Washington and Pyongyang have their respective needs to mitigate the DPRK nuclear problem and the tension it causes: the former needs, first of all, to concentrate its attention and available resources on the pacification and stabilization of Iraq, together with the management of the Middle and Near East situation that is closely related to the anti-terrorist priority; while the latter needs, first of all, outside assistance to mitigate its serious economic difficulties, as well as chances to broaden the division in attitudes toward it between the US and the ROK, on the one hand and the US and China on the other, and thereby improve its problematic position in international politics. These, together with efforts by China and the ROK, in particular, for a peaceful solution, will probably lead to step-by-step progress in the Six-Party Talks, to the extent that the crisis is mitigated or even passed over in the next year or a little longer. This means that the Talks would probably produce, in the end, a final agreement, somewhat similar in essence to the 1994 Framework Agreement, giving Pyongyang, first of all, some written security assurance as well as economic and energy assistance, in exchange for Pyongyang's promise and some inspected implementation of non-nuclearization.

However, there will be another aspect of the "settlement." Pyongyang has very strong and insistent motivation, resulting from various profound causes, both international and domestic, to possess a nuclear-arms capability. The mutual distrust between the US and the DPRK is not hard to imagine. A sufficiently coherent and coordinated international concert including five powers aimed at complete non-nuclearization by peaceful means is also very difficult, perhaps impossible, to realize. All these mean that an assured complete de-nuclearization of the DPRK (or in President Bush's definition, a "visible, verifiable, and irreversible" de-nuclearization) is probably something beyond practical possibility, at least in the present international and domestic conditions. In other words, speculating from a likely "worst case" scenario, years after the "settlement" there might break out a new "North Korean nuclear crisis," and on the first day of this new crisis one might be confronted by a cruel fact, i.e. that Pyongyang would already have a substantial nuclear arsenal. If that were so, the international dangers would be much graver.

The above is a prudently optimistic or, one might say, prudently pessimistic prediction; "partial settlement" is better than a protracted stalemate of "non-settlement." The latter will let the DPRK have time to develop its nuclear-arms programme further and further. However, while the international community should endeavour to realize the probable prospect, it also should strive peacefully, with stronger determination, and more appropriate strategy, for the improbable best – an assured complete non-nuclearization of North Korea.

VII

What about the building up of East Asian regional security regimes? The question mark here is significant when the North Korean nuclear problem is discussed. It means that, up to now, the relevance and significance of China's experience of security multilateralism on the North Korean nuclear problem are still limited, uncertain, and tentative.

The general context for judging the relevance and significance referred here may be several difficulties particularly relating to China in the making of multilateral security regimes in East Asia. The Chinese leaders recognize more and more in these years the beneficial functions and effects of international regimes or institutions in general. This, combined with their willingness to develop China's constructive influence in East Asia, has led them to hope in principle that the East Asian multilateral cooperative regimes could be gradually created and developed. However, what they have seriously considered and practised up to now are largely those in the economic sphere. In their thinking and practice on the mitigation or solution of East Asian security problems by means of multilateral security regimes, their ideas have been rare and insufficiently concrete. The exception was about the Six-side Talks on the North Korea nuclear problem, now unfortunately dormant.

Moreover, statesmen frequently encounter opposition between ideas and reality. They know in theory the benefits of multilateral security regimes, but things often become not so simple when they encounter concrete international security issues. For example, at present the concrete issues in this field are, first of all, the disputes about maritime territories, territorial waters, and rights over exclusive economic zones in South and East China Seas. In theory, the principle of international cooperation and security regimes is especially fitted to deal with this kind of matter, but in practice, traditional international politics are still the essential rules of the game, and domestic opinion in disputing countries far from willing to pursue the untraditional and more hopeful approach of international cooperation.

Even more important in impeding the development of security multilateralism in China's foreign policy is the protracted tension in, and deterioration of, the Sino-Japanese political relations, a development resulted from various profound and dynamic causes, among them the historical issue being only the most apparent and emotional one. From the negative side, it influences strongly almost the whole range of China's East Asian multilateral cooperation, whether in economics or in security. In addition to this, the United States focus of policy attention on the bilateral military alliances in the region and shows remarkable passivity toward the pan-regional or sub-regional multilateralism in this part of the world, while China's almost suddenly emerged "energy obsession" is complicating her external relations, raising the possibility of friction, excessive competition, or confrontation between her and some of her neighbours. All of these are definitely unfavourable to the creating, fostering, and developing of security multilateralism in East Asia.

Another problem that negatively influenced China's active inclination to build up East Asia multilateral regimes has become somewhat notable recently. Especially since the East Asian Summit held in December 2005, Washington has developed concern that China might use multilateralism and an integration process to reduce and, finally, to exclude American power and influence in East Asia. Events have proved in general what the leading ROK English newspaper, the *Korea Herald* predicted a year before the East Asian Summit. It said in the last day of 2004 that

> Whether the United States is willing to play second fiddle in this [East Asian Community building] process will depend on Washington's percep-

tions and assessment of China's position in Asia. If the Americans think the EAC [East Asian Community] has not only strengthened China's eminent economic position but also emboldened its strategic imperatives at US expense, then, the United States is not likely to stand idly by while its security advantages and influence are diminished. That would put pressure on Japan and to a lesser extent South Korea, which are staunch US regional allies.

In fact, partly from their own worries and partly because of American influence, "In negotiations leading up to the summit, Japan, Singapore and Indonesia fought hard to broaden the membership to include Australia, New Zealand and India," as the *Washington Post* reported during the Summit. America's worry in turn has made China substantially reduce her endeavour toward East Asian multilateralism for fear that the American feeling of being challenged by "Chinese expansionism" may develop to the point of seriously damaging China–US political relations and so promote a strong US strategic and diplomatic reaction against China. This indicates a degree of caution on the part of China that surely will last into the predictable future.

Lastly, but far from least, it is important to point out that the lack of China–US systematic and institutional strategic negotiation, and thereby the lack of a related system of norms, on the most critical strategic issues (Taiwan, strategic weapons, China's security relations with US military presence in East Asia and West Pacific, and with US–Japan and US–ROK military alliance, and the Sino-American long-term strategic mutual mistrust, etc.) between these two great powers makes the emergence of an East Asia multilateral security regime impossible.

As to the relevance and significance of China's experience of multilateralism on the North Korea nuclear problem, what we can say at present is that these depend to a great degree on what kind of final result is produced by the Chinese government's protracted and determined efforts, to sponsor the Beijing Six-side Talks and, on the other, to pursue Pyongyang and Washington, (as well as to deal with Seoul, Tokyo, and Moscow), through many bilateral diplomatic contacts and meetings. The final result will probably be very much mixed, i.e. some limited success, or from another perspective, some limited failure. The developments since the North Korean launching of missiles in early July 2006 have made even this cautious prediction appear too optimist. Moreover, what kind of memory has the Chinese government of the behaviour of the US and Japan during the process of solution to the North Korea nuclear problem, up to now? No doubt, this memory is complicated and far from good. The above major factors are certainly not very encouraging to China in her perception of the feasibility of East Asia security multilateralism in regard to the most important regional security issues.

7 China and SCO

Towards a new type of interstate relations

Jianwei Wang

Entering the twenty-first century, multilateral diplomacy has increasingly become an integral part of Chinese foreign policy at both a global and a regional level. Particularly in its regional or peripheral diplomacy, multilateralism is consciously and unconsciously pursued by the Chinese leadership as a less threatening and more effective instrument to create economic and other functional interdependence with neighbouring countries, to enhance Beijing's profile and influence, and to resolve real and potential conflict. In this regard, the Shanghai Cooperation Organization (SCO) could be seen as a benchmark of this paradigmatic shift from being bilaterally oriented to multilaterally driven in China's regional strategy.

SCO possesses the necessary critical mass to be pivotal in the Eurasian international relations. It covers a total area of more than 30 million square kilometres, or three-fifths of Eurasia, with a population of 1.455 billion, almost a quarter of the world's human beings, and $1.57 trillion of GDP. If one adds the four observer states, it covers four-fifths of the Eurasian continent and makes up almost half of the world's population.[1] It is the first multilateral, regional, international organization born in the twenty-first century. More significantly, it is the first multilateral security organization in which China has played a leading role from the very beginning.[2] This can be easily seen from the fact that it is named after a Chinese city. In addition, the permanent body of SCO – the Secretariat – was set up in Beijing. Finally, a Chinese diplomat was appointed as the first Secretary-General of the organization. All of these are remarkable and unprecedented in China's foreign policy in general and its multilateral diplomacy in particular. It provides an interesting case for studying the change and continuity in Chinese multilateral diplomacy from both policy and theoretical perspectives.

Put functionalism upside down

Shanghai Cooperation Organization (SCO) originated from the military confidence-building measures (CBMs) between China and Russia, as well as the other three former Soviet republics with which China shares common borders: Kazakhstan, Kyrgyzstan, and Tajikistan. In 1996, the presidents of the five countries met for the first time, in Shanghai, to sign the landmark treaty of CBMs in the border region. The presidents also decided that they would hold a regular summit every year, thus indicating the establishment of the "Shanghai Five" meeting mechanism. In 1997, another treaty featuring a mutual reduction of military force in the border region was signed in Moscow. These two treaties were aimed at building trust and confidence and reducing tension in the border area. From 1998 on, the summit of the Shanghai Five began to expand the scope of its agenda to include other security issues, such as the three antis (anti-terrorism, anti-separatism, and anti-extremism), and non-security issues such as economic cooperation and cultural exchanges. Each summit resulted in a signed agreement or statement dealing with major security issues in the region as well as expressing common positions on major international issues. At the fifth summit, held in July 2000, the joint statement explicitly stated that all parties would work to turn the Shanghai Five into a regional mechanism to conduct multilateral cooperation in all areas. Eventually, the Shanghai Five mechanism evolved into a formal regional organization – the SCO, in June 2001, at the sixth summit meeting. Uzbekistan was admitted as the new founding member of SCO, thus expanding Shanghai Five to Shanghai Six.

The evolution of SCO and China's embrace of multilateralism in Northeast and Central Asia have pointed to remarkable changes in the geopolitical landscape in this sub-region and in China's periphery diplomatic strategy. The multilateralism exemplified by SCO also shows some interesting features that are different from multilateralism elsewhere in Asia and the world at large.

Unlike Southeast Asia, where ASEAN has been the main engine of multilateralism for decades, Northeast Asia and Central Asia have had little tradition of multilateralism, due to the polarizing effect of the Cold War. In other words, in this sub-region, multilateralism has to be developed from scratch. In this respect, the split of the Soviet Union provides a new geopolitical reality that calls for an adjustment of Chinese foreign policy. Needless to say, China could deal bilaterally with the Soviet Union as well as other former Soviet republics bordering China. But China chose a different approach. Here the issue of border disputes common to all parties involved facilitated this choice. It is fair to say that, initially, Beijing did not have a clear strategy of multilateralism; neither did any of the other five parties involved. To a great extent, multilateralism in this area is more an unintended result of practice rather than of design. Indeed, the Shanghai Five was initially designed to be bilateral rather than multilateral. The first two CBM agreements, mentioned earlier, were signed between China as one side and Russia and three Central Asian countries as the other side. So, it was a bilateral negotiation of five countries. During the process, however, the bilateral mechanism gradually transformed into a multilateral mechanism, as the agenda of the summit moved away from pure border management. At the summit in 1998, the bilateral talk formally became a multilateral talk among five countries rather than between two sides of one and four. This multilateral consultation mechanism eventually developed into a formal regional organization that no party, including China, had foreseen.

In many ways, the multilateralism centred round SOC is different from its Southeast Asian, as well as its Western European, counterparts. For example, instead of small-country-driven multilateralism, as in the case of ASEAN, the multilateralism in Northeast Asia and Central Asia is driven to a greater extent by major powers. China and Russia are more in the driver's seat to guide the direction of SCO. In its multilateral diplomacy in the Asia-Pacific region, China was more sceptical about multilateralism in security areas. The Chinese often argued that it was unnecessary or even undesirable to establish a formal and institutionalized security regime in the Asia-Pacific region. Multilateral security dialogue and consultation would be sufficient to address the countries' security concerns. But in Northeast and Central Asia, China became a strong advocate of security multilateralism. No student of Chinese foreign policy ever predicted that China would so soon embrace a formal security-oriented regional organization with its former enemies in this region.

The organizational and functional evolution of SCO is also distinct from the development of the regional multilateralism in the European Union, which is a typical example of the traditional functionalism.[3] The multilateralism in Western Europe took off in non-political issue areas – economic integration. Then the cooperative habits formed in the process of economic integration gradually spilled over to the political and security areas. The evolution of SCO turned functionalism upside down. In other words, SCO started with a security-oriented mandate. It was the function of a highly successful cooperation in security areas that eventually spilled over to other, non-security, areas, such as foreign-policy coordination, economic cooperation, and cultural exchanges. The scope of security co-operation widened gradually. Initially, the focus of the Shanghai Five was quite narrow: maintenance of stability and peace in the border area. After territorial disputes among the five had basically been settled and with the mutual trust nurtured through border settlements, the Shanghai Five moved to address broader security issues, such as terrorism and separatism. Before SCO was formed in 2001, it became evident that security alone was not enough to sustain the momentum of institution-building. Therefore, the mandate of SCO is defined as promoting comprehensive cooperation in all domains among members, rather than just in security issues. Jiang Zemin described security cooperation and economic cooperation as two indispensable "wheels" of SCO. They are equally important and mutually reinforcing.[4] In short, SCO progressed from a one-dimensional security-consulting mechanism to a comprehensive formal regional organization.[5]

Related to the pattern of security first, economy second, another interesting feature in the development of SCO is that it took a top-down rather than bottom-up approach. It started with the summit in which top leaders of five countries were committed to the Shanghai Five mechanism. Then, foreign ministers, defence ministers, and ministers of internal security, trade and economic ministers, transportation ministers – and now prime ministers and ministers of cultural affairs – began to meet on a regular basis, thus creating a multiple-layer, multiple-area, consulting mechanism. In terms of institutionalization, the development of SCO is also somewhat different from that of another regional organization, ASEAN. The formation of ASEAN was declared in 1967, but it did not institutionalize until ten years later. The launch of SCO, however, was quickly followed by further measures of institutionalization. It could be argued that, compared with ASEAN, SCO has a more solid basis, as it had accumulated five years of experience before the formation.

The expansion of security mandate

The security mandate of SCO started with a multilateral confidence-building regime initiated by the leaders of China, Russia, Tajikistan, Kazakhstan, and Kyrgyzstan. They signed two agreements on confidence-building and arms reduction in 1996 and 1997. The initial purpose of these two agreements was to create a stable and peaceful border of more than 7,000 km – one of the longest common borders in the world. Through these two treaties, the five countries were committed to downsizing troop levels, reducing military activities, limiting the deployment of weapons, and increasing security transparency. Among other things, China and the four former republics of the Soviet Union agreed on a partial pullout of troops from the 100 km zone along their mutual border. The agreements also envisaged the renunciation of any military exercise in the zone involving more than 40,000 troops and the reduction of troop strength on each side to no more than 139,000. A joint monitoring group was established in 1999 to oversee the implementation of CBMs in the two agreements. This group holds two sessions each year to draw up mutual inspection plans and to supervise the implementation of the two agreements.[6]

These measures created a favourable security environment in which China successively settled its border disputes with Russia, Kazakhstan, Kyrgyzstan, and Tajikistan.

During the process, the multilateral security consultation at the highest level became a regular mechanism of the "Shanghai Five," with the objective of maintaining peace and stability along China's lengthy border with Russia and the three former Soviet republics. The disintegration of the Soviet Union, however, created a new security situation in Central Asia characterized by a host of ethnic, religious, and territorial disputes in the region. To various degrees, the Shanghai Five all suffered from the rise of Islamic fundamentalism in Central Asia facilitated by the power vacuum resulting from the collapse of the Soviet Union. Shanghai Five therefore provided a forum to address the common new security challenges collectively. Consequently, the agenda for security consultation gradually expanded beyond the border issue to other security issues of common concern, and from traditional security issues to non-traditional security issues, from one-dimensional military cooperation to more comprehensive security cooperation. For example, at the fourth summit in 1999, the five leaders issued a statement to strengthen cooperation on fighting crime and drug traffic across their borders. This broad policy statement was then implemented by specific agencies in the respective countries. Soon after the fourth summit, officials of the public-security and law-enforcement agencies met to sign a memorandum agreeing to strengthen mutual cooperation in fighting international terrorism, nationalist separatism, religious fundamentalism, and organized crime.[7]

In recent years, the security agenda of Shanghai Five-SCO has more clearly shifted to the so-called "three evils." It is fair to say that "Shanghai Five" is the earliest regional multilateral mechanism calling for cooperative actions against terrorism in Central Asia. SOC took on international terrorism as its major target at the very time of its establishment. On the day of its public formation in June 2001, member states signed the Shanghai Convention against Terrorism, Separatism, and Extremism. The convention gives conceptual and operational definitions of terrorism, separatism, and extremism, and lays down a legal basis for member states to combat terrorism. It claims that these three evils impose serious threats to the territorial integrity, social and political stability, and the national security of member states and calls for concerted action, including intelligence exchanges, extradition, coordinating policy in international organizations, taking preventive actions, inquiry for assistance, and so on. The convention is also committed to establishing a regional anti-terrorism centre.[8] Uzbekistan's new membership in SCO also indicated the shift of SCO's priority from border settlement to regional security concern. Uzbekistan is the only country that does not share the border with China, but it does have a frontier with Afghanistan, where Islamic terrorists were the most active in the region.

However, less than three months after the establishment of the organization, the viability of SCO was put to a serious test in the aftermath of the September 11 terrorist attack. The attack dramatically changed the geopolitical configuration in the region. As a consequence of the war on terror, the United States, for the first time since the Second World War, has established a significant military and political presence in Central Asia. With a series of geopolitical changes, SCO seemed to have been sidelined. The United States–Russia relations dramatically improved. Other smaller members of SCO took, in various degrees, more pro-Western policies. Uzbekistan, Kyrgyzstan, and Tajikistan, for example, allowed the United States to establish military bases and deploy military forces on their territories. The three countries strengthened their anti-terrorist cooperation with the United States through bilateral channels rather than through SCO. In light of these developments, Chinese analysts worried that the United States might turn its temporary anti-terror arrangements with the Central Asian states into a formal, United States-dominant, regional-security mechanism, thus making SCO irrelevant. Consequently, China's strategic position "has eroded substantially" in Central Asia.[9] Western observers have predicted a possible early demise of this infant multilateral organization.[10]

China and Russia realized the danger and made an effort to offset the adverse effect of the US war on terror on SCO. Among other things, they attempted to make SCO more relevant in the war against terror. On September 14, immediately after the September 11 attacks on the United States, prime ministers who were attending the Prime Ministers' Conference of the SCO at the Alma-Ata, Kazakhstan, issued a joint communiqué in which they denounced the terrorist attacks while expressing condolences and sympathy for the American people. The joint communiqué declared that the SCO was ready to closely unite with all countries and international organizations and that effective measures would be taken to wage an unremitting struggle to eradicate all global risks brought about by terrorism.[11] However, because of the lack of a coordination and institutional infrastructure, SCO was unable to take more forceful and concerted action against terrorism.

To regain the initiative of anti-terrorism, China arranged the extraordinary meeting of the SCO Foreign Ministers in Beijing in January 2002. The joint statement after the meeting pointed out that the recent development in Afghanistan vindicated the view that SCO's pre-9/11 decision to focus on striking against "three evil forces" was farsighted. Long before the 9/11 attacks, SCO had warned the international community several times about the danger of terrorism.[12] The meeting also approved the SCO principles of an emergency reaction mechanism to deal with future 9/11-type crises as an organization. It also reiterated SCO's decision to set up an anti-terrorist structure in the near future. In April, attending another SCO foreign ministers meeting in Moscow, the Chinese foreign minister, Tang Jiaxuan, claimed that SCO is not "a club for empty discussions, but a viable institution capable to make an important contribution to the international war on terror."[13]

Actually, the idea of establishing an anti-terrorist mechanism was put forward by the Shanghai Five as early as 1999, when the first meeting of the leaders of law-enforcement agencies was held. The meeting made the decision to found the so-called "Bishkek group" to exchange intelligence and carry out cooperation in judiciary and law-enforcement fields.[14] But the formal institutionalization of this mechanism was stalled due to the different interests of member states. Some SCO members did not want to see too much militarization of the organization, fearing the apprehension of the United States and other Western countries.[15] The September 11 terrorist attack gave this anti-terrorist initiative new momentum. SCO members became more aware of the urgency of setting up such a mechanism. China pushed hard for the institutionalization of a regional anti-terrorism centre. In early 2002, Chinese President Jiang Zimin declared that the setting up of such a centre is, "the most urgent thing at present."[16] An agreement signed in June 2003 to establish the SCO Regional Anti-terrorism Structure in Bishkek[17] realized China's intention. The agreement stipulates that this centre should become operational no later than January 2004. Furthermore, Beijing would like to see SCO members' anti-terrorist cooperation with the United States conducted in the framework of SCO.[18]

To infuse more substance into the SCO anti-terrorist cooperation, China pioneered a joint military exercise among SCO members. The Chinese troops conducted a joint military exercise with the Kyrgyz forces in October 2002, within the framework of SCO. By doing so, the Chinese military set a precedent for conducting military missions in other countries during peacetime.[19] At the Moscow summit in May 2003, pushed by the SCO leaders, the SCO defence ministers signed a memorandum on joint military exercises to be carried out in autumn 2003.[20] The first multilateral anti-terrorist military exercise of SCO was therefore conducted in August 2003. The drill had two phases, carried out, respectively, in Kazakhstan and China, and included war games against terrorists and a hostage-rescue operation. For China, the significance of this military exercise goes beyond SCO. It is the first large-scale multilateral anti-terrorist exercise in which the Chinese Army has participated, and it is the first time that China has invited foreign armies into its territory.[21] To maintain this momentum, China conducted a ground-breaking joint military exercise with Russia in August 2005 within the framework of SCO. The exercise involved nearly 10,000 troops from both sides and was the first ever to involve ground, sea and air forces together.[22] In August 2006, China's border police and anti-terror special force conducted its first joint anti-terror with Kazakhstan. This is the first of its kind between two countries' law enforcement bodies.[23] In September 2006, China held, and Tajikistan also held, its first anti-terrorist military exercise.[24] At the SCO defence ministers' meeting in April 2006, it was decided that the six members of the SCO will hold another anti-terrorism drill in Russia in 2007. According to Russian Defence Minister Sergel Ivanov, the military exercise could simulate one member country being attacked by armed groups while other member countries come to its aid.[25]

From settling border disputes to managing international terrorism in the region, the security mandate of the SCO has been shifting from traditional security issues to non-traditional security issues. Besides anti-terrorism, Chinese leaders also emphasized the function of SCO to manage other non-traditional security threats, such as drug trafficking, weapon smuggling, transnational monetary crimes, and so forth.[26] For example, the SCO leaders decided to set up an anti-narcotic drugs cooperative mechanism as soon as possible.[27] During this process, security and military consultations between SCO member states have been further regularized and institutionalized. For instance, a plan for regular meetings for secretaries of the national security councils of SCO member states was created in 2004.[28] To facilitate communication between the SCO military bodies, China also held a symposium for officers of member countries in Beijing.[29]

Institutionalizing "Shanghai Five"

China's push for the establishment of the SCO regional anti-terrorist mechanism was part of its broad effort to beef up the institutionalization of the organization. This is a remarkable change in China's attitude towards regional multilateralism which formerly was often characterized by a tendency against institutionalization. In the early stages of Shanghai Five, China was quite comfortable and satisfied with its remaining solely a forum and meeting mechanism. In recent years, however, China has become the driving force, striving for the institutionalization of the Shanghai Five. Particularly after the 9/11 attacks that put SCO's validity to the test, China was convinced that "internal institutional building is an important way to strengthen cohesiveness and enhance the vitality of the organization."[30] Chinese Premier Zhu Rongji, while attending the first SCO Prime Ministers' Conference, in Alma-Ata, Kazakhstan, in 2001, suggested that SCO should put its emphasis on two tasks: to finish drafting the SCO charter as soon as possible and to step up the establishment of the anti-terrorism centre.[31] To make the SCO more functional before the charter and permanent agency of SCO had been put into place, SCO foreign ministers agreed, in January 2002, during the SCO foreign ministers meeting, to some transitional measures. The joint statement issued after the meeting established a contingency mechanism that included the emergency meeting of foreign ministers and the statement of foreign ministers to express the common position of the SCO members.[32]

After the declaration of the formation of the SCO in June 2001, the first step for institutionalization was to draft various legal documents to bind member states together and increase the normative stake for possible defection. At the second summit of SCO, held in St. Petersburg on 7 June 2002, the six members approved a series of documents, including the charter of the SCO, an agreement on the establishment of a regional anti-terrorism agency, and the declaration of presidents of SCO members. The most important document is the SCO Charter. The charter provides purposes, principles, structure, and operational rules of the organization, laying a legal foundation for its construction and development. An institutional structure for the organization was set up by the charter. It has two parts: the meeting mechanism and the permanent organs. The highest SCO authority is the Council of Heads of State that holds regular sessions once a year. Below it there are the Council of Heads of Government, the Council of Ministers of Foreign Affairs, and the Conference of Heads of Agencies. All these are basically meeting mechanisms. In addition, there is the Council of National Coordinators that coordinates and manages the daily activities of the organization and makes preparation for the meetings of other councils. SCO also has two permanent agencies: the Secretariat and the Regional Anti-Terrorism Structure (RATS).[33]

The success in further institutionalizing SCO at the St. Petersburg summit suggests that, to some extent, SCO regained some vitality in a post-9/11, new environment. Jiang Zemin noted in his meeting with Kazakh President Nazarbayev that SCO has vitality in that it conforms to the practical needs of the region, the interests of the SCO member countries, and the trend of development of history. As Kyrgyz President Akayev put it, SCO has withstood the test over the past year.[34] China's effort to expedite the process of institutionalization continued after the summit. At the Moscow summit in May 2003, Chinese President Hu Jintao emphasized that institutional building was the top priority of SCO. He urged member states to work even harder to make sure that the Secretariat could be operational by 2003 and that the anti-terror centre should be created as soon as possible.[35] The six leaders signed a declaration to confirm the legal standing of the SCO charter and to indicate the common position on major international issues. The summit approved about ten legal documents regarding the institutionalization of the meeting mechanism of various councils and two permanent bodies – the Secretariat and the Regional Anti-terrorism Structure. As a result of these documents, the issues of finance, personnel, and material for the two permanent agencies were largely settled.[36] Russian President Vladimir Putin commented that the summit marked the first time the SCO has become an international cooperation organization "in a real sense."[37]

The SCO Moscow summit in May 2003 set a timetable to launch the Secretariat and the Regional Anti-terror Structure at a date no later than 1 January 2004.[38] China was eager to make the Secretariat operational earlier.[39] To meet the timelines of institutionalization set by the Moscow summit, Beijing was willing to provide some concrete "public goods." As the host country of the SCO Secretariat, the Chinese government decided to provide free office facilities for the Secretariat in Beijing.[40] China was also willing to pay the lion's share of the SCO budget. The annual budget for the two standing organs of SCO is $3.5 million. China and Russia each pay 24 per cent of the budget while other members share smaller percentages.[41]

The formal take-off of the two permanent bodies of SCO was a little behind schedule. The Secretariat was not officially launched in Beijing until 15 January 2004. Zhang Deguang, former Chinese Vice Foreign Minister and former Chinese Ambassador to Russia, was appointed the first SCO Secretary-General. The term is three years and officials from member states will take the position in turn in the Russian alphabetic order.[42] The launch of the SCO Regional Anti-terrorism Structure (RATS) was even later. It came into operation in Tashkent, Uzbekistan, in June 2004. The purpose of the anti-terrorist structure is to coordinate the fight against the "three evils" in a more effective way. The primary objectives and functions of this anti-terrorist organ include maintaining working contacts with main administrative bodies of member states and strengthening coordination with international organizations on matters of combating the "three evil forces" of terrorism, separatism, and extremism, drafting international legal documents on matters of combating the "three evil forces," gathering and analysing information provided by member states on "three evil forces," creating a data bank of anti-terrorist structure, and holding research conferences to exchange experiences on combating the "three evil forces."[43] To further substantiate the RATS, the SCO 2005 summit decided to set up an institution of permanent representatives of member states to the body.[44]

With both the Secretariat and the Anti-terrorism Centre up and running, the Tashkent Declaration of the SCO signed by the presidents of the six SCO members declared that the SCO had finished its preliminary stage of establishing an organization and had begun a new stage of full-range cooperation.[45]

With the SCO legal and organizational framework well set, SCO began to contemplate its external relations with other countries and international organizations. According to its charter, membership in SCO is open to other countries in the region. A number of Asian countries already have expressed interest in joining the organization.[46] But, so far, the consensus of the SCO members is that it is not in a hurry to admit new members, as the enlargement of the organization will inevitably lead to complication of management and decision-making.[47] At this stage, however, SCO is willing to invite non-member states to attend some

SCO programmes or activities.[48] At the Tashkent summit in 2004, SOC's expansion took a small but important step and Mongolia was formally accepted as its first observer.[49] In the meantime, the SCO Council of Ministers of Foreign Affairs adopted an interim scheme of relations between SCO and other international organizations and states. The scheme provides that other countries and international organizations may be invited to attend as guests the meeting of the SCO Council of Ministers of Foreign Affairs and diplomatic consultations. By the same token, SCO may also send representatives to attend activities of other international organizations. To date, SCO has made some substantial progress in its external relations and enlargement. In December 2004, SOC was given observer status at the UN General Assembly and became engaged in active cooperation with the UNESCAP, UNDP, and other UN-related agencies.[50] SCO has also signed Memorandums of Understanding with the Secretariats of ASEAN, CIS and the Eurasian Economic Community (EURASEC), established contacts with the European Union, the OSCE and other international organizations.[51] At the 2005 SCO summit in Astana, Pakistan, Iran and India were also granted observer status.[52] These observer countries, together with Mongolia, attended the fifth SCO summit in June, 2006 in Shanghai. They were also joined by the president of Afghanistan, representatives of CIS and ASEAN, who participated in the meeting as guests of the host country. At the summit, the heads of state entrusted the SCO Council of National Coordinators to make recommendations on the procedure of SCO membership enlargement.[53]

The two-track strategy

For a long time, the Shanghai Five regime was almost exclusively security-oriented. It was fine as long as it remained as a semi-institutionalized, one-dimensional, consultative, mechanism. However, when Chinese leaders attempted to transform this security regime into a fully-fledged regional organization, they soon found that security issues, no matter how broadly they are defined, are not sufficient to sustain the dynamics of institutionalization and economics and that other functional dimensions need to be added. In other words, even before September 11, the Chinese came to the conclusion that for SCO to become a viable regional organization, security multilateralism was insufficient. Without substantial economic multilateralism, SCO was likely to be "hollowed out."[54]

As a matter of fact, the four smaller Central Asian countries are more interested in economic, than security or military, cooperation. They particularly need their participation in SCO to yield tangible economic benefits for their sluggish economies. Chinese analysts therefore predicted that promoting economic cooperation could constitute a new growth point to increase the coherence of SCO. Compared with the situation in Southeast Asia, economic and trade relations among SCO members were underdeveloped. The level of economic integration in SCO is much lower but the development of economic multilateralism in SCO members faces different hurdles. Among other things, the Chinese business community is not particularly interested in the region, given the backward infrastructure and poor market mechanism in these economies. For that reason, member governments need more political will to take action to initiate and support some major projects and thereby to increase the member states' stake of economic interdependence within the organization.[55]

The process of economic cooperation started with the first SCO prime ministers' meeting in September 2001. That meeting was interrupted by the 9/11 terrorist attacks and no specifics about economic cooperation were worked out. At the SCO summit in Moscow in May 2003, the importance of economic cooperation was particularly emphasized. The Chinese President made a strong appeal for an early focus on building transportation infrastructure through multilateral treaties.[56] At the SCO prime ministers meeting in September 2003, the member countries signed a framework agreement called "Programme of Multilateral Trade and Economic Cooperation of SCO Member States" that set the long-, intermediate-, and short-term, goals for economic cooperation among the member states, including the realization of the free movement of commodities, capital, service, and technology in SCO within 20 years.[57] Chinese Premier Wen Jiabao for the first time proposed to establish a free trade area (FTA) among SCO members, similar to its initiative to ASEAN countries.[58]

In pursuing the economic function of the SCO, China obviously enjoys greater advantages vis-à-vis other member states, including Russia. Smaller member states in SCO are eager to get on the bandwagon of China's economic boom. For example, Kazakhstan has proposed four times to establish a free-trade zone along the border of the two countries. During President Hu Jintao's visit to Kazakhstan in September 2003, President Nazarbayev again outlined a potential China–Kazakhstan free-border-trade zone located between the Yili Kazak Autonomous Prefecture, Xinjiang, and Almaty, Kazakhstan as part of the China-Central Asia free-trade zone proposed by Premier Wen Jiabao. If successful, it can serve as an example for other Central Asian countries.[59] At the fifth SCO annual meeting of prime ministers, Chinese Premier Wen Jiabao pledged to double its trade with the SCO members by the end of 2010, from $40 billion to $80–100 billion.[60]

At the Tashkent summit in June 2004, promoting intra-SCO economic relations became a major item on the agenda. Leaders decided to establish five specialized working groups concerning e-commerce, customs, quality inspection, investment promotion, and transportation facilitation. Chinese President Hu Jintao urged that five groups should start to work as soon as possible and put forward proposals for closer economic cooperation of the members.[61] Again, China was willing to take a lead. Hu declared that China decided to offer a total of $900 million of preferential buyers credit loans to the other five members of the SCO to promote their trade relations with China.[62] To further promote economic relations among member states, the leaders at the Tashkent summit also agreed to create the SCO Development Fund and the SCO Business Council and charged the SCO secretariat to prepare relevant documents on realization of these projects as soon as possible.[63] At the third SCO prime ministers' meeting in Bishkek in September 2004, government leaders approved the Action Plan on

Implementation of the Programme of Multilateral Trade and Economic Cooperation. They agreed to focus on the cooperation in the energy and natural resources sector including oil and gas exploitation, oil pipeline construction, petrochemicals, hydropower development, and mining. They also called for the completion of drafting a multilateral agreement on international road transportation facilitation before the end of June 2005.[64] Altogether, more than 127 projects in 11 areas about multilateral trade and economic cooperation have been approved during the meeting.[65] So far, the SCO Business Council and Interbank Association have been established and began to operate. The SCO Development Fund is in a process of formation.[66]

With these initiatives, economic cooperation, along with security, has become one of two main pillars that are mutually complementary in sustaining the dynamics of SCO. In recent years, the mandate of SCO has become increasingly comprehensive and multi-dimensional. SCO is committed to "expand cooperation among the member states in political, economic and trade, cultural, scientific and technological and other fields."[67] A very extensive meeting mechanism of the heads of various ministries has been established and constantly expanded. This meeting mechanism not only includes foreign ministers and defence ministers, but also includes ministers of economy, transportation, culture, and education, emergency measures, parliament speakers, heads of law-enforcement bodies, public prosecutors, and presidents of supreme courts.

For example, in recent years, the SCO emphasize the so-called cooperation in the humanities. The SCO cultural ministers started to meet in 2002 to promote mutual understanding and dialogues between different civilizations and religions. Some Chinese scholars point out that the two fundamental problems in Central Asia are economic poverty and a very complicated cultural background. It is an area in which a variety of civilizations, including Chinese, Islamic, Slav, and Indian, intertwined. The security environment in the area will not be significantly improved without effective addressing of these two problems. SCO could provide a platform for conversations between different civilizations in the region.[68] At the SCO 2006 summit in Shanghai, Chinese President Hu Jintao further stressed the importance of the cooperation in humanities so as to consolidate the social basis of the organization.[69] The heads of SOC member states also pledged to "institutionalize bilateral and multilateral cooperation in culture, arts, education, sports, tourism and media."[70]

Building a normative international order

Just like other major powers' involvement in regional and global multilateralism, China's participation in, and promotion of, SCO are underlined by some instrumental motives: either to manage border disputes in the narrow sense or offset US influence in Central Asia in the broad sense. The Western media and analysts tend to portray SCO as Beijing's and Russia's attempt to establish a condominium in Central Asia and a mini-NATO to counterbalance US dominance.[71] There is some truth in such an argument, but it is hardly the only, or even the most important, motive for Beijing. It is fair to say that the initiation of the Shanghai Five was largely motivated by the concerned parties' desire to find a resolution to the border disputes and had little to do with external balancing. When "Shanghai Five" has evolved into a regional organization, Beijing certainly has some geopolitical objectives in its mind. Among other things, Beijing wants to use SCO to "fill the geopolitical vacuum on the Eurasian continent" to stabilize the volatile area.[72] Second, SCO can also serve the function of "improving the balance of forces in the world and promoting the process of multipolarity,"[73] a coded phrase, really for the effort against the US-dominant unipolarity. In this regard, the public demand by the SCO that the United States should set a final timeline for the use of military facilities on the territories of some SCO member states highlights Beijing and Moscow's intention to reduce the US influence in the region.[74]

But equally important, from the very beginning the Shanghai Five-SCO reflected Beijing's desire in establishing a norm-based and new kind of post-Cold War security order in the region. Starting from 1996, the same year Shanghai Five signed the first CBMs treaty, China has strongly advocated and consciously cultivated the so-called "new concept of security" on various occasions. The elaboration of the new concept of security in the official documents and speeches has been more systematic and sophisticated in recent years. It "has become an important component of China's foreign policies."[75]

According to the Chinese official interpretation, the core of such a new security concept is characterized by mutual trust, mutual benefit, equality, and coordination.[76] While these terms are not new in the Chinese diplomatic vocabulary to define interstate relations, they are new in a sense that they are used to define security – a domain that used to be considered quite sensitive and only related to terms such as military, strength, power, and force.

In one senior Chinese official's opinion, the new security concept takes the best from various Western security concepts: common security, mutual security, cooperative security, comprehensive security, and collective security.[77] More specifically, the new security concept first and foremost means "common security," which transcends the traditional one-sided security. It is based on common interest.[78] Second, the new security concept also means "cooperative security," namely, seeking security through cooperation. Under the condition of interdependence and globalization, the security of all states is interdependent. Without international cooperation, no state can maintain its security single-handedly, no matter how powerful the country is.[79] Therefore, "dialogue and cooperation are indispensable."[80] Third, the new security concept means that a county's security is no longer one-dimensional; rather, it is meant to be multi-fold, including not only military and political security, but also economic, scientific, technological, environmental, and cultural, as well as many other areas of non-traditional security.[81] In other words, the new security concept means "comprehensive security" and is no longer military centred. Fourth, related to the "comprehensive security," the new security concept also emphasizes the importance of non-traditional security including terrorism, drug trafficking, weapon proliferation, the spread of disease, and environmental degradation.[82] These non-traditional security threats are often intertwined with one another, making the security situation more complicated and imposing bigger challenges to global security.

To deal with these new security challenges, China should come up with new approaches to security. First, military means are not the only way, probably not even the most effective way, to achieve security. The means to seek security are being diversified. Force is not always the most desirable way to do the job. "The security concept and regime based on the use of force and the threat to use force can hardly bring lasting peace."[83] The traditional means of maximizing security, such as military alliance, is no longer a valid instrument of foreign policy. International cooperation in the fields of economics, the environment, and social affairs can also promote China's security.[84] Second, cooperation under the new security concept should be flexible and diversified in forms and models. It could be a multilateral security plan of relatively strong binding force, or it could be a forum, like a multilateral security dialogue, a confidence-building bilateral security dialogue, or an academic, nongovernmental, dialogue.[85] Third, since security among nations is interdependent rather than one-sided, international politics is no longer a zero-sum game and the security policy of a country should seek win-win results rather than unilateral advantages.

Under the new international circumstances, and with a new understanding of international security dynamics, multilateralism has been increasingly regarded as a more effective means to address China's security concerns. Instead of just reacting or responding to the call of multilateralism by others, China "should vigorously promote multilateralism."[86]

The practice of SCO is exactly the embodiment of the new security concept elaborated above.[87] Chinese President Jiang Zemin made it very clear in 2000 that the purpose of SCO was not just to find a way to promote friendly cooperation among member countries, but, more important, it was an experiment to explore "new interstate relations, new security concept, and new model of regional cooperation" that goes beyond the Cold War mentality.[88] In this context, Shanghai Five-SCO may point to the gradual evolution from an instrumental order to a normative-contractual order in this specific sub-region.[89]

In terms of the nature of the organization, China advocated that SCO follow the principle of nonalignment, without prejudice against any third country or region, but open to all, including non-members.[90] In terms of norms governing the relationship among member states, China emphasized that SCO is underlined by the so-called "Shanghai Spirit." At the St. Petersburg summit in June 2002, Jiang defined the "Shanghai Spirit" in the following terms: "mutual trust, mutual advantages, equality, joint consultation, respect for cultural diversity, and the desire for common development."[91] It was summarized by a Chinese scholar as the five Cs: confidence, communication, cooperation, coexistence, and common interest.[92]

These norms are consistent with the new concepts of security advocated by China in recent years. As Jiang Zemin indicated, China wants to use SCO as a catalyst to promote a new type of international relations based on these new concepts of security. To further institutionalize these norms of new type of interstate relations, Chinese leader Hu Jintao further proposed at the jubilee summit of SCO in June 2006 that member states sign a multilateral treaty on long-term neighbourly and amicable cooperation.[93] The summit adopted this idea and instructed the Council of National Coordinators to conduct consultations on concluding such a treaty.[94]

These norms, needless to say, are still closely attached to the Westphalia international order, as well as to the realist framework. However, it could be argued that the realism implicit to SCO is at least not the hardcore Hobbesian version described by some scholars as "particularly acute" in Chinese foreign policy.[95] In addition, by the practice of SCO, China is advocating some post-Cold War norms that are different from what Beijing perceived as the outdated Cold War mentality manifested by the American post-Cold War foreign policy.

Beijing attempts, among other things, to demonstrate through SCO that, first, countries with different civilizations and social systems could coexist in peace without democratizing domestic systems, as the democratic peace advocates would argue. Peaceful relations among nations could simply be the result of learning from past mistakes. Second, the era of "either enemy or ally" is gone, as declared by Chinese President Hu Jintao in his visit to the United States in early 2002. Interstate relations could be something between these two extremes. SCO, unlike NATO, is not a traditional military alliance.[96] It strives for a relationship among members that is neither confrontational nor collusive. It is called a "partnership without alliance."[97] In Beijing's view, this is a right approach to maintain regional stability and peace and to avoid repetition of the polarization.[98] Third, Beijing intends to develop a model of cooperation in which major powers and smaller powers can collaborate on an equal footing. One device for such equality is consensus-building in decision-making that gives all members virtually the veto power. Although member states shoulder different proportions of the SCO budget, each has an equal right in decision-making. In SCO Secretary-General Zhang Deguang's words, "There is no veto in the SCO, so no major country can outweigh others."[99] The SCO charter legalized this mechanism. It stipulates that decisions in SCO are made by non-voting consultation and the passage of resolutions needs unanimous consent from the member states.[100] Another feature of decision-making reflecting the non-alliance nature of SCO is the voluntary principle. Member states could decide whether to participate in or stay out of the cooperative projects endorsed by SCO. Non-participation in some projects does not affect a country's full membership.[101]

While Chinese scholars admit that these norms still sound idealistic under current circumstances, such norms could nevertheless play a constructive role in moulding the behaviour of member states.[102] The "Shanghai Spirit" was formally enshrined in the Declaration of Shanghai Cooperation Organization and the Charter of the Organization. Some evidence shows that the norms of the "Shanghai Spirit" are being increasingly accepted by the member states, at least in their diplomatic discourse.[103]

Conclusion

Over the time span of five years or so, Shanghai Five has evolved into a relatively fully-fledged regional international organization – Shanghai Cooperation Organization. During the process, it has experienced transformation from being traditional security to non-traditional security-oriented, single dimensional to comprehensive, and a non-institutional meeting mechanism to a formally institutionalized structure. It also has withstood the storms of the September 11 terrorist attack and the "colour revolution" in Central Asia. China has played pivotal roles in all these changes and made great efforts to enable SCO to "translate consensus into action and render plans into reality" and to prevent the organization from becoming a mere "discussion club."[104]

Needless to say, Beijing's pursuit of multilateralism in this sub-region is mainly motivated by instrumental purposes. Ever since the disintegration of the Soviet Union, China has been concerned with the instability and uncertainty brought about by the dramatic geopolitical changes in the region. China's active involvement in Shanghai Five and SCO is mainly aimed at creating a more peaceful and favourable regional environment for China's economic development, resolving long-standing border disputes, managing new sources of threat, raising Beijing's positive profile in the region, dispelling misgivings and concerns about China's growing economic and military might, and offsetting the influence of outside, as well as indigenous, major powers, such as the United States. In doing so, Beijing increasingly perceived multilateral diplomacy as a more effective and less alarming strategy to advance China's national interest and to project China's influence. The long-term goal of Beijing is to turn Central Asia into China's stable "strategic backyard." Overall, the Shanghai Five-SCO has been successful in nurturing mutual trust and cooperative habits among member states, mitigating the fallout of the "three evils," and maintaining a relatively stable security order in the region. For example, SCO is becoming an important partner in helping Afghanistan fight against drug-trafficking and terrorism.[105] The President of Afghanistan was invited to attend the SCO summit and the two sides signed the Contact Group Protocol to institutionalize cooperation. As one Chinese scholar put it, "We can say without any exaggeration, if there were no 'Shanghai Five' – SCO mechanism, the Afghan conflict would already have spread to Tajikistan and Uzbekistan, and maybe to Pakistan as well."[106]

On the other hand, China's multilateral diplomacy in Shanghai Five-SCO is driven by more than just geopolitical or utilitarian calculations. It also reflects China's intention to coordinate interstate relations and establish order on the basis of "generalized" principles of conduct.[107] China firmly believes that the new reality of world politics requires some norms and principles that are different from those that regulated interstate relations in the Cold War period. China is determined to have a say in formulating these new norms and principles. Its tireless advocacy of "new security concepts" as well as the configuration of these concepts in forms of "Shanghai Spirit" in the case of SCO points to the increasing weight of norm and rule-making in China's foreign policy.

The experiment of SCO also indicates a significant departure of China's foreign policy from its bilateral and non-aligned tradition. Even since the 1980s, China pursued a standard independent foreign policy pledging that it will not enter alliance with any big power or group of countries, and will not establish any military bloc.[108] China's practice of SCO has clearly diverged from that standard. It is true that SCO and the Shanghai Five was initially conceived as a non-military meeting mechanism aimed primarily at solving issues such as border delimitation. However, the setting up of the anti-terrorist mechanism and joint military exercises among SCO members made some analysts call SCO by-and-large a military alliance. While it is still perhaps too early to call SCO a military alliance in the traditional sense,[109] it nevertheless already contains some military elements.[110] Some Chinese scholars started calling SCO a "political and security coalition." In accordance with the change in China's diplomatic practice, Jiang Zemin's political report at the 16th Party Congress dropped the "non-alliance" clause used in the report at the 15th Party Congress in 1997.[111]

However, China's perceptual and behavioural changes reflected in its SCO behaviour do not necessarily mean that it will endorse highly institutionalized multilateralism across the board. What China embraced in its peripheral diplomacy is the so-called "flexible multilateralism."[112] It means that China will not follow a unified model. Instead, it will take different modes of multilateralism to fit different geopolitical and geo-economic conditions. For example, in the Southeast Asia and the broadly defined Asia-Pacific region, China evidently prefers a loosely structured and open-ended multilateralism but in the case of Shanghai Five-SCO, China spared no effort to push for institutionalization. The priority of issue in China's multilateral diplomacy could also be different from one sub-region to another. While Beijing started with economic multilateralism in Southeast Asia, it took a "security first and economy second" approach in North and Central Asia that challenged the logic of traditional functionalism. But in a final analysis, Beijing concluded that a mere security rationale featured by a threat or enemy is not enough to sustain regional multilateralism. Economic integration is also the key for the sustainability of SCO.

Notes

1 Zhang Deguang, "Generalizing experience, deepening cooperation, leading the SCO towards new great achievements." Online. Available: www.sectsco.org/html/01007.html.
2 Yu Jianhua, "The Development of SCO and the Exploration of New Interstate Relations," *Chinese Diplomacy*, no. 7, 2003, p. 28.
3 For traditional functionalism, see David Mitrany, *A Working Peace System*, London: Royal Institute of International Affairs, 1946.
4 "President Jiang Zemin's Speech at the SCO St. Petersburg Summit, 7 June 2002," *Collection of Shanghai Five – SCO Documents*, Center for Studies of SCO, Shanghai Academia of Social Science, 2003, p. 72.
5 Chinese scholars hold that this security-driven multilateralism has a merit of building up trust among parties involved first and then spreading cooperation to other functional areas. Pang Guang, "An Analysis of the Prospect of 'Shanghai Five,'" in

Ling Rong (ed.) *Thinking of the New Century*, Beijing: Chinese Central Party School Press, December 2002, p. 111.
6 "Disarmament Helps Improve Border Security," *Xinhua News Agency*, 30 October 2004.
7 "China, Russia, Kazakhstan, Kyrgyzstan, and Tajikistan Signed a Joint Memorandum to Fight International Terrorism," *Chinesenewsnet*, 3 December 1999.
8 "Shanghai Convention on Shanghai Convention against Terrorism, Separatism, and Extremism," *Collection of Shanghai Five – SCO Documents*, Center for Studies of SCO, Shanghai Academia of Social Science, 2003, pp. 19–25.
9 David Sands, "China Counters US Influence," 11 January 2002. Online. Available: www.mail-archive.com/muttil@taklamaka.org010 27.html.
10 Here are some of descriptions about SCO's state of affairs after the September 11 attacks: "The SCO has cracked at the first serious test;" "The SCO went into cardiac arrest;" "SCO stood as exposed as irrelevant;" SCO is a "stillborn" organization; and "the SCO will lose viability as a regional security and political forum." See Sean L. Yom, "Geopolitics in Central Asia: The SCO and Its Future," *Journal of World Affairs and New Technology* 5, October 2002. Online. Available: www.world-affairs.com/54sco.htm; *Monitor*, Jamestown Foundation 7, no. 217, p. 27 November 2001. Online. Available: www.russia.jameston.org/pubs/views/mon_007_217_ 000.htm; *Russia's Week*, Jamestown Foundation 7, no. 2, 16 January 2002. Online. Available: www.russia.jamestown. org/pubs/view/bul_007_ 002_001.htm.
11 *Kazakhstan News Bulletin*, 14 September 2001.
12 "The Joint Statement of the SCO Foreign Ministers Meeting," 7 January 2002 in *Collection of Shanghai Five – SCO Documents*, Center for Studies of SCO, Shanghai Academia of Social Science, 1993, pp. 30–2.
13 *Eurasia Insight*, "Shanghai Cooperation Organization Prepares for New Role," 29 April 2002. Online. Available: www.eurasianet.org/ departments/insight/articles/eav042902.shtml.
14 Press release on the meeting of the representatives of law-enforcement agencies of the Republic of Kazakhstan, People's Republic of China, Russian Federation, Kyrgyz Republic and the Republic of Tajikistan – members of the "Bishkek group" of the Shanghai Organization of Co-operation, 23 May 2002. Online. Available: www/mfa.kz/ english/sco_230502.htm.
15 Pang Guang, "SCO Under New Circumstances: Challenge, Opportunity and Prospect for Development," *Journal of International Studies*, no. 5, 2002, p. 40.
16 "Jiang Zemin Calls for Regional Anti-terrorism Mechanism between SCO," 7 January 2001. Online. Available: www.genevamissiontoun.fmprc.gov.cn/eng/23370. html.
17 The location of the centre was later moved to Tashkent at the request of Uzbek President Islam Karimov. "SCO Foreign Ministers Converge in Tashkent." *Muslim Uzbekistan*, 6 September 2003. Online. Available: www.muslimuzbekistan.com/eng/ennews/2003/09/ennews06092003_2.html.
18 Some Chinese analysts argue that the SCO plays a particular role in the US antiterrorism strategy and that such a role cannot be entirely replaced by any other organization. Therefore, it is necessary for the United States to cooperate with SCO to deal with international terrorism. Bei Zhou, "After the St. Petersburg Summit," *Beijing Review*, 4 July 2002, pp. 8–9.
19 It is reported that according to one of the unpublished terms of the SCO, China could send troops to Central Asia to combat Islamic extremism, if requested to do so. "Shanghai Grouping a 'Military Alliance,'" *Strait Times*, 21 July 2001.
20 Xu Tao, "SCO: Example for the World," *Beijing Review*, 12 June 2003, p. 27.
21 Xu Tao, "Exercising for Regional Defense Fitness," *Beijing Review*, 21 August 2003, pp. 42–3.

22 "Joint military drill with Russia begins," *Xinhua*, 18 August 2005.
23 "China, Kazakhstan stage joint anti-terror drill." Online. Available: www.chinanews.cn, 25 August 2006.
24 "China, Tajikistan holds military exercise." Online. Available: www.chinanews.cn, 23 September 2006.
25 Joint military drills target terrorism," *China Daily*, 27 April 2006.
26 "SCO Foreign Ministers Release Communiqué," *People's Daily*, 25 November 2002.
27 "Shanghai Cooperation Organization," 7 January 2004. Online. Available: www.fmprc.gov.cn/eng/topics/sco/t57970.htm.
28 "SCO achieves 'impressive progress,'" *People's Daily Online*, 14 January 2005.
29 "China confident and pragmatic in military exchanges," *People's Daily Online*, 7 January 2005.
30 Xu Tao, "SCO: Example for the World," *Beijing Review*, 12 June 2003, p. 27.
31 Pang Guang, "The Development of Sino-Russian Relations and the SCO under the New Situation," *Chinese Diplomacy*, no. 4, 2003.
32 Pang Guang, "The Development of Sino-Russian Relations and the SCO under the New Situation," *Chinese Diplomacy*, no. 4, 2003, p. 41.
33 "Chart of Shanghai Cooperation Organization," *Collection of Shanghai Five–SCO Documents*, Center for Studies of SCO, Shanghai Academia of Social Science, 1993, pp. 36–42.
34 "St. Petersburg Summit of SCO Concludes with Rich Fruit," *Xinhua News Agency*, 8 June 2002.
35 "Chinese President Urges Great Efforts to Fight Terrorism," *People's Daily*, 30 May 2003.
36 Xu Tao, "SCO: Example for the World," *Beijing Review*, 12 June 2003, p. 27; Zhang Wenwei and Xu Jing, "SCO's New Development and New Prospect," *International Strategic Studies*, no. 1, 2004, pp. 27–8.
37 Xu Tao, "SCO: Example for the World," *Beijing Review*, 12 June 2003, p. 26.
38 "The Third SCO Summit Meeting Held in Moscow," 30 May 2003. Online. Available: www.fmprc.gov.cn/eng/topics/hjtcf/t23117.htm.
39 China hoped that the secretariat could be officially open after the summit in 2003 or in November of that year. "SCO Foreign Ministers Release Communiqué," *People's Daily*, 25 November 2002; "Five Department Director-General Talk about Hu Jintao's Trips to Europe and Asia," *World Affairs*, no. 13, 2003, p. 17.
40 "Hu Jintao's Speech at the SCO Moscow Summit," 29 May 2003, *People's Daily*, 30 May 2003.
41 "China Shoulders 24 Percent SCO Annual Fee," *People's Daily Online*, 16 January 2004.
42 According to Zhang, the qualification for the candidates is pretty high. He or she has to have worked in the diplomatic fields for more than 15 years and know Russian well. "SCO Enjoys Bright Future: Secretary-General," *People's Daily*, 13 January 2004.
43 *Xinhuanet*, "SCO Launches Regional Anti-Terrorist Body," 17 June 2004.
44 Declaration of Heads of Member States of Shanghai Cooperation Organization," Astana, 5 July 2005.
45 *Xinhuanet*, "Hu Proposed SCO on Security, Economy," 17 June 2004.
46 Pakistan, India, Mongolia, Iran, and Turkmenistan have all expressed an interest. It is said that even the United States would like to join SCO. John Daly, "'Shanghai Five' Expands to Combat Islamic Radicals," *Janes Terrorism and Security Monitor*, 19 July 2001.
47 Xu Tao, "SCO: Example for the World," *Beijing Review*, 12 June 2003, p. 27.
48 For example, the Mongolian foreign minister, on an official visit to China, was invited to attend inauguration ceremony of the SCO secretariat in January 2004.

Afghan President Hamid Karzai attended the Tashkent summit in June 2004 as an honorary guest.
49 "Shanghai Cooperation Organization Accepts Mongolia as Observer," *People's Daily Online*, 17 June 2004. But SCO Secretary-General Zhang Deguang made it clear at the beginning of 2005 that the introduction of any new members or even observers is "not on the SCO's agenda." "SCO achieves 'impressive progress,'" *People's Daily Online*, 14 January 2005.
50 See "Speech by Secretary-General of the Shanghai Cooperation Organization Zhang Deguang at the 60th High-level plenary meeting of the United Nations General Assembly," New York, 16 September 2005. Online. Available: www.sectsco.org/html/00515.html.
51 Zhang Deguang, "Generalizing experience, deepening cooperation, leading the SCO towards new great achievements." Online. Available: www.sectsco.org/html/01007.html.
52 "Declaration of Heads of Member States of Shanghai Cooperation Organization," Astana, 5 July 2005. Online. Available: www.sectsco.org/html/00500.html.
53 *Xinhua*, "Joint Communique of 2006 SCO Summit," 15 June 2006.
54 Pan Guang, "An Analysis of the Prospect of 'Shanghai Five,'" in Ling Rong (ed.) *Thinking of the New Century*, Beijing: Chinese Central Party School Press, December 2002, p. 114.
55 Pan Guang, "An Analysis of the Prospect of 'Shanghai Five,'" in Ling Rong (ed.) *Thinking of the New Century*, Beijing: Chinese Central Party School Press, December 2002, pp. 114–15.
56 "Hu Jintao's Speech at the SCO Moscow Summit," 29 May 2003, *People's Daily*, 30 May 2003.
57 "SCO and Regional Cooperation," *Contemporary International Relations*, no. 6, 2004, p. 33.
58 "China Proposes Free Trade Zone between SCO Members," *China Daily*, 24 September 2003.
59 "Work on Free Trade Zone on Agenda," *China Daily*, 2 November 2004.
60 Online. Available: www.chinanews.cn, "Premier Wen: SCO trade is set to double," 16 September 2006.
61 *Xinhuanet*, "Hu Proposes SCO Focus on Security, Economy," 17 June 2004.
62 *Xinhuanet*, "China Offers 900 Million US Dollars in Credit Loans to SCO Members," 17 June 2004. The loans became available early 2006. Online. Available: www.chinanews.cn, "Premier Wen: SCO trade is set to double," 16 September 2006.
63 *Pravda*, "SCO Summit in Tashkent," 17 June 2004.
64 *Xinhuanet*, "Premier Wen Urges Closer Cooperation Among SCO Members," 23 September 2004.
65 "Foreign Minister Li Zhaoxing talks about the achievements of Premier Wen Jiaobao's Visit: 'Friendly Neighbours and Sincere Friends'," 28 September 2004. Online. Available: www.fmprc.gov.cn/eng/ topics/wjacfdo/t162457.htm.
66 Zhang Deguang, "Generalizing experience, deepening cooperation, leading the SCO towards new great achievements." Online. Available: www.sectsco.org/html/01007.html.
67 "Declaration of Shanghai Cooperation Organization," 15 June 2001, *Collection of Shanghai Five – SCO Documents*, Center for Studies of SCO, Shanghai Academia of Social Science, 2003, p. 18.
68 Li Fengling, "SCO Entered in A New March," *International Strategic Studies*, no. 1, 2004, p. 30; "SCO and Regional Cooperation," *Contemporary International Relations*, no. 6, 2004, p. 36.
69 Hu Jintao made four proposals to build a harmonious region," *People's Daily*, 16 June 2006.

70 Declaration on 5th Anniversary of SCO," Shanghai, 15 June 2006.
71 Willy Wo-Lap Lam, "Beijing's NATO' Hits Stumbling Block," CNN.com, 16 May 2002. Some alarmists even see the SCO as China's Warsaw Pact. Western intelligence circles describe SCO merely a synergistic tool and framework for Russia and China to court Central Asian countries and to establish the strategic Sino-Russian condominium over Central Asia against the United States and NATO. See Matthew Oresman, "The SCO: A New Hope or to the Graveyard of Acronyms?" *PacNet* newsletter, no. 21, 22 May 2003. Online. Available: www.csis.org/pacfor/pac0321.htm; Sean L. Yom, "Geopolitics in Central Asia: The SCO and Its Future," *Journal of World Affairs and New Technology* 5, October 2002. Online. Available: www.world-affairs.com/54sco.htm; *Newsmax.com*, "China, Russia form Anti-US Axis," 16 June 2001.
72 Zhang Deguang, "Generalizing experience, deepening cooperation, leading the SCO towards new great achievements." Online. Available: www.sectsco.org/html/01007.html.
73 Ibid.
74 See "Declaration of Heads of Members States of Shanghai Cooperation Organization," Astana, July 2005.
75 "China's Position Paper on the New Security Concept," 6 August 2002. Online. Available: www.un.fmprc.gov.cn/eng/33462.html.
76 "China's Position Paper on the New Security Concept," 6 August 2002.
77 Xiong Guangkai, "The New Security Concept Advocated by China," a speech at the London Institute of International Strategic Studies, *Study of International Strategy*, no. 3, 2002, p. 2.
78 "China's Position Paper on the New Security Concept," 6 August 2002.
79 Statement by Ambassador Hu Xiaodi, head of the Chinese delegation, at the First Committee of the Fifty-eighth Session of the United Nations General Assembly, New York, 7 October 2003.
80 "Global Problems Call for Global Answers: Chinese FM," *People's Daily*, 18 January 2002.
81 "China's Position Paper on the New Security Concept," 6 August 2002.
82 "To Enhance the Role of the United Nations, in Promotion of Peace and Development," statement by Chinese Foreign Minister Li Zhaoxing at the general debate of the Fifty-eighth Session of the United Nations General Assembly, 24 September 2003. Online. Available: www.un.fmprc. gov.cn/eng.56633.html.
83 "China's Position Paper on the New Security Concept," 6 August 2002.
84 "Chinese Foreign Policy after the 16th CPC National Congress," *China Daily*, 18 July 2003.
85 "China's Position Paper on the New Security Concept," 6 August 2002.
86 Statement by Ambassador Hu Xiaodi, head of the Chinese delegation, at the First Committee of the Fifty-eighth Session of the United Nations General Assembly, New York, 7 October 2003.
87 Chinese Vice Foreign Minister Wang Yi's comments, see Martin Sieff, "China wants its own 'new world order' to oppose US version," *UPI*, 6 February 2002.
88 See Yu Jianhua, "The Development of SCO and the Exploration of New Interstate Relations," *Chinese Diplomacy*, no. 7, 2003, p. 29.
89 For the discussion of instrumental and normative-contractual order, see Muthiah Alagappa, "Constructing Security Order in Asia: Conception and Issues," in Muthiah Alagappa (ed.) *Asian Security Order, Instrumental and Normative Features*, Stanford: Stanford University Press, 2003, pp. 41–52.
90 "Declaration of Shanghai Cooperation Organization," 15 June 2001, *Collection of Shanghai Five – SCO Documents*, Center for Studies of SCO, Shanghai Academia of Social Science, 2003, p. 18.
91 "President Jiang Zemin's Speech at the SCO St. Petersburg Summit," 7 June 2002,

Collection of Shanghai Five – SCO Documents, Center for Studies of SCO, Shanghai Academia of Social Science, 2003, p. 73.
92 Lu Zhongwei, "The Evolution of the Geo-Strategic Structure in Eurasia" in *Shanghai Cooperation Organization – New Security Concept and New Mechanism*," Beijing: Current Affairs Press, 2002, p. 10.
93 "Hu Jintao made four proposals to build a harmonious regaion," *People's Daily*, 16 June 2006.
94 "Joint Communique of 2006 SCO Summit," *Xinhua*, 15 June 2006.
95 Thomas Christensen, "Pride, Pressure, and Politics: The Roots of China's Worldview," in Deng and Wang, *In the Eyes of the Dragon*, Lanham, Md: Rowman and Littlefield, 1999, p. 240.
96 SCO Secretary-general Zhang Deguang declared that SCO will never become a geopolitical military bloc. It does not have hypothetical adversaries. The real enemies of SCO are terrorism, separatism and extremist, poverty, ignorance, and backwardness. "The speech of the Secretary-General of the Secretariat of Shanghai Cooperation Organization Zhang Deguang at the International Conference, 'The Shanghai Cooperation Organization: A New Model of Regional Cooperation,'" 17 August 2004. Online. Available: www.sectsco.org/news_detail.asp?id= 208&LanguageID=2.
97 Wang Jincun, "An Advance of Historical Significance – from 'Shanghai Five' to 'Shanghai Cooperation Organization,'" *World Economics and Politics*, no. 9, 2001, p 80.
98 As one Chinese scholar observed, "Because of China's participation, the SCO is quite different in nature from other big powers and blocs in the region," "SCO embarks on key development stage," *People's Daily Online*, 14 June 2004.
99 "China Shoulders 24 Percent SCO Annual Fee," *People's Daily Online*, 16 January 2004.
100 This mode of decision-making of course will become more difficult with the possible expansion of membership of SCO in the future.
101 "Chart of Shanghai Cooperation Organization," *Collection of Shanghai Five – SCO Documents*, Center for Studies of SCO, Shanghai Academia of Social Science, 1993, p. 41.
102 Xu Tao, "Shanghai Cooperation Organization under New Situation," *Cotemporary International Relations*, no. 6, 2002, p. 13.
103 As Russia's foreign ministry spokesman pointed out, the SCO is based on the principles of equality and consensus. It does not necessarily follow one country's leader, and it does not have "leading" members or nations to be "led." Sergei Blagov, "Shanghai Cooperation Organization Prepares for New Role," *Eurasia Insight*, 29 April 2002. Online. Available: www.eurasianet.org/departments/insight/articles/eav)42902.shtml.
104 See "President Hu: SCO future hinges on action," Xinhua, 6 July 2005; Zhang Deguang, "Generalizing experience, deepening cooperation, leading the SCO towards new great achievements." Online. Available: www.sectsco.org/html/01007.html.
105 *Pravda,* "SCO summit in Tashkent," 17 June 2004.
106 Pan Guang, "China-Central Asia-Russian Relations and The Role of SCO in the War on Terrorism," paper presented at Stanford University, University of California-Los Angeles, RAND, Monterey Institute of International Studies, University of Cambridge, and Carleton University, 2002, p. 4.
107 John Gerard Ruggie, "Multilateralism: The Anatomy of an Institution," *International Organization* 46, no. 3, Summer 1992, p. 571.
108 Jiang Zemin, "Hold High the Great Banner of Deng Xiaoping Theory for an All-round Advancement of the Cause of Building Socialism with Chinese Characteristics into the 21st Century – Report delivered at the 15th National Congress of the

Communist Party of China on 12 September 1997. Online. Available: www.china.org.cn/english/features/45607.htm.
109 SCO Secretary-General Zhang Deguang declared that "The SCO countries will never grow into a military bloc nor resume military confrontation as in the Cold War," "China, Russia, other SCO nations aim for economic integration: official," *People's Daily Online*, 18 August 2004.
110 It is not accidental that the first SCO anti-terror military drill was named "Coalition2003."
111 Ye Zicheng and Mu Xinhai, "From independence to common development," *Studies of International Politics*, no. 1, 2003, p. 61.
112 Pang Zhongying, "China's Asian Strategy: Flexible Multilateralism," *World Economy and Politics*, no. 10, 2001, pp. 30–5.

8 Chinese and ASEAN responses to the US Regional Maritime Security Initiative

Gaye Christoffersen

Introduction

Most of the world celebrates "World Maritime Day" during the last week of September. China, which only began celebrating World Maritime Day in 2005, celebrates in July on a date which commemorates the 600th anniversary of Zheng He's voyages. Zheng He was a Ming Dynasty admiral, and a Muslim, who made several journeys through Southeast Asia. Zheng He has become a symbol of the longevity of Chinese–Southeast Asian maritime connections. During July 2005, Malaysia's Prime Minister launched a Zheng He exhibit called "Envoy of Peace from China." Although China and Malaysia established diplomatic relations only three decades ago, the Chinese Ambassador stressed that Zheng He, during his five visits to Malacca, had launched Chinese Malaysian friendship.

The Chinese theme of the 2005 observance of World Maritime Day was "love the motherland, be good friends with neighbouring countries and navigate scientifically." The second observance of World Maritime Day in 2006 was used by the Chinese government to call for greater public awareness and interest in China's million square miles of "blue territory" with the theme of "love the blue territory, develop ocean shipping."[1]

Although the Zheng He exhibit seemed to be a rather contrived performance to create public awareness of China's maritime interests in Southeast Asia, it was effective as a Sino-Malaysian project to establish a lengthy lineage of China's interests in the Malacca Straits.

However, these celebrations and exhibits by themselves did not establish China's role in the Malacca Straits. This chapter argues that China's role in the region was clarified as a consequence of East Asia's reaction to the US proposal for the Regional Maritime Security Initiative (RMSI), a proposal to send US Special Forces into the Malacca Straits. RMSI, announced in March 2004, assumed for its implementation of the hub-and-spokes pattern of US foreign policy, and challenged an emerging East Asian security order that Japan, China, and ASEAN are constructing, a "multi-layered security order" with Asian regional organizations.[2] The RMSI met with intense regional opposition, leading to its eventual disappearance.

Japan had initiated the East Asian multilayered security order in the early 1990s, at the end of the Cold War, when it began to hedge the US–Japan Defense Treaty with multilateral regimes, such as the ASEAN Regional Forum (ARF).[3] Japan and ASEAN intended to use the ARF to facilitate integration of China into the East Asian order. Japan would help establish ASEAN Plus Three (APT, ASEAN countries plus Japan, China, and South Korea) in the late 1990s. The Japanese Ministry of Foreign Affairs took a multi-tiered approach which allowed it to pursue both Asian multilateralism and the bilateral US–Japan Defense Treaty simultaneously.

Although theoretically it is possible to achieve an Asian maritime security order through some combination of American hegemony, bilateral agreements, and globa/regional regimes,[4] there is no littoral state or user state of the Malacca Straits that accepts all pathways with the exception of Japan. ASEAN fragmented over RMSI – Malaysia and Indonesia rejected the initiative in Southeast Asia while Singapore was publicly supportive. Southeast Asia's response to the RMSI made it clear that the littoral states would collectively provide for the security of the Malacca Straits.

China's initial response was to voice concern over Malacca but to not confront the US directly. Rather Beijing let Malaysia take the lead in resisting US leadership in Malacca. Beijing was noticeably silent, although it conferred with Kuala Lumpur periodically and began to discuss more its "Malacca Strait Predicament" and fears that the US would physically control the Strait and strategically deny it to Beijing at some future time. Beijing is dependent on, and benefits from, American protection of the SLOCs, and would not want maritime terrorists cutting off its supply line from the Middle East.

China's response to RMSI reflected its standard approach during the 1990s in the ARF and APEC as a regime-taker rather than a regime-creator. By the late 1990s, Chinese initiatives for a multilateral security regime and adoption of cooperative security in the "new security concept paper" indicated the influence of socialization under the ARF process.[5] The formation of ASEAN plus three (APT) in 1997, under which China–ASEAN relations strengthened, encouraged China to take greater initiative and contribute to the organization's institutionalization.

Beijing's foreign-policy initiatives towards ASEAN countries following announcement of RMSI demonstrate an effort to have a greater voice in the East Asian maritime order, working through Asian multilateral regimes. This would culminate in a larger role for China in the Malacca Straits.

RMSI: an American initiative

Terrorists are suspected of plotting to disrupt the Malacca Straits. The Malacca Straits, only 1.5 miles wide, at its narrowest point is an oil transit choke point. Every day 11 million barrels of oil pass through Malacca. An oil tanker that was grounded in the Strait could block the channel, forcing the 50,000 ships/year that pass through there to find other routes, increasing the requirement for vessel capacity that could absorb all excess capacity of the world fleet.[6]

Admiral Thomas Fargo, commander of the US Pacific Command (PACOM), during his annual US PACOM Posture testimony to the House Armed Services Committee, March 2004, mentioned RMSI as a US initiative to operationalize the Proliferation Security Initiative (PSI).[7] He claimed RMSI was needed because there were vast stretches of the oceanic world that were uncharted territory, unmanaged by the US, which needed to be put under firmer control. RMSI would create an architecture that would allow the US to share information and put standing operating procedures in place in East Asia.[8] He claimed that vast stretches of Southeast Asian sea space were ungoverned, especially "… the ungoverned littoral regions of SE Asia" which he felt were fertile ground for proliferation, terrorism, and piracy.[9]

Admiral Fargo also mentioned during Q&A that the US planned to deploy Marines and Special Forces on high-speed vessels along the Malacca Straits. This would later be downplayed, and initially, Secretary of Defense Rumsfeld denied that it was ever said. Eventually, however, it became part of the written record. Admiral Fargo had assumed widespread ASEAN consensus based on his meetings with Singaporeans.[10]

US counter-terrorist effort in Southeast Asia, organized on the hub-and-spokes pattern, had limitations. Success would depend on the willingness and capacity of individual states to cooperate. In early 2001, prior to 9/11, the US had indicated interest in establishing bases in Southeast Asia – in the Philippines, Thailand, Singapore, and even Vietnam, for the purpose of containing China.[11] Post 9/11, the US made Southeast Asia the second front in the war on terrorism, and the purpose of proposed military bases became to contain China and counter terrorists. The goal was "places not bases," a search for "lily pads" to store equipment and arms until needed, a result of the Department of Defense transformation strategy, the *Global Posture Review*. The expectation was that the US could organize the hub-and-spokes pattern of bilateral military alliances into a collective security arrangement of the "like-minded," an "Asian NATO," or if that proved unworkable, an ad hoc "coalition of the willing," as needed.

China had acquiesced to a US initiative to put terrorism on APEC's agenda at the Shanghai meeting in October 2001, even though APEC was created as an economic forum and does not have an institutionalized focus on security. China was not very alarmed when the US–ASEAN Joint Declaration on Combating Terrorism was signed in August 2002 because several ASEAN nations opposed US military forces engaged in counter-terrorism in Southeast Asia, the agreement left it up to individual nations whether they would let US forces into their country, and anti-American sentiment among ASEAN nations' domestic populations would limit the extent of cooperation.[12]

In 2003, prior to the announcement of RMSI, China participated in several multilateral initiatives that would address maritime security and counter-proliferation in Asia. The APT had a project on piracy initiated by Japan. APEC held a Conference on Maritime Security in September 2003. The Joint Declaration of ASEAN and China on Cooperation in the Field of Non-Traditional Security Issues, issued November 2002, included piracy and terrorism. In December

2002, the UN General Assembly had adopted a resolution on "Oceans and the Law of the Sea," which directed the International Maritime Organization to address threats to maritime security. In August 2003 China held a conference "SLOC Security and Sino-US Nuclear Non-proliferation," jointly sponsored by the China Institute of Contemporary International Relations (CICIR) and the Ford Foundation. Participants discussed the prospects for US–China maritime cooperation, the threat of WMD and terrorism to SLOC security, and called for a new regional economic and political order.[13]

However, the Chinese questioned RMSI and PSI which gave secondary importance to these kinds of multilateral efforts. In September 2003, PSI held its first training exercise in counter-proliferation on the high seas, "Pacific Protector," off the coast of Australia. At that time PSI had 11 members but only two from the Asia-Pacific – Japan and Australia. The US had expected that ASEAN and South Korea would soon be joining.

China doubted the legitimacy of this US-led exercise with only two members from Asia, suspecting that it was directed at the DPRK, and suggested that other approaches would have greater efficacy than interception. China and ASEAN countries forged a common criticism of PSI that focused on its US-driven character outside the UN system. Critics claim the legitimacy of PSI is undermined by the secrecy of PSI interdictions. Asian nations fear that the US will change international law to legitimize pre-emptive interventions on the high seas or on sovereign territory.[14]

ASEAN+3

During the time when the response from Southeast Asia was overwhelmingly negative to the US initiative RMSI, Japan held a workshop on piracy, as it had done before, within the framework of APT. Japan has selectively used APT for security issues. Prime Minister Koizumi in January 2002 made APT the framework for an East Asian Energy Security Community.[15] The Japanese Foreign Ministry utilized APT as the framework for managing piracy which it called "piracy" rather than "maritime terrorism" in deference to the sensitivities of ASEAN states.

Both Japan and China have been edging towards promoting APT as a security forum. At the 1999 APT summit, Zhu Rongji had stated that "China was ready" for security to be placed on the agenda.[16] The 1999 APT issued a Joint Statement on East Asian Cooperation that primarily focused on economic and trade issues, briefly mentioning the political-security area where they agreed to increase mutual understanding and trust.

At the 2000 APT summit, it was Japanese Prime Minister Mori who suggested that cooperation should be expanded to include political and security cooperation. Mori proposed anti-piracy as a basis for APT cooperation, suggesting the holding of the "Asian Cooperation Conference on Combating Piracy and Armed Robbery against Ships."[17]

In 2000 Japan offered its coast guard to the three littoral states to conduct joint patrols of the Malacca Strait but was turned down by all the littoral states. Japan instead opted for the indirect approach, dispatching coast guard patrol vessels to conduct joint exercises and train personnel.[18] Japan has maintained a ship in the vicinity of the Straits which it declared is for training purposes.

The November 2001 APT meeting achieved greater clarity on the issue of taking on a security function. Former Chinese Premier Zhu Rongji presented a five-point proposal to further institutionalize APT in areas that included non-traditional security and terrorism.[19] Prime Minister Koizumi followed up on Mori's suggestion of the year before, proposing a "Regional Cooperation Agreement on Combating Piracy and Armed Robbery Against Ships in Asia" (ReCAAP). At the trilateral meeting of Japan, China and South Korea, which occurs in conjunction with APT, the three countries agreed to cooperate against terrorism and piracy.[20]

However, ASEAN rejected the Japanese proposal to issue a joint anti-terrorism statement and consider joint counter-terrorism activities. The proposal had divided ASEAN – Thailand and the Philippines favoured the statement while Malaysia and Indonesia did not. ASEAN itself would issue the 2001 ASEAN Declaration on Joint Action to Counter Terrorism which condemned terrorism, treating it as a transnational crime rather than a military issue, and called for greater cooperation among law enforcement agencies rather than militaries.

In 2003, Chinese proposals to treat APT as a security regime also met resistance from ASEAN. When Chinese Premier Wen Jiabao suggested making APT the main channel of security dialogue between China and ASEAN at the Bali II Summit in October 2003, ASEAN made it clear to Beijing that APT would not replace the ARF. Beijing appeared to have acquiesced to this ASEAN preference, submitting at ARF's November 2003 Intercessional Group meeting a proposal for an ARF Security Policy Conference (ASPC). The ASPC met for the first time in Beijing in November 2004, an ARF defence ministers' meeting.

Japan continues to use the APT and APEC frameworks in a limited way for some security issues. In June 2004, the Japanese Ministry of Foreign Affairs issued a report on the APEC Counter-Terrorism Capacity Building Initiative, and listed the ways in which Japan was assisting Southeast Asian nations to expand their capacity in counter-terrorism, such as a "Port Security Seminar in Southeast Asian Countries" to help them implement the SOLAS/ISPS code which came into effect 1 July 2004.[21] Tokyo also hosted the Asian Coast Guard Agencies Meeting in June 2004 to continue building cooperative relations and information sharing in maritime security.[22] Despite Japan's careful multilateral approach, Singaporeans suspected that Japan and India were capitalizing on the US anti-terror campaign to establish a maritime presence in the Malacca Straits.[23]

China had signed the Treaty of Amity and Cooperation (TAC) during the Bali Summit II in October 2003. Once China had signed it in 2003, all other Asian powers followed which put great pressure on Japan to follow suit. After much internal debate, Tokyo signed TAC at the July 2004 ARF meeting, committing itself not to militarily intervene in Southeast Asia or challenge ASEAN sovereignty. Japan had hesitated signing TAC out of concern that it would conflict with the US–Japan Defense Treaty and close off the option of joint US–Japan military interventions in Southeast Asia. ASEAN had first asked the US and other outside powers to sign it in 1992. ASEAN's stress on TAC in 2003 is no doubt a response to President Bush's announcement of PSI in May 2003.[24]

During a January 2004 maritime security conference, a former Vice Admiral of Japan's Self-Defence Forces, complained that two contending strategies, one Japanese and the other American, hampered the formation of a regional framework for a maritime security coalition. Japanese preferred strengthening the ARF into a multilateral cooperative security framework inclusive of all Northeast and Southeast Asia. The Americans preferred a maritime "coalition of the willing" to undertake maritime security maintenance in the Malacca Straits, excluding those nations that were not like-minded.[25] The inference was that the US strategy, narrowly based, was undermining the Japanese strategy which was more inclusive.

Japan's efforts to organize the region against maritime terrorism within an APT framework bore results in November 2004 when Tokyo hosted a meeting of 16 nations that adopted a resolution on "Regional Cooperation Agreement on Combating Piracy and Armed Robbery Against Ships in Asia" (ReCAAP) which would set up a Regional Information Centre in Singapore. ReCAAP promotes anti-piracy cooperation amongst the ASEAN+3 (APT) countries plus India, Sri Lanka, and Bangladesh. ReCAAP required ten countries to ratify it before it could come into force.

Malaysian and Indonesian responses

The US had apparently decided on the RMSI after prior consultation with Singapore but not with the other littoral states of Malaysia and Indonesia. Singapore as a non-Muslim State in post-9/11 was predisposed to the US War on Terrorism (WOT) because it corresponds with traditional threat perceptions that Singapore is surrounded by a menacing Muslim Malay world. Singapore has taken a leadership role in Southeast Asia to counter Jemaah Islamiyah (JI) following arrests of JI cells in the city and uncovering a JI plot to attack US naval ships in port. The Singapore government produced a White Paper on the Jemaah Islamiyah Arrests and the Threat of Terrorism in January 2003.

Traditionally, Indonesia has preferred an autonomous regional order with no role for foreign military powers, while Singapore preferred foreign military alliances with outside military powers as a guarantee against neighbouring countries. Singapore has used balance of power politics to prevent dependence on any one outside power. ASEAN differences over a preferred regional order spilled over into ASEAN differences over WOT. Muslim and non-Muslim ASEAN members diverged over US treatment of Muslims in the Iraq War. Friction was ongoing between Singapore and Indonesia over Jakarta's refusal to acknowledge the existence of Jemaah Islamiyah and an overall Indonesian reluctance in the war on terrorism.

The 2003 Shangri-La Dialogue in Singapore focused on Asia's response to the US pre-emptive strike doctrine, the 2002 National Security Strategy of the United States of America, called the "Bush Doctrine." At that time, Admiral Fargo introduced the concept of Regional Maritime Security Initiative, using phrases such as, "expeditionary military capabilities," and, "robust maritime interdiction forces," but there were not many details, no mention of the Malacca Straits, and not much regional reaction.[26]

However, when Admiral Fargo discussed RMSI in March 2004 before Congress, the Malaysian reaction was immediate and unambiguous, heatedly rejecting RMSI. The Malaysian Defence Minister announced that before any foreign military could join security operations in the Straits of Malacca, it would need permission from Malaysia and Indonesia.

The Malaysian Deputy Prime Minister, Datuk Sri Najib Tun, accused the United States of, "looking for an excuse to be a hero in the Straits of Malacca," claiming the US presence in the Straits was a source of instability rather than a force for order because the US was a magnet for terrorists rather than a deterrent. Malaysia had not invited the US to guard the Malacca Strait, and thus an American presence in the Strait lacked legitimacy.

Indonesia had even more reason to fear the RMSI, having been referred to as a "failed state" by the US in the past and thus a target rather than a partner in WOT. US pre-emptive strike doctrine resonates with traditional Indonesian threat perceptions on national integrity and survival. Indonesia, as a Muslim State, after 9/11 had been in denial over the terrorist problem. After the October 2002 Bali bombing, Indonesian leaders began to acknowledge the existence of JI, but threat perceptions focused on a fear of becoming the target in WOT.

In 2003, Indonesian analysts suggested changing Indonesia's traditional strategy of autonomy to a mix of balance of power strategies integrated with Asian multilateralism, seeking support from other major powers within multilateral regimes to counter the US, thus both transnational terrorism and US unilateralism were constituted as threats to Indonesia.[27] One consequence of this strategy shift would be improved relations with China and Russia.

The Indonesian military (TNI) used the Iraq War to generate a debate over the nature of threats to Indonesia. Megawati claimed if the country was attacked by a foreign country (meaning the US), it could not survive one week because of the poor quality of Indonesian weaponry. Military analysts claimed Indonesia could counter a foreign assault with guerilla tactics by paramilitaries that could last 100 years.

The Indonesian Defense White Paper claimed Indonesia's greatest threats were domestic, and required TNI to be given back its domestic security role, *dwifungsi* (dual function). Domestic dangers included: separatist movements in Papua and Aceh, radical Islamic movements, ethnic and communal conflicts, and terrorism. TNI meant to open a domestic debate to increase budgetary allocations, and legally sanction the military approach to separatism and terrorism but instead, opened a debate on paramilitary groups.

Muslim organizations, which have been a force for democratization and civilian control of the military, opposed a strengthening of TNI's *dwifungsi* role. Hamzah Haz, then Vice President and an Islamist, disputed the need for TNI-controlled paramilitary groups. Hamzah supported Muslim paramilitaries defending themselves against TNI and foreign invaders. The paramilitary debate was linked to the debate over what is the nature of threats facing Indonesia, domestic insurgencies or a US pre-emptive strike. If it were Islamist paramilitary groups, among whom JI could submerge itself, than paramilitaries should be abolished. If the real threat were the US, then paramilitaries would be needed for defense against a US pre-emptive strike.

The US had assured Jakarta without success that it would not be considered a "failed state," and thus potentially another target on the Afghan model. Although it would be logistically impractical, Indonesians' greatest perceived threat is a military invasion by the US. Admiral Fargo's initial presentation on RMSI, referring to American Special Forces unilaterally patrolling the Malacca Strait, gave a tangible reality to these Indonesian threat perceptions.

As Thailand countered Muslim separatist violence in the south, the US offered to set up a military base in Thailand to help quell the Islamic violence, and had reportedly offered to send Special Forces to fight alongside Thai soldiers in the South. The offer was declined.[28] Malaysia heatedly objected to US military bases in Thailand or anywhere else in Southeast Asia, consistent with its rejection of a US military presence in the Malacca Strait. Thailand stated it backed the US on RMSI, but not the deployment of US forces in the Strait.[29]

Southeast Asian scholars argue that although collaboration between ASEAN and partner countries' intelligence services in the war on terror has been fairly effective, unenthusiastic regional responses to terrorism are partly a reaction to the highly militarized and unwelcome counter-terrorism strategy pursued by the United States.[30]

The US continued to work on a strategic framework agreement on security and defense with Singapore, and attempted to manage the diplomatic debacle with Malaysia and Indonesia by backtracking from its original position, reaffirming its respect for the littoral states' sovereignty and capacity to manage terrorism.

During this US–Southeast Asian discord, China and Japan both remained relatively silent, although not disinterested. Beijing used the *People's Daily* to voice official concerns over US hegemonic designs in the Malacca Strait, and used it as an opportunity to justify the Chinese Navy's expansion to defend the country's maritime security.[31]

At the end of May 2004, Malaysian Prime Minister Abdullah Ahmad Badawi, visited Beijing where he discussed strengthening bilateral ties, and developing APT into an East Asian Community with economic and security functions. The issue of China's role in the Malacca Straits was discussed, and the two countries found they had a common position on the Straits.

RMSI and PSI were hotly debated at the May 2004 CSCAP meeting in Hanoi. It was a joint session of the Confidence and Security Building Measures and Maritime Cooperation Working Groups. As a Track II group supporting ARF, it was a good sounding board outside the ARF meeting. Asian participants questioned PSI's legality and Washington's willingness to act outside of international law, mentioned because the US had not yet ratified the UN Convention on the Law of the Sea (UNCLOS). Japan and Singapore, the only two Asian countries participating in PSI, were not critical during the meeting. However, the extra-legality of PSI was underscored by other ASEAN participants.[32]

The Chinese participant clearly sided with Malaysia and Indonesia in opposing outside military intervention, although he recognized that China benefits from the US maintenance of SLOC security.[33]

The US presented a proposal paper on the RMSI at the annual ASEAN Regional Forum (ARF) in May 2004 with a much greater emphasis on multilateral cooperation. The ARF deliberated over an Indonesian proposal for an ASEAN Security Community, a framework to manage security issues multilaterally and regionally, rather than with outside powers. Southeast Asian nations meant to displace RMSI with their own proposals.

Malaysia passed the MMEA Act in July 2004 to establish the Malaysian Maritime Enforcement Agency (MMEA), created to enforce Malaysian federal laws and UNCLOS in the Malaysian maritime zone. The MMEA would strengthen Malaysian state capacity for better and more effective governance of the maritime zone. The Japanese Coast Guard assisted in the establishment of MMEA, part of Japan's programme to strengthen the capacity of littoral states.

In July 2004, the navies of Indonesia, Malaysia, and Singapore, with 17 ships, initiated Operation MALSINDO for coordinated patrols to create greater security for the Strait of Malacca. The three countries created a hot-line to be used when one nation is in hot pursuit into another's territorial waters. MALSINDO was meant to prevent intervention by outside powers.

By the end of 2004, Southeast Asians felt the US had "backed down" from its initial position on RMSI. A Malaysian analyst argued that it was because Malaysia had stood firm in rejecting US patrols in the Malacca Strait despite structural power differences between the two countries.[34]

Chinese initiative

China and ASEAN had promoted a potential Asian maritime security regime in November 2002 when they signed the Declaration on the Conduct of Parties in the South China Sea, committing themselves to observing UNCLOS, and combating transnational crime including piracy.

It was during 2003–04 that China developed a "Malacca Strait Predicament" which was constituted a "crisis" requiring several measures that would create alternative routes to the SLOCs passing through the Malacca Straits.[35] An oil pipeline from China to Myanmar was proposed by Chinese scholars who claimed it was made more urgent by the US RMSI. Chinese suspected RMSI was meant to control the Strait of Malacca to contain China and not just to fight terrorism in Southeast Asia.[36]

The China Institute of Contemporary International Relations (CICIR) merged energy and maritime security issues in an analysis supportive of regional energy cooperation and Chinese naval development. The Chinese author argued that China's position was becoming increasingly vulnerable as its oil import dependence grew, because it lacked the diplomatic and military influence of a country such as the US. Because the Chinese Navy could not secure the SLOCs from the Middle East as the US Navy could, the author felt China should not adopt an energy security policy modelled on that of the US; rather, China would have to coordinate with other net oil importers in Asia.[37]

The Chinese Navy's maritime mission, initially focused on coastal defence, is evolving to a mission of "green water active offshore defence," in a sphere that stretches from Vladivostok to the Malacca Straits, and out to the "first island chain." This is said to be an intermediate stage on the way to a blue-water naval capability, with aircraft carriers capable of securing the SLOCs. *Jiefangjun Bao* lobbied for aircraft carriers without which the PLA Navy lacked capacity to counter pirates in the Malacca Strait.[38]

According to Hong Kong newspapers, the military used the "Malacca Strait Predicament" as an opportunity to call for expansion of its budget, and perhaps its mission, but not to acquire aircraft carriers.[39] The Malacca Strait Predicament did not succeed in promoting an aircraft-carrier-building programme. Instead, alternative routes to bypass the Strait were initiated.

The Chinese were alarmed at the possibility of the US stationing troops in the Malacca Strait and establishing a military base there but were gratified that Malaysia and Indonesia opposed an American military presence in the Strait. Chinese criticism of RMSI emphasized East Asian solidarity.[40]

A Chinese scholar commenting on the RMSI, noted that, in his view, the "US has long wanted to control the Strait, and anti-terrorist operations provide the US with the best pretext and opportunity."[41] He noted that many Chinese believe that RMSI contravenes the UN Convention on the Law of the Sea (UNCLOS). Although China is concerned about who is in control of the Strait, he argued that RMSI was not designed solely to block China's access to oil supply from the Middle East. China supported counter-terrorism initiatives and was, "willing to participate in regional cooperation to guarantee SLOC security." China expected that a multilateral framework to guarantee the Strait's security would be created according to the principles of UNCLOS and in consultation with the littoral states.[42]

ASEAN's negative response to RMSI and search for alternatives opened up a possibility for China to contribute to SLOC security under international law and in collaboration with ASEAN nations. However, there was no multilateral mechanism for either counter-terrorism collaboration or regional consideration of China's role.

At the ASEAN–China Forum held by ISEAS, June 2004, there were panels on ASEAN–China Maritime Security Cooperation. Conference participant Colonel Wang Zhongchun (Deputy Director, National Defence University, Beijing) mentioned that China was concerned about the US RMSI proposal for the Malacca Strait, and proposed that China and ASEAN might jointly safeguard regional maritime security, engage in joint patrols of the Strait, and hold joint maritime military exercises in non-traditional security issues that included piracy and terrorism.[43]

ASEAN responded negatively to Wang's proposal. The organization was not ready to consider China's military role in the region. ASEAN participants suggested that China contribute to ASEAN maritime security in a manner similar to Japan's through financial and technical assistance to the littoral states. Although China's role was left unclear, Chinese and Southeast Asians achieved a consensus on opposition to RMSI.[44]

The contrast between American and Chinese soft power grew stronger on the issue of maritime security. Southeast Asians felt Chinese ratification of UNCLOS gave China and ASEAN nations a common legal basis for maritime cooperation. Singapore Ambassador-at-large Tommy Koh had argued at the 2004 Shangri-la Dialogue that UNCLOS ratification was the condition for outside powers' participation in the Malacca Straits, claiming the US would be part of a common legal framework between littoral states and user states if it ratified UNCLOS.[45] He implied that UNCLOS ratification gave China a stronger legal basis for participation in Malacca Strait security than the US had. Also, the US had not signed ASEAN's Treaty of Amity and Cooperation (TAC) that forbids military interventions in Southeast Asia, while China, Russia, India, Japan, Australia, and South Korea are all signatories.

At a conference organized by the Maritime Institute of Malaysia in October 2004, The Straits of Malacca: Building a Comprehensive Security Environment, Chinese Foreign Ministry Counselor Zhao Jianhua urged a common legal basis for maritime security cooperation. Zhao questioned whether bilateral agreements between ASEAN countries and outside powers would be compatible with multilateral agreements. He described China's role in the Straits of Malacca as defined by UNCLOS, the 2002 Declaration on the Conduct of Parties in the South China Sea, the 2004 China–ASEAN MOU on Cooperation of Non-traditional Security Issues, and other China–ASEAN agreements. Acknowledging that China has a vital interest in the security of the Malacca Straits, he offered Chinese cooperation with ASEAN nations to combat maritime security threats.[46]

The discursive construction of China's role and identity in the Malacca Straits was clear. The ASEAN conference participants spoke of China as a "user state" in the Malacca Straits, part of the East Asian user states, which they distinguished from user states outside the region (Russia, India, Canada, Australia, and the US). Because of geographic proximity, the East Asian user states had a different and closer relationship to the Straits than had the outsiders.

A Chinese volume written by CICIR, Sea Lane Security and International Cooperation, outlined the maritime security strategies of China, ASEAN, Japan, and the US. It included sections on US–Chinese maritime security cooperation, ASEAN maritime cooperation, and the necessity of cooperation for China. Its purpose seemed to be to explain to Chinese domestic audiences the necessity of maritime cooperation.[47]

China's role in Southeast Asian counter-terrorism was strengthened in November 2004, when Beijing hosted the ARF Security Policy Conference

(ASPC), the first meeting of ARF defence ministers. ASPC pledged that member countries would collectively play a constructive role in fighting terrorism through coordination and cooperation, in conformity with international laws. The 100 military participants from 24 countries agreed to strengthen cooperation against non-traditional security threats such as terrorism and piracy. The meeting was closed to the press but it can be surmised that it was an effort to construct an Asian multilateral regime as an alternative to the American RMSI and the western-influenced Shangri-la Dialogue.

Beijing's critics claimed this defence ministers' forum was China's attempt to marginalize and displace the US in regional security forums. Some read Beijing's actions as contributing to the restructuring of the East Asian order, away from the hub-and-spokes pattern.

In November 2004, the UN's International Maritime Organization (IMO) called for a ministerial conference in 2005 to construct a collaborative framework to secure the Malacca Straits through joint naval exercises hosted by the littoral states with outside stakeholders (user states) participating. The United Nations General Assembly had passed a resolution on 10 November 2004 on Oceans and Law of the Sea that directed the IMO to work on collaboration between the littoral states and user states.[48]

In March 2005, Singapore and the US co-hosted the ARF CBM on Regional Cooperation in Maritime Security. Singapore briefed on the progress of the Regional Cooperation Agreement on Anti-Piracy and Armed Robbery Against Ships in Asia (ReCAAP) and the related Information Sharing Centre that would be based in Singapore. Singapore's Defence Minister reiterated the three principles that an East Asian regional consensus had formed around: (1) the littoral states had primary responsibility; (2) there is a role for all stakeholders in the Malacca Straits; and (3) cooperation would proceed in accordance with international law and on the basis of consultation.[49] ReCAAP exemplified implementation of the three principles.

At the 2005 meeting, the US proposed the littoral states participate in the Maritime Domain Awareness (MDA) initiative which could identify and monitor vessel traffic in the Malacca Strait and provide actionable intelligence to the littoral states, providing them with an early warning system. Malaysians suspected MDA was a means to justify a US naval presence in the Malacca Strait, and would give the US the ability within the Strait to "see without being seen."[50]

A Malaysian researcher claimed that the real reason the US wanted to increase its presence in the Malacca Straits was to interdict Chinese oil-supply lines from the Middle East. He argued a subsequent Sino-American shooting war in the Straits was not in the interests of the littoral states who should instead keep the Strait open for international navigation according to the principles of UNCLOS. Malaysia felt itself pressured by both the US and China, caught between overt US efforts to expand an American presence in the Straits, and covert Chinese efforts to defend its SLOCs and maintain unfettered access to the Straits.[51]

At the June 2005 Shangri-La Dialogue, the Malaysian Defence Minister explicitly laid out what would not be tolerated: no American bases on Malaysian territory; no foreign warships patrolling in the littoral states' territorial waters or escorting ships; and no use of "private-security companies" (covert operations). Only capacity-building aid to the littoral states was acceptable and especially welcome for the "eyes in the sky" programme; foreign powers might be allowed to fly the aircraft but only littoral-state nationals could control the surveillance equipment. The Malaysian proposal was meant to be a counter-proposal to the RMSI that had been discussed at the 2004 Shangri-La Dialogue and rejected by Malaysia. Malaysia had in 2004 claimed there would be no more "free riders" in the Malacca Straits, i.e. user states that did not share the financial burden of maintaining Straits security.

At the June 2005 Shangri-La Dialogue, the Singaporean Defence Minister also stressed that the littoral states had primary responsibility for Malacca Strait security while the American PSI could play a supporting role. He suggested the ARF should be the vehicle for multilateral coordination.[52]

ASEAN's insistence that the ARF be the primary vehicle for regional management of terrorism and maritime security was undermined at the ARF July 2005 meeting. The US Secretary of State, Condoleeza Rice, did not attend, nor did the Japanese or Indian foreign ministers. The Chinese foreign minister, Li Zhaoxing, was there but left early.

In July 2005 additional pressure was put on the littoral states when Lloyd's of London put the Malacca Straits on the list of high-risk zones, making insurance costs much higher for ships that pass through the straits.

In August 2005 the littoral states initiated an ASEAN-led project, the "Eyes in the Sky" programme, a maritime air patrol, to supplement the coordinated naval patrols. During the ASEAN Regional Forum's meeting on Confidence-Building Measures and Preventive Diplomacy in Honolulu in October 2005, the littoral states provided an update on the "Eyes in the Sky" initiative in the Straits. The meeting discussed possible roles for user states in the initiative and considered a proposal by Singapore for a maritime capacity-building exercise under the auspices of the ARF.[53]

Within the UN's International Maritime Organization, China's role in Malacca expanded. At the UN's IMO meeting in September 2005, held to consider collaboration between littoral and user states, Beijing offered assistance to the littoral states to guard the Malacca Straits. It was the first time China had officially offered aid for maritime security to ASEAN. The meeting issued the "Jakarta Statement" which acknowledged littoral and user states' rights and obligations in the Malacca Straits under UNCLOS, especially Article 43 which requires littoral and user states to cooperate in the Straits. The Statement called for littoral states' to identify needs and priorities, and user states to identify types of assistance they would provide through burden sharing.

By October 2005, Beijing and Singapore had signed an agreement for Chinese assistance in Malacca Strait security. The Singaporean Prime Minister clarified that Singapore did not want to be dependent on China, but would rather have China take a role similar to that played by the US, Japan, and India, and assist in constructing Asia's regional security architecture.[54] In December 2005,

China and Malaysia issued a *communique* mentioning that "Malaysia welcomes China's participation in security cooperation in the Malacca Strait" and agreed to discuss the forms the security cooperation would take.[55]

By the end of 2005, Singaporeans thought Beijing was less anxious about the Malacca Straits than it had been since Admiral Fargo's comments in March 2004. This was due to the littoral states' strengthening of their own capacity to maintain Straits security which reassured Beijing that the US would not be directly involved in securing the Straits.[56] It was also a result of US–China relations being less tense following Deputy Secretary of State, Robert Zoellick's reference to China as a "responsible stakeholder" in September 2005, a country the US would cooperate with to uphold the international system rather than a country needing to be contained.[57]

Although China was less anxious, Malaysia remained suspicious of the US maritime initiative. According to Malaysian commentary, the US had exerted enormous pressure on the littoral states for greater access to the Malacca Straits, and it was expected that China would also pressure Malaysia for unfettered access.[58]

The US had always considered RMSI to be an evolving initiative. As regional resistance grew to the initiative, its notoriety made it unworkable, and eventually, sometime between late 2004 and early 2005, RMSI seemed to disappear from discussion and PACOM websites.

By 2006, there was still disagreement over which framework would be the vehicle for maritime-security cooperation. Asia-Pacific support for the PSI was still weak with few Asian countries willing to be associated with it. Only Japan and Singapore had participated in its exercises. China, India, Malaysia, Indonesia did not. PSI continued to be viewed as a US-dominated operation, and the RMSI had become a non-topic.[59]

Chinese began to suggest that the ASEAN-China Joint Declaration on the Strategic Partnership for Peace and Prosperity, signed in Bali in October 2003, might be the appropriate vehicle within which to cooperate on maritime security issues. According to Chinese analysts, maritime-security issues and SLOC security have increased in significance for China–ASEAN relations although ASEAN countries are divided on cooperation with China. Additionally, Chinese note that the US and Japan could be expected to be alarmed by closer ASEAN–China cooperation, interpreting this as an effort by China to expand its role in Southeast Asia for the purpose of weakening the positions of the US and Japan.[60]

Chinese Defence Minister Cao Gangchuan visited Malaysia and Singapore's Changi Naval Base in April 2006. His purpose was to expand bilateral military ties with ASEAN countries, and suggested maritime exercises with the PLA-Navy such as search and rescue exercises. Discussions emphasized security cooperation within the framework of ARF. During the Chinese Defence Minister's visit, Singaporean Senior Minister Goh Chok Tong (former Prime Minister) called for China to play an active role in establishing a regional security architecture, and to increase its role in maritime security.[61]

On 21 April 2006, Singapore, Malaysia and Indonesia signed an agreement to coordinate patrols in the Straits of Malacca, the Terms of Reference (TOR) of the Malacca Strait Patrol (MSP), the standard operating procedures, and Joint Coordinating Committee (JCC). The three countries' navies had increased their surveillance of the Straits since July 2004, and since 2005 had used 'Eye-in-the-Sky' aerial surveillance. On 21 April, these initial efforts were formalized as the Malacca Strait Coordinated Patrol network, codenamed "MALSINDO."[62]

Indonesia indicated all three states would not reject technical assistance from the United States and Japan which, using the language of UNCLOS, it referred to as user states and stakeholders in the security of the Malacca Straits. Indonesia's maritime patrol planes needed spy devices which it would request from the US at the 4th Indonesia–United States Security Dialogue (IUSSD).[63] The IUSSD would also clarify for Jakarta the nature of the bilateral relationship, whether it was a strategic partnership within which both countries would cooperate.[64] In 2004, Indonesia had felt more like a target than a partner. The US had lifted its embargo on military and security cooperation only in November 2005. The US would provide an early warning system to Indonesia to be used in the Malacca Straits on maritime patrol aircraft and at points along the waterway. The US had assured Jakarta that US military forces would not be physically present.[65]

While the US faltered on gaining greater Asian compliance on the PSI, and had stopped discussing RMSI, Japan's initiative that began within the APT framework, the Regional Cooperation Agreement on Combating Piracy and Armed Robbery Against Ships in Asia (ReCAAP), achieved success. In June 2006, Singapore announced that ReCAAP had obtained ratification by 11 countries and would enter into force in September 2006. Press reports noted that ReCAAP was the first regional government-to-government agreement to combat piracy at sea, and that it was a Japanese initiative but there was little mention of APT.[66]

Three countries – China, Indonesia, and Malaysia – had not yet ratified ReCAAP but this was viewed by Japanese as not detrimental to ReCAAP's success. Indonesia and Malaysia had given verbal assurances, although Jakarta would later state it was determined to postpone ratification of ReCAAP because the pact impinged on Indonesian sovereignty. The Indonesian Defence Minister Juwono Sudarsono claimed that, if in the end Indonesia did decide to ratify ReCAAP, Jakarta would remain vigilant in protecting national interests.[67] Beijing would probably eventually join because ReCAAP would reinforce China's newly recognized status as a user state in the Malacca Straits.

In September 2006, the UN's International Maritime Organization and the littoral states held an international meeting in Kuala Lumpur, Meeting on the Straits of Malacca and Singapore: Enhancing Safety, Security and Environmental Protection. Its purpose was to create a cooperative mechanism for the Straits and sort out the responsibilities of user and littoral states in burden sharing and capacity building. Thirty-one countries attended and adopted the "Kuala Lumpur Statement." The conference identified six major projects that would cost $50 million over the next five to ten years. The meeting expressed appreciation for the establishment of ReCAAP.[68]

The head of the Chinese delegation stressed how ready China was to support the littoral states and participate actively in Straits security under the multilateral mechanism created by the IMO.[69] Other user states – the US and South Korea – had indicated intent to support the six projects. However, a Malaysian official noted that "China in particular has come forward and made a commitment in principle to support some of the six projects proposed by the three littoral states."[70] China had also offered to provide training at a Chinese maritime university.

The September 2006 IMO conference created a cooperative mechanism for the Malacca Straits that drew on an East Asian consensus that had formed over the previous decade. Joint resistance to the American RMSI proposal had helped China and Malaysia form a consensus on appropriate policies for the Malacca Straits. The Zheng He exhibit in Malaysia in July 2005 was a concrete manifestation of that consensus.

Conclusion

This case study of the emergence of China's role in the Malacca Straits against the background of East Asian responses to the US RMSI and PSI leads to several conclusions:

1 A cooperative maritime security regime evolves through interactions of participant nations over time rather than being written in concrete from the beginning. A regional consensus is a necessary prerequisite before a multilateral framework can be adopted.
2 Without the US RMSI proposal, Asia might not have been jolted into serious measures against maritime terrorism because Asian nations put greater priority on maritime issues other than piracy/terrorism. These include overlapping resources claims, poaching and military surveillance in EEZs (US in China's EEZ; China in Japan's EEZ; Japanese poaching in Russia's EEZ; and multiple disputes in the South China Sea).
3 Japan's pursuit of a regional multilayered security architecture facilitates China's dual approach to both include and exclude the US in regional security multilateralism within the ASEAN institutional complex.
4 American lukewarm support of Asian multilateralism has not had the intended effect of blocking increasing institutionalization but, rather, has had the effect of marginalizing the US. By 2006, the US was in the position of asking not to be left out of the Asian institutional process, fearing displacement by China.
5 China's approach to multilateralism is interactive, and cannot be understood separately from American, Japanese, and ASEAN, approaches to security multilateralism.
6 Studying Asia's response to RMSI and PSI offers some empirical evidence regarding China's socialization into Asian multilateralism and has greater explanatory power than a narrower focus on Chinese foreign-policy behaviour alone.

7 China's role as a user state in the Malacca Straits was not formed militarily, but rather was a negotiated identity, discursively shaped within Asian multilateral dialogues and regimes, using the language of UNCLOS.

Notes

1 "China Celebrates 'Blue Territory' on Maritime Day," *People's Daily*, 12 July 2006. Online. Available: www.english.people.com.cn/200607/12/eng20060712_282182. html.
2 Muthiah Alagappa (ed.) *Asian Security Order: Instrumental and Normative Features*, Stanford University Press, 2004.
3 Kuniko Ashizawa, "Japan's Approach toward Asian Regional Security: From 'Hub-and-spoke' Bilateralism to 'Multi-tiered,'" *Pacific Review* vol. 16 no. 3, Sept. 2003, pp. 361–82.
4 Jean-Marc Blanchard, "Maritime Issues in Asia: The Problem of Adolescence," in Alagappa, *Asian Security Order*, pp. 424–57.
5 Alastair Iain Johnston, "Socialization in International Institutions: The ASEAN Way and International Relations Theory," in John Ikenberry and Michael Mastanduno (eds) *International Relations Theory and the Asia-Pacific*, Columbia University Press, 2003, pp. 107–62.
6 *World Oil Transit Choke Points*. Online. Available: www.eia.doe.gov/cabs/choke.html.
7 The Proliferation Security Initiative (PSI) is a US-led international network to block the spread of weapons of mass destruction (WMD) through interdiction on land, sea, and air, and to prevent WMD from falling into the hands of hostile states and terrorists. The US has encouraged other states to adhere to PSI principles. PSI is a "coalition of the willing" rather than an international organization.
8 Testimony of Admiral Tom Fargo, USN Commander, US Pacific Command, before the House Armed Services Committee, United States House of Representatives, Q&A Session, 31 March 2004. Online. Available: www.pacom.mil/speeches/sst2004/040331hasc-qa.shtml.
9 Testimony of Admiral Tom Fargo, USN Commander, US Pacific Command, before the House Armed Services Committee, United States House of Representatives, Regarding US Pacific Command Posture, 31 March 2004. Online. Available: www.pacom.mil/speeches/sst2004/ 040331housearmedsvcscomm.shtml.
10 Testimony of Admiral Tom Fargo, USN Commander, US Pacific Command, before the House Armed Services Committee, United States House of Representatives, Q&A Session, 31 March 2004. Online. Available: www.pacom.mil/speeches/sst2004/040331hasc-qa.shtml.
11 Zalmay Khalilzad *et al.*, *The United States and Asia: Toward a New US Strategy and Force Posture*, RAND MR-1315-AF, 2001. Online. Available: www.rand.org/pubs/monograph_reports/MR1315/ index.html.
12 Liao Xiaojian, "ASEAN–US Anti-Terrorist Honeymoon," *Liaowang* no. 33, 12 August 2002, pp. 57–9, in FBIS, CPP20020819000062.
13 XINHUA, "Seminar on Maritime Safety Held in Beijing," www.chinaview.cn, 7 August 2003. Online. Available: news.xinhuanet.com/english/2003–08/07/content_1015676.htm.
14 Mark Valencia, "Bring the Proliferation Security Initiative into the UN," Policy Forum Online 05–101A, Nautilus Institute, 20 December 2005. Online Available: www.nautilus.org/fora/security/05101Valencia.html.
15 Gaye Christoffersen, "The Politics of Oil Security," presented at the Global and Regional Security Governance Workshop, Institute on Global Conflict and

Cooperation and Institute for International, Comparative and Area Studies, University of California, San Diego, 3 October 2002.
16 "China, Japan, and South Korea Agree with ASEAN on Trade Cooperation," *International Herald Tribune*, 29 November 1999. Online. Available: www.iht.com/articles/1999/11/29/asean.2.t_1.php.
17 Summary of ASEAN+3 (Japan, People's Republic of China, the Republic of Korea) Summit Meeting, 24 November 2000. Online. Available: www.mofa.go.jp/region/asia-paci/asean/conference/asean3/summary0011.html.
18 "Planning National Strategies – Marine Interests at Stake; Guarding Malacca Strait Crucial," *The Daily Yomiuri*, Tokyo, 10 June 2006.
19 *XINHUA*, "Chinese Premier Zhu Rongji Presents Five-Point Proposal on ASEAN Plus Three Cooperation," 5 November 2001.
20 "Opening Statement by Prime Minister Junichiro Koizumi at the Press Conference Following the ASEAN+3 Summit Meeting," 6 November 2001. Online. Available: www.mofa.go.jp/region/asia-paci/asean/ conference/asean3/state0111.html.
21 The UN International Maritime Organization (IMO) conference on Maritime Security, held December 2001, adopted changes to the 1974 International Convention on Safety of Life at Sea (SOLAS) and adopted the International Ship and Port Facility Security Code (ISPS) in December 2002, which went into effect July 2004.
22 "MOFA Report on Japan's Commitment in Counterterrorism Initiative in APEC Region," Ministry of Foreign Affairs, 24 June 2004, found at: Foreign Broadcast Information Service (hereafter FBIS), JPP20040629000050.
23 MAJ Irvin Lim Fang Jau, "Fireball on the Water: Rolling Back the Global Waves of Terror ... from the Sea," *Pointer: Journal of the Singapore Armed Forces*, vol. 29 no. 4, Oct.–Dec. 2003. Online. Available: www.mindef.gov.sg/safti/pointer/back/journals/ 2003/Vol29_4/6.htm.
24 Kavi Chongkittavorn, "US changes tone and approach on ASEAN policies," *The Nation*, 24 April 2006. Online. Available: nationmultimedia.com/2006/04/24/opinion/opinion_30002362.php.
25 Hideaki Kaneda, "Regional Assessment of Northeast Asia: Pursuing a Maritime Security Coalition in the Asia-Pacific Region," presented at Maritime Security in East Asia conference, organized by the Centre for Strategic and International Studies and American-Pacific Sealanes Security Institute, Honolulu, January 2004.
26 Admiral Thomas B. Fargo, Commander, US Pacific Command, Shangri-La Dialogue, 4th Plenary Session – "Maritime Security after 9–11," 1 June 2003. Online. Available: www.pacom.mil/speeches/sst2003/030601shangrila.shtml.
27 Andi Widjajanto, International Fellow, National Defense University, Washington, DC, "Transnational challenges to RI's security," *Jakarta Post*, 6 January 2003.
28 "Bush offers to set up US military base in Thailand" Bangkok *The Nation*, 4 May 2004. Online. Available: www.nationmultimedia.com/search/page.arcview.php?clid=3&id=98235&usrsess.
29 "Bangkok Backs US in Straits Initiative," *Bangkok The Nation*, 25 June 2004. Online. Available: www.nationmultimedia.com/search/page.arcview.php?clid=4&id=101302&usrsess.
30 See Seng Tan, Kumar Ramakrishna. "Interstate and Intrastate Dynamics in Southeast Asia's War on Terror," *SAIS Review* 24, 1, Winter 2004, pp. 91–105.
31 Zuo Liping (Naval Research Institute), "Countries Scramble to Build up Naval Forces as Maritime Conflicts Increase Amid Rising Competition for Maritime Resources," *People's Daily*, 26 April 2004.
32 Pacific Forum CSIS. "Countering the Spread of Weapons of Mass Destruction: the Role of the Proliferation Security Initiative." *Issues and Insights*, vol. 4 no. 5, July 2004. Online. Available: www.csis.org/media/csis/pubs/v04n05%5B1%5D.pdf.
33 Su Wei, CSCAP China, "China's Views on PSI," Ibid., 32.
34 Helen E.S. Nesadurai, *Malaysia and the United States: Rejecting Dominance,*

Embracing Engagement, IDSS working paper no. 72, Singapore: Nanyang Technological University, Institute of Defence and Strategic Studies, December 2004, 4. Online. Available: www.ntu.edu.sg/idss/WorkingPapers/wp72.pdf.
35 Zhang Yuncheng, "The Malacca Strait and World Oil Security," *Huanqiu Shibao*, 5 December 2003, in FBIS, CPP20031217000202.
36 "Build Oil Pipeline from China to Burma," *Singapore Straits Times*, 15 July 2004, in FBIS, CPP20040715000042.
37 Zhang Wenmu, "China's Energy Security and Policy Choices," *Shijie jingji yu zhengzhi*, no. 5, 14 May 2003, pp. 11–16, in FBIS, CPP20030528000169.
38 Lou Douzi, "Looking at Navy and Air Force Dispositions Following Establishment Restructuring," *Jiefangjun Bao*, 14 July 2004, in FBIS, CPP20040715000074.
39 "Military Calls for Stepping Up National Defense Construction," *Ming Pao* (Hong Kong), 3 February 2004.
40 Luo Yuan and Shi Xiaoqin, "Troubled Waters: East Asian Countries Unhappy with the US Proposal to Send Troops to Assist in Patrolling the Waters of the Malacca Strait," *Beijing Review*, 15 July 2004, p. 14.
41 Ji Guoxing, "US RMSI Contravenes UN Convention on the Law of the Sea," *Pacnet* 29, 8 July 2004. Online. Available: www.csis.org/pacfor/pac0429.pdf.
42 Ibid.
43 Wang Zhongchun and Li Yaqiang, "China–ASEAN Maritime Security Cooperation Situation and Proposals," in Saw Swee-Hock, Sheng Lijun, and Chin Kin Wah (eds) *ASEAN–China Relations: Realities and Prospects*, Singapore: ISEAS, 2005, pp. 187–98.
44 Lee Kim Chew, "China Could Play Part in ASEAN's Maritime Security: Dialogues can be Started and Joint Exercises can Help Fight Criminal and Terror Activities, says Chinese official," *Singapore Straits Times*, 24 June 2004.
45 Woon Wui Tek, "KL Open to Talks on Maritime Security Plan," *Singapore Straits Times*, 7 June 2004.
46 Zhao Jianhua, "The Straits of Malacca and Challenges Ahead: China's Perspective." Online. Available: www.mima.gov.my/mima/htmls/conferences/som04/papers/zhao-jianhua.pdf.
47 Zhongguo xiandai guoji guanxi yanjiuyuan. *Sea lane security and international cooperation (haishang tongdao anquan yu guoji hezuo)*. Beijing: Shishi Chubanshe, 2005.
48 *IMO to take Straits initiative*, 19 November 2004. Online. Available: www.imo.org/home.asp.
49 Speech by Mr Teo Chee Hean, Minister for Defence, at ASEAN Regional Forum Confidence Building Measure, 2 March 2005. Online. Available: www.mindef.gov.sg/imindef/resources/speeches/2005/02mar05_speech.html.
50 By Mokhzani Zubir, *Should Malaysia Join the US Maritime Domain Awareness Scheme?* Maritime Institute of Malaysia, 2005. Online. Available: www.mima.gov.my/mima/htmls/papers/pdf/mokhzani/usmda.pdf.
51 Mokhzani Zubir and Mohd Nizam Basiron, *The Straits of Malacca: the Rise of China, America's Intentions and the Dilemma of the Littoral States*, Maritime Institute of Malaysia, April 2005. Online. Available: www.mima.gov.my/mima/htmls/papers/pdf/mokhzani/mz-mnb.pdf.
52 "Speech by Mr Teo Chee Hean, Minister for Defence, at the Fourth Shangri-La Dialogue Plenary Session, Asia-Pacific Armed Forces and Counter-Terrorism," 5 June 2005. Online. Available: www.mindef.gov.sg/imindef/news_and_events/nr/2005/jun/05jun05_nr.html.
53 *Co-Chairs' Summary Report of the First Meeting of the ASEAN Regional Forum Inter-Sessional Support Group on Confidence Building Measures and Preventive Diplomacy*, Honolulu, Hawaii, United States of America, 17–19 October 2005. Online. Available: www.dfat.gov.au/arf/ intersessional/report_interses_05_06.html.
54 "China to work with Singapore and region to fight terror and sea piracy," *Channel-

newsasia, 25 October 2005. Online. Available: www.channelnewsasia.com/stories/singaporelocalnews/view/175279/1.html.
55 "China and Malaysia study economic pact," *Financial Times*, 16 December 2005.
56 Michael Richardson, "China Relaxes as Region Addresses Maritime Piracy," *Straits Times*, Singapore, 27 December 2005.
57 Robert B. Zoellick, Deputy Secretary of State, "Whither China: From Membership to Responsibility?" Remarks to National Committee on US–China Relations, New York City, 21 September 2005. Online. Available: www.state.gov/s/d/rem/53682.htm.
58 Mokhzani Zubir and Mohd Nizam Basiron, "The Strait of Malacca: the Rise of China, America's Intentions and the Dilemma of the Littoral States," *Maritime Studies*, Australia, 141, March/April 2005.
59 Michael Richardson, *The Proliferation Security Initiative (PSI): An Assessment of its Strengths & Weaknesses, with Some Proposals for Shaping its Future*. Trends in Southeast Asia Series: 3, 2006, p. 15. Online. Available: www.iseas.edu.sg/tr32006.pdf.
60 Guo Xinning, *Anti-Terrorism, Maritime Security, and ASEAN–China Cooperation: A Chinese Perspective*. Trends in Southeast Asia Series: 15, 2005. Online. Available: www.iseas.edu.sg/tr152005.pdf.
61 Joanne Leow, "SM Goh calls on China to contribute to peace and stability," *Channel NewsAsia*, 13 April 2006. Online. Available: www.channelnewsasia.com/stories/singaporelocalnews/view/202899/1/.html.
62 "Singapore, Malaysia, Indonesia Sign Pact on Malacca Strait Patrols," *Channel News Asia*, 21 April 2006. Online. Available: www.channelnewsasia.com/stories/singaporelocalnews/view/204221/1/.html.
63 "Indonesia to Seek US Technical Aid to Support Patrols in Malacca Strait," *People's Daily*, 20 April 2006. Online. Available: www.english.people.com.cn/200604/20/eng20060420_259607.html.
64 "RI to Seek US Affirmation on Proposed Strategic Partnership," Jakarta *ANTARA News*, 19 April 2006. Online. Available: www.antara.co.id/en/seenws/?id=11472.
65 "US Offers Early Warning System to Secure Malacca Strait," www.chinaview.cn, 22April 2006. Online. Available: www.news.xinhuanet.com/english/2006–04/22/content_4459918.htm.
66 Donald Urquhart, "Regional Anti-piracy Initiative Gets the Green Light; 11 of 16 Countries Involved have Ratified the RECAAP Agreement," *The Business Times Singapore*, 22 June 2006. The website for RECAAP's Information Sharing Centre is at: www.recaap.org/html.
67 "Indonesia Determined to Postpone Ratification of Malacca Strait Pact," *Antara*, 25 September 2006.
68 IMO Briefing 32, "States Make Progress in Co-operation to Enhance Safety of Navigation, Security and Environmental Protection in Straits of Malacca and Singapore," 22 September 2006. Online. Available: www.imo. org/home.asp.
69 "China Ready to Contribute to Safeguarding Security of Malacca Straits: Official," *People's Daily*, 19 September 2006. Online. Available: www.english.people.com.cn/200609/19eng20060919_304037.html.
70 Clarence Fernandez, "Malacca Strait Users Agree to Back Safety Projects," DefenseNews.com, 20 September 2006.

9 Maritime security and multilateral interactions between China and its neighbours

Keyuan Zou

Introduction

Maritime security is one of the most concerning issues in the world, particularly after the September 11 terrorist attack. Maritime security in this chapter covers both traditional security issues, such as military activities, and non-traditional security issues, such as piracy and maritime terrorism. Since there are so many maritime-security issues in East Asia, this chapter is only able to identify and address some of the most pressing in the multiple interactions by China with its neighbours, including the South China Sea dispute, military activities in the exclusive economic zone, suppression of piracy and maritime terrorism, and China's response to the Regional Maritime Security Initiative.

International law is a typical product of multilateralism since it is formulated through the efforts of the whole world community. The general legal framework which governs maritime security is centred on the 1982 United Nations Convention on the Law of the Sea (LOS Convention),[1] which is commonly known as the Constitution of Oceans and has incorporated almost all previously existing conventional and customary rules and norms concerning the oceans. Pursuant to the provisions of the LOS Convention, a coastal state has the right to establish maritime zones under its jurisdiction: internal waters inside the baselines which are used to measure the extent of the territorial sea and other jurisdictional waters, the territorial sea of 12 nautical miles (nm), the exclusive economic zone (EEZ) of 200 nm, and the continental shelf of 200 nm (or up to 350 nm in some cases), outward from the baselines.

Different maritime zones have different legal status. Internal waters and territorial sea are treated as part of the coastal state's territory and that state enjoys full sovereignty there except innocent passage for foreign vessels in its territorial sea. The sovereignty of the coastal state over the territorial sea extends to the airspace above the territorial sea as well as to its bed and subsoil.[2] For some jurisdictional purposes, such as prevention and punishment of infringement of its customs, its fiscal, immigration or sanitary laws and regulations, a coastal state has the right to establish the contiguous zone which may extend not more than 24 nm from the baselines from which the breadth of the territorial sea is measured. However, it should be noted that in comparison with the territorial sea or the EEZ, the contiguous zone is not a complete maritime zone; rather, it is subsidiary to the territorial sea for the coastal state to control certain matters of territorial nature while, at the same time, it is part of the EEZ, in another sense.

As to the EEZ and continental shelf, the coastal state, according to the LOS Convention, only enjoys sovereign rights and certain kinds of jurisdiction. The coastal State enjoys sovereign rights to the living and non-living resources in the EEZ and continental shelf, and exercises its jurisdiction over matters relating to "the establishment and use of artificial islands, installations and structures," "marine scientific research," and "the protection and preservation of the marine environment."[3] The coastal state has the exclusive right to authorize and regulate drilling on the continental shelf.[4] The EEZ and the continental shelf are identical in terms of sovereign rights and jurisdiction of a coastal State. For that reason, the EEZ and the continental shelf are not part of the high seas, or part of the territorial sea. The EEZ is a maritime zone *sui generis*. However, there is at least one similarity between the territorial sea and the EEZ in the sense that they both are maritime zones within national jurisdiction.

China is a coastal state with very long coastlines. The coastline of the mainland is more than 18,000 km from the mouth of the Yalu River in Liaoning Province in the north to the mouth of the Beilung River in the Guangxi Autonomous Region in the south. The seas adjacent to China are the Bohai Sea, the Yellow Sea, the East China Sea, and the South China Sea. The Bohai Sea is China's internal sea, surrounded by the Shantong Peninsula and the Liaotong Peninsula, with an area of about 77,000 square km and an average depth of 18 m with a maximum depth of 70 m. The Bohai Sea is linked to the Yellow Sea by the Bohai Strait, which is 45 nautical miles (nm) wide. The Yellow Sea is about 380,000 km^2, 44 m of depth on average with a maximum depth of 140 m. It is a continental shallow sea. The East China Sea is a wider shallow sea with an average depth of 370 m and 770,000 km^2. The South China Sea is bounded on the north by mainland China, on the east by the Philippine archipelago, on the south by Kalimantan, and on the west by the Malay Peninsula and Vietnam. The area of the South China Sea is about 3,500,000 km^2 with an average of 1,212 m and a maximum depth of 5,559 m.[5] The total areas of the above seas are equivalent to about half of China's land territory (more than 4,730,000 km^2),[6] with abundant natural resources which can be exploited and utilized by the Chinese and other peoples, and which have served as a tie of friendly intercourse between the Chinese and other nations. For example, in ancient times there existed a "silk road at sea" just like the silk road on land to the West. The seas are also natural barriers safeguarding China's land territory. All the seas described above, except for the Bohai Sea, which is part of China's internal waters, are semi-enclosed seas, as defined by the LOS Convention.[7]

Based on the international law of the sea, China has established legal regimes for its maritime zones, including the territorial sea, EEZ, and the continental shelf, through its domestic legal procedures. Among all the domestic laws and regulations (see Table 9.1), the most important one is the 1992 Law on the Territorial Sea and the Contiguous Zone,[8] which has improved the territorial sea regime established under the 1958 Declaration on the Territorial Sea. China has set its territorial sea at a breadth of 12 nm and the contiguous zone of 24 nm, measuring from its baselines. Merchant ships enjoy the right of innocent passage through China's territorial sea but foreign warships are subject to the requirement of prior permission. China uses the method of straight baselines to define the limits of its territorial sea and in May 1996, part of such baselines around the mainland and the Xisha Islands was publicized.[9] In addition to the above fundamental stipulations, the law provides that all international organizations, foreign organizations or individuals should obtain approval from China for carrying out scientific research, marine operations or other activities in China's territorial sea and comply with relevant Chinese laws and regulations (Art. 11). The Chinese competent authorities may, when they have good reasons to believe that a foreign ship has committed violations, exercise the right of hot pursuit against the foreign ship (Art. 14). This law applies to all of China, including Taiwan and various islands located in China's adjacent seas.

The other equivalent important law is the 1998 Law on the Exclusive Economic Zone and the Continental Shelf.[10] This law is designed to guarantee China's exercise of sovereign rights and jurisdiction over its EEZ and continental shelf, and to safeguard China's national maritime rights and interests. According to this law, China's EEZ is the area beyond and adjacent to China's territorial sea, extending up to 200 nm from the baselines from which the breadth of the territorial sea is measured.

The legal regime of the continental shelf is closely related to that of EEZ, though different under the LOS Convention. For the purpose of natural resource development, the former is more concerned with non-living resources and the latter with living resources. That is why in state practice the two regimes are found together in legislation, as exemplified in the above Chinese law. In addition to enjoying the same rights and jurisdiction as in the EEZ regime, coastal states like China enjoy the exclusive right to authorize and regulate drilling on the continental shelf for all purposes.[11] The continental shelf of China comprises the sea-bed and subsoil of the submarine areas that extend beyond China's territorial sea throughout the natural prolongation of its land territory to the outer edge of the continental margin, or to a distance of 200 nm from the baselines where the outer edge of the continental margin does not extend up to that distance. It is interesting to note that, although the provision to define the EEZ is just a copy of the relevant provision of the LOS Convention, the provision regarding the continental shelf has something new with Chinese characteristics, that is, the emphasis on the natural prolongation of China's rights to the continental shelf, which bears strong implications for the delimitation of the continental shelf in the East China Sea.

After the entry into force of the LOS Convention in 1994, the legal situation of maritime zones in East Asia has become more complicated. Most of the East Asian countries have become parties to the LOS Convention (see Table 9.2), and have enacted their corresponding domestic laws governing the maritime zones entitled under the LOS Convention. However, since the seas adjacent to China

Table 9.1 Selected marine laws of the People's Republic of China

State	Date of ratification
Declaration on the Territorial Sea	4 September 1958
Regulations Governing Non-Military Foreign Vessels Passing Through the Qiongzhou Strait	8 June 1964
Regulations on Sea-Port Pilotage	12 November 1976
Regulations Governing Supervision and Control of Foreign Vessels	22 August 1979
Regulations on the Exploitation of Offshore Petroleum Resources in Cooperation with Foreign Enterprises	30 January 1982 (amended 23 September 2001)
Law on Marine Environmental Protection	23 August 1982 (amended 25 December 1999)
Maritime Traffic Safety Law	2 September 1983
Regulations Concerning Environmental Protection In Offshore Oil Exploration and Exploitation	29 December 1983
Regulations Concerning the Prevention of Pollution of Sea Areas by Vessels	29 December 1983
Regulations Concerning the Dumping of Wastes at Sea	6 March 1985
Fisheries Law	30 January 1986 (amended 31 October 2000)
Mineral Resources Law	19 March 1986 (amended 29 August 1996)
Regulations Concerning the Prevention of Environmental Pollution by Ship-Breaking	18 May 1988
Regulations on the Management of Laying Submarine Cables and Pipelines	11 February 1989
Regulations on the Protection of Underwater Cultural Relics	20 October 1989
Regulations Governing the Investigation and Settlement of Marine Traffic Accidents	11 January 1990
Regulations Concerning the Prevention of Pollution Damage to the Marine Environment by Coastal Construction Projects	25 May 1990
Regulations Concerning the Prevention of Pollution Damage to the Marine Environment by Land-Based Pollutants	25 May 1990
Law on the Territorial Sea and the Contiguous Zone	25 February 1992
Measures on the Management of Foreign Merchant's Participation in the Salvage of Sunken Vessels and Sunken Objects in China's Coastal Waters	12 July 1992
Regulations on the Management of Marine Navigational Warnings and Navigational Notices	22 December 1992
Regulations on Inspection of Ships and Offshore Installations	14 February 1993
Regulations on the Protection of Aquatic Wildlife	17 September 1993
Regulations Concerning Navigation Marks	3 December 1995
Measures on the Management of Marine Nature Reserves	11 May 1995
Decision on Ratification of the United Nations Convention on the Law of the Sea	15 May 1996
Regulations on the Management of Foreign-Related Marine Scientific Research	18 June 1996
Law on the Exclusive Economic Zone and the Continental Shelf	29 June 1998
Law on the Management of the Use of Maritime Areas	27 October 2001

Source: Prepared by the author.

are all semi-enclosed seas with multiple coastal States, maritime boundary delimitation becomes another maritime issue in East Asia. Although China has resolved the maritime boundary issue in the Gulf of Tonkin with Vietnam, it still has to negotiate maritime boundary delimitation with its neighbouring countries in the Yellow Sea, East China Sea, and South China Sea. The maritime boundary delimitation, if involving territorial disputes over islands, will be more difficult to undertake, as manifested in the East China Sea, regarding the Tiaoyu/Senkaku Islands dispute between China and Japan, and in the South China Sea, regarding the Spratly Islands, claimed by five countries/six parties.

The South China Sea dispute

The political situation in the South China Sea is complicated, as it contains the potential of conflict with different national interests. In terms of the islands groups, because of their geographical differences, their political situations are accordingly different from each other. The Pratas Islands are under the firm control of the Taiwan Chinese. No competing claims exist there under the "one China" conception. For the Macclesfield Bank, the only claimant is China, including Taiwan.[12] Nevertheless, if the Scarborough Reef is considered part of the Macclesfield, then the recent developments indicate that the Philippines has also lodged its territorial claim over the Reef, then over Macclesfield, if the

Table 9.2 Contracting parties to the LOS Convention in East Asia

States	Date of ratification[a]
Brunei Darussalam	5 November 1996
Cambodia	–
China	7 June 1996
Indonesia	3 February 1986
Japan	20 June 1996
Korea (North)	–
Korea (South)	29 January 1996
Laos	5 June 1998
Malaysia	14 October 1996
Myanmar	21 May 1996
Philippines	8 May 1984
Singapore	17 November 1994
Thailand	–
Vietnam	25 July 1994

Source: United Nations Office for Ocean Affairs and the Law of the Sea, "Status of the Convention and of Related Agreements, as at 8 January 2002". Online. Available: www.un.org/Depts/los/convention_agreements/ convention_agreements.htm (accessed 15 January 2002).

Notes
a The date here is the date when the depository the United Nations received the instrument of ratification.
b Taiwan is not a member of the United Nations and not qualified to be a signatory of the LOS Convention.

former is regarded as its part. The Paracel Islands are under the control of China, though contested by the Vietnamese. Because of the firm control by the Chinese, the political situation around the Paracels is relatively calm and stable in comparison with that around the Spratly Islands. The dispute over the Spratly Islands is most complicated since it has been lingering on for a long time and involves as many as five states, i.e. China, including Taiwan, Malaysia, Vietnam, the Philippines, and Brunei. It is not usual in the history of international relations that so many countries make claims over the whole or part of such so-small islands, as the Spratly Islands and their surrounding waters. As many predict, if the issue of the Spratly Islands is not well handled, it could produce a threat to the peace and security of the East Asian region and of the world. In China's view, the issue of disputes over boundaries and sovereignty over areas of the South China Sea form one of the three main factors that might trigger military conflicts in the Asia-Pacific region.[13]

There were two armed skirmishes between China and Vietnam which happened in the South China Sea, in 1973 and 1988, over the dispute of the South China Sea islands. The 1995 tension between China and the Philippines over Mischief Reef also invited high-profile exposure in the mass media. Recently, some countries have occupied new reefs, in a "sneaky" or "stealthy" way. For example, during 1999 and 2000, Malaysia grabbed three new reefs it had claimed in the South China Sea without any report appearing in major newspapers around the world. Arrests of fishing boats and fishermen are frequent. The claimant states blame one another for incursions in the disputed areas.[14] In June 2002, Vietnam lodged a protest against China's live ammunition exercises in the South China Sea, but China dismissed Vietnam's protest and stated that the drill fully complied with international law.[15] Thus, the South China Sea is one of the thorniest issues in the Sino-ASEAN relations.

Since 1992, the Association of Southeast Asian Nations (ASEAN) member states have taken a concerted stance towards the South China Sea issue by jointly signing the Declaration on the South China Sea, which, for the first time, unanimously expressed their resolve to explore the possibility of cooperation in the South China Sea and to establish a code of international conduct there.[16] In 1995, in response to the Mischief Reef incident, the ASEAN foreign ministers reiterated the letter and spirit of the 1992 Declaration and expressed their concerns with the tensions in the South China Sea.[17] The most significant move by the ASEAN is its untiring push to adopt a code of conduct for the South China Sea.

As a key player, China's efforts and cooperation are indispensable in the preparation of the South China Sea code of conduct. Originally, however, China was very reluctant to negotiate a code of conduct at a multilateral level with ASEAN, though it had a bilateral code of conduct with the Philippines. It is recalled that during the 9th South China Sea Informal Workshop in December 1998, China opposed the proposal to negotiate a code of conduct for the interested parties concerned. The reasons behind this included, *inter alia*: (1) China did not want to receive additional burdens or pressure resulting from the code of conduct if it were formulated. Though a code of conduct bears no legal binding force, it is, after all, a "gentlemen's agreement," and should be complied with, *bona fide*. Any violation would be condemned by other parties. (2) China did not consider the workshop an appropriate forum to negotiate such a code of conduct. The workshop was informal and the participants were present in their personal capacity. The process of formulating a code of conduct would imply that such an informal workshop could turn into a formal one and the personal capacity might become an official capacity. China did not want to see such a scenario, particularly in the circumstances, as delegates from Taiwan also participated in the workshops. (3) China preferred bilateral negotiations to resolve the South China Sea issue rather than multilateral negotiations. If a code of conduct were necessary, it should be done through a bilateral diplomatic channel, just as manifested by the 1995 Code of Conduct between China and the Philippines.

Nevertheless, China gradually changed its attitude and began to consider the possibility and the benefits of negotiating a code of conduct at the regional level. The change may have resulted from two forces, one internal, the other external. Internally, China carried out a pragmatic foreign policy and "stabilizing the neighbouring regions" (*wending zhoubian*) is one of its top priorities. Based on this, China had to maintain a stable environment in the South China Sea. Externally, the pressures and efforts made by ASEAN countries convinced the Chinese that cooperation with ASEAN was inevitable if China desired a stable environment in the South China Sea. As a result, China put forward its own proposal on the code of conduct in 1999 as a response to the ASEAN counterpart one.[18] There were differences between the two proposals, so that the two sides undertook negotiations to reach an agreed document. ASEAN countries, together with China, have held several rounds of discussion to formulate a Code of Conduct for the South China Sea.[19]

On 4 November 2002, China and all the ASEAN member States signed the Declaration on the Conduct of the Parties in the South China Sea (the 2002 Declaration) in Phnom Penh, Cambodia.[20] It is the most remarkable document ever signed between China and ASEAN countries. The Declaration is designed to consolidate and develop the friendship and cooperation existing between China and ASEAN, to promote a peaceful, friendly, and harmonious, environment in the South China Sea, and to enhance the principles and objectives of the 1997 Joint Statement of the Meeting of the Heads of State/Government of the Member States of ASEAN and President of the People's Republic of China.

The Declaration reaffirms the Parties' commitment to the use of international law, and in particular, the LOS Convention, to conduct confidence-building and cooperation. The Parties ensure the freedom of navigation in, and overflight above, the South China Sea. They promise to resolve their territorial and jurisdictional disputes by peaceful means, without resorting to the threat or use of force. They intend to cooperate in the following matters:

- marine environmental protection;
- marine scientific research;

- safety of navigation and communication at sea;
- search and rescue operation; and
- combating transnational crime, including, but not limited to, trafficking in illicit drugs, piracy and armed robbery at sea, and illegal traffic in arms.

The modalities, scope and locations, in respect to bilateral and multilateral cooperation, should be agreed upon by the Parties concerned prior to actual implementation.[21] They promise to resolve their territorial and jurisdictional disputes by peaceful means, without resorting to the threat or use of force, and to continue their dialogues on the South China Sea and restrain themselves from taking any provocative actions in the area.

In comparison, the 2002 Declaration absorbed many elements from the previous Chinese proposal, including, but not limited to, the cooperative matters. China's signature can be regarded as a goodwill gesture to show China's willingness to resolve the South China Sea issue by peaceful means. It may be perceived, therefore, that there will be no major conflicts in the South China Sea in the near future. On the other hand, the Parties still face a series of tasks to be accomplished in accordance with the Declaration. The 2002 Declaration itself, though being a first step, is not the code of conduct, and the Parties concerned will have to work on its adoption in the years to come.

There are different views regarding the Declaration of the Conduct of the Parties. It is doubted whether the Declaration can play its intended role in maintaining peace and security in the South China Sea, bearing in mind that there have already been two bilateral codes of conduct, between China and the Philippines, and Vietnam and the Philippines, respectively,[22] which had not been able to stop clashes between the claimants in the past. Some have even called it "a flimsy piece of paper," "a self-deceiving exercise," and "a flawed attempt," which is doomed.[23] However, the prevailing view is that the 2002 Declaration has value as "a referent," and modifies the behaviour of the parties to the South China Sea dispute; it provides a basis for China and ASEAN to continue their efforts in mitigating the tensions in the South China Sea and paving the way to resolving the dispute in the end, despite the fact that it is a political document without legal binding force.

In fact, since the signing of the 2002 Declaration, the exercise of self-restraint in the South China Sea has been evident. For example, China and the Philippines downplayed their navy drills, stating that they were not related to the maritime territorial disputes. In addition, there is further cooperation between China and ASEAN members concerning the South China Sea. On 11 November 2003, the CNOOC and the Philippine National Oil Company agreed to jointly explore oil and gas in the South China Sea through a letter of intent between the two sides. A joint committee will be set up to help select exploring areas in the South China Sea. They also agreed to a programme to "review, assess and evaluate relevant geographical, geophysical and other technical data available to determine the oil and gas potential in the area."[24] In the Joint Communiqué between China and the Philippines issued in September 2004, the two sides emphasized the importance of maintaining peace and stability in the South China Sea and continuing the discussion of "joint development."[25] According to China, the Sino-Philippine agreement is an important undertaking in the implementation of the 2002 Declaration by the two countries, and China is also willing to discuss ways and means of joint development with other ASEAN countries, including Vietnam.[26] However, while it is good to improve the Sino-Philippine relations, it has invited protests from other claimants, such as Vietnam. In this sense, any joint development arrangement for living or non-living resources in the South China Sea should accommodate all the ASEAN members concerned.

The 2002 Declaration excluded Taiwan due to its peculiar legal status in the international community. However, as it is one of the major claimants in the South China Sea, the exclusion may bring about some negative consequences, as Taiwan can easily become a "trouble-maker" to disrupt any cooperative efforts between China and ASEAN or do something extreme on the pretext that it is not bound by any agreement made between China and ASEAN governing state behaviour in the South China Sea.

Military activities in the exclusive economic zone

The 2001 US EP-3E spy airplane incident[27] triggered a serious legal issue in international law relating to maritime security, i.e. whether military activities can be conducted in the EEZs of other countries in time of peace. According to the LOS Convention, all the seas in the world shall be used peacefully, and any threat or use of force against the territorial integrity or political independence of any state, or action in any other manner inconsistent with the principles of international law embodied in the Charter of the United Nations, shall be prohibited.[28] From this basic legal principle, military activities with threatening potentials should not be carried out in the EEZs of other countries. But, though it is extremely difficult to differentiate what is threatening from what is not, what about foreign military activities without threatening potentials?

According to one scholar, military use of oceans consists of two categories: movement rights and operational rights. The former embraces the notion of mobility and includes such legal rights as transit passage through straits used for international navigation, innocent passage in territorial seas and archipelagic waters, and high-seas freedom of navigation and overflight. The latter includes such activities as task force manoeuvring, anchoring, intelligence collection and surveillance, military exercises, ordnance testing and firing, and hydrographic and military surveys.[29] For the purpose of this Article, military activities refers to those activities in the second category, as defined above, i.e. other than simple navigation or overflight.

As we know, there is a controversy over whether the conducting of military activities in the EEZ of another country is legitimate. Some states may invoke Article 58(1) of the LOS Convention to justify their military activities in other countries' EEZs. The provision reads:

[i]n the exclusive economic zone, all States, whether coastal or land-locked, enjoy, subject to the relevant provisions of this Convention, the freedoms referred to in Article 87 of navigation and overflight and of the laying of submarine cables and pipelines, and other internationally lawful uses of the sea related to these freedoms, such as those associated with the operation of ships, aircraft and submarine cables and pipelines, and compatible with the other provisions of this Convention.

Freedoms in the high seas provided in Article 87 are thus applicable to the EEZ as long as they are not contrary to other provisions of the LOS Convention. According to maritime powers such as the United States, the wording "freedoms" "associated with the operation of ships, aircraft" implies the legality of naval manoeuvres in a foreign EEZ.[30] One view even considers military exercises, aerial reconnaissance, and all other activities of military aircraft freedom of high seas if due regard is paid to the rights and interests of third states.[31] As advocated, since the LOS Convention mainly provides the rights of navigation and overflight, while keeping silent on the rights of military activities, a maritime superpower must defend and enforce such rights for its security interests.[32]

Then there is the question of whether military use constitutes an internationally lawful use of the ocean. The LOS Convention does not mention the military use, so that it becomes a grey area which leads to different interpretations. This non-mention is criticized as being one of the major defects in the new LOS Convention.[33] It is argued that without an express mention in the Convention, military use can hardly be regarded as one of such lawful uses. However, such an argument may not be convincing. According to a fundamental legal principle, nothing is illegal if there is no law to make it so.[34] Following this train of thought, military use is not prohibited since there is no such prohibition in the LOS Convention. Second, as the LOS Convention affirms, matters which are not regulated under it should be governed by general international law, including customary law. If the matter is traced back in history, military activities were consistently allowed under customary international law, though in the implied form. Third, it is admitted that there is a difficulty in inferring from the text and legislative history of Article 58 of the LOS Convention[35] that the establishment of the EEZ has limited foreign military operations other than pure navigation and communication.

The allowance of military activities under international law does not mean that they may be conducted in the EEZ without any regulation. It should be borne in mind that the circumstances now are fundamentally different from those in the past. There was, and still remains, no controversy regarding the military activities conducted on the high seas which were and are open to all. The EEZ is different from the high seas in that it is an area under national jurisdiction. While military activities are allowed there, the factor of national jurisdiction must be taken into account. There should be some kind of check-and-balance mechanism for foreign military activities in the EEZ. It is hard to understand the logic of the argument that while marine scientific research in the EEZ is subject to the consent of the coastal State, military activities may be conducted freely without any check by the coastal State. On the other hand, even if the military use is an internationally lawful use, it can be argued according to the LOS Convention that it is limited to navigation and overflight, and other rights, as provided in Art. 87 of the Convention. This can be seen from some domestic EEZ legislations, such as Surinam's.[36]

In practice, coastal states, including Bangladesh, Brazil, Cape Verde, India, Malaysia, Pakistan, and Uruguay, explicitly restrict unapproved military exercises or activities conducted by other countries in or over their EEZs. The other typical country is Iran which also lays down laws restricting foreign military activities in its EEZ by stipulating that "[f]oreign military activities and practices, collection of information and any other activity inconsistent with the rights and interests of the Islamic Republic of Iran in the exclusive economic zone and the continental shelf are prohibited."[37] Because of this legal provision, there was a diplomatic row between Iran and the United States. The United States lodged a protest against it by stating that the prohibition of military activities contravenes international law and the United States reserves its rights in this regard. In reply to the United States protest, the Iranian diplomatic note states that, due to the multiplicity of economic activities, it is possible that such activities, for which the coastal State enjoys sovereign rights, could be harmed by military practices and manoeuvres; accordingly, those practices which affect the economic activities in the EEZ and the continental shelf are thus prohibited.[38] It is interesting to note that the Iranian explanation does not deny the right of foreign military activities in the EEZ and the only reason for their prohibition results in their possible harm to economic activities there.

The regulations above are made under the rationale that military activities are inherently potential threats to the peace and good order of the coastal states. While such regulations are understandable, it should be borne in mind that not all military activities are threatening. Contrarily, some military activities, such as the activities undertaken by the UN peacekeeping forces, are indispensable to maintaining peace and good order. By the same thinking, some civilian activities also may be threatening and this can be illustrated by a severe marine pollution accident caused by a civilian activity or illegal fishing in the EEZ. In such a context, what we should look into is not the form of a certain activity, but its nature. If a military activity is threatening in nature and is conducted with clearly bad intention and/or in a hostile manner, it should be banned in the EEZ. Otherwise, it should be allowed under certain conditions laid down by the coastal State, similar to the marine scientific research regime under the LOS Convention. There is no reason why the coastal state should be prevented from regulating foreign military activities in its EEZ, while it is allowed to regulate foreign marine scientific research there.

While the coastal state is allowed to enact relevant laws and regulations to govern the activities in the EEZ, an issue arises when such certain law is not consistent with, or not expressly permitted by, the LOS Convention. As shown above, the laws governing foreign military activities are challenged by the United States and some other Western countries. Under such circumstances, the question of whether a certain activity is "legal" or "illegal" becomes controversial and such controversy, in turn, affects the normal enforcement of its law by the coastal state, as well as possibly causing conflicts between the countries concerned.

In order to resolve differences and conflicts, states usually resort to diplomatic channels. In 1998 China's Ministry of National Defence and the United States Department of Defense signed an agreement on establishing a consultation mechanism to strengthen military maritime safety.[39] Under the agreement, both sides agree that their respective maritime and air forces operate "in accordance with international law, including the principles and regimes reflected in the United Nations Convention on the Law of the Sea" (Art. 1), and consultation could be focused on "measures to promote safe maritime practices and establish mutual trust as search and rescue, communications procedures when ships encounter each other, interpretation of the Rules of the Nautical Road, and avoidance of accidents at sea" (Art. 2). It is unfortunate that this agreement was unable to help prevent contention between the two sides concerning the military air crash over the South China Sea. It is reported that after the spy airplane incident, the two sides held several rounds of discussion on military aviation technical issues which had been largely ignored before.[40] That indicates that since the spy airplane incident, China and the United States have paid more attention to the "rules of the road" in the air so that they can avoid such incidents in the future.

It is to be noted that after the EP-3 Incident, the United States began to consider seriously the issue of military and intelligence-gathering activities in the EEZs, as the East–West Centre sponsored a series of workshops on this topic. The first one was held in Bali, Indonesia, in June 2002, and focused on identifying disagreements and contrasting positions as well as on areas of possible mutual understanding and agreement.[41] The Tokyo Meeting in February 2003, acknowledged that with the technology advances in the EEZs, intelligence-gathering activities would increase.[42] The Honolulu Meeting in December 2003, went further and some guidelines for military and intelligence-gathering activities in the EEZs were drafted.[43] Through these efforts, it is hoped that some consensus can be reached in the world community regarding military and intelligence-gathering activities in the EEZs, particularly in connection to a possible review of the LOS Convention after it has been in force for ten years.

Piracy and maritime terrorism

Piracy continues to exist in modern times and became a serious problem after the 1990s. According to the statistics collected by the International Maritime Organization (IMO), cases of piracy have risen sharply since 1994. Pirate attacks jumped 28 per cent in the first quarter of 2002. The total number of piratical incidents from 1984 to the end of April 2003 was 3,073.[44] According to a report issued by the International Maritime Bureau (IMB), pirate attacks have tripled in the last decade. The number of attacks in the first quarter of 2003 already equalled the total number of recorded pirate attacks for the whole of 1993,[45] and for the first half of 2003 the figures were the worst since 1991, with a record of 234 piratical attacks. In 2002, there were 171 attacks, but in 2003, we see an increase by 37 per cent.[46]

Sea piracy is usually linked to maritime terrorism. As early as December 1985, the United Nations General Assembly called upon IMO "to study the problem of terrorism aboard or against ships with a view to making recommendations on appropriate measures."[47] After the 11 September disaster, piracy has been firmly connected to maritime terrorism, though there is no universally accepted definition of terrorism. The Bush Administration tried to convince the world that terrorism was just as immoral as piracy, the slave trade, and genocide.[48] The IMB issued a warning in its annual piracy report for 2002 on the vulnerability of shipping to terrorist attacks. Attacks like the one in the Gulf of Aden in October 2001, when the French tanker *Limburg* was rammed by a boat packed with explosives, are difficult to prevent.[49] In March 2003, two Chinese fishing vessels, operating in the sea off Sri Lanka, were attacked suddenly by unidentified armed vessels and sank. Of the 23 crew members, only eight were rescued.[50] Such blatant armed attack is more serious than piracy and can be well defined as a terrorist attack.

Piracy existed in the East Asian region as early as the fourteenth century. During Zheng He's seven voyages to the Indian Ocean in the Ming Dynasty (1405–33), he undertook some action to suppress pirates in the South China Sea and Southeast Asia for the purpose of maintaining peace and bringing order to the region.[51] Currently, piracy has revived on a serious scale in the region, endangering the safety of navigation, persons, and property. More than two-thirds of the world's pirate attacks are in Asian waters. In the 2000 figure, piracy in the region accounted for 65 per cent of the world's total number. In 2002, Indonesian waters were, and remain, the world's most pirate-infested, with 22 of 87 attacks reported world-wide (32 in the Southeast Asian seas) from January to March.[52] Incidents in the South China Sea increased from 120 in 2001 to 140 in 2002.[53]

The term "piracy" usually refers to a broad range of violent acts at sea. The LOS Convention defines it as:

> Piracy consists of any of the following acts: (a) any illegal acts of violence or detention, or any act of depredation, committed for private ends by the crew or the passengers of a private ship or a private aircraft, and directed to: (i) on the high seas, against another ship or aircraft, or against persons or property on board such ship or aircraft; (ii) against a ship, aircraft, persons or property in a place outside the jurisdiction of any State; (b) any act of voluntary participation in the operation of a ship or of an aircraft with knowledge of facts making it a pirate ship or aircraft; (c) any act of inciting or of intentionally facilitating an act described in subparagraph (a) or (b).[54]

However, the above definition has limitations. First, it defines "piracy" as only for "private ends" and terrorist acts at sea for political ends are generally excluded. That is why, after the *Achille Lauro* incident in 1985,[55] the world community needed the Convention on the Suppression of Unlawful Acts against the Safety of Maritime Navigation (the SUA Convention). Second, according to the above definition, piracy *juris gentium* presupposes that a criminal act be exercised by passengers or the crew of a ship against another ship or persons or property on board. The two-vessel requirement is an ingredient of the crime of piracy, unless a criminal act occurs in *terra nullius*.[56] Thus "internal seizure" within the ship is hardly regarded as "act of piracy" under the definition of the LOS Convention.[57] Finally, piracy must occur on the high seas and piratical acts within territorial waters are not subject to the above definition.

To remedy these limitations, IMO has attempted to divide acts of piracy into two categories by geographical and legal division of maritime zones: piracy on the high seas is defined as "piracy" under the LOS Convention definition, while acts of piracy in ports or national waters (internal waters and territorial sea) are defined as "armed robbery against ships."[58] However, we may note that the shortcoming of such a division is obvious: piracy is not equivalent to armed robbery and it may also include other violent acts such as murder, assault, and rape.

For most of the countries in East Asia, piracy may be subject to punishment in the name of robbery, murder, larceny, or kidnapping, according to their criminal laws. In this context, the international definition does not carry a significant meaning when piratical activities occur in the waters within national jurisdiction and subject to the domestic criminal law of a coastal state. However, at the regional level, particularly with a view to regional cooperation, the definition under international law is meaningful and consists of the legal concept of a crackdown on piracy. It should be pointed out that with the legal developments in the international arena the definition provided by the IMO has been gradually accepted world-wide, as manifested in numerous international documents, including those UN documents relating to the LOS Convention.[59]

The geographic features of the East China Sea and the South China Sea are very complex. The complicated topography and the vast size of the sea may enable pirates to commit their crimes more frequently than in other regions of the world. It is noted that effective law enforcement is extremely difficult in the South China Sea because of its vastness (more than 200 nautical miles wide) and due to the fact that it is dotted with numerous uninhabited islands to which pirates can retreat.[60] The sea area, with its points in Hong Kong, Luzon Island, and Hainan Island, is called "the Hainan Triangle," a pirate haven.

The LOS Convention is the major international convention for the suppression of piracy at the global level. China signed the LOS Convention in 1982 and ratified it in 1996. In addition, China also ratified the 1988 SUA Conventions and its Protocol against maritime terrorism. In addition, China has participated in activities relating to the piracy issue sponsored by relevant international organizations such as IMO.

International law has established an obligation for states to cooperate in the

Maritime security and multilateral interactions 161

suppression of piracy and grants states certain rights to seize pirate ships and criminals. Article 100 of the LOS Convention provides that "All States shall cooperate to the fullest possible extent in the repression of piracy on the high seas or in any other place outside the jurisdiction of any State." Article 105 further provides that

> on the high seas, or in any other place outside the jurisdiction of any State, every State may seize a pirate ship or aircraft, or a ship or aircraft taken by piracy and under the control of pirates, and arrest the persons and seize the property on board. The courts of the State which carried out the seizure may decide upon penalties to be imposed, and may also determine the action to be taken with regard to the ships, aircraft or property, subject to the rights of third parties acting in good faith.

However, only warships or military aircraft or similar governmentally authorized ships or aircraft have the power to seize a pirate ship or aircraft on the high seas. It should be noted that the above piracy provisions are also applicable to the EEZ, though it is within the national jurisdiction.[61] This is particularly important to the China Seas since most, if not all, of the sea areas are now within the national jurisdiction.

The SUA Convention applies to all maritime terrorist acts, whether private or political. The significance lies in that, if terrorist acts may not be punished and suppressed under the LOS Convention, they may still be so under the terms of the SUA Convention. This means that any maritime terrorist or piratical act cannot escape justice. The other twin instrument is the 1988 Protocol for the Suppression of Unlawful Acts against the Safety of Fixed Platforms Located on the Continental Shelf (the SUA Protocol),[62] which was adopted at the same time as the SUA Convention and contains similar provisions. It is relevant to the China Seas in the context that the seas are rich in oil and gas and the coastal states have already launched exploitation projects, either by themselves or jointly with foreign oil companies. It is said that offshore oil and gas installations are potential targets of piracy.[63] Should any terrorist or piratical attack be against oil platform(s) or artificial islands located in the China Seas, it could be suppressed under this protocol. As of March 2003, the SUA Convention has been ratified by 87 States, representing 75.74 per cent of world merchant shipping tonnage and the SUA Protocol has been ratified by 79 States, representing 75.41 per cent of world merchant shipping tonnage.[64] So far, as of September 2006, there are nine countries in East Asia which have ratified the SUA Convention.

Regional cooperation is a necessity to effectively combat piracy in the region. For China, suppression of piracy is undertaken under the regional cooperative framework of managing non-traditional security issues. In April 1997, China initiated the concept of new security which contains the core elements of mutual trust, mutual benefit, equality, and coordination. In May 2002, China submitted to the ASEAN Regional Forum (ARF) Senior Officials' Conference the document concerning China's stand in strengthening cooperation in non-traditional security fields. In November, the Joint Declaration of ASEAN and China on Cooperation in the Field of Non-Traditional Security Issues (the Joint Declaration) was adopted, which initiated full cooperation between ASEAN and China in the field of non-traditional security issues and listed the priority and form of cooperation. The priorities at the current stage of cooperation include "combating trafficking in illegal drugs, people-smuggling, including trafficking in women and children, sea piracy, terrorism, arms-smuggling, money-laundering, international economic crime, and cyber crime." As to the multilateral and bilateral cooperation, it aims to, "(a) strengthen information exchange, (b) strengthen personnel exchange and training and enhance capacity-building, (c) strengthen practical cooperation on non-traditional security issues, (d) strengthen joint research on non-traditional security issues, and, (e) explore other areas and modalities of cooperation."[65] In addition, the 2002 Declaration on the Conduct of the Parties in the South China Sea also mentions the suppression of piracy and armed robbery at sea.

Multilateral interactions among the countries in East Asia have produced some positive results in regional cooperation in this regard. For example, heads of coastguard agencies from 16 countries and one region (ten ASEAN countries, India, Sri Lanka, Bangladesh, South Korea, China, Hong Kong, and Japan) attended the first regional conference held in April 2000, where three documents were adopted. In a statement "Asia Anti-Piracy Challenge 2000," the coastguard authorities expressed their intention to reinforce mutual cooperation in combating piracy and armed robbery against ships. The "Tokyo Appeal" calls for the establishment of contact points for information exchange among relevant authorities as well as for the drafting of a national anti-piracy action plan. The Model Action Plan states specific counter-measures based on the Tokyo Appeal.[66] At the bilateral level, China and the Philippines discussed the possibility of their cooperation in combating piracy and drug-trafficking in the South China Sea, including the possible establishment of special joint patrol teams.[67] In October 2004, China's Maritime Safety Administration and the Philippine Coast Guard held a joint table search and rescue (SAR) exercise to strengthen capabilities in the region and make the sea safer for the public and ships.[68] In the East China Sea, China and Japan signed an agreement on police cooperation between the Ministry of Public Security of China and the Police Bureau of Japan, which is helpful in the taking of common measures against piracy.[69]

A most significant development recently is the ARF Statement on Cooperation against Piracy and Other Threats to Maritime Security which was issued on 19 June 2003 in Phnom Penh, Cambodia, during the tenth ASEAN Regional Forum. It is acknowledged that piracy and armed robbery against ships has been a significant problem in the Asia-Pacific region and effective responses require "regional maritime security strategies and multilateral cooperation in their implementation."[70] It is noted that the ARF countries express their commitment to becoming parties to the SUA Convention if they have not yet done so. In addition to undertaking necessary actions such as exchange of information, consideration, and discussion of new IMB proposals on prescribed traffic lanes for large supertankers with coastguard or naval escort, provision of technical assistance and capacity-building infrastructure for countries that need help, they commit to "endorse the ongoing efforts to establish a legal framework for regional cooperation to combat piracy and armed robberies against ships."[71] Based on this, a regional treaty on anti-piracy is currently being negotiated among the Asian countries and the parties decided recently to establish a Centre for Information Exchange in Singapore.[72]

China's response to the Regional Maritime Security Initiatives

Closely related to the suppression of piracy and maritime terrorism is the Regional Maritime Security Initiative (RMSI). It was formally put forward in March 2004, by Admiral Thomas B. Fargo, Navy Commander of the US Pacific Command, in his testimony regarding US Pacific Command posture, before the House Armed Services Committee of the US House of Representatives.[73] According to Fargo, the RMSI is designed to implement the "President's Proliferation Security Initiative (PSI)[74] and State Department's Malacca Strait Initiative," with the approach that detailed plans are provided "to build and synchronize interagency and international capacity to fight threats that use the maritime space to facilitate their illicit activity." From Fargo's remarks, it is obvious that this Initiative is designed for the East Asian region, particularly focusing on the safe navigation in the Strait of Malacca. Furthermore, Fargo emphasized that in order to conduct effective interdiction in the sea it is necessary to use high-speed vessels equipped with Special Operations Forces or Marines. To implement the PSI, the United States signed non-proliferation ship-boarding agreements with Liberia (11 February 2004), Panama (12 May 2004), and Marshall Islands (13 August 2004). According to such agreements, if a ship with either party's flag is suspected of carrying proliferation-related cargo, either party can request the other to confirm the nationality of the ship and, if necessary, to authorize the boarding, search and possible detention, of the ship and its cargo. These agreements, together with PSI partners, cover more than 50 per cent of commercial shipping fleet dead weight tonnage, which is subject to rapid action consent procedures for boarding, search, and seizure, by the United States.[75]

Responses from Asian countries to this Initiative are various: some countries, such as Japan, Singapore, and South Korea, immediately rendered their support. For example, Japan hosted the PSI Maritime Interdiction Exercise off the coast of Sagami Bay and off the Port of Yokosuka from 25–27 October 2004.[76] Yet some other countries, such as Malaysia and Indonesia, are doubtful of the RMSI and whether it can really play a positive role in curbing piracy and maritime terrorism. They are also suspicious of the American intention and whether it would infringe upon their national sovereignty and territorial integrity. In order to prevent potential American military intervention in Strait affairs, Malaysia and

Indonesia decided to formulate a joint patrol to protect this international waterway. Singapore later joined. The tripartite patrol consists of 15–20 military vessels and patrols in the Strait all the year round.[77]

China's feeling is complex. On the one hand, China needs the safety of navigation in the Strait of Malacca since most of China's imported oil reaches China through this strait, but China is concerned by the American intervention in the Strait, fearing that a military presence of the United States in the Strait may block China's oil transportation if their bilateral relations deteriorate, due to some disputes, concerning, say, the Taiwan issue. For that reason, China has been considering the construction of an oil pipeline from Myanmar to China to reduce its dependence on shipping oil imports through the Strait of Malacca.[78] As stated by a Chinese diplomat, maritime security is of vital importance for the welfare and economic development of the region, and regional cooperation is indispensable for maritime security.[79] However, China has doubts whether the principles embodied in international law, including the UN Charter, "would be or could be strictly observed in real actions against maritime threats. Extreme care and sensitiveness is need when it comes to military involvement.[80] In a word, China prefers a regional arrangement of maritime security for the Strait of Malacca.

In addition, China has a bitter experience regarding the interdiction at sea. On 7 July 1993, the Chinese freighter the *Milky Way* (*yinhe*) departed from Tianjin to the Middle East with the destination port of Kuwait. On 23 July, the United States accused China of sending to Iran chemical materials (thiodiglycol and thionyl chloride) to be used for making chemical weapons and demanded an inspection on board by the American side. From 1 August, several American warships followed the *Milky Way*, monitoring its movement and taking photos so that the Chinese ship could not sail normally. Due to the American pressure, the *Milky Way* was refused permission to anchor in port and remained on the high seas until late August. Finally, on 29 August, China agreed to check the containers on board together with the Saudi Arabia representative and American experts. The investigation result proved that there were no chemical materials such as the United States had alleged. On 4 September 1993, the Chinese Foreign Ministry issued a statement, condemning the American hegemonic attitude and its groundless accusation.[81]

Chinese legal scholars accused the United States of having violated international law, including the freedom of the high seas, and maintained that the United States should bear legal liability to compensate for the economic loss of the Chinese freighter.[82] From this incident, it may be assumed that China is very averse to the RMSI when military interdiction at sea is involved. This also can be seen from China's basic policy regarding the South China Sea as China has always reiterated that it will maintain the freedom of navigation and overflight in the South China Sea; it has never interfered in such free passage and will not do so in future.[83] However, for some reasons, China might not always oppose military interdiction or naval inspection. A Taiwanese scholar recently wrote a piece about how China can stop the United States from selling weapons to Taiwan. One of the alternatives, as he proposed, could be the use of the American experience in blockading Cuba in the 1960s. China can select some American merchant vessels for inspection by applying the 17 August Communiqué and also learn lessons from the *Milky Way* incident, to negotiate with the Americans.[84] The American-sponsored RMSI, once fully implemented in East Asia, may give China the right of inspection and apply it towards American vessels more justifiably.

Conclusion

From the above assessment of the recent interactions between China and its neighbouring countries, we can draw a number of preliminary conclusions.

First, law, particularly international law, has begun to play a more and more important role in China's diplomacy and its intercourse with other countries. As described above, the marine legal order in East Asia is based on the universally accepted principles of international law, including the LOS Convention, which most of the East Asian countries, including China, have ratified. Although there are various definitions on rule of law, one thing is clear: the rule of law principle at the international level requires states to use international law rather than power, the will of individuals, or even force, to govern state-to-state relations. It is of paramount importance that countries, particularly those big countries in the region, behave responsibly.

It is remarkable that China, for the first time, expressed clearly that rule of law should be implemented in international relations in 2004. In the Four Opinions of China regarding the work of the United Nations, one of the opinions is the rule of law in international relation. According to China, rule of law is fundamentally important in maintaining world peace and security, enhancing development and protecting human rights. The pick-and-choose mentality towards international legal norms is of no help in promoting and realizing the rule of law and justice in the world community.[85] In this sense, the principle of rule of law has been implanted into the foreign relations of China, though it is only at the beginning of its implementation.

More reliance on international law to develop China's diplomacy at the bilateral, regional, and global levels is actually a timely reflection of the changed perception of the current Chinese leadership in understanding the law, as well as in terms of governance at the domestic level. As it is recalled, rule of law was officially incorporated in 1999 into the Chinese Constitution, in which China pledged to "implement law to govern the State and construct the socialist country with the rule of law."[86] Following this new change, the Chinese government, as well as the Chinese Communist Party, has implemented the new policy towards political reforms, which is called "governance in accordance with law" (*yifa zhizheng*) and "administration in accordance with law" (*yifa xingzheng*). The new internal policy and changed governmental behaviour have no doubt influenced China's external relations.

Second, China has realized, though with some reluctance, that regionalization of the maritime-security issues such as the South China Sea dispute is an inevitable trend, which China is unable to prevent but must adapt itself to, so that it still can play a significant role in dealing with regional maritime security issues. In fact, vibrant regional cooperation and a regional mechanism for maintaining and improving the marine legal order in China's adjacent seas with other countries are required by international law, including the LOS Convention, which obliges coastal states to cooperate between/among themselves:

- to coordinate the management, conservation, exploration and exploitation of the living resources of the sea;
- to coordinate the implementation of their rights and duties with respect to the protection and preservation of the marine environment;
- to coordinate their scientific research policies and undertake where appropriate joint programs of scientific research in the area; and
- to invite, as appropriate, other interested States or international organizations to cooperate with them in furtherance of the provisions of this Article.[87]

The most active area for regional cooperation is the protection of the marine environment through two regional programmes such as the East Asian Seas Program sponsored by the International Maritime Organization, the Global Environment Facility, and the UN Environment Program (UNEP), and implemented in 1994 with the participation of 11 countries (Brunei, Cambodia, China, Indonesia, Malaysia, North Korea, the Philippines, Singapore, South Korea, Thailand, and Vietnam), and the Regional Seas Program sponsored by the UNEP for the Northwest Pacific (involving China, Japan, North Korea, Russia, and South Korea). The existing cooperative experiences in the area of marine environmental protection can be extended to apply to other areas in the context of maritime security. At present, non-traditional security issues have become a focal priority in the China–ASEAN regular talks. On the other hand, China's preference for regionalization of some security issues is intended to prevent them from become internationalized. The Spratly Islands issue is a typical example.

Third, while having accepted regionalization and international law, China still firmly sticks to the principle of sovereignty in its multiple external interactions. According to China, sovereignty can be interpreted as independence, including the internal power of independence (such as legislation, establishment of national system, etc.), and external power of independence (such as freedom to deal with international affairs, participation in international conferences and signing treaties).[88] It is acknowledged that strict adherence to the principle of the inviolability of sovereignty has become a distinctive feature of foreign policy of the PRC and is treated as the basis of international relations and the cornerstone of the whole system of international law.[89] Thus, as to China's external power inherent in the principle of sovereignty, China will not allow any violation or infringement of its sovereignty and political independence.

Related to sovereignty are the famous Five Principles of Peaceful Coexistence, which include: (1) mutual respect for each other's sovereignty and territorial integrity; (2) non-aggression; (3) non-interference in each other's internal affairs; (4) equality and mutual benefit; and (5) peaceful coexistence. The Five Principles first appeared in the Agreement between the Republic of India and the People's Republic of China on Trade and Intercourse between Tibet Region of China and India, signed on 29 April 1954.[90] Since then, the Five Principles have been reiterated in China's foreign policy documents as well as in agreements, declarations, and joint statements signed between China and other countries that are willing to incorporate those principles into the relevant documents. In China's view, these principles have become the universally applicable principles among the States, thus becoming fundamental principles of international law. In this sense, China's advocacy of rule of law in the world community seems strengthening, rather than decreasing, the applicability of China's long-maintained and implemented Five Principles of Co-existence in its diplomacy. The question is whether the "co-existence" mentality has hampered and will hamper China's attempts to make active diplomatic interactions with its neighbouring countries and the entire world community.

Notes

1. 21 ILM (1982) 1261. The Convention was open for signature on 10 December 1982 and came into effect on 16 November 1994. As of December 2004, there were 146 Contracting Parties to it, including one international organization.
2. Art. 2 (2) of the LOS Convention.
3. Art. 56 (1) (b) and Art.77 (1) of the LOS Convention.
4. Art. 81 of the LOS Convention.
5. See *Marine Affairs of the Contemporary China* (in Chinese) in Luo Yuro and Zeng Chengkui (eds), Beijing: Social Sciences Press, 1985, pp. 1–2.
6. For details, see *China Natural Resources Series: Ocean* (in Chinese) in Committee of Editors of the *China Natural Resources Series* (ed.), Beijing: China Environmental Science Press, 1995, pp. 35–45.
7. Article 122 of the Convention defines "enclosed or semi-enclosed sea" as "a gulf, basin, or sea surrounded by two or more States and connected to another sea or the ocean by a narrow outlet or consisting entirely or primarily of the territorial seas and exclusive economic zones of two or more coastal States."
8. An English version may be found in Office of Ocean Affairs, Bureau of Oceans and International Environmental and Scientific Affairs, US Department of State, *Limits in the Seas*, no. 117, Straight Baselines Claim: China, 9 July 1996, pp. 11–14.
9. Declaration on the Baseline of the Territorial Sea of the People's Republic of China, 15 May 1996, see Office of Ocean Affairs, ibid., pp. 9–10.
10. An English version translated by this author is available in *MIMA Bulletin*, 1999, vol. 7 (1), pp. 27–29.
11. Art. 4 of the EEZ Law. It is borrowed from Art. 81 of the LOS Convention.
12. A main reason that there is no other claimant for the Macclesfield Bank is that this Bank is permanently submerged under the water. Otherwise, Vietnam or the Philippines might have claimed it, as well.
13. The other two factors are: military confrontation in the Korean Peninsula, and the controversial US–Japan military alliance and Taiwan's separatist activities. See Yan Xuetong, "Co-operation Key to Regional Peace," *China Daily*, 27 March 1998, p. 4.
14. For example, the Philippines expressed its alarm over increasing Vietnamese military

and fishing vessel incursions into the waters off the disputed Spratly Islands in the South China Sea and there were 205 Vietnamese vessels in areas claimed by the Philippines in the first 10 months in 2001. See "Philippine alarmed over increasing Vietnamese incursions in Spratlys," *Agence France-Presse*, 16 November 2001.
15 See "Vietnam Protests China's Exercises in 'Off-limits Zone,'" *Voice of Vietnam*, Hanoi, 11 June 2002; and "China Dismisses Vietnam's Protest over Naval Exercise," *Xinhua News Agency*, Beijing, 11 June 2002.
16 "ASEAN Declaration on the South China Sea," Manila, Philippines, 22 July 1992. Online. Available: www.aseansec.org/5233.htm (accessed 27 October 2004).
17 "Recent Developments in the South China Sea," 18 March 1995. Online. Available: www.aseansec.org/5232.htm (accessed 27 October 2004).
18 These two proposals are reprinted in Hainan Research Institute for the South China Sea (ed.), *Selected Foreign and Chinese Articles on the South China Sea (2001)* (in Chinese), Hainan, China, March 2002, pp. 180–3.
19 The drafts of the Code of Conduct both from ASEAN and China are reprinted in Hainan Research Institute for the South China Sea (ed.), *Collection of Selected Foreign and Chinese Papers on the South China Sea* (in Chinese), Hainan: Haikou, 2002, pp. 180–3.
20 The whole text is available in the ASEAN website. Online. Available: www.aseansec.org/13163.htm (accessed 18 November 2004).
21 Ibid.
22 For details, see Nguyen Hong Thao, "Vietnam and the Code of Conduct for the South China Sea," *Ocean Development and International Law*, vol. 32, 2001, pp. 105–30.
23 See Ronald A. Rodriguez, "Conduct Unbecoming in the South China Sea," *PacNet*, no. 22A, 21 May 2004.
24 "Chinese, Philippine Firms Join Forces to Look for Oil in South China Sea," *Agence France Presse*, 13 November 2003.
25 See "The Joint Communiqué of the Government of the People's Republic of China and the Government of the Republic of the Philippines," *People's Daily* (in Chinese), 4 September 2004, p. 3.
26 See "Ministry of Foreign Affairs: China Seriously Requests Vanuatu to Keep its promise on Taiwan," 18 November 2004. Online. Available: www.people.com.cn/GB/shizheng/1027/2997844.html (accessed 19 November 2004).
27 On 1 April 2001, while the US EP-3E Aries II airplane was conducting espionage activities near the Chinese coast in the South China Sea, it was intercepted by two Chinese F-8 fighter jets and then collided with one of the jets. The damaged Chinese jet crashed into the water and the pilot died. The damaged American airplane made an emergency landing at Lingshui in China's Hainan Island and all the crew members were safe. The incident immediately became a diplomatic row between China and the United States. China accused the United States of encroaching on China's territorial sovereignty and of violation of international law as well as of relevant Chinese laws, and demanded an apology and compensation from the American side. The United States responded that the reconnaissance airplane was operating outside China's territorial waters and that the airplane had landed in distress. For that reason, the United States refused to render an apology; and instead demanded that China immediately return the American crew and the airplane. After several rounds of diplomatic contacts, the United States finally sent a letter to China on 11 April 2001, expressing its sincere regret over the Chinese missing pilot and aircraft and used the word "sorry" for their loss. The letter also used the word "sorry" for the American airplane's entering of China's airspace and landing without verbal clearance. On the next day, China allowed all 24 crew members to leave China. However, the damaged American spy airplane did not leave China until 3 July 2001 after it had been dismantled and packed. The Chinese side asked for $1 million for the costs relating to the aircraft but the Americans only offered the amount of $34,567 which was refused by the Chinese.

The compensation for the cost is still a pending issue to be resolved between the two sides.
28 See Art. 301 of the LOS Convention.
29 Charles E. Pirtle, "Military Uses of Ocean Space and the Law of the Sea in the New Millennium," *Ocean Development and International Law*, vol. 31, 2000, p. 8.
30 See Boleslaw Adam Boczek, "Peacetime Military Activities in the Exclusive Economic Zone of Third Countries," *Ocean Development and International Law*, vol. 19, 1988, p. 450.
31 Kay Hailbronner, "Freedom of the Air and the Convention on the Law of the Sea," 77 AJIL, 1983, p. 503.
32 See Pirtle, *supra* note 29, 8–9.
33 Shao Jin, "Legal Problems Concerning Military Use of Exclusive Economic Zones and Continental Shelves," *Chinese Yearbook of International Law* (in Chinese), 1985, p. 183.
34 For example, *"nullum crimen sine lege"* (no crime without law); and *"nullum crimen nulla poena sine lege"* (no criminal punishment without law).
35 Francesco Francioni, "Peacetime Use of Force, Military Activities, and the New Law of the Sea," *Cornell International Law Journal*, vol. 18, 1985, p. 216.
36 "As it provides, all nations, with the observance of the international law, enjoy: ... 4. Freedom to exercise internationally recognized rights in connection with navigation and communication," Art. 5 of Law concerning the extension of the territorial sea and the establishment of a contiguous economic zone of 11 June 1978, in Division for Ocean Affairs and the Law of the Sea, Office of Legal Affairs, United Nations, *The Law of the Sea: National Legislation on the Exclusive Economic Zone*, New York: United Nations, 1993, p. 351.
37 Art. 16 of Act on the Marine Areas of the Islamic Republic of Iran in the Persian Gulf and the Oman Sea, 1993, in Division for Ocean Affairs and the Law of the Sea, Office of Legal Affairs, United Nations, *The Law of the Sea: Current Developments in State Practice No. IV*, New York: United Nations, 1995, p. 67.
38 See Protest from the United States of America, 11 January 1994; and Comments from the Islamic Republic of Iran concerning the viewpoints of the Government of the United States of America regarding the Act on Marine Areas in the Persian Gulf and the Oman Sea, in Division for Ocean Affairs and the Law of the Sea, Office of Legal Affairs, United Nations, 1995, ibid., pp. 147–51.
39 It was signed on 19 January 1998. Text is reprinted in 37 ILM 530 (1998).
40 See Qian Chuntai, "Analysis on Sino-U.S. Consultation Mechanism for Military Maritime Safety," *Contemporary International Relations*, no. 4 (in Chinese), 2002, p. 10.
41 For details, see East–West Center, *Military and Intelligence Gathering Activities in Exclusive Economic Zones: Consensus and Disagreement: A Summary of the Bali Dialogue*, East–West Center, 2002.
42 For details, see East–West Center, *The Regime of the Exclusive Economic Zones: Issues and Responses: A Report of the Tokyo Meeting*, East–West Center, 2003.
43 See Hasjim Djalal, Alexander Yankov, and Anthony Bergin, "Draft guidelines for military and intelligence gathering activities in the EEZ and their means and manner of implementation and enforcement," *Marine Policy*, vol. 29 (2), 2005, pp. 175–83.
44 See "Reports on Acts of Piracy and Armed Robbery against Ships," issued monthly – acts reported during April 2003, IMO Doc. MSC.4/Circ.35, 7 May 2003.
45 "Pirate Attacks Have Tripled in A Decade, IMB Report Finds." Online. Available: www.iccwbo.org/home/news_archives/2003/ stories/piracy-quarter-1.asp (accessed 19 July 2003).
46 See "Piracy Soars as Violence against Seafarers Intensifies." Online. Available: www.iccwbo.org/ccs/news_archives/2003/piracy_report_second_quarter.asp (accessed 25 July 2003).
47 "Convention for the Suppression of Unlawful Acts against the Safety of Maritime

Navigation, 1988." Online. Available: www.imo.org/home.asp?topic_id=161 (accessed 2 July 2003).
48 "Pentagon Policy Chief: Terrorism as Immoral as Genocide," *Dow Jones International News*, 8 May 2002.
49 See "High Seas Terrorism Alert in Piracy Report." Online. Available: www.iccwbo.org/home/news_archives/2003/stories/piracy%20_report_2002.asp (accessed 19 July 2003).
50 "Families of Victims Who Died in the Sri Lanka Attack to Institute Compensation Lawsuits in Fujian," *China Ocean News* (in Chinese), 4 July 2003.
51 See Wang Li, "Zheng He's Voyage and Solution of Pirates Issue," in *Chinese Heading for the Sea* (in Chinese), Nanjing Zheng He Study Association (ed.), Beijing: Sea Tide Publishing House, 1996, pp. 311–19.
52 "Pirate Attacks Jumped 28 per cent in First Quarter," *The Shipping Times*, Singapore, 10 May 2002.
53 "Reports on Acts of Piracy and Armed Robbery against Ships," IMO Doc. MSC.4/Circ.32, 17 April 2003.
54 Article 101 of the LOS Convention.
55 On 3 October 1985, a group of Palestinian guerrillas hijacked the Italian cruise ship *Achille Lauro* while it was in Egyptian territorial waters. The hijackers demanded the release of 50 Palestinians held in Israel in return for the release of the passengers. They ordered the ship to sail to Syria, which refused them port entry. The hijackers then on 8 October killed an American passenger. Several days later the four hijackers gave themselves up to the Egyptian authorities. On 11 October an Egyptian civilian aircraft was intercepted by United States military aircraft over the Mediterranean Sea and instructed to land at an air base in Sicily. Four Palestinians on board were detained by the Italian authorities and subsequently indicted and convicted in Genoa for offences related to the hijacking of the ship and the death of the American passenger.
56 Natalino Ronzitti, "The Law of the Sea and the Use of Force against Terrorist Activities," in *Maritime Terrorism and International Law*, N. Ronzitti (ed.), Dordrecht: Martinus Nijhoff, 1990, p. 1.
57 A different view holds that internal seizures could be piracy. See Samuel P. Menefee, "Piracy, Terrorism, and the Insurgent Passenger: A Historical and Legal Perspective," in Ronzitti (ed.), ibid., 60. In addition, it is acknowledged that even internal seizure was not a piratical act in international law, it is still a one under municipal law of the flag state.
58 See Birgit S. Olsen, "Piracy and the Law," paper presented to the IMO Seminar and Workshop on Piracy and Armed Robbery against Ships, Singapore, 3–5 February 1999, p. 2. (on file with the author).
59 See, for example, "Oceans and Law of the Sea," Report of the Secretary-General, UN Doc. A/57/57, 7 March 2002, pp. 27–9.
60 See "IMO to Organize Missions, Rregional Seminars on Piracy," IMOFAX 05/98, 8 April 1998. Online. Available: www.imo.org/imo/briefing/1998/fax05.htm (accessed 17 June 1998).
61 Provisions on the high seas of the LOS Convention are applicable to the EEZ as long as there is no contradiction.
62 27 ILM, 1988, p. 685.
63 See Sam Bateman and Doug MacKinnon, "The Role of Port States to Suppress Acts of Piracy in Their Waters," paper presented to the 3rd ICC-IMB International Meeting on Piracy and Phantom Ships, 1–2 June 1998, 5, Kuala Lumpur (on file with the author).
64 "Legal Committee, 86th Session: 28 April – 2 May 2003." Online. Available: www.imo.org/home.asp?topic_id=161 (accessed 2 July 2003).
65 See Joint Declaration of ASEAN and China on Cooperation in the Field of Non-

Traditional Security Issues, 6th ASEAN–China Summit, Phnom Penh, Cambodia, 4 November 2002. Online. Available: www.aseansec.org/13185.htm (accessed 2 July 2003).
66 See Japanese Ministry of Foreign Affairs, "Diplomatic Bluebook 2001." Online. Available: www.mofa.go.jp/policy/other/bluebook/2001/chap2-4-d.html (accessed 26 January 2002).
67 See *Lianhe Zaobao*, Singapore, (in Chinese), 15 July 1999.
68 "Country runs exercise with the Philippines," *China Daily*, 22 October 2004.
69 See Yu Qing, "China and Japan Signed the Minutes of Police Co-operation," *People's Daily* (in Chinese), 26 August 1999.
70 Text is available online. Available: www.aseansec.org/14838.htm (accessed 18 July 2003).
71 Ibid.
72 See "Asian countries decide to establish anti-piracy information center in our country," *Lianhe Zaobao* (in Chinese), 13 November 2004. The countries involved in the negotiations include Bangladesh, Brunei, Cambodia, China, India, Indonesia, Japan, Laos, Malaysia, Myanmar, the Philippines, Sri Lanka, Singapore, South Korea, Thailand, and Vietnam.
73 The whole text of the Testimony is available online. Available: www.pacom.mil/speeches/sst2004/040331housearmedsvscomm.shtml> (accessed 11 November 2004).
74 PSI is an effort to consider possible collective measures among the participating countries, in accordance with national legal authorities and relevant international law and frameworks, in order to prevent the proliferation of weapons of mass destruction, missiles, and their related materials that pose threats to the peace and stability of the international community. The PSI is administered by the "core group" countries, which, at present, consist of 15 countries (Japan, US, UK, Italy, the Netherlands, Australia, France, Germany, Spain, Poland, Portugal, Singapore, Canada, Norway, and Russia). See "The Proliferation Security Initiative (PSI) Maritime Interdiction Exercise hosted by Japan," 18 October 2004. Online. Available: www.mofa.go.jp/policy/un/disarmament/arms/psi/exercise-2.html (accessed 11 November 2004).
75 See "US–RMI Agreement: Maritime Security Initiative Signed," 15 August 2004. Online. Available: www.yokwe.net (accessed 11 November 2004).
76 See "The Proliferation Security Initiative (PSI) Maritime Interdiction Exercise hosted by Japan," *supra* note 74.
77 See "Indonesia and Malaysia Jointly Oppose American Army to Patrol in the Strait of Malacca," *Lianhe Zaobao* (in Chinese), 8 May 2004; and "Piratical attacks are more fierce in the Strait of Malacca, Indonesia, Malaysia and Singapore will prevent this jointly," 9 October 2004. Online. Available: www.people.com.cn/GB/guoji/1029/2905373.html (accessed 9 October 2004).
78 See "Chinese Scholars Propose Way to Reduce Dependence on Malaccan Strait," *Alexander's Oil & Gas Connections*, vol. 9, Issue 15, 4 August 2004. Online. Available: www.gasandoil.com/goc/news/nts43127.htm (accessed 11 November 2004).
79 Zhao Jianhua, "The Straits of Malacca and Challenges Ahead: China's Perspective," paper presented to the Conference on "Straits of Malacca: Building a Comprehensive Security Environment," 11–13 October 2004, Kuala Lumpur (on file with the author).
80 Zhao Jianhua, ibid., p. 4.
81 See "Milky Way event." Online. Available: www.china.org.cn/chinese/HIAW/109186.htm (accessed 20 November 2004); and "The United States Forced our Yinhe Freighter to Stay on the High Seas for 33 Days." Online. Available: www.news.163.com/2004w09/12686/2004w09_1096092272435.html (accessed 20 November 2004).
82 For details, see Zhao Lihai, *Studies on the Law of the Sea Issues* (in Chinese), Beijing: Peking University Press, 1996, pp. 237–44.
83 See "China's Basic Position on the South China Sea Issue and Its Policy Assertion on

the Settlement of the South China Sea Dispute," *China Ocean News* (in Chinese), 23 April 2004.
84 See Shih Chi-yu, "Beijing May Inspect American Merchant Vessels," *Lianhe Zaobao* (in Chinese), 17 August 2004.
85 See "Zhang Yishang Put Forward Four Opinions on the Work of the United Nations in the General Assembly," 8 October 2004. Online. Available: www.people.com.cn/GB/guoji/14549/2904212.html (accessed 9 October 2004).
86 See Art. 5 of the amended Constitution. For a detailed analysis of the 1999 Amendment, see Zou Keyuan and Zheng Yongnian, "China's Third Constitutional Amendment: A Leap Forward towards Rule of Law in China," *Yearbook Law and Legal Practice in East Asia*, vol. 4, 1999, pp. 29–41.
87 Art. 123 of the LOS Convention.
88 See Bai Guimei, "Basic Rights and Obligations of the State," in *International Law* (in Chinese), Wang Tieya (ed.), Beijing: Law Press, 1995, pp. 107–8.
89 J.A. Cohen, "Attitudes toward International Law," in *Contemporary Chinese Law: Research Problems and Perspectives*, J.A. Cohen (ed.), Cambridge: Harvard University Press, 1970, p. 287.
90 Text in UNTS 299:59 (1958).

Part IV
Peaceful rise?

10 Intentions on trial
"Peaceful Rise" and Sino-ASEAN relations

Yongnian Zheng and Sow Keat Tok

Coping with the rise of new powers in the international system appears to be one of the most intriguing exercises of international politics. This is an important issue pertinent not only to the international society at large, but also to the rising power itself which needs to come to terms with the changes in its fortune. We thus see in Thucydides' *The History of the Peloponnesian War* the intense debate relating to the rise of Athens that was as alive in the Hellenic world as within the city-state. If the collection of *The Federalist Papers* was inadequate in conveying an expression to manage America's rise in world politics (especially vis-à-vis Europe), many other policy guidelines like the Monroe Doctrine in 1823 or Woodrow Wilson's Thirteen Points, clearly contemplated the impact of the rise of the United States. These self-reflecting and soul-searching processes were found also in eighteenth-century Japan and Germany, where the intelligentsia and governing elites were locked in debates over the handling of the impending rise of each respective state. The rise of China is now set to be the new intrigue of the post-Cold War twenty-first century; Napoleon's "sleeping giant" is awakening, and while the world looks on in earnest, the giant is himself trying to come to terms with his self-perceived role in the international order.

Against this backdrop, the concept of "peaceful rise" (*heping jueqi*), or "peaceful development" in some official versions, mooted by China's fourth generation leadership positively identified the path that the world's newest power intends to follow. The concept aims at dispelling the myths of "China threat" theories that abounded in the international relations (IR) literature in the 1990s by emphasizing the peaceful way in which China could emerge as a world power. It is an active effort to provide a countervailing view to the erstwhile realism-dominated discourse by highlighting China's inherent, self-limiting, complexities, and its cultural-historical tendencies that could be translated into China's peaceful (re)introduction into the world's power structure.

Given the anxieties over China's rise in international politics, the pertinent question is: will it be possible for China to keep its word to "rise peacefully"? Commentaries have reasonably pointed out that Beijing's future handling of cross-strait relations is the critical test.[1] Indeed, few could dispute this argument. After all, with Taiwan's domestic dynamics gaining a life of their own, Beijing is now confronting rising nationalisms and growing nationalistic differences on both sides of the strait; with its diminished capacity to influence developments over the strait, war can be a very tempting option for Beijing when it comes to the crunch. So, is this "peaceful rise" rhetoric doomed to fail right from its conception? What if we have an impasse over the so-called "Taiwan issue"? Can there be other reasons to believe that China will continue with its "peaceful rise" endeavours outside the context of Taiwan Strait?

In this chapter, we attempt to go beyond the Taiwan Strait to look at how China can actively pursue its "peaceful rise" intentions. We identify the Association of Southeast Asian Nations (ASEAN) as the alternative testing ground for Beijing. We argue that – on the condition that the status quo is maintained over the strait – Beijing's approach and attitude towards Sino-ASEAN relations becomes the important litmus test to its new foreign-policy commitment. This argument is presented and substantiated in the following way.

The first section answers the questions of What, Who, How, and Why. *What* is the case presented by Beijing? *Who* are the intended audiences given the conditions under which the idea was floated? *How* does China intend to pursue this policy? And most important, *why* "peaceful rise"? These are crucial questions that require some unpacking before any meaningful assessment can be conducted. This section carries the reader through the events that can throw some light on these queries. Follow-on discussions include the significance of Beijing's new rhetoric, and raise the challenge for Beijing to "operationalize" its idea.

Through the concept of "peaceful rise," the Chinese leadership aims to send the United States a strong message, that is, that China has no capability or willingness to challenge its hegemonic position. In other words, China is for now more than willing to accept the US-defined status quo, and work within the current international structure that the US helped shape and has dominated. However, instead of directly applying the concept to Sino-US relations, the Chinese leadership appears to have chosen ASEAN as the test bed for "peaceful rise." Inevitably, the question is: why ASEAN? This section provides an analysis of the weight, and role, of ASEAN in China's foreign policy. It first briefly covers the evolution of Sino-ASEAN relations in the context of multilateralism. The main focus is directed at analysing the impact of ASEAN's corporate policy towards China since 1978, especially that of "constructive engagement" in the 1990s. We find that this policy has benefited China as well as ASEAN states, and enabled them to develop shared interests. Through the ASEAN channel, China gained access to the international space that it was punitively denied after the Tiananmen Incident, and Beijing in turn rewarded ASEAN members with trade and investment opportunities in the largely untapped China market. Even as China slowly emerges out of the shadows of Tiananmen by the turn of the century, ASEAN still carries considerable weight in Beijing's overall diplomatic and strategic interests.

The third section examines the emerging structure of Sino-ASEAN relations which is in favour of "peaceful rise." By placing the "peaceful rise" concept in the context of Sino-ASEAN multilateralism, this section explains why it is conducive to the application of Beijing's rhetoric. We argue that, beyond the friendly relationship established over the years, ASEAN's relative weakness (vis-à-vis China), together with the extensive institutionalization of the "ASEAN way," has created a favourable environment for the experimentation of "peaceful rise." Nevertheless, despite this rosy picture, China's realization of "peaceful rise" in ASEAN must ultimately meet the challenge of the uncertainties in Sino-US relations; the successful reception of the concept among ASEAN member states still hinges on an accommodating atmosphere between Beijing and Washington.

"Peaceful rise": what, who, how, and why?

> As a whole, for the next ten to twenty years, or even the first half of the twenty-first century, Asia is blessed with a historically unique opportunity to rise peacefully. China's peaceful rise is but part of Asia's peaceful rise. This not only means that the process of modernization and reform, and the rise of China, are directly connected to the experiences and developments of other Asian countries; more to that, it signifies that China, as a member of Asia, will have an increasingly positive effect on the development, prosperity and stability of other Asian countries, especially its immediate neighbours.[2]

What? First floated by China's then Vice-President of the Central Party School, Mr Zheng Bijian, to a largely Asian audience during the Boao Forum for Asia in Hainan province in 2003, the concept of "peaceful rise" provides the international audience with an introductory glimpse of China's new strategic thinking. This concept, interestingly, was later eclipsed by the concept of "peaceful development," which appeared on many key speeches and official documents. The two concepts, however, are essentially one and the same. Their share similar intellectual roots and assumptions, and basically operate on the same policy package. For fear that the word "rise" may give its intended audience the wrong impression, a milder version that emphasizes "development" is used instead, even though Zheng himself has kept alive the "peaceful rise" version in many of his speeches and writings, even till today.

The core argument begins with the assumption of the structural impediments to China's rise "with two simple equations, one involving multiplication, another of quotient." The argument goes as follows: even the most insignificant and trivial economic and social challenges would be issues of enormous magnitude when "multiplied" by 1.3 billion (China's population); likewise, seemingly limitless capital and material capability have but relative insignificance once divided by 1.3 billion. While the argument recognizes the massive potential behind the numbers, given that China has to "do its utmost" to deal with all its domestic challenges and to improve the livelihood of its people, China will likely be kept "very busy," perhaps "too busy," to harbour any wish to challenge the existing international order.[3]

The same arguments were presented by China's Premier, Wen Jiabao, during his visit to the US in early December 2003. Speaking to a Harvard congregation, he said it more blatantly: "A large population and underdevelopment are the two facts China has to face ... for China to reach the level of the developed countries, it will still take the hard work of several generations, a dozen generations, or even dozens of generations."[4] State President Hu Jintao reiterated the new concept, not once, but several times – first during a Mao Zedong commemorative function in late December 2003 in Beijing, then during his visit to France in January 2004, and then during a regular meeting of the Political Bureau in February – giving wide media attention to Beijing's shifting international philosophy.[5]

The concept recognizes and accepts the apprehension that a rising China could bring to the rest of the world. It argues that given the "inevitability" and "reality" of China's rise as a world power, the real issue lies with the Chinese attitude towards the undertaking of its new-found status and power. Beijing is increasingly conscious of the obstacles posed by "China threat" perceptions in China's membership to the league of powers. Moreover, as much as sceptics see the enormous threat China can be, they have ignored the equally huge, if not greater, opportunities China could offer to the international community.

By adopting a conciliatory posture, Beijing hopes to convey the idea that a rising China does not necessarily need to disrupt the existing international order, at least not if China conscientiously opts for a "peaceful" approach. Accepting the status quo is the key to China's peaceful rise, so the argument extends, and China has to – *must* – do just so. In short, China's "peaceful rise" presents "opportunities, not threat; status quo, not change; (co-)prosperity and progression, not instability or regression."[6] As a matter of fact, the leadership has commissioned research into the historical experiences of rising powers to explore their respective international behaviours and their subsequent impacts on the international system.

Who? The fact that "peaceful rise" was first brought up on various occasions in the international forums clearly indicates that the concept was conceived initially with external audiences in mind. This argument is geared towards alleviating the concerns over the destabilizing effects a rising China could have on the international order, a strand of thought shared by many mainstream international relations scholars, especially those from the realist tradition. The gist of the realist discourse is that all rising power, China being no exception, will eventually challenge the international power configuration since all politics are essentially the pursuit of power.[7] Indeed, Zheng Bijian's inspiration of the concept arose during his official visit to the US in December 2002, where he reportedly experienced, first-hand, the pervasive discourses of "China threat" and "China collapse" theories in the States.[8] The concept was soon accepted by the top leadership. Beijing counters the "China threat" concept by emphasizing the "peaceful" intentions of the rising Chinese nation that are underpinned by a Confucian pluralistic worldview: harmony in diversity (*he'er butong*). This thinking advocates the benevolent acceptance of differences between individuals or entities without wavering from one's own original standpoint. The term "harmony" extends to a wide interpretation that can be used to encompass reaching agreement in almost anything, which, in the case of the Chinese leadership, renders to "independently and freely develop socialism of Chinese characteristics," meanwhile embracing and being actively involving in the interconnected processes of economic globalisation.[9] In the context of Sino-US relations, this is an apparent attempt to send an important message to Washington: China, as a rising power, will not seek to challenge the US hegemonic position, even though it will continue to practise its own style of socialism.

The concept soon acquired its domestic character when Hu spoke of it on various occasions aimed at a domestic audience. Despite its early negligence towards the domestic audience, "peaceful rise" came under the spotlight as a new item on Beijing's domestic agenda. Countless discussions on the concept littered the major state dailies between December 2003 and May 2004, and as recently as October 2004, one commentator ostensibly close to Beijing contributed an article on "peaceful rise" to *Xin Bao* (Hong Kong economic journal), arguing the need to develop "comprehensive nationalistic quality" (*guojia guomin zonghe suzhi*) that encompasses "nationalistic drive that is devoted to positive undertakings, rather than that defined in narrow or xenophobic terms."[10] This again reflects Beijing's acknowledgement of the internal challenges, like rising nationalism and growing social woes, it faces in its pursuit of "peaceful rise," calling upon its people to work together to fulfill the national objective.

How? To this end, the Chinese leadership seems ready to apply the new concept to China's neighbours. In this context, Premier Wen Jiabao forwarded five guiding principles to "peaceful rise" during the Second Meeting of the Tenth National People's Congress on 14 March 2004. These five principles bear some striking resemblances to former Premier Zhou Enlai's "Five Principles of Peaceful Co-existence" that purportedly kicked off the non-alignment movement in the 1955 Bandung Conference. First, China's rise needs to take full advantage of the peaceful international environment to focus on developing and strengthening China, while at the same time utilizing the fruits of China's development to defend world peace. Second, its foundation should rest on its own independent efforts. Third, it is inseparable from the rest of the world; China must persevere in its "open-door" policy and stand by the principles of equality and reciprocity to develop economic and trade links with all friendly nations. Fourth, it is a long-term project that requires consistent efforts and attention. Fifth, it should not inconvenience, hinder, threaten, or sacrifice the interests of other nations, and will not seek domination, much less harbour hegemonic ambitions, be it in the present or in the future.[11]

In addition, this should be achieved within a "socialist market economy and democratic system" by taking in and reflecting upon the historical lessons of human civilization while propagating the Chinese culture and civilization, and by taking into account the "complexity of interests" (*gezhong liyi guanxi*) between state-local, human-environment, domestic-international, and so on.[12]

Some core elements and their respective significance from the Chinese rhetoric can be identified. The appeal to focus on economic issues may be nothing new for a world that has undergone a quarter century of China's "open door" policy and economic modernization, but for Beijing to recognize its own internal weaknesses is an interesting development in the new Chinese strategic thinking. This is a rare phenomenon by all accounts. Furthermore, this comes with Wen's subtle admission that human rights conditions in China are "not impeccable,"[13] a manifestation both of Beijing's sensitivity to the global discourse and of its changing attitude towards gradual acceptance of an international standard of human rights norms. The conciliatory tone is unmistakable. This acknowledgment, however, has a caveat, which leads to a second core element that highlights China's "differences." The argument is that if China can recognize the different value systems between itself and the rest of the world (mainly the West, though), and will try to work towards a consensus, the latter should also try to accommodate current differences and allow China the political space to work on the consensus.

Most significant, though, is China's increasing appreciation of the importance of "soft power" in modern international politics. This is probably a due realization that China lacks the legitimate tools to partake in the global discourse in its own right, for the objective reality remains that one has to speak *the* language in a largely American-dominated intellectual field.[14] Simply to assert that China can become a responsible power using a uniquely Chinese standard of civilization is ineffective in breaking down this dominance; Beijing has to nurture its soft appeal. By conflating the Confucian "harmony in diversity"[15] argument with the subject of international standards of civilization, Beijing tries to effectively create an intellectual space for itself in the global discourse, finding an unlikely but credible ally in the Western pluralist school. This serves to underscore Beijing's growing understanding that any changes that it desires have to be initiated from within the system, which in turn draws our attention to one of the preambles Beijing attaches to its rise in world politics: that it will not play the role of an antagonist to the existing order. More specifically, by first raising the issue in the US, China's leadership is in effect sending a signal to Washington that Beijing has no intention of challenging US hegemony. Compared with the United Front forged with Russia in the early post-Cold War years against US "hegemonic ambitions," Beijing's attitudinal changes towards US domination in the system are certainly remarkable.

Why? Beijing's rationale for "peaceful rise" is manifold. This can be viewed from three different levels: leadership, domestic, and international.

The "peaceful rise" concept carries with it a strong correlation to China's recent leadership transition. As a new group of leaders emerged from the sixteenth Party Congress, there appears to be an urgent need to put together a new set of ideas to guide policies. In line with the Chinese Communist Party's (CCP) teaching "to use theory to guide practice" (*lilun zhidao shijian*), the Hu-Wen fourth generation leadership is merely following a well-trodden path that Beijing's previous patriarchs have travelled. Scores of examples of such a tradition can be found in all eras since 1949. During Mao Zedong's era, the paramount leader came out with the "leaning to one side" (*yibiandao*) (alliance with the Soviet Union) of the 1950s, and to "Three Worldism" (*sange shijie*) of the 1970s. After Mao, the rise of Deng Xiaoping set in motion ideas like "Four Modernizations" and *taoguang yanghui, yousuo zuowei* (literally, "hiding one's capabilities to bide one's time while accomplishing something worthwhile"). The former was conceived in line with Deng's "open-door" policy that characterized his time in power. The latter, when first conceptualized by Deng, was a response to an emerging post-Cold War international environment characterized by the fall of communism and hostile international sentiments towards the Tiananmen Incident. The essence of Deng's philosophy was to lie low (*taoguang yanghui*) and to wait for China's turn to make a meaningful impact (*yousuo zuowei*).

When coming to the third generation leadership, Jiang Zemin inherited Deng's legacy of stressing the concept of "comprehensive power" (*zonghe guoli*) in China's external affairs. This reflected the period of China's post-Tiananmen diplomatic revival and phenomenal economic growth.[16] "Peaceful rise" is a continuation of this leadership tradition. Apparently, the new concept is related to another new concept that the fourth generation leadership raised over domestic affairs – "New Three Principles of People" (*xin sanmin zhuyi*). While trying to establish a pro-people image internally, the leadership is also making efforts to create a peace-love image externally.

Lucian Pye uses the term "symbolism" to describe such a practice, arguing that "policy questions are often floated as part of the process of consolidating power."[17] More than that, however, it offers a chance for the Hu-Wen leadership to build up a political legacy; an essential ingredient for effective leadership in the Chinese context. Only if this is done will the young leaders be able to command the huge Chinese bureaucratic machinery to respond to the bidding of the new leadership.

Besides, Beijing needs a peaceful domestic transition. After two decades of "open-door" policy, the vast demand for continuing economic growth forms part of the political reality in China today. Having tasted the fruits of economic modernization, it is now quite inconceivable for the CCP to roll back its economic reforms to return to the austerity of the immediate post-revolutionary years. The legitimacy of the regime is increasingly resting on its capability to bring in economic goods.[18]

To this end, the CCP has so far performed exceptionally. Economic growth averaged 9.4 per cent since 1979, making China one of the world's fastest-growing economies of the late twentieth century. Exports experienced an average growth of 16 per cent, and China became the world's fourth largest exporter of manufactured goods in 2003. Its foreign-exchange reserve now stands at approximately $470 billion, surpassing Japan in Asia, and second only to the US.[19] Yet on the other hand, new domestic challenges are on the rise in China, and these issues are well-documented.[20] Social issues like drug-abuse, AIDS, and moral decay exist alongside other concerns like environmental degradation, income disparities, rampant corruption, to name but a few. Beijing's efforts to alleviate these conditions through reforming its state and its socio-economic structures are often hampered by prevalent social and political practices like factionalism and vested interests. Thus far, the rise of domestic woes seems to outpace the ongoing reform processes.

In part to rein in social discontent, in part to counter the "China collapse" arguments, which highlight the dangers of China's mounting social issues, the CCP runs an aggressive campaign to introduce the "peaceful rise" concept to the domestic audience.[21] The Party is again attempting to manage the agenda by playing its economic cards. When China's leaders introduced the concept of peaceful rise to their domestic audience, they tried to send out an important message: a peaceful domestic transition (both in terms of economic and politics) is the precondition for China's rise. If China collapses, as many in the West have argued, China's rise is out of the question.

This has the effect of dampening the rising nationalistic fervour on mainland China. Especially with respect to the issue of national unification, the concept provides a framework to legitimize Beijing's more reconciliatory approach towards "domestic" disputes like Taiwan and Hong Kong. It helps to provide an ideological constraint on the strong nationalistic discourses that have dominated such policy areas. It is also part of the strategy of "winning the hearts and minds" of the people in the peripheries by emanating "benevolence" and peace from the centre. This move will set the stage for Beijing to develop itself as a responsible power from within – through legitimacy and accountability to its people.

In addition, with China fast emerging as a great power, Deng's *taoguang yanghui* philosophy was gradually perceived as an anachronism from the immediate post-Tiananmen years.[22] It became infeasible, and highly impractical, for Beijing to follow the words that were contrived for a different context. As China's growing stature is fast becoming a reality, the strategy of biding its time appears increasingly irrelevant. Mounting disillusionment with Deng's strategy requires either a philosophical alternative or reinterpretation. "Peaceful rise" is deemed the solution.

The international environment today is marked by the process of accelerated economic globalization and interdependency. China found itself posited right at the heart of these global phenomena. Beijing is beginning to grasp that while China's continuing economic success remains dependent on a benign international environment, what happens inside China will also affect the rest of the world. This impression intensified after the 9/11 tragedy. Overnight, with the images of the Twin Towers carried across the television networks and the Internet to even the most remote corners of the earth, the politically weak suddenly found themselves empowered by the latest discovery of global politics – terrorism. This, coupled with the revival of nationalism and separatist movements in the late 1990s, and the aroused US' unilateral tendencies following the 9/11 tragedy, poses a great challenge to the existing international structure. China is not excluded from this grand shift in international politics. For example, tensions in the Middle East are accentuating Beijing's anxiety. To China, this is more than an issue of energy security. While Beijing needs to concern itself with the US's aggressive Middle East policy that can potentially disrupt the flow of energy resources and threaten China's economic interests, it also has to take into account the impacts of US international activities on its ethnically and religiously diversified western provinces. Meanwhile, as China is fast becoming an important actor in global issues, Beijing is well aware of the increasing spillover effects of its domestic developments. Recent economic overheating in China shows how domestic developments can adversely affect the rest of the world. Certainly, the resource-hungry Chinese economy has contributed to the recent hike in oil prices and steel prices, too. It is to be expected that China's international weight will continue to increase with its growing economy. Faced with this new circumstance, China's top leaders felt the urgent need to actively mould its environment to suit its national goals.

Needless to say, as an aspiring power, Beijing needs the recognition of the international community in general, as English scholars have argued.[23] China is expected to live up to its role as a great power if it is to be regarded as one, and, in an interdependent world, this role includes acknowledging, respecting, and maintaining, each others' dependencies. Adding to this understanding are the challenges posed by "China threat" theories that have flooded academic and policy-making circles since the early 1990s. With the advancement of the information age, China development of what Joseph Nye termed "soft power" is deemed increasingly important.[24] Effective counters to China's negative image are urgently needed; the "peaceful rise" concept provides the means.

Between discourse and policy

Evidently, the wide agenda and the fact that new ideas are still continually being thrown into the fray suggest that the concept "peaceful rise" is still very much in its formulation and nascent stage. Given the complexity of interests in China's domestic politics, different voices will continue to articulate different versions of "peaceful rise," only to crowd the literature with even more different interpretations. One example was the idea put forward by the Vice-Chairman of the Central Military Commission (CMC), General Cao Gangchuan, in late March 2004, that "the international society needs to reciprocate by understanding and supporting China's policy to maintain its own internal social stability and territorial integrity, since China's rise is integral to the world."[25] Although this is presumably CMC's knee-jerk reaction to the brewing separatist sentiments in Taiwan following the Presidential election and referendum in 2004, some of these conflicting and shifting statements are bound to send rather confusing signals to China's international audience. In this case, is Beijing arguing that an armed conflict along Taiwan Strait should not affect international opinions towards China's peaceful intentions?

In another instance, the need to pay lip service to all these interests leads to unnecessary phrase-mongering. What does Beijing mean when it says, on one hand, that China needs to rely on its own means to "independently and autonomously" (*duli zizhu*) manage its rise, while on the other hand, insist that China's rise is "integral to" or "inseparable from" the world (*li bukai shijie*)? The readers were presumably overwhelmed and baffled by these slogans and catchphrases, wondering exactly what they allude to and how they are related to the concept. Indeed, experience with China's past philosophical approaches – United Front, Three-World theory, Five Principles of Peaceful Co-existence, "hiding one's capacity while biding one's time," to name a few – only raised more questions than answers, giving the impression that Chinese responses are often "long on rhetoric and short on critical analysis."[26]

Despite all these potential confusions, policy discourse matters in the context of Chinese politics. Earlier on, Lucian Pye pointed out the fact that Chinese leaders, being expected to fulfil policy-initiation roles, often "act out of inspiration rather than in response to bureaucratically defined problems ... Thus, pronouncements of policy usually occur before feasibility has been determined." Yet Pye also reminded us of the importance of such rhetoric. He observed, "The use of extensive ceremony when advancing new policies accentuates, and also explains, the symbolic uses to which the new programs can be put ... The initiation of a new program usually starts with a symbolic slogan ... the proclamation from on high alerts lesser cadres to what at least some elements of the elite consider to be good."[27]

In other words, given the benefit of the doubt, the Chinese leadership is probably sincere about leading China to "rise peacefully." But considering the nature of Chinese politics – the gap between political symbolism and policy implementation – the real test for the "peaceful rise" concept is to "operationalize" the concept, that is, convert rhetoric to action. Without further elaborations backed by concrete action from Beijing, excessive rhetoric will only continue to frustrate observers, both within and outside China alike.

ASEAN as the test bed to China's "peaceful rise"

So, to whom can Beijing carry its words? How can China convince others about its cause? The answers to these questions lie not too far away: Southeast Asia. While "peaceful rise" remains to be tested in the context of Sino-US relations, the Chinese leadership appears keen to apply the concept to augment China's existing policy of good neighbourliness, particularly that vis-à-vis ASEAN. Indeed, many existing factors in Sino-ASEAN relations make it conducive for Beijing to first test the concept in its immediate neighbourhood.

Structural factors

Southeast Asia has been an important region in China's foreign policy as far as recent memories are concerned. Not only does China share the same Asian land mass as Southeast Asia, the latter's narrow strategic waterways have, for centuries, been the most important maritime gateways for China's link with the West. This geographical proximity is readily translated to close trade and demographical links following centuries of interaction. Southeast Asia's trade links with China can be traced back to the times of Chinese imperial courts, and the region is China's fifth largest trading partner today. Meanwhile, the demographical and cultural dimensions of the relationship are underpinned by the millions of ethnic Chinese who have, over the centuries, migrated to, and assumed citizenship in, many Southeast Asian states.

Southeast Asia then became a contested region in Cold War politics. During the early days before the Beijing–Moscow schism, promotion of socialist revolution in Southeast Asia states, most of which were then colonies of the western powers, fell within the responsibility of Mao Zedong's regime. It is thus no surprise that for the first two-and-a-half decades after the establishment of the People's Republic of China (PRC), ideological and ethnic contradictions marred Sino-Southeast Asian relations. In fact, barring a short decade of diplomatic honeymoon between Mao's China and Sukarno's Indonesia right up till 1965, and notwithstanding China's logistical support for Vietnam during the early days of the Vietnam War, China's relations with the rest of the Southeast Asian states have been controversial at best. Beijing's policies after 1949, often seen as "erratic and often ambiguous," did little to assure the political leaders of Southeast Asia.[28] PRC's efforts to provide material and moral support for various communist insurgencies plagued regimes in Southeast Asia lasted through the 1950s to the 1980s.[29] In other words, while China diplomatically gained little ground, if any at all, in Southeast Asia during the pre-ASEAN days, Southeast Asia was then a focal point in Beijing's pan-Asian ideological campaign and, therefore, its political attention, especially given the geographical and demographical intimacy.

When ASEAN was formed in 1967 out of the wave of decolonization in Southeast Asia and the *Confrontasi*, Beijing had little to do with the Association, denouncing the latter as a "reactionary military alliance" directed against China, and whose members were derided by Beijing as "stooges of the West."[30] This early animosity was, however, interrupted by Richard Nixon's visit to China and the resulting Shanghai Communiqué in 1972. Already deeply alarmed in the late 1960s by the British "East-of-Suez" policy, as well as by the Guam Doctrine, which were seen as Western withdrawal from Southeast Asia, the humiliating defeat of the US in Vietnam and an imminent communist victory in Indochina struck fear in the original ASEAN member states. For many of these states, the sustaining of their newfound nationhood and the maintenance of a stable regional order amid great power interests became important tasks. China was deemed a decisive variable in the pursuit of these objectives. Thus, in May 1974, Malaysia became the first of the original ASEAN member state to establish a diplomatic relationship with China. This was followed closely by the Philippines (June 1975) and Thailand (July 1975),[31] paving the way for Deng Xiaoping's whirlwind tour of Southeast Asia in late 1978, during which he acquired a tacit agreement from most ASEAN members to conduct punitive action against Vietnam in January 1979. By the early 1980s, Beijing's ASEAN policy became the next most important expression of China's foreign policy towards the Cold War ideological divide outside the Sino-US–Soviet Union nexus, culminating in a 1982 declaration by then-Premier Zhao Ziyang to cease all material support to Southeast Asian communist parties. Zhao also promised that Beijing's relations with these parties would not affect existing friendly relations with Southeast Asian states.[32]

ASEAN's status in China's foreign policy was then raised to an unprecedented level in the aftermath of the Tiananmen Incident. The draconian measures taken during the students' movement in 1989 discredited China's hitherto untarnished image as a progressive, reformist, communist state. This was followed by the dissolution of virtually every communist regime in Eastern Europe in the latter half of the year, and eventually, the collapse of the Soviet Union in 1991. By then, China found itself in an unfamiliar international position: whereas in early 1989 it was still hailed as the most boldly reforming communist state, by 1990 it was "widely regarded as an international outlaw, ruled by retrograde communists who would massacre their own citizens in order to maintain their outmoded grip on power."[33] External and domestic pressures mounted, and many western countries, including the US, imposed economic sanctions and terminated all high-level talks and military exchanges with China. These events, however, had not affected Sino-ASEAN relations; as a matter of fact, Sino-ASEAN relations were "greatly improved after the Tiananmen Incident." This can be observed through Beijing's re-establishment of diplomatic ties with Indonesia in 1990, and the exchange of embassies with Singapore and Brunei (the latter joined ASEAN in 1984), in 1991. There were also frequent high-profile state visits between China and ASEAN leaderships in late 1989 and 1990.[34]

Thus, in perhaps the most challenging moments since its "open-door" policy, Beijing expanded its international reaches through ASEAN: China gained observer status in ASEAN in 1992, joined the ASEAN Regional Forum (ARF) upon its launching in 1994, becoming a full dialogue partner of ASEAN in 1996, and participated in the ASEAN+3 Summit upon its inauguration, which paved the way for the ASEAN–China Summit, in 1997, among others.[35] Also, ASEAN has from the beginning strongly backed China's bid to join the WTO. ASEAN thus positioned itself as a staunch supporter of China and chose the path of "constructive engagement" when the latter was desperately in need of international space.[36] Beijing will not easily forget this cause for gratitude.

Furthermore, this was apparently not a one-sided affair, as the parties found common agendas to lend each other support against "outsiders." Pressure exerted by the west on the issues of human rights and democracy precipitated a consensus between China and ASEAN. By the early 1990s, China and ASEAN began to bandwagon against western intervention in internal affairs, rallying around the notion of "Asian value." In the Bangkok Summit Declaration in 1995, China endorsed the affirmation to "economic growth, community interests, non-interference ... and respect for each other's different socio-economic, historical, and cultural background."[37] In the issue of Myanmar, Beijing and ASEAN are experiencing convergence of interests as both "put national security above concern with human rights in neighbouring countries."[38] As these political exchanges deepened, ASEAN gradually became a stage for Beijing to showcase its benign intentions and cooperative behaviour.

It is also worthy to note that the rapid expansion of ASEAN between 1995 and 1999 to include Vietnam (joined 1995), Laos, Myanmar (both 1997) and Cambodia (1999) reintroduced the geo-strategic component to Beijing's perception towards the region and the Association. In the earlier days of ASEAN, none of its member states actually share a common land border with mainland China (though there were shared maritime boundaries); the inclusion of the four mainland Southeast Asian states changed all that. While these land boundaries, when considered individually, are considerably less than that shared between China and Russia (3,645 km), or between China and India (3,380 km), they form a contiguous border that stretches 3,889 km, by far the longest land border China shares with any single political bloc today.[39] Some of these borders are still contested by various parties, and the delicate ethnic and cultural issues that exist across these state boundaries are still haunting regimes on both sides. This is in addition to outstanding maritime issues in the South China Sea. Faced with a strengthened ASEAN bloc, China will have to devote more resources to these questions than ever before.

Contextual factors

Considering the weight of ASEAN in Beijing's foreign policy, the Association appears to be a natural platform for Beijing to stage its bid for "peaceful rise." But so far, the argument presented does not explain why Beijing *should* do so. Why does Beijing not test the concept to its other important relations like Russia and Central Asia, the European Union (EU), Latin America, or even Africa, for that matter? Two main contextual factors have dictated Beijing's choice.

First, is China's economic rise. The economy is a subject that carries a huge security dimension in both China and ASEAN, and their respective views on this issue are by no means contradictory. Compared with other areas such as strategic and military affairs, economics is an important area where both China's and ASEAN's interests overlap. It is thus unsurprising that at the centre of these intensifying political engagements was the increasing interdependency between the two regional economies.

China's economic rise seems to have been in favour of ASEAN's economic considerations. Within ASEAN, security policies of the various states are far from unified and homogeneous. This can be attributed to the region's diverse historical experiences and demographic compositions, such that each state has its own characterizing strategic perception, some overlapping, some entirely unique.[40] Within this diversity, however, there exists a common, overwhelming, desire to maintain a sense of "regional order" that is independent of external influence and is conducive to national and domestic developments. The main security functions of ASEAN, as Shaun Narine describes, are to "benefit economic development in the member states and by extension, contribute to political stability by helping to alleviate the domestic social conditions nurturing communist insurgency," as well as to "make its members less vulnerable to the machinations or outside powers."[41] This is based on the "belief that local disputes were wasteful and self-defeating" and that "(p)olitical consultation to resolve local problems and to present a united front against external challenges would enhance the ability of each state to ensure its own integrity."[42] The idea of "ASEAN" is thus built on the objective to maintain an ordered externality, which the ruling elite perceive as key to stable internal environments. The political legitimacy and longevity of the respective regimes in ASEAN thrive with the presence of such "order," and are augmented by achieving a perceptible level of economic well-being. The latter task is, in turn, made possible only with a stability-induced investing environment.[43]

This common outlook has a bearing on the united security policy fronts of ASEAN and its activities. China would technically become the world's largest economy in the year 2010 and is thus an important economic partner for ASEAN into the twenty-first century.[44] In absolute terms, mutual trade between China and ASEAN has expanded tremendously. It grew an average of 20 per cent annually since 1990, reaching $78.3 billion in 2003, and is expected to pass the $100 billion mark in 2005.[45] Moreover, China is gradually establishing itself as a stabilizer in regional economic development. The 1997 Asian economic crisis all but entrenched its role as a responsible economic player in the ASEAN community. Distressed by the tepid response from the US towards the economic crisis, and IMF's draconian intervention in regional economies, Beijing's move not to devalue the *yuan* came as a long-awaited relief to ASEAN. This move was followed by Beijing's $1 billion financial assistance to Thailand, and $4–6 billion for the IMF programmes to support Southeast Asia.[46]

This economic relation is again a two-way exchange. China's domestic situation is quite similar to that faced by ASEAN states: both sides are counting on their ability to continue to bring in economic goods to sustain their respective domestic legitimacy. This shared experience could have bolstered the efforts of the two parties to engage each other in the pursuit of common interests. No doubt, ASEAN has never been, and perhaps may never be, the top economic partner of China; as a trading partner, the Association has consistently hovered in the mid-table of China's top-ten trading nations in the last decade; as an investor, it currently accounts for about 6.5 per cent of China's total paid-up investments, less than that from Hong Kong, Taiwan, and Japan.[47] But to China, ASEAN's significance is not so much an issue of absolute numbers. It is all about the timing and nature of economic exchanges.

ASEAN intensified its economic links with China at the time when the latter was still scorned by the West in the early 1990s. For example, in terms of foreign direct investment (FDI), a group of researchers in Hong Kong pointed out that "China's FDI had increased by 13-fold in terms of real value between 1990 and 1997, but FDI from ASEAN had increased by 57 times … Investment from ASEAN has become increasingly important since 1992."[48] The fact that ASEAN is formed by a collection of relatively small, developing, states in China's geographical vicinity can only make this economic relation politically more significant. While what ASEAN's deepened engagement with China in the early years after Tiananmen could be no more than a choice made out of practical consideration of their respective national interests, from Beijing's perspective, the worth of every dollar made out of Sino-ASEAN economic exchange may well make up for many times that value when trading with either Japan or the US.

Then it comes to the mutual accommodation of the ASEAN way and Chinese multilateralism. Beijing has so far played its role as a "responsible power" well; it now has to maintain its hard-earned creditability by acting even more "responsibly" in regional affairs. The nature of Sino-ASEAN relations presents a typical big-power-versus-small-states scenario. There is little question that China will carry more weight when dealing with ASEAN than with other political and economic blocs or major powers. Moreover, as is ever being emphasized, the physical intimacy between China and Southeast Asian is a geo-strategic reality. It is thus far easier for Beijing to earn credit for its peaceful rhetoric by showering goodwill on states that it is in the position to threaten directly, as opposed to those out of its reach. As S.D. Muni was quoted, "China's close relations with the new ASEAN members enables [sic] it to 'project itself as a stabilizing force and mature power in the Asia-Pacific region.'"[49]

Moreover, the nature of ASEAN as a regional multilateral organization helps to promote Beijing's "peaceful rise" agenda. ASEAN's emphasis on economic issues sits nicely in the basic thrust of Beijing's rhetoric: the need for the Chinese leadership to satisfy domestic demands and meet domestic challenges through economic modernization; due to China's inherent weaknesses, this will be a long process and will exhaust China's national efforts to pursue other courses of activities. This complementarity in both ASEAN's and Beijing's interest has obviously prompted the China–ASEAN Free Trade Agreement (CAFTA), and is bound to be given greater emphasis in the years ahead.

The dedication to the so-called "ASEAN Way" adds the icing to the Sino-ASEAN relations cake under "peaceful rise." By "ASEAN Way," it basically refers to an informal code of conduct established to help to alleviate the historical animosity and suspicion among ASEAN member states during the early days of the Association. In the words of Rodolfo Severino, Secretary-General of ASEAN,

> Southeast Asians' way of dealing with one another has been through manifestations of goodwill and the slow winning and giving of trust. And the way to arrive at agreements has been through consultation and consensus – *mushawara* and *mufakat* – rather than across-the-table negotiations involving bargaining and give-and-take that result in deals enforceable in a court of law.[50]

This approach involves some of the most highly ritualized processes that are consistent with core Southeast Asian cultural values: non-confrontational, sensitive, behind-the-door, elitist politics and negotiations, and non-legalistic. The focus is on the *means* of achieving goals, and not on the goals themselves.[51] China has long discovered the merits of this framework of interaction and decision-making, and has grown to be comfortable with it.[52] To Beijing, the ASEAN Way promotes more than just a simple multilateral approach – yet another thrust in the "peaceful rise" rhetoric – it enables Beijing to enjoy a certain level of anonymity, and hence, flexibility, in its involvement. Besides, this is one platform that has commanded the ears of major powers with interests in the region. Compared with the more transparent processes in the United Nations Security Council, China is able to engage both ASEAN members states and their major dialogue partners like the US, Russia, EU, Japan and India in a more discreet manner as it feels its way towards the path of "peaceful rise."

Towards the end of "operationalizing" the "peaceful rise" concept in ASEAN, Beijing may be expected to pursue several policies at the same time. Beijing's future economic decisions certainly will be major concerns to ASEAN. Coincidentally, China's economic boom in the late 1990s corresponded with the Asian financial crisis; the shrinking of the Southeast Asian economy and the collapse of the East Asian economic miracle raised the fear that China's economy will hollow out other Southeast Asian economies. Already, Beijing is trying ways to allay such fears; as mentioned, resisting the temptation to devalue the *yuan* and initiating the CAFTA, being two instances. These are in turn built on a growing Sino-ASEAN trade in favour of the latter, and Beijing's "going out" (走出去 *zou chuqu*) policy: an effort to encourage Chinese enterprises to invest overseas. By the last count in 2003, China ran a total of $16.4 billion trade deficit with ASEAN; as a latecomer in the FDI business, China's total investment in ASEAN passed $941.1 million, or eight per cent of all China's investment overseas.[53] Continuing such sound and responsible financial and macroeconomic policies which could benefit Beijing's ASEAN partners will definitely be crucial to winning the hearts and minds of these governments and their peoples.

Needless to say, Taiwan will be a complication. As far as Beijing is concerned, Taiwan remains a domestic issue and is barred from all official discussions in international forums. However, with globalization of the world's economy, it is almost impossible for any national economies, let alone neighbouring ASEAN economies, not to suffer the repercussions of a Taiwan Strait conflict, should such an event occur. The world community has a keen interest in the Taiwan issue. To Beijing's benefit, Taiwan is already an item on the ARF unofficial agenda – that is to say, the issue is discussed at private meetings during the forum but the conclusions are not made public. In the recent Taiwanese Presidential election in 2004, Beijing also changed its position to engage Washington over Strait affairs. These are positive moves, but greater assurances could be offered to the international community. The ARF presents by far the best platform to do so. At the least, discussions on the Taiwan issue can be made more transparent through issuing statements, and, given the nature of the ASEAN Way, this should not hurt China's core national interests in any way that Beijing may have perceived.

Beijing–Washington mutual accommodation?

"Peaceful rise" in Sino-ASEAN relations, nevertheless, will have to endure the test of developments in Sino-US relations. The pertinent question is: can China and the United States accommodate each other in ASEAN?

In April 2002, then-Prime Minister of Singapore, Goh Chok Tong was quoted, speaking to Hu Jintao, who was then Vice-President of China "... the US–China relationship is crucial. If this relationship is stable, it will have a calming effect on the entire region. If it is upset, it will unsettle the region."[54] This indicates an understanding among ASEAN leaders that stability of post-Cold War Southeast Asia rests heavily, if not solely, on Sino-US relationship. To translate to the context of this discussion, the state of Sino-US relationship will determine if Beijing will be able to operationalize its "peaceful rise" in Southeast Asia. In its bid to greatness, China will undoubtedly face many difficult choices. At the end of the day, will Beijing accept a prominent US presence, or will it try to diminish US influence? Will China cooperate with the US, or thwart all efforts to maintain a regional order? While these questions do not imply that China has to play second-fiddle to the US in regional matters, China needs to keenly seek US participation or endorsement. This should alleviate the fear that a rising China would of its own accord upset the current great power structure in the region. Notwithstanding existing ASEAN institutions like the ASEAN Summits, the ARF, ASEAN+3, others like the Asia-Pacific Economic Cooperation (APEC), the Six-Party Talks on North Korea and the many regional Track-Two mechanisms can all serve to engage the US by initiating collective policies.

Apparently, Washington's response to China's peaceful overtures remains a key issue. In the end, it is one thing for Beijing to extend its olive branch, it is another thing for Washington to accept it; it takes two to make things happen. Randell Scheweller has warned that to deprive a rising power of a stake is to run the danger of nurturing a dissatisfied, maybe even revolutionary, actor in the system.[55] If the most powerful nation on earth today were to treat China as a threat it could well end by creating what it fears.

Though still a long way from the hyped-up depiction of the superpower rivalry of the twenty-first century, there are many issues that have the potential to rupture Sino-US relations. It is fortunate that Sino-US relations are "at their best" for more than 30 years, as then-Secretary of State Colin Powell proclaimed in September 2003,[56] and Beijing could well capitalize on this cordial opportunity while it lasts. The outlook was not so rosy, when the Bush administration first came to office in 2000. The neo-conservative tendencies in the US administration indulged in a world vision in which US hegemony would be unchallenged, a *Pax Americana* that would seek to stifle competitors before they emerged.[57] This naturally translates to skepticism about China's rise as a power.[58] In view of this bad start, the 9/11 incident may be seen as a blessing in disguise for Sino-US relations. Almost overnight, China was transformed from a strategic competitor to a strategic partner in the US war on terror. China is still an important coordinator to a resolution of the Korean Peninsula nuclear crisis. In fact, the outlook is so optimistic at this moment that in the 2004 run-up to the US Presidential election, "China-bashing," a common campaign strategy in the previous campaigns, has never materialized as a campaign issue.

Nonetheless, this is a window of opportunity that may not last forever. For all the goodwill that exists between Beijing and Washington today, a cruel fact remains: as long as China is not perceived as a democracy by Washington's power brokers, Beijing faces the uphill task of convincing its counterparts of its "peaceful" intentions. This was the case in the pre-Tiananmen years; this continues to be the case today. Especially following Taiwan's Presidential election and referendum – notwithstanding the legitimacy of the results – authoritarianism on mainland China now stands in even sharper contrast to the budding democratic polity on Taiwan. Besides, this is but one of many outstanding issues, from trade imbalances to military build-up, between Beijing and Washington today.

A confrontation of whichever sort between China and the US will certainly undermine the existing regional order in Southeast Asia. An intensified Sino-US rivalry will pose great difficulties for the ASEAN states, as the latter will have less room to manoeuvre, and may be forced to make a choice between the two. In this trial, the US could be *the* wild card and the ensuing Sino-US relationship will persistently return to haunt Sino-ASEAN relations under "peaceful rise."

Concluding remarks

The "peaceful rise" concept is an interesting phenomenon in China's foreign policy. Through the concept, we are observing a China that is beginning to come out of its shell to adopt an internationalist agenda. It reflects, to a certain degree, its appreciation of the workings of the post-Cold War international society. Beijing acknowledges, as it has never done before, the potential threat that China can be to the rest of the world, and with that, it relates the role that it intends to play in the foreseeable future. "Peaceful rise" is a commitment to respecting the international structure and adhering to existing international norms in China's pursuit of great power status. Not only is this a far cry from the stubborn assertions that Beijing used to deliver in the past, this is also a refreshing shift from the simmering Sino-US rivalry following the Tiananmen incident and the collapse of the Soviet Union.

Beyond rhetoric, though, Beijing urgently needs to inject more credit into its new promise, and creditability is something that has to be earned. The task at hand is to translate the "peaceful rise" rhetoric into real policy initiatives. Due to the unique structural and contextual nature of Sino-ASEAN relations, ASEAN could be an ideal testing ground for Beijing to operationalize this concept. The common outlook shared by Beijing and the other capitals of ASEAN member states, the interests of major powers towards the region, the institution of the ASEAN Way, to name but a few, all contribute to a conducive environment in which China can have a freer hand to forward the corresponding programmes.

So, is ASEAN no more than an utilitarian afterthought in Beijing's foreign policy? This question is undoubtedly pertinent to our exploration of China's new international philosophy, but, as of now, is difficult to answer. Although some scholars (as in this volume) have argued that, for China, engaging ASEAN has become valued in itself, this chapter has not taken up the challenge to answer beyond Beijing's more realistic considerations. Till today, it remains questionable if ASEAN has effectively transformed itself from its origins as a Cold War organization to one that can tackle post-Cold War issues. Its failure to act as a corporate whole during the Asian financial crisis, for example, underlines ASEAN's struggle with its new agenda. Until ASEAN steers clear of its organizational lethargy, this question shall be left open for further observations.

Can China eventually make true its words in its relationship with ASEAN? Many challenges lie ahead, but it may eventually boil down to the shape of Sino-US relations. While Beijing can confidently push the initiatives in other issues – including the Taiwan Strait – the highly complex nature of the Sino-US relationship spells that the success of a Chinese experimentation of "peaceful rise" may not entirely rest in Beijing's hands. The underlying tensions and contradictions between the two great powers make it difficult for Beijing to make a reality of its peaceful overtures. This worry may be overstated, given the cordiality of the two nations in the past years, but it will be, without question, the most decisive variable in China's bid to "peaceful rise," much as it is to ASEAN, as well as to the rest of the world.

Notes

1 See, for example, Zhenhai Qiu, "Call for New Thinking in Beijing's Hong Kong and Taiwan Policies," *Lianhe Zaobao*, Singapore, 20 January 2004; Yan Chen. "Speaking of China's 'Peaceful Rise'," *Xin Pao*, Hong Kong, 21 January 2004; Frank Ching, "China's Actions must Match its Words," *Business Times*, Singapore, 27 February 2004.
2 Zheng Bijian, "The New Path of China's Peaceful Rise and the Future of Asia," (translated by authors) speech delivered during Boao Forum for Asia, 31 October–4 November 2003. Chinese transcript available at www.cas/as/cn/html/Dir/2003/12/25/0112.htm (accessed 17 February 2004).
3 Ibid.
4 Wen Jiabao, "Turning Your Eyes to China," speech delivered at Harvard 10 December 2003. English transcript available at the website of Ministry of Foreign Affairs of the People's Republic of China. Online. Available: www.fmprc.gov.cn/eng/ (accessed 17 February 2004).
5 "Hu Jintao: Speech During a Seminar Conducted in Commemoration of the 110th Birth Anniversary of Comrade Mao Zedong," *Xinhua News Agency*, 26 December 2003. In Hu's speech during the opening of Boao Forum for Asia in April 2004, he mentioned the word "peace" on no less than 11 occasions. See "Full text of Hu Jintao's Speech at BFA Annual Conference 2004," china.org.cn. Online. Available: www.china.org.cn/english/features/93897.htm (accessed 5 July 2004).
6 Wen, op. cit.
7 Or "survival" in the case of neorealist. See Hans J. Morgenthau, *Politics Among Nations: The Struggle for Power and Peace*, 6th edn, New York: Alfred A. Knopf, 1985; A.F.K. Organski, *World Politics*, New York: Alfred A. Knopf, 1968; for a

neorealist account, see Kenneth Waltz, *Theory of International Politics*, Reading, Mass.: Addison-Wesley, 1979.

8 "Heping jueqi: Zhongguo tese shehui zhuyi de yige jiqi zhongyao di Zhongguo tese" (Peaceful Rise: An Important Chinese Characteristic of Socialism with Chinese Characteristics), an interview with Zheng Bijian, *Study Times*, no. 239, 14 June 2004, p. 1.

9 This has been the common component in the speeches of Zheng *et al.*, op. cit.

10 Huiwen Ren, "The Bumpy Road to China's Rise" (translated by authors), *Xin Pao*, Hong Kong, 22 October 2004.

11 "Questions and Answers of Wen Jiabao's Press Conference," *Xinhua Net*, 15 March 2004. Online. Available: news.xinhuanet.com/newscenter/2004–03/15/content_ 1365856_1.htm (accessed 8 June 2004).

12 "Zheng Bijian: The New Path of China's Peaceful Rise" (translated by authors), *Wen Wei Po*, Hong Kong, 21 March 2004.

13 Wen, "Turning Your Eyes to China."

14 For an interesting discussion of this issue, see Robert M.A. Crawford and Darryl S.L. Jarvis (eds) *International Relations – Still an American Social Science?: Toward Diversity in International Thought*, Albany, NY: State University of New York Press, 2001.

15 Wen Jiabao, "Vigorously Pushing Forward the Constructive and Cooperative Relationship between China and the United States – In commemoration of the 25th Anniversary of China–US Diplomatic Relations" (translated by Zhou Wenzhong), 7 February 2004, English transcript available at the website of Ministry of Foreign Affairs of the People's Republic of China. Online. Available: www. fmprc.gov.cn/eng/ (accessed 9 February 2004).

16 For a discussion of the concept of "comprehensive national power," see Yongnian Zheng, *Discovering Chinese Nationalism in China*, Cambridge: Cambridge University Press, 1997, pp. 114–22.

17 Lucian W. Pye, *The Dynamics of Chinese Politics*, Cambridge, Mass.: Oelgeschlager, Gunn and Hain, 1981, p. 159.

18 Guoguang Wu, "Legitimacy Crisis, Political Economy, and the Fifteenth Party Congress," in Andrew J. Nathan, Zhaohui Hong and Steven Smith (eds) *Dilemmas of Reform in Jiang Zemin's China*, Boulder, Colo.: Lynne Rienner Publishers, 1999, p. 14.

19 Figure as of June 2004, available on the website of The People's Bank of China. Online. Available: www.pbc.gov.cn/english/diaochatongji/tongjishuju/gofile.asp?file=2004S6.htm (accessed 2 November 2004).

20 For more comprehensive discussions on China's internal challenges and their impacts, see Elizabeth J. Perry and Mark Selden (eds) *Chinese Society: Change Conflict and Resistance*, New York: Routledge, 2000; Gungwu Wang and Yongnian Zheng, *Reform, Legitimacy and Dilemmas: China's Politics and Society*, Singapore: Singapore University Press and World Scientific, 2000; Shaoguang Wang, "The Social and Political Implications of China's WTO Membership," *Journal of Contemporary China*, vol. 9: 25, 2000, pp. 373–405.

21 For an example of the "China collapse" theories, see Gordon G. Chang, *The Coming Collapse of China*, New York: Random House, 2001.

22 "Zhong Weizhi: The Debate for China's *Taoguang Yanghui* Strategy Becoming More Intense," *Chinese News Net*, 28 March 2003. Online. Available: www1.chinesenewsnet.com/gb/MainNews/Opinion/2003_3_27_21_22_33_414.html (accessed 30 March 2004).

23 See Hedley Bull, *The Anarchical Society: A Study of Order in World Politics*, 3rd edn, Basingstoke: Palgrave Macmillan, 2002.

24 Joseph S. Nye, Jr, *Bound to Lead: The Changing Nature of American Power*, New York: Basic Books, 1990, ch. 1, 6; see also Joseph S. Nye, Jr, *The Paradox of Amer-*

ican Power: Why the World's Only Superpower Can't Go It Alone, New York: Oxford University Press, 2002, pp. 4–12.
25 "Cao Gangchuan's Speech in Thailand: China is Determined to Rise Through Peaceful Means" (translated by authors), *Zhongguo Wang* (China Net), 31 March 2004. Online. Available: www.china.org.cn/chinese/zhuanti/hp/531266.htm (accessed 12 April 2004).
26 Herbert Yee and Ian Storey (eds) *The China Threat: Perceptions, Myths and Reality*, London: RoutledgeCurzon, 2002, 11.
27 Pye, op. cit., 164–74.
28 Peter Polomka, "ASEAN Perspective on China: Implications for Western Interests," *The Australian Journal of Chinese Affairs* 0: 8, July 1982, pp. 86–7.
29 Robert A. Scalapino, "China's Role in Southeast Asia," in Richard L. Grant (ed.) *China and Southeast Asia: Into the Twenty-first Century*, Washington: CSIS, 1993, p. 61.
30 Muthiah Alagappa, "The Major Powers and Southeast Asia," *International Journal* XLVI, Summer 1989, p. 565.
31 Because of ASEAN's complex relationship with China, it is useful to look at the diplomatic history of Sino-ASEAN relationship through the association's expansion over the years. Technically, Indonesia established diplomatic ties with China in April 1950, though the relationship summarily broke down following the *Gestapu* (acronym for *Gerakan September Tiga Puluh*, literally "Thirtieth of September Movement") Incident in 1965. Thus at the time when ASEAN was established, no member state of the founding ASEAN-5 (Indonesia, Malaysia, Philippines, Singapore, and Thailand) had official representations in Beijing. Meanwhile, other current members like Vietnam (January 1950), Myanmar (June 1950), Cambodia (July 1958), Laos (April 1961) all established diplomatic ties with Beijing well before most of the founding members, but did not join the association until the 1990s.
32 John W. Garver, *Foreign Relations of the People's Republic of China*, New Jersey: Prentice Hall, 1993, pp. 166–7.
33 Kenneth Lieberthal, *Governing China*, New York: Norton & Co, 1995, p. 332; see also Denny Roy, "The 'China Threat' Issue," *Asian Survey* 36: 8, August 1996, p. 758.
34 Lai To Lee, "Domestic Changes in China since the 4 June Incident," *Contemporary Southeast Asia* 13: 1, June 1991, pp. 37, 40.
35 See Mely Caballero-Anthony, "Major Milestone in ASEAN–China Relations," *Perspectives*, Singapore: Institute of Defence and Strategic Studies, November 2002. Online. Available: www.ntu.edu.sg/idss/Perspective/Research_050230.htm (accessed 1 November 2004).
36 Segal, Gerald, "East Asia and the 'Constrainment' of China," *International Security* 20: 4, Spring 1996, pp. 107–35; Ian J. Storey, "Living With the Colossus: How Southeast Asian Countries Cope With China," *Parameters*, Winter 1999/2000. Online. Available: global.umi.com (accessed 22 May 2002).
37 Quoted in, Joseph Y.S. Cheng, "Sino-ASEAN relations in the Early Twenty-first Century," *Contemporary Southeast Asia* 23: 3, December 2001, p. 422. See also Allan S. Whiting, "ASEAN Eyes China: The Security Dimension," *Asian Survey* 37: 4, April 1997, p. 301; Lai To Lee, "ASEAN–PRC Political and Security Cooperation: Problems, Proposals, and Prospects," *Asian Survey* 33: 11, November 1993, p. 1103; Stephen A. Douglas and Sara U. Douglas, "Economic Implications of the US–ASEAN Discourse on Human Rights," *Pacific Affairs* 69: 1, Spring 1996, pp. 71–87.
38 Wayne Bert, "Chinese Policies and US Interests in Southeast Asia," *Asian Survey*, 33: 3, March 1993, p. 331.
39 The figure is derived from the sum of all land borders China shares with Vietnam (1,281 km), Laos (423 km), and Myanmar (2,185 km), according to Central

Intelligence Agency, *The World Factbook 2004*. Online. Available: www.cia.gov/cia/publications/factbook/geos/ch.html#Geo (accessed 1 November 2004).
40 For good overviews on the (internal and external) security perceptions of ASEAN and its member states, refer to Justus M. van der Kroef, "ASEAN's Security Needs and Policies," *Pacific Affairs* 47: 2, Summer 1974, pp. 154– 70; Jusuf Wanandi, "Politico-Security Dimensions of Southeast Asia," *Asian Survey* 17: 8, August 1977, pp. 771–92; Sheldon W. Simon, "ASEAN's Strategic Situation in the 1980s," *Pacific Affairs* 60: 1, Spring 1987, pp. 73–93; Leszek Buszynski, "Southeast Asia in the Post-Cold War Era: Regionalism and Security," *Asian Survey* 32: 9, September 1992, pp. 830–47; Robert O. Tilman, *The Enemy Beyond: External Threat Perceptions in the ASEAN Region*, Singapore: ISEAS, 1984.
41 Shaun Narine, "ASEAN and the Management of Regional Security," *Pacific Affairs* 71: 2, Summer 1998, p. 196.
42 Shelton W. Simon, "ASEAN Security in the 1990s," *Asian Survey* 29: 6, June 1989, p. 581.
43 Tim Huxley, "Southeast Asia in the Study of International Relations: the Rise and Decline of a Region," *Pacific Review* 9: 2, 1996, pp. 211–12, 218. See also Amitav Acharya, *The Quest for Identity: International Relations of Southeast Asia*, Singapore: Oxford University Press, 2000, pp. 51–63.
44 In Allan Collins' words, "China's economic growth and its future potential has enabled China to have a direct bearing on the stability of ASEAN economies." See Allan Collins, *The Security Dilemmas of Southeast Asia*, New York: St Martin's Press, 2000, p. 138; Michael Yahuda, *The International Politics of Asia Pacific 1945–1995*, London: Routledge, 1996, p. 189.
45 Statistics tabulated based on data extracted from Ministry of Commerce of the People's Republic of China. Online. Available: www.mofcom.gov.cn/jinchukou2003.shtml, and a presentation made by Zhou Hongli, "ASEAN–China: The New Economic Partnership," February 2004. Online. Available: sg.mofcom.gov.cn/table/cafta_final.ppt (both accessed 2 November 2004).
46 Cheng, op. cit., 425; Vassily Mikheev, "The Financial Crisis in Asia and Its Economic and Political Consequences," *Far Eastern Affairs* 2, 1998, p. 52.
47 Zhou, op. cit.
48 Mee Kau Nyaw, Gordon Chi Kai Cheung, and Chak Yan Chang, "Money Migration: An Assessment of ASEAN's Investment in China with Special Reference to Overseas Chinese Investment After 1979," *Journal of World Investment* 2: 3, September 2001, pp. 439–55.
49 Amitav Acharya, "Seeking Security in the Dragon's Shadow: China and Southeast Asia in the Emerging Asian Order," *IDSS Working Paper No. 44*, Singapore: Institute of Defence and Strategic Studies, 2003, p. 15.
50 Rodolfo C. Severino, "The ASEAN Way and the Rule of Law," address delivered at the International Law Conference on ASEAN Legal Systems and Regional Integration, Kuala Lumpur, 3 September 2001. Online. Available: www.aseansec.org/2849.htm (accessed 2 November 2004).
51 Hadi Soesastro (ed.) *ASEAN in a Changed Regional and International Political Economy*, Jakarta: Centre for Strategic and International Studies 1995, pp. iii–ix.
52 Rosemary Foot, "China in the ASEAN Regional Forum: Organizational Processes and Domestic Modes of Thoughts," *Asian Survey* XXXVIII: 5, 1998, pp. 425–40.
53 Zhou, op. cit.
54 Quoted in Evelyn Goh, "Singapore's Reaction to Rising China: Deep Engagement and Strategic Adjustment," *IDSS Working Paper No. 67*, Singapore: Institute of Defence and Strategic Studies, May 2004, pp. 14–15.
55 Randell L. Schweller, "Managing the Rise of Great Powers: History and Theory," in Alastair Iain Johnston and Robert S. Ross (eds) *Engaging China: The Management of an Emerging Power*, London: Routledge, 1999, pp. 19–26.

56 "Powell Hails Good Sino-US Relations," *China Daily*, 8 September 2003.
57 Nicholas Lemann, "The Next World Order," *The New Yorker*, 1 April 2002. Online. Available: www.theconversation.org; Joseph Gerson, "American Icarus: Goals, Dangers, and Resistance to Bush's Imperial Aggression," *Peacework* 30: 334, April 2003, p. 4.
58 See "Quadrennial Defense Review Report," US Department of Defense, 30 September 2001, p. 4. Online. Available: www.defenselink.mil/pubs/qdr2001.pdf (accessed 1 November 2004).

11 Peaceful rise? Soft power?

Human rights in China's new multilateralism

Jeremy Paltiel

If we judge China's progress in relation to the process of socialization of international human-rights norms into domestic policies as outlined by Thomas Risse and Katharyn Sikkink, China has come a long way from mere instrumental adaptation and strategic bargaining (Risse and Sikkink 1999: 4–5). They outline a five-phase "spiral model" of normative adaptation:

1 repression and activation of international networks
2 denial
3 tactical concessions
4 prescriptive status – where the actors regularly refer to human-rights norms to describe and comment on their own behaviour and that of others, including the ratification and implementation of human-rights instruments
5 rule-consistent behaviour.

Chinese public behaviour has gone well beyond denial and tactical concessions, and could, in important aspects, be considered to have moved into the fourth phase. Major obstacles to full implementation of international human-rights norms remain. However, the logic of China's international status in multilateral institutions keeps China fully engaged, and prevents China from slipping backwards. China has achieved considerable tactical success through acknowledging international human-rights norms while vigorously rejecting their transnational implementation.

China's behaviour in the area of multilateral human rights, as well as Risse and Sikkink's idea of a "boomerang effect" of resistance to human-rights norms (Risse and Sikkink 1999: 23), illustrates very clearly the logic of resistance that Immanuel Wallerstein has outlined:

> When an anti-systemic movement organizes to overthrow or replace existing authorities in a state, it provides itself with a very strong political weapon designed to change the world in specific ways. But, by so organizing, it simultaneously integrates itself and its militants into the very system it is opposing. It is using the structure of the system to oppose the system, which, however, partially legitimates these structures. It is contest-

ing the ideology of the system by appealing to antecedent, broader ideologies (that is, "universal" values), and by so doing is accepting in part the terms of the debate as defined by the dominant forces.

(Wallerstein 1997: 100)

Illiberal internationalism?

China's multilateral engagement since the 1990s has aimed to reassure China's neighbours, as well as the international community in general, of China's peaceful intentions. An explicit commitment to peace as the best environment within which to sustain China's economic and all-round development has matched a growing awareness of, and emergent commitment to, China's own responsibilities as a great power in shaping an environment conducive to "peace and development." This context continues to shape China's multilateral engagement in the area of human rights. China's concern has been to identify itself as a responsible member of the international community, on the one hand, and to pre-empt invidious comparisons and condemnation on the other. China wishes to prevent its isolation within the international community and in order to do so, it also tries to shape an international consensus with which it can identify.

I shall not attempt in this chapter to give a comprehensive overview of China's multilateral engagement in the human-rights area. That topic has been well covered elsewhere (Kent 1999; Foot 2000; Wan 2001). Instead, this chapter tries to look at what China's multilateral engagement in the area of human rights can tell us about Chinese-style multilateralism. Previous studies have focused on the impact of the multilateral human-rights regime on China's domestic behaviour, or on the details of China's human-rights diplomacy. This chapter seeks to place China's multilateral engagement in the area of human rights within the overall context of Chinese foreign policy. The chapter will look at the evolution of China's engagement, the relationship between this type of engagement and domestic institution-building and the impact of the perceived "rise of China," and its diplomacy in the area of international human rights.

Inauspicious beginnings

China's concern over international human rights came out of its isolation following the Tiananmen repression of 1989. China was shocked by its condemnation in Geneva at the Sub-Commission on Human Rights meeting in August 1989 (Kent 1999: 56–60; Wan 2001: 111). While the Chinese delegate rejected the resolution and pronounced it "null and void," China did not walk out. Following this experience China had to build up an infrastructure designed to counter international criticism of China's human-rights record and to shape an international human-rights diplomacy. This culminated in China's issuing its first human rights White Paper in 1991.

It is not surprising that China began to place much greater emphasis on international human rights and the international human-rights regime in the years following the suppression of the Tiananmen demonstrations in 1989 and the criticism China sustained as a result. The Propaganda Department of the Central Committee of the Chinese Communist Party (recently renamed in English the "Publicity Department") organized a meeting to refute the notion that "human rights have no borders," on 10 November 1989 (Guo 1998: 376). General Secretary Jiang Zemin called for research to settle the issue of how "democracy, freedom, and human rights should be looked at from a Marxist viewpoint." "We must explain how our democracy is the most extensive peoples' democracy and explain how socialist China is most respecting of human rights." "Human rights in China are exemplified by Chapter II of the Constitution: Fundamental Rights and Duties of the citizens." Accordingly, the Central Committee issued a directive: "We must boldly propagate our country's viewpoint regarding human rights, democracy, and freedom and the true circumstances of our protection of human rights and practice of democracy. We must hold the banner of human rights democracy and liberty in our own hands" (Dong 2004). By October 1990 the Party had organized the translation and publication of the major international human-rights instruments (Dong 1991). At the same time, Party General Secretary Jiang Zemin mobilized the scholarly community and issued a directive on 2 March 1991. This directive called for opening research in eight areas:

1 Marxist theory of human rights
2 Western human-rights theories
3 Human rights in developing countries
4 Human-rights outlooks of socialist and social-democratic parties
5 The construction of human rights in China
6 Human rights charters of various countries
7 International human-rights instruments
8 Human-rights diplomacy by Western countries. (Guo 1998: 379)

The Chinese Association for the study of Human Rights, which is the official "NGO" in the human rights area, is a creature of the CPC Propaganda department. Its officials including its first head, Zhu Muzhi, a lifelong official in the CPC's propaganda apparatus, are self-conscious agents in the realm of ideological struggle, and define human-rights diplomacy in those terms.[1] The achievement of this institution-building exercise was the issuing of China's first-ever White Paper, the "White Paper on Human Rights Conditions in China," issued by the State Council Information Office on 1 November 1991. That document attempted to present a distinctly Chinese approach to conformity with human-rights norms. For one thing, it set up a hierarchy of rights with the so-called "right to subsistence" as the core human-rights value (Li and Wan 1992: 31–2).

China's adherence and conformity to the international (multilateral) human rights system is seen by some as a test of regime theory and the ability of the international community to enforce its norms on a member state (Kent 1999; Foot 2001).[2] The literature on regime theory and norm compliance postulates that where an "epistemic community" comes into being surrounding a given body of norms, these can become institutionalized in a form described as "cognitive compliance" (Johnston 1996). The difficulty is that the institutional actors designated by the Chinese state to engage in international human-rights dialogue are selected with a view to their participation in a "struggle" and are predisposed to regard their foreign interlocutors in invidious terms (Li and Wan 1992: 3–27).

This makes me less sanguine about the role played by epistemic communities in fostering inter-subjective transnational discourse and normative conformity with international regimes. The China Association for the Study of Human Rights is the official dialogue partner for the human-rights dialogues fostered by the Chinese government. Its members are recruited to play a role as agents in an ideological struggle. Following China's embarrassment at the UN subcommittee, at the meeting of the full Commission on human rights in 1990, China forged a new tactic at the UN Commission on Human Rights in Geneva by inventing the procedural stratagem of a "take no action" resolution (Kent 1999: 61). China's Premier Li Peng actually interrupted his report to the National People's Congress to "announce the good news" from the podium (Beijing Review 1994).

Anne Kent, in *China The United Nations and Human Rights*, is explicitly committed to testing a hypothesis about international regimes and compliance. The book is, therefore, heavily weighted towards measuring the degree of compliance and the types of compliance possible when dealing with a large and increasingly powerful state. Her explicit premise is that the international regime is the causal factor that encourages either instrumental adaptation or normative learning. In other words, it assumes that both norms and structures are initially *external* to the Chinese state.

> China's compliance or non compliance with the norms of the human rights regime constitutes the most rigorous test of international citizenship, for human rights present an immediate challenge to the principle of state sovereignty. Unlike the international political economy regime, it is a moral regime whose norms currently conform not the goals of the Chinese state, but rather to the ideals of a politically conscious stratum of its domestic population.
>
> (Kent 1999: 2)

This approach practically ignores the identity issues inherent in conformity and implicitly posits conformity as an unalloyed good. Rosemary Foot's approach is similar, but instead of being premised on regime theory, is implicitly rooted in the "international society" approaches of the 'English School' pioneered by Hedley Bull and first applied to China by Gerrit Gong (Gong 1984). Elsewhere, Foot has explicitly applied these notions in the construction of the concept of China as a 'responsible great power' (Foot 2001). Both these approaches bestow agency primarily to the Western and European community in promoting change within China. In this approach, the Chinese state is left only two options, passive conformity or resistance. While the possibility of creative participation is not excluded, it is not seen as most pertinent. Learning is seen as part of a process of compliance and implementation rather than a means to weave norms into a new narrative of Chinese (and potentially global) identity. Crude comparison of external criticisms and Chinese reactions only yields a partial view of the underlying processes of normative adaptation. The state, is, after all, an instrument for resisting foreign pressure. We *should* expect to see both resistance and instrumental compliance in response to external pressure. A more nuanced view of normative learning is possible when looking at changes *outside* the context of immediate foreign pressure.

The double resistance of the Chinese state to human rights

As we have already seen, the Chinese state resists the imposition of international human-rights standards, and refuses to engage over particular cases of human-rights abuses, due to a particular concept of Chinese sovereignty. That concept of sovereignty is informed by the derogation of Chinese sovereignty China experienced during the nineteenth century and, in particular, the institution of extraterritoriality which removed foreign citizens from the jurisdiction of Chinese law. The resistance of the Chinese state to foreign human-rights claims is paralleled by resistance by the Chinese state to domestic human-rights claims. At its root, this resistance is informed by a certain concept of sovereignty and its relationship to the rule of law.[3] Contemporary rule of law discourse in China tends to emphasize the universal jurisdiction of the state and its universal competence to regulate society through law. In this sense, the rule of law is an expression of sovereignty. Human-rights claims (as distinct from programmatic expressions by the Chinese state that Chinese citizens "enjoy" rights, and characterization of Chinese social and economic policy as protection and promotion of the "right to subsistence") are viewed (correctly) as a constraint on the authority of the state (Shi 1995) The Chinese state refuses to recognize any claim that implicitly limits its own authority. As distinct from a conception of law that sees it as part of the relationship between state and (civil) society or the body politic, the Chinese state sees law as the universal and only legitimate expression of authority in society, authority exclusive to the state. Domestically, sovereignty is a logical prerequisite for the supremacy of law. Internationally, sovereignty is the legal category establishing a state system. However, should the rule of law become a criterion for sovereignty and its recognition, this would entail setting up invidious standards whereby some political entities might be excluded from the state system. Of course this is precisely what happened when "the standard of civilization" was applied in the nineteenth century. This then begs the question of minimal thresholds for the rule of law and benchmarks for graduation into the state system. The so-called "standard" becomes an excuse for orientalism and racism if these threshold standards are not consistently or universally applied, a condition that is impossible to meet in a world dominated by Great Powers.[4]

Human rights in China's new multilateralism 203

The primary argument employed by Chinese officials and the Chinese state is to insist on the logical and legal priority of state sovereignty over human rights. The argument that human rights constitute a substrate of norms underlying the state system is associated with a cosmopolitan world view (Held 1995; Evans 1996: 21). The Chinese position, articulated in numerous documents, is clearly statist, and makes state sovereignty a value in itself.[5]

> [S]tatist discourse ... views regimes within the framework of rules of practical association. Since this conception stresses those rules considered necessary for coexistence and the maintenance of the international system, rather than human aspirations and values, cooperative arrangements like regimes are seen as practical structures designed to secure order and increase predictability ... there remains a powerful, if tacit implication that practical rules must take priority over purposive rules. That is the preservation of the existing society of states is taken as an end in itself.
> (Evans 1996: 22)

Furthermore, Chinese scholars and officials argue, if human rights were taken as a subject of international obligations, this in turn would exacerbate international conflict, thereby undermining the basic principle of international relations, which is the preservation of peace:

> One of the aims of modern international law is to advance the cause of international peace and international cooperation, not to provoke or expand international disputes. Although human rights are important, nevertheless, if they are to be made a fundamental principle of modern international law, enabling other countries to arbitrarily judge other countries' human rights situation according to their own standards, this will form an objective viewpoint inevitably exacerbate the contradictions among countries and would be most unfavourable to the maintenance of world peace and cooperation.
> (Li and Wan 1992: 124)

Underlying China's position on human rights is a particular view about the relationship between human rights, the state, and sovereignty:

> If one were to characterize the main differences between the human rights philosophies and systems in the West and China, it would be that the former emphasizes the universal and abstract nature of the individual civil and political rights, with social rights as secondary, concrete, non-universal and contingent, and that the latter emphasize social and economic rights, but views all rights as collectively based, concrete, nonuniversal, and subordinate to the state.
> (Kent 1993: 30)

The Chinese state interpreted resolutions that condemned or criticized China's human-rights record as an attack on the legitimacy of the Chinese state and an effort to subvert its regime.

> Western politicians are concerned most with their own interests. Western civilization is used as an instrument to pursue their interests. Human rights, a part of the Western civilization, are most widely applicable. Western politicians view human rights diplomacy as their 'sophisticated weapon' and the most important advantage of the liberal democratic nations in the struggle to expand their influence. Some western countries led by the United States have launched attacks time and time again at meetings of the UN Human Rights Commission. Those that have been accused are invariably developing nations. They are insufferably arrogant, because they think their heavenly mission is to make so-called freedom and social justice popular among the whole of mankind through their democratic demonstration. To them, the Western lifestyle is the beacon to be imitated by other countries and the Western social system is the role model to be followed by other countries. ... Obviously human rights are used to interfere in the sovereignty of others, to violate the sovereignty of others, and even to subvert the regimes of other nations. This is the essence of Western human rights diplomacy.
>
> (Zhu 2002: 207–8)

While China has consistently appealed to the defence of sovereignty and the principle of non-interference as its first line of defence against human-rights criticisms (Kent 1999: 62; Foot 2000: 122), participation in the international human-rights regime has rendered absolute reliance on the doctrines of sovereignty unpersuasive and obsolete. Nevertheless, in order to avoid isolation China had not only to develop a domestic infrastructure capable of engaging the international community, but also to make an effort to forge an international consensus favourable to China's views. China could not insist on a rigid and absolute defence of state sovereignty without appearing to contradict the purposes of the United Nations, the values enunciated in the Universal Declaration of Human Rights, and the development of the entire United Nations human-rights system, together with the major international human-rights covenants.

China's earliest efforts to construct a favourable interpretive community came in the lead-up to the Vienna International Conference on Human Rights in 1993. China actively participated at the Bangkok regional conference and proclaimed its close association with the Bangkok Declaration (Wan 2001: 117–18). Thus, while China sought to avoid censure by manoeuvring Third World delegates to the Human Rights Commission in Geneva, it also endeavoured to pour new meaning into human-rights norms in a way that would make China less susceptible to international isolation and condemnation. The core thread in this strategy was to be found in the "right to development" and right to subsistence. In addition to the cultural-relativist implications of the Bangkok Declaration and its association with the Asian Values debate, China sought to adopt a developmental-relativist position, whereby human-rights obligations become a progressive process relative to the accomplishment of economic development.

By juxtaposing rights and development, China seeks to build an interpretive community in common with other developing countries designed to counter Western human-rights criticisms. This interpretive community is explicitly fostered by Chinese officials (*People's Daily* 2001). Chinese officials habitually treat rights as goals or ideals that are meant to be addressed in the course of overall development. Since development is seen primarily as the result of state policy this places human rights in a position that appears as subordinate to state policy. This way of seeing rights strikes the Western observer as wrong, in a reading that Maurice Cranston articulated well in *What are Human Rights*:

> Various statements of human rights – even some of the United Nations' own literature commenting on the Universal Declaration – describes the rights of man as 'ideals'. This is an unfortunate word. An ideal is something which belongs to the realm of imagination and aspiration. It is something one yearns for, but cannot expect immediately to realize. But a right is not like this. It is something which *can* and should be recognized in the here and now. What ought to be done is not an ideal; what is right, what is a duty, what is just is not what would be wise to see some day in a better future. It is something demanded what Kant called the categorical imperative.and there can be no excuse for *not* doing it.
> (Cranston 1973: 37–8)

However, Chinese leaders specifically appeal to human rights as ideals when they speak about their conformity to the international human-rights regime. As China's first White Paper on human rights put it:

> In the practice of protecting and guaranteeing human rights, China has experienced various vicissitudes. At present, although we have made great achievements in the promotion and protection of human rights, there still however, exist many areas awaiting perfection. To continuously promote the development of human rights, to diligently achieve the lofty goal of realizing comprehensive human rights demanded by China's socialism, remains a long term historical duty of the Chinese government and people.
> (State Council 1991)

Again, one reason for the glaring discrepancy in understanding what human rights are derives from a different understanding of the relationship of the individual to the state:

> Looking more closely at China's concept of civil and political rights, it can be seen to assume a different relationship between the citizen, the state, and the law from that which pertains in the West. Thus, while in the west the legal system, through the individual's invocation of his civil rights

> interceded between the sovereign individual and the state, claiming for the individual rights of immunity, as well as of political participation and welfare consumption, in China the legal system, to the extent that it is invoked, intervenes on behalf of the collective interests of all individuals vested in the sovereignty of the state.
>
> (Kent 1993: 30)

Following the Vienna International Conference on Human Rights, which overwhelmingly endorsed a universalist interpretation of human rights against the narrower, more relativistic, interpretation that China favoured, China sought to shape the international agenda and build a broader interpretive community around itself. Nevertheless, China could take comfort in the fact that the Vienna Declaration, which affirmed the universality, interdependence, and inseparability of human rights (including women's rights) also endorsed the right to development (Broadbent 1993: 6).

China's agreement and desire to host the International Conference of Women's Rights in Beijing in 1995 was motivated in some substantial measure by two perceptions. One was that by successfully hosting such an event, China would gain prestige on the international stage and second, that it would in some measure outflank criticisms of China's own human-rights record by highlighting an area where China's leadership believed, somewhat naively, China's record was relatively progressive and enlightened.

With the end of the Cold War, China confronted a much greater risk of isolation, for the first time since before the First World War, and faced an international society that was more coherent and far more institutionalized than ever before. Unlike a century earlier, "international society" was no longer coterminous with "the West." Moreover, the exigencies of China's development policies, especially once Deng Xiaoping had squarely staked the Party's legitimacy on high-speed economic development based on market reforms and the open policy of international trade and investment, determined that it was contrary to China's national interest to foster such a perception, either domestically or internationally. Chinese reacted with alarm and dismay to Samuel Huntington's, "Clash of Civilizations" hypothesis. A trend developed whereby China began to consciously identify with "international society." At first, this concept was used without specific normative connotations along the lines suggested by the work of Hedley Bull and the so-called English School. "International society" was, instead, employed as a descriptive term denoting a sphere of activity, namely organized state interactions in international institutions and organizations, most specifically, the UN. However, by the end of the 1990s, "international society," in Chinese usage, increasingly takes on a normative hue, corresponding very much with the notions advocated by the English School – a sphere of normative activity guiding the behaviour of states, a collectivity defining proper behaviour among nations. "International Society" increasingly identifies the opposing counterpart to "hegemony."

By the time of the UN's Millennium Summit of 2000, China has come to identify a concept of international society that is pluralistic at the level of culture, and "democratic" with respect to the equal participation of various forms of social system and state organization. The priority values espoused by the Chinese state in its international dealings can be gathered from the speech given to the Millennium Summit of the United Nations by Chinese President Jiang Zemin on 6 September 2000. In it, he mentioned *independence* three times; *sovereignty* seven times; *democracy* five times; *equality* seven times; *peace* 25 times; *development* (or developing states) 45 times; and *human rights* only three times.

In the short paragraph devoted to human rights, sovereignty clearly had an edge:

> Dialogue and cooperation in the field of human rights should be undertaken on the basis of respect for state sovereignty. This is the most fundamental and effective path to protect and promote the cause of human rights. As long as borders continue to exist in the world and people continue to live separately within their own states, the protection of each state's independence and sovereignty is the highest interest of the government and people of each state. Without sovereignty, there are no human rights to speak of.
> (Jiang 2000)

The consistent line defended by China at the Human Rights Commission in Geneva has been the priority of development over individual rights:

> To realize civil and political rights in all around way is a comprehensive project, requiring simultaneous and balanced promotion of economic social and cultural rights. Just as stated in the Vienna Declaration and Action Program all human rights as universal, inseparable, interdependent and interconnected. Economic development promotes open thinking, progress of civilization and social development. In recent years, the construction of China's democracy and rule of law has proceeded in a continuously quickened pace, keeping pace at each step with China's rapidly developing economy. In areas where economic conditions are relatively superior, people's legal consciousness and rights consciousness is relatively superior to those areas where the economy is relatively backward. When the economy develops relatively quickly then the enjoyment of people's citizen rights and political rights rises relatively more quickly. For this reason, if international society wishes to further promote and guarantee civil and political rights, then it must at the same time promote the comprehensive economic social and cultural development of various countries. Only by looking at both types of human rights on the same level can the cause of human rights be promoted in a balanced and comprehensive manner.
> (Shen 2003)

Opposing a vision of invidious comparison and value hierarchy identified with US hegemony and Western concepts of liberal democracy and human rights,

China proposes a "democratic" vision based on peaceful coexistence, cultural and ideological pluralism, along with a more equitable redistribution of the world's economic resources.

In "The Logic of the Rise of Great Powers," the editor of the influential Chinese periodical *Strategy and Management*, Zhang Wenmu, argues that the sustainable rise of a great power requires the recognition of limits to expansion. In particular, Zhang refers to limited resources. He highlights China's growing dependence on the import of natural resources and argues that a sustainable rise requires the maintenance and defence of a "democratic world order." "The ultimate goal of the international system is to distribute world resources. However, the system has never been a democratic one, as it has been defined and maintained violently by hegemonic powers. China's rise will inevitably pose a challenge to the existing unequal world resource distribution system."

He defines a democratic world order as an order of sovereign states where each state has "equal access to international markets and world resources, and the right to use sea passages freely." This kind of equality is not defined, nor does the author identify which institutions sustain the equal distribution of world resources. Nevertheless, he contrasts "democracy" with hegemony: "International hegemony is the opposite of international democracy." At the same time however, he recognizes that a sustained rise requires building what he calls "political civilization." Most important in this is the development of citizenship:

> Citizenship, resulting from consensual transfer of "popular" and "national" autonomy to the state, implies a contractual relation with the state. At the core of citizenship is a system of rights and obligations: while citizens are obliged to pay taxes and remain loyal to the state, it is the duty of the state to protect its citizens according to their legal rights. The state mobilizes its citizens to the maximum in the counterbalance of right and obligation.

He concludes, "a government by the people serves as a premise for China in its construction of the political civilization and its efforts to dialogue with the world." Zhang recognizes the link between domestic and international sovereignty, although, in typical fashion, he places national sovereignty in the first place:

> sovereignty provides the metalogic and starting point of modern state theory. As the rise of a state to a great power requires adequate resources, resources become the first link in the logic of their rise, from which derive concepts like strength, power, rights and state institutions.

In 2004 Chinese theorists and ideologist began to articulate a comprehensive vision of Chinese internationalism crystallized in the notion of China's "peaceful rise." Zheng Bijian, an academic director of the Communist Party of China's Central Party School, and a key advisor to Hu Jintao, argues first of all that China's development strategy is inseparable from the forces of globalization.

Human rights in China's new multilateralism 209

Moreover, that China's rise must be peaceful since the history of all rising powers has shown that those powers that engage in a struggle for hegemony and territorial expansion have always ended in defeat (Zheng 2004: 1).

Zheng identified the strategy of "peaceful rise" with close relations with Europe and common strategic aims, namely, an international environment of peaceful development, mutual trust and mutual interest, and common enrichment; support for multilateral diplomacy, respect for cultural pluralism, and the democratization of international relations by revising the irrational elements of the current international system in the spirit of the rule of law (Zheng 2004: 2).

The notion of a peaceful rise is a development and extension of China's rhetorical posture since the late 1990s of identifying itself as a "responsible Great Power." As Xu Jian argues, developing the concept of a "peaceful rise" requires a concept of international cooperation that transcends ideology and narrow nationalism by injecting new content into China's views of sovereignty, human rights, and national humiliation:

> China's view of sovereignty is currently combining with its outlook of ... the Three Represents for the Chinese Communist Party. [T]o represent the advanced forces of production and advanced culture requires ... China to transcend the ideological outlook in managing the relationship between China and the world, and builds a basis for China to absorb the outstanding fruits of material, spiritual and political civilization of humanity ... this not only encourages extensive cooperation and engagement with the various countries of the world, it should also make us more willing to listen to constructive criticism and reasonable concern from international society and be more daring in absorbing useful international experience including those of Western states in order to improve ourselves ... Secondly China's concept of international cooperation is combining with an outlook on human rights more consistent with cosmopolitan values. The political concept ... of representing the basic interests of the widest mass of the people, ... also propels the Chinese outlook on human rights in the directions of progress and development.
>
> (Xu 2004: 27)

Xu accepts the notion that China must engage international society on questions of human rights:

> China's colouration in the area of international human rights cooperation has changed from passive to active, with richer theoretical assertions going from opposing interference to promoting dialog from emphasizing the class nature of human rights to acknowledging civil rights from stressing the right to subsistence and the right to development to simultaneously paying attention to political rights. The development and progress in China's views of human rights and development has engendered a reorientation in China's human rights and security policies. For instance, in the area of humanitarian

intervention, China has come from criticism and negation to conditional acceptance and participation.

(Xu 2004: 28)

Domestic concerns

The idea that China should conform more fully to the mainstream ideas of "international society" in the area of human rights does not come solely from the desire for a more harmonious relationship with the international community. It also flows from a recognition that the norms values enunciated in the international human-rights instruments correspond to China's domestic developmental needs and the efforts to build a rule of law state. Li Buyun distinguishes the commitment to "regulate the country by relying on law" and building a "rule of law state" (Li 1999). The former he sees as a programmatic goal involving two elements: the first is that the long-term viability of the state depends on authoritative laws and systems and not on sage rulers and the second as an action plan for state rule, which eschews simple reliance on the wisdom of rulers for the laws embodying the laws of nature, the spirit of the times and socialist ideals, rather than making power superior to the law.

By contrast, to build a rule of law state is a strategic objective involving the particular choice of a legal-political system. Li Buyun identifies the protection of human rights as one of the most important benchmarks of a rule of law state:

> Human rights are the rights that ought to accrue to human beings with accordance their natural and social being. Their content includes the rights of the person and personality, political rights and freedoms as well as economic social and cultural rights. Human rights are the concentrated expression of human dignity and human value and are the general reflection of human needs and happiness. To deny that human beings ought to enjoy rights of their own in society is to treat them as something less than human. People do not exist for the sake of the state and its laws, but rather that law and the state exist for the sake of human beings ...
>
> (Li 1999: 15)

One of the most important steps that Li Buyun lays out as benchmarks towards implementing the rule of law in China is the ratification of the two Human Rights Conventions, ICCPR and the ICESR:

> This can not only raise our international authority with respect to human rights questions, but may also promote a further improvement of the system of human rights protection in our country through this important measure, such as establishing a system of social insurance, a law on religions which is based on rights protection, a law on family planning, a law on social organization, a news media law, a law on publications, a law for the rights of dispersed minority populations; it can promote the reduction control of

the use of the death penalty, the abolition or improvement of the system of education through labour, reform of the system of legal representation, strengthening the role of labor unions and the legal entitlement of the right to strike.

(Li 1999: 15)

Li Buyun is not alone in rejecting China's official position concerning the relationship of human rights to sovereignty. Other Chinese scholars have pointed out the contradictions in China's official posture. Lu Shilun joins the attack from a Marxist perspective. He attacks the position that sovereignty is a precondition for human rights and that sovereignty is higher than human rights as a form of "state superstition." He gives three reasons for rejecting the official view:

1   That Karl Marx had evidently made *Civil Society* the premise and basis of human rights.
2   The position that sovereignty is the premise of human rights makes no distinction between types of state one is talking about. It could be raised by socialist states, capitalist states ... even fascist states. In that case would not the proletarian struggle for human rights be rendered superfluous and redundant?
3   Proletarian internationalism has as its mission the emancipation of the entire human race.

Lu, from a position of Marxist internationalism rejects the official Chinese view of the relationship of sovereignty and human rights and instead argues forthrightly that "the correct way of speaking is that in its fundamental aspect, universal human rights should be higher than state sovereignty" (Lu 1998: 390).

Further on the issue of whether there are hierarchies of human rights, there is also dissent within the Chinese legal community, with scholars rejecting the notion of a distinction between human rights and "fundamental" human rights, the rights of subsistence being foremost among them (Bai 1999).

International society and international citizenship

There is evident tension between Chinese appeals to international society as a means of enhancing the Chinese state's "international citizenship" together with the universality of the state system, and the concept of human rights as universal norms underlying the sovereignty of states. Acknowledging the latter makes the Chinese state vulnerable to invidious comparisons, while the former is made attractive and possible because China's rising economic and political power gives it substantial weight in forming "international society," with participation in international society serving as the benchmark of China's achievement of global status as a great power. To be a great power is to be a player in international society, but, an "international society" must embody a set of norms. Insistence on cultural and ideological pluralism with sovereignty as the sole common denominator of international society disables China from the production of norms of international society. Increasingly, China also seeks to pursue "soft power" (Xinhua 2004). The pressure of China's "peaceful rise" pushes China in the direction of greater conformity with the "embedded liberalism" of international society which, in turn, puts pressure on the CPC regime's domestic posture.

The process of China's adhesion to the two basic covenants of the United Nations Human Rights regime is instructive. China signed the UN Covenant on Economic and Social and Cultural Rights (UNESCR) immediately before Chinese President Jiang Zemin's departure for the US in October 1997; it signed the UN Covenant on Civil and Political Rights (UNCCPR) on the eve of the meeting of the UN Human Rights Commission in March 1998, and it is broadly understood to have been a quid pro quo for an American decision to drop sponsorship of a resolution criticizing China, and part of a package meant to smooth President Clinton's June 1998 visit to China (Mann 1999: 354–63; Foot 2000: 209–20).

This illustrates the ways in which China has attempted to manage the human-rights issue in the post-Tiananmen period through trading off bilateral and multilateral relationships. Whereas the Chinese signature on the ICCPR and ICESCR is closely related to Sino-American relations, China has also held out bilateral human-rights dialogues in exchange for countries dropping their sponsorships of resolutions critical of China at the UN Human Rights Commission (Wan 2001: 71–3).

In parallel with efforts to deflect critical resolutions through offers to promote bilateral dialogue, China also began to promote engagement with UN human-rights institutions. Beginning in 1994, China invited the UN Special Rapporteur on Religious Intolerance (1994) the UN Working Group on Arbitrary Detention (1996) and in September 1998 invited the UN High Commissioner for Human Rights, Mary Robinson, and signed a Memorandum of Intent on a technical cooperation program (State Council 1999: 35).

China identifies with international society as a means of "soft" counter-hegemony. This means identifying with secondary powers as a normative means of constraining US hegemony. This can be distinguished from balancing in a balance of power system by the absence of an overt power or security dimension. Instead, China sees itself as a consensus power upholding traditional Westphalian concepts of sovereignty against a US power that threatens to undermine these concepts. The irony in this posture is that for it to be effective China must identify with other multilateral actors, principally European, who promote a distinctively liberal version of multilateralism.

> Participation in multilateral cooperation is a major step in China's acceptance into international society. It is a subjective requirement for the realization of state prosperity and strength (*fuqiang*) and national revival, and is an intrinsic guarantor of national interests, is a new and important channel for safeguarding regional and global stability, improving and strengthening

security relations with the nations of the world, developing friendly cooperative relations with neighbouring countries, an important channel for improving mutual understanding and trust, and is a new development and new instantiation of China's independent foreign policy in the new era.

(Meng 2001: 29)

Of course, such glowing praise also hides deep misgivings. Multilateral cooperation is both an "opportunity" and "a challenge" that requires the Chinese to "emancipate their minds" and overcome mistaken perceptions.

We should not look only at the way that the major powers of the West have used multilateral organizations to press their hegemonic policies, but ignore, or rarely look at how [multilateralism] represents the tidal trend of peaceful development, and instantiates the wishes of the great majority of nations. Moreover to a certain extent it has the positive significance of blocking hegemonism and promoting the formation of a new international security order. We should not see only how it has been the tool which some relevant states, especially Western states have used to restrict the development of other states, but ignore or mainly overlook how to various extents it restrains all participating parties. We should not look only at how some countries struggle to establish a leading role, and overlook the significance of establishing normative frameworks and rules to the maintenance of the external security of states and to the realization of security interests. One should not only look at how joining and participation may to some extent require giving up a certain amount of freedom of action and overlook how states can acquire security guarantees of much greater scope over a much longer time frame.

(Meng 2001)

Chinese-style internationalism involves neither balancing nor bandwagoning. China remains keenly aware of the 'embedded liberalism' (Ruggie 1983) of the multilateral order and continues to associate the multilateral systems promoted by liberal internationalists such as Woodrow Wilson and Franklin Roosevelt with US hegemony (Yu 2001). A multilateral order offers the most effective means to counter hegemonism and secure China's sovereignty, yet, at the same time, "soft" counter-hegemonism through multilateralism does not contradict the maintenance of positive bilateral relations with the US. What China fears about rule-driven multilateralism is the elective affinity between rules-based multilateralism and liberal governance under the rule of law. The fear is that rules will define the regime, whereas China's Communist Party regime wishes to define itself and the rules under which it chooses to operate. Obviously, there is tension between this and China's commitment to rules-based orders as part of its participation in trade and transnational flows. China needs rules and appreciates their value. However, it remains protective both of its national sovereignty and its regime.

There is already increasing pressure on the regime both domestically and internationally to conform to a rules-based system. The tension is likely to be expressed at the local level, in conflict over rules-based adjudication and the principle of territorial Party control, a principle that has strong patrimonial overtones. At some point the Communist regime faces a choice between patrimonialism and the rule of law. Party patrimonialism means that the Communist Party literally directs the legal regime and Party institutions (as distinct from Party members) are not directly accountable before the law.

Internationally, therefore, China cannot afford to promote a strictly sovereignty-based, "illiberal, internationalism." Instead, China continues passively to accept liberal norms while working actively to shape the ways in which these are implemented at the national and international level. For this reason the Chinese regime sees no contradiction in promoting rules-based multilateralism in the WTO while continuing to block specific resolutions condemning China's human-rights practices at the UN Human Rights Commission in Geneva. However, rather than proclaim its exception to the UN human rights system, China promotes dialogue and cooperation with the UN High Commissioner for Human Rights and begins to selectively and conditionally participate in humanitarian interventions.

In general, Zhu Feng's proposition may be right, that the desire to conform is much more effective in promoting domestic human-rights change than the threat to exclude.[6] However, the experience of China's interaction with the multilateral human-rights system in the 1990s suggests that the initial threat of exclusion had a substantial impact in promoting engagement with the multilateral human-rights system. Moreover, this engagement, even where initially aimed at resistance, and effective in parrying efforts to promote domestic regime change, nevertheless did not result in the formulation of a consistent alternative to Western human-rights ideas, still less an alternative human-rights system or regime. Instead, Chinese participation in the multilateral human-rights regime, like its participation in other multilateral projects, tends selectively to reinforce and reaffirm liberal vales and norms in the effort to find a congenial consensus around Chinese interests and goals consistent with the shifting coalitions with which China associates. The key to this process is a growing identification with the norms of "international society" as a means of restraining unilateralism and mitigating the effects of a hegemonic order.

> The characteristic of the current era is a struggle between two types of world order: On the one hand, the sole superpower, the US, attempts through multilateral (as well as bilateral) diplomacy to prolong, expand and consolidate its own global hegemony. In recent years, the US relying on its own strong economy and military power, is increasingly unwilling to accept the restraints of international society and international law, and is actively employing unilateral to seek hegemony in its own exclusive interest. On the other hand, the vast majority of states in the world, including China, hope to establish a new democratic, just and reasonable international order – we

term this a multi-polar global structure, and towards it we have opened up an active multilateral and bilateral diplomacy. The characteristic of multilateral diplomacy in the new era is broad participation in the search for peace and cooperation.

(Shen 2001: 21)

During the 1980s China gradually took on a strategic and diplomatic posture that finally recognized "one world."[7] This policy did not come into full play until the 1990s. "Soft" counter-hegemonism requires China to adhere to a posture that aims at projecting greater respect for global institutions and regional sensitivities than the US, and indirectly more consistent support for rules-based orders and multilateral decision-making than the US. Barry Buzan has propounded a theory of international society as a composite of two principles of association: a *gemeinschaft* aspect of shared values and cultural orientations, and a *geselschaft* of contractual relations based on common interests and shared commitment to rules (Buzan 1993, 1996). According to Mark Evans, China, as a weak and peripheral state in the international system, has made great strides in integrating itself along *geselschaft* lines in international society but faces severe obstacles, particularly in relation to human rights and domestic governance, in integrating itself along *gemeinschaft* lines (Evans 2004).

China will oppose a "holy alliance" of democratic states led by the US in favour of traditional Westphalian sovereignty that leaves ideology to the territorial state. In recent years, especially since the crack in the Western Alliance surrounding US intervention in Iraq, China has both embraced and identified itself as an integral part of "international society" with the US on the outside.[8] This is a kind of soft counter-hegemonism. Soft counter-hegemonism differs from traditional balance of power diplomacy by not directly aiming at building a coalition to confront the dominant power. China is committed to maintain the shape of the international system against what it sees as twin threats: *one* is the threat posed to the territorial state by global terrorism, *the other* is the threat to sovereignty posed by unilateralist policies of humanitarian intervention and pre-emptive strikes.

Internationally, we see a new appreciation of the role of legal sovereignty in negotiating rules and adjudicating concerns about managing and encouraging transborder flows. For the first 30 years of the People's Republic, the overriding aim of security policy was in hardening the external shell of the regime and the state and making the frontier rigid. For the past quarter century, the main trend of China's domestic and foreign policy was in accelerating transborder flows and evolving the legal and institutional machinery as well as the diplomatic tools required to manage such flows. The current contradiction in China's attitudes towards the frontier and towards sovereignty is a growing disjuncture between the ways in which transborder flows are managed internationally and in dealings with multilateral organizations and the ways in which domestic governance is conceived. In international dealings, "sovereignty" is parcelled out to specialized institutions and managed according to explicit and specialized rules.

Domestically, sovereignty is poised in an ambiguous posture between the people and its representative institutions, and the reality of Party leadership and its de facto sovereign power. Pitman Potter sees the Chinese system of power as one of patrimonial sovereignty. "Drawing on traditional norms of Confucianism combined with ideals of revolutionary transformation drawn from Marxism-Leninism and Maoism, regulatory culture in China tends to emphasize governance by political authority that remains largely immune to challenge" (Potter 2004: 476). Today, there is an increasing effort to try to square the circle by having the Party conform to rules-based governance internally. But this process founders on the key question of *custodies quis custodiet* (who takes care of the care-takers). The monolithic hierarchy of the Party organization does not allow for specialized adjudication in accordance with law, a fact that is recognized in the state by vesting the power to interpret the law in the hands of the legislative (National People's Congress) Standing Committees rather than the courts.

Essentially, China's exceptionalist posture with respect to human rights and many other issues touching on sovereignty and the rule of law, stems from the problem of accounting for the peculiar system of sovereignty operating domestically – formal sovereignty of the people with de facto Party patrimonialism. This is more than a matter of face or ideology. Unless the contours of sovereignty can be defined juridically through independent judicial bodies that respond to the law and not to the secret internal dictates of the Party hierarchy, there will be a permanent gap between the principles at work in adjudicating transborder flows and the workings of domestic governance. The Chinese state cannot easily maintain two contradictory logics of authority.

By trumpeting its role as the sole defender of China's sovereign interests, the Party disqualifies itself from adjudicating the contours of sovereignty in a manner that might satisfy parties in a transborder dispute. And yet, by jealously guarding its prerogatives, the Party also places itself in the direct line of criticism where domestic norms fall short of internationally recognized standards. By deploying sovereignty in this manner, the Chinese Communist Party leaves the Chinese state as a whole liable for all the shortcomings of legal norms and institutions, whereas by relaxing its grip and devolving autonomy to specialized institutions the critics would be required to take account of such autonomous action in directing criticisms at the Chinese state. The Chinese Communist Party, by seeking to reap all the credit for the Chinese *nation*, places itself in the awkward position of taking all the blame for the shortcomings of the Chinese *state*. Eventually the Party will have to relinquish some authority in order to bolster its legitimacy.

Conclusion

Today, the Communist Party of China is in the peculiar position of advocating pluralism and democracy in the inter-state system while seeking to curtail and control the expressions of the same domestically. My contention is that domestic and international sovereignty are not two incommensurable concepts but interlinked notions of authority. If so, China is today an anomaly. Note, however, that official Chinese statements assert China's adherence to the *values* of democracy and the rule of law. Chinese dissent in the multilateral human-rights regime is less ideological than institutional. The effort to uphold Party patrimonialism runs against the pluralizing tendencies of China's market economy, whereas the resulting friction in a society that is increasingly open to transborder flows of information, people, and goods, will be taken up by transnational NGOs and reflected in the multilateral human-rights regime, regardless of China's growing global influence.[9] Managing China's "peaceful rise" will inevitably engage domestic and international human rights, however awkward the consequences. Here, as in other areas, despite strong gestures of dissent, China's foreign-policy makers are pulled in the direction of a liberal consensus. This can hardly be considered a viable long-term strategic option. China is playing out what Sikkink and Risse call the "boomerang effect" of the effort to deny international scrutiny. Structural forces, engaged both by domestic actors and international opinion, propel China along the path of conformity with international liberal norms. The regime throws up a flimsy screen of nationalism to resist liberal forces and aligns itself with fellow dissenters from the Euro-American liberal consensus, but is both unable and unwilling to mount a challenge to liberal norms and institutions.

Notes

1 See, for example, Wang 2004.
2 Kent makes human rights the test of international citizenship arguing from the premise that, unlike the political economy regime, its principles directly challenge sovereignty.
3 For a perspective from a well-known Chinese scholar who develops this theme, see Zhu 1996. Zhu argues that the primary problem in China is the lack of separation between state and society. He rejects the notion that foreign pressure can have any positive effect on human rights, implicitly because it forces the state into a defensive position to defend its sovereign prerogatives:

> The social composition of modern nation-states reflects different levels and forms of separation between economics and politics, the state and the individual. In a system of nearly total government and party control, such as existed previously in China, moving toward the separation mentioned here is an very complicated and painful process of partition and disconnection ... What China needs at present is greater freedom and the rule of law with political and economic reforms in process now. These have a direct relationship to human rights and will advance the popularity of human rights thinking. This will in turn aid the process of democratic development. The dynamism of keeping the advancement of human rights can only derive out of China's internal evolution.
>
> (41, 57)

4 For example,

> a punitive approach isolates alleged violators while a constructive approach includes them. Furthermore, inconsistency exposes the [aid] donor country to charges not only of imposing its values on another country but also of selectivity in the application of those values. In fact, the perception that the West, particularly the United States, operates according to double standards has been a key concern of Asian governments.
>
> (Zhu 1996: 57–8)

5 There can be no clearer demonstration of this than the arguments put forward by Deng Xiaoping:

> After we put down the rebellion [referring to 4 June 1989 and the Tiananmen demonstrations], the Group of Seven summit meeting issued a declaration imposing sanctions on China. What qualifies them to do that? Who granted them the authority? Actually, national sovereignty is far more important than human rights, but they often infringe upon the sovereignty of poor, weak, states.
>
> (Deng 1992a)

> Actually, in Chinese Deng does not use the formal term for sovereignty *zhuquan* but rather *guoquan*, or state power or state rights. He used this term earlier also in his conversation with Former US President Richard Nixon: "People who value human rights should not forget the rights of the state."
>
> (Deng 1992b)

6 A similar point was made recently with respect to bilateral sanctions policies (Li and Cooper Drury 2004).
7 Wu Zichen sees China's adoption of a foreign-policy posture of "peace and development" as the marker of this transition (Wu 2001).
8

> Since the 9/11 incident US security strategy has undergone momentous reorganization, but the goal of proselytizing US values globally and establishing a global order under US power has not changed. Under the pretext of eliminating global terrorism and preventing the proliferation of weapons of mass destruction it has already fomented two wars, in Afghanistan, and in Iraq. With respect to the latter in particular, the US has stood against the strong opposition of international society (including some of the major allies of the US itself) for sidestepping the UN Security Council.
>
> (Zheng Ruixian 2004: 8)

9 The repression of the Falungong is an outstanding example of the internationalization of a purely domestic movement.

References

Bai, Guimei, "Are there any Hierarchies of Human Rights in International Law" in P. R. Baerhr *et al.* (eds) *Human Rights: Chinese and Dutch Perspectives,* The Hague: Kluwer, 1999, pp. 133–42.
Beijing Review, "Western Anti-China Draft Rejected," *Beijing Review*, vol. 32, no. 12, 21–27 March 1994, p. 32.
Broadbent, Ed., "Democracy Capitalism and Foreign Policy: Ten Propositions About the New World Order," *Canadian Foreign Policy*, vol. 1, no. 2, Spring 1993.
Buzan, Barry, "From International System to International Society: Structural Realism and Regime Theory Meet the English School," *International Organization*, vol. 47, no. 3, Summer 1993.
—— "International Society and International Security" in Rick Fawn and Jeremy Larkins (eds) *International Society After the Cold War: Anarchy and Order Reconsidered*, London: Macmillan, 1996, pp. 261–87.
Cranston, Maurice, *What Are Human Rights*, London: Bodley Head, 1973.
Deng Xiaoping, "The United States Should Take the Initiative in Putting an End to the

Strains in Sino-American Relations," 31 October 1989 in *Selected Works*, vol. 3, 1992b. Online. Available: english.peopledaily.com.cn/ dengxp/vol3/text/d1060.html.

—— "We Must Adhere to Socialism and Prevent Peaceful Evolution Towards Capitalism," 23 November 1989, *Selected Works*, vol. 3, 1992a. Online. Available: english.peopledaily.com.cn/dengxp/vol3/ text/d1090.html.

Dong, Yunhu and Liu, Wuping (eds) *Shijie renquan yuefa zonglan* [World Documents of Human Rights – the title in English appears on the cover, though the materials are all in Chinese translation], Chengdu: Renmin Chubanshe, 1991.

Dong, Yunhu, "'Renquan' ruxian: Zhongguo Renquan fazhan de zhongyao lichengbei" ['Human Rights' enter the constitution: an important milestone in the development of human rights in China] *Renmin Ribao*, 15 March 2004.

Evans, Mark D., "Weak States, State Making and Humanitarian Intervention with a view from the People's Republic of China," in Mark Davis, Wolfgang Dietrich, Bettina Scholdan and Dieter Sepp (eds) *International Intervention in the Post-Cold War World: Moral Responsibility and Power Politics*, Armonk, NY: ME Sharpe, 2004, pp. 104–22.

Evans, Tony, *US Hegemony and the Project of Universal Human Rights*, London: Macmillan, 1996.

Foot, Rosemary, *Rights Beyond Borders: The Global Community and the Struggle over Human Rights in China*, New York: Oxford University Press, 2000.

—— "Chinese Power and the Idea of A Responsible State," *The China Journal*, no. 45, January 2001, pp. 18–19.

Gong, Gerrit, *The Standard of Civilization in International Society*, Oxford: Oxford University Press, 1984.

Guo, Daohun, "Guan yu 1991 Disan Qi *Faxue* ben kan pinglunyuan wenzhang 'Shenru kaizhan renquan yu fazhi de lilun yanjiu'" [on the 1991 commentator's article "Deepen the Study of the Theory of Human Rights and the Rule of Law" in Guo Daohun, Li Buyun, Hao Tiechuan (eds) *Zhongguo dangdai faxue zhengming shilu* [Documentary reports of contemporary controversies in Chinese jurisprudence], Changsha: Hunan Renmin Chubanshe, 1998.

Held, David, "Democracy and the New International Order," in Daniele Archebugi and David Held (eds) *Cosmopolitan Democracy: An Agenda for a New World Order*, Cambridge: Polity Press, 1995, pp. 96–120.

Jiang, Zemin, "Zai Lianheguo Qiannian shounao huiyi shang de jiang hua 2000. 9.6," *Renmin Ribao*, OE, 7 September 2000, p. 1.

Johnston, Alastair Iain, "Learning Versus Adaptation: Explaining Change in Chinese Arms Control Policy in the 1980s and 1990s," *The China Journal*, no. 35, January 1996, pp. 27–62.

Kent, Anne, *Between Freedom and Subsistence: China and Human Rights*, New York: Oxford University Press, 1993.

—— *China, the United Nations, and Human Rights*, Philadelphia: University of Pennsylvania Press, 1999.

Li, Buyun, "Shishi Yifa zhiguo zhanlue lungang' [a programme for the realization of ruling the country by relying on law] *Xinhua Wenzhai*, no. 9, 1999, pp. 12–15.

Li, Long and Yuxiang, Wan, *Renquan lilun yu guoji renquan* [Human Rights Theory and International Human Rights], Wuhan: Wuhan Daxue Chubanshe, 1992.

Li, Yitan and Drury, A. Cooper, "Threatening Sanctions when Engagement Would be More Effective.: Attaining Better Human Rights in China," *International Studies Perspectives*, vol. 5, no. 4, November 2004, pp. 378–94.

Lu, Shilun and Shi Zhong, "Suowei 'buheshiyi' de renquanlun" [A so-called 'untimely' view of human rights] in Guo Daohun, Li Buyun, Hao Tiequan (eds) *Zhongguo dangdaifaxue zhengming shilu*, [transcripts of contemporary controversies in Chinese jurisprudence], Changsha: Hunan Renmin Chubanshe, 1998, pp. 382–90.

Mann, James, *About Face: A History of America's Curious Relationship to China from Nixon to Clinton*, New York: Knopf, 1999.

Meng, Xiangqing, "Canyu duobian anquan hezuo: jishi taozhan, ye shijiyu" [participation in multilateral security cooperation: both an opportunity and a challenge], *Shijie Jingji yu Zhengzhi*, no. 10 (254), 2001, pp. 25–9.

Potter, Pitman, "Legal Reform in China: Institutions, Culture and Selective Adaptation," *Law and Social Inquiry*, vol. 29, no. 2, Spring 2004.

Risse, Thomas and Sikkink, Katharyn, "The Socialization of International Human Rights Norms into Domestic Practice," in Thomas Risse, Stephen Ropp, and Katharyn Sikkink (eds) *The Power of Human Rights: International Norms and Domestic Change*, Cambridge: Cambridge University Press, 1999, pp. 1–38.

Ruggie, John G., "International Regimes, Transactions, and Change: Embedded Liberalism in the Postwar Economic Order," in Stephen Krasner (ed.) *International Regimes*, Ithaca: Cornell University Press, 1983, pp. 195–231.

Shen, Jiru, "Duobian waijiao he duoji shijie" [Multilateral diplomacy and a multipolar world], *Shijie Jingji yu zhengzhi*, no. 10 (254), 2001.

Shen, Yongxiang, 中国代表团副代表沈永祥在第59届人权会关于公民权利和 政治权利首页>外交部>组织机构>国际司>国际组织与会议>联合国>中国在 人权领域的活动中国代表团副代表沈永祥在第59届人权会关于公民权利和政 治 2003/06/27 (Deputy director of the Chinese delegation on Civil and Political Rights, 2003).

Shi, Xiuyin, "Zhongguo Shehui zhuanxing shiqi de quanli yu quanli: guannian fenxi" [Public Power and Rights during the Transformational Period in China] in behind Xia Yong, *Zouxiang Quanli de Shidai* [Towards an Era of Rights], Beijing: Zhongguo Zhengfa Daxue Chubanshe, 1995, pp. 70–134.

State Council Information Office, *The Condition of Human Rights in China*, Beijing: State Council Information Office, 1991.

—— *Progress in China's Human Rights in 1998*, Beijing: China Intercontinental Press, 1999.

Wallerstein, Immanuel, "The National and the Universal: Can There be Such a Thing as World Culture?" in Anthony D. King (ed.) *Culture, Globalization and the World-System*, Minneapolis: University of Minnesota Press, 1997.

Wan, Ming, *Human Rights in Chinese Foreign Relations: Defining and Defending National Interests*, Philadelphia: University of Pennsylvania Press, 2001.

Wang, Linxia, "Jianlun Woguo renquan lilun jianmshe de lishi yu fazhan" [A brief discussion of the history and development of the construction of human rights theory in our country], *Renmin Daxue baokan fuyin ziliao, Zhongguo zhengzhi*, no. 7, 2004, pp. 41–51.

Wu, Zichen, "China's Twisted Road to Coexistence," *Heartland*, no. 2, 2001, p. 37.

Xinhua, "Guoqing tegao: heping fazhan de Zhongguo zhuoli cengqiang ruan shili," 2004, [Special feature: China's peaceful development powerfully strengthens "soft power"]. Online. Available: www.news.xinhuanet. com/newscenter/2004–09/27/content_2029983.htm (accessed 27 September 2004).

Xu, Jian, "Heping jueqi shi Zhongguo Zhanlue Kuaize" [Peaceful Rise is China's Strategic Choice], *Zhongguo Waijiao*, no. 5, 2004, pp. 27–8.

Yu, Yixuan, "Yalta lixiang, Wilson juyi yu hezuoanquan" [The Yalta Ideal, Wilsonism, and cooperative security], in Xu Yihua (ed.) *Shiji zhijiao de Guoji Guanxi*, Shanghai: Yuandong Chubanshe, 2001, pp. 131–59.

Zhang, Weumu, "Daguo jueqi de lueji" [the logic of the rise of Great Powers] Zhongguo Shehuikexue, no. 5, 2004, pp. 50–4.
Zheng, Bijian, "Heping Jueqi de Xin daolu" [The New Road of Peaceful Rise], *Xinhua wenzhai*, no. 10, 2004, p. 1.
Zheng Ruixian, "Heping gongchu wuxiang yuanzi chansheng de lishi beijing he shidai yiyi," [The Historical Background to the Five Principles of Peaceful Coexistence and Their Epochal Importance] *Contemporary Asia-Pacific Studies*, no. 6, 2004.
Zhu, Feng, "Human Rights and the International Community: The Case of China," in *Prime*, no. 4, July 1996, pp. 37–60.
Zhu, Majie, "Contemporary Culture and International Relations," in Yu Xintian *et al.*, *Contemporary World Configuration*, Shanghai: Shanghai Institute of International Studies, 2002.

12 China's petroleum diplomacy
Hu Jintao's biggest challenge in foreign and security policy

Willy Wo-Lap Lam

Securing reliable supplies of energy and raw materials – particularly oil and gas – to sustain record-high growth rates is one of the most daunting tasks facing the leadership of President Hu Jintao and Premier Wen Jiabao. In the short to medium term, the People's Republic of China (PRC) seems to have enough foreign-exchange reserves as well as investment capital to purchase adequate amounts of oil and other resources on the international market, as well as to acquire mines and exploitation rights all over the world. However, what the Chinese Communist Party (CCP) leadership calls "energy security" can only be guaranteed by multi-pronged manoeuvres in the fields of foreign trade, foreign aid, military affairs, and, above all, diplomacy and multifarious geopolitical manoeuvres. Aggressive moves made by Beijing in the past year or two to win friends and lock up long-term supplies of oil and other resources have had a significant impact on the country's relations with dozens of countries on five continents.

This chapter will examine diplomatic efforts made by Beijing to achieve the following energy-related goals: diversifying supplies of oil and gas to lessen its reliance on Middle East crude; securing supplies from countries that have already made similar commitments to countries not friendly with China; ensuring the safety of sea lanes and other channels through which oil and other minerals will be shipped to China; handling diplomatic disputes that have arisen owing to Chinese efforts to prospect for oil and gas in territories also claimed by other nations; and using unconventional means such as military assistance and shipment to win the favour of – and contracts with – oil-exporting regimes such as Sudan and Angola. While China is also short of minerals and resources ranging from water to uranium, this chapter will mainly focus on diplomacy relating to oil and gas.

Discussion will be conducted on how the CCP leadership's multi-dimensional efforts to attain "energy security" has exacerbated the country's already fragile and problematic ties with other countries, including the US and Japan. The Hu-Wen team's energy search – which includes looking for oil and gas in areas with disputed sovereignty – could militate against two of China's much-ballyhooed foreign-policy initiatives in the early 2000s: the policy of good neighbourliness and the "peaceful rise" theory of non-aggressive development.

Petroleum-based diplomatic problems have been exacerbated by the fact that major economic players near China, ranging from Japan and India, are also frantically engaged in the same difficult game (*New York Times*, 19 February 2004).[1]

Moreover, Beijing's support and sponsorship of pariah states such as Myanmar, Sudan, and Venezuela could undercut its claim to be the leader of the under-developing world – and cast into doubt China's qualifications for being a responsible, law-abiding, member of the global community. Moreover, the PRC's energy obsession could, because of these and other reasons, undercut Beijing's moral authority and hamper its recent attempts at diplomatic multilateralism, particularly in areas such as the North Korea nuclear crisis, where Beijing is well placed to make contributions to global stability.

The sudden urgency of petroleum diplomacy

"Energy diplomacy" is expected to play an increasingly vital role in the Hu-Wen team's foreign and security policy. Compared with the previous administration under ex-president Jiang, the new leadership has put a higher priority on ensuring the reliable supply of energy, minerals, and raw materials. And diplomats as well as cadres in the three major state oil companies are very conscious of the fact that they must use diplomatic, economic, military, and other means to gain the friendship, or at least, acquiescence, of foreign countries from which Beijing must secure petroleum and other resources. As Chinese Academy of Sciences (CASS) expert Shen Jiru – one of the first academics to use the term "energy diplomacy" – noted in mid-2004, the question of energy was "inextricably linked to state security, strategic economic interests and foreign policy maneuvres" (*China News Service*, 27 July 2004).[2]

It is unquestionable that of all the resources and minerals, oil and gas stand out as the most crucial. This is despite the fact that China's search, for example, for water resources has also figured prominently in diplomatic wrangling with countries such as Myanmar, Vietnam, Thailand, and India. China is consuming some 5.5 million barrels of oil a day, two million barrels of which have to be imported. The PRC surpassed Japan as the second largest importer of crude in 2003, when the country's degree of dependence on imports reached a horrendous 37 per cent (*Businessweek*, 15 November 2004).[3] Most estimates say China may have to import as much as six million bpd by 2015. And by 2020, China's foreign-oil dependency may reach 60 per cent, and the PRC will surpass the US as the world's premier crude importer. Meanwhile, domestic oil reserves have dwindled to 23.7 billion metric tonnes, or barely 2.1 per cent of the world total. Quite a big proportion of oil finds in Xinjiang or along the Chinese coast has proven to be either not as voluminous as forecast or too expensive to excavate (*Wen Wei Po*, 13 March 2004).[4]

Not long after he became premier in March 2004, Wen announced that China must vastly expand its emergency oil reserves, from the current seven days to about a month. The State Council in early 2004 set aside six billion yuan to build up storage facilities in four major port areas. Moreover, the CCP Leading

Group on Foreign Affairs (LGFA) – China's foremost policy-making on diplomacy and security, headed by Hu – has pulled together the country's top cadres and experts from the fields of diplomacy, defence, intelligence, energy, and foreign trade, to handle this priority mission (Bloomberg news service, 14 December 2004).[5]

However, China's energy game plan has been rendered even more difficult by the unexpected price hike of crude in mid-2004. While coal still provides 70 per cent of China's energy supply, aggressive exploitation of China's reserves of around 114 billion metric tones – about 11.6 per cent of the world's – has led to the death of some 6,000 miners a year. Despite Beijing's heavy investment in nuclear power generation, nuclear stations are not expected to contribute more than 3 per cent of fuel needs by 2010. And while Beijing has already made sizeable investment in hydro-electricity, hydropower has yet markedly to improve China's dependence on imported energy supplies (*Time* Asia edition, 25 October 2004).[6]

The energy imperative has become even more pronounced in light of the Hu-Wen leadership's so-called *jiyu lun*, or "the theory of catching opportunities." This is a reference to the dictum, first issued by patriarch Deng Xiaoping in the 1990s, that China faces a golden opportunity in economic takeoff during the first two decades of this century, after which conditions both inside the country and internationally may not be as favourable. In the words of President Hu, "we must take a firm grip – and make good use – of the period of strategic opportunity when the country is faced with profound changes in the international situation" (New China News Agency, 25 November 2003; *People's Daily*, 9 August 2006).[7] However, from 2003 onwards, the leaps-and-bounds growth of the "world factory" along China's eastern coast has engendered a severe shortage of resources ranging from iron and cement to electricity. The fear of somehow letting slip the once-in-a-lifetime *jiyu* has further galvanized the Fourth-Generation leadership into devoting all the resources it can muster to tackle the energy imbroglio.

Securing long-term oil supplies vs. great power rivalry

Minimizing the impact of American preponderance in the Middle East

Given that China gets more than 60 per cent of its crude oil from the Middle East, a top priority of the PRC's energy diplomacy is to ensure and even boost its supplies from this key oil-producing region. However, even before the start of the Iraq War, Beijing had realized its oil prospects there were under threat. This was despite Beijing's sterling relationship with most Middle East regimes, which had been built on decades of support for causes such as Palestinian statehood and the curbing of Israeli "expansionism." Beijing, however, has been unable to stop fast-growing US influence in the unstable region. Soon after the 11 September 2001 events, Chinese strategists had warned against the right-wing and "unilateralist" White House using the pretext of fighting terrorism to gain control, first over Afghanistan and then, the Middle East (*Outlook Weekly*, 21 February 2005).[8] Yet there was little that the CCP leadership could do except go along with France, Germany, and Russia in opposing America's incursion into Iraq.

However, there are indications that particularly after the re-election of George Bush in November 2004, the Hu leadership was determined to apply more diplomatic and other pressure to prevent the US from expanding its perceived military occupation of, and influence in, several Middle East countries. President Hu's advisers thought that, in his second term, Bush might apply his "policy of pre-emption" to Iran, which was suspected by Washington to have been surreptitiously developing weapons of mass destruction (WMD) behind the façade of the peaceful use of nuclear energy. Moreover, Iranian agents had reportedly infiltrated Iraq and wreaked havoc on US and British forces stationed there. The LGFA concluded at the time that there was a good possibility that Bush may next target Iran, with or without the blessings of the United Nations Security Council (UNSC).

In November, Beijing made it known that it objected to the Iranian issue's being referred to the UNSC; Beijing instead backed negotiations between Tehran and EU countries for the suspension of Iran's production of enriched uranium. Chinese diplomats also dropped strong hints that Beijing would cast its veto if the UNSC were to vote on sanctions or military action against Iran at a later time. This was at variance with Beijing's attitude in the run-up to the Iraq War, when it was understood that China would abstain from an UNSC ballot on using force against Iraq. China's much more assertive stance regarding Iran was due to its great expectations that the latter would remain its major Middle East oil supplier in the coming decade or so (*Asia Times Online*, 30 November 2004).[9]

Foreign Minister Li Zhaoxing pledged strong diplomatic and economic support for Iran during a brief but high-profile trip to Tehran in early November. Chinese diplomats privately admitted that should Washington decide to use military force against Iran while bypassing the UNSC, there was nothing much China can do in practical terms. But Beijing seemed determined to persuade Britain and Australia – and other possible members of a new "coalition of the willing" under Washington's direction – not to follow the lead of the US this time. Beijing was quite amply rewarded for its apparent determination to lock horns with the US over Iran. In October, Sinopec signed multiple contracts worth close to $100 billion for items including annual imports of ten million tonnes of liquefied natural gas for 25 years as well as exploitation rights to the Yadavaran oil field near the Iraq border. And during Li's visit, the Iranian Petroleum Minister, Bijan Zanganeh, expressed the hope that China would soon displace Japan as the largest importer of Iranian crude and gas (*International Herald Leader*, 12 November 2004).[10]

From the larger perspective, the LGFA felt strongly that while oil prices had shown signs of edging down by the end of 2004, they would still stay at intolerably high levels unless the situation in the Middle East were stabilized. There was no lack of conspiracy theorists in Beijing who claimed that it was a "US plot" to spike oil prices so as to hurt the PRC economy and "to prevent China's rise." Referring to the possibility that Bush might again start military action in the Middle East, President Hu reportedly said at a LGFA meeting in late 2004 that China "must do all it can to ensure a favourable international climate for its economic development." For Hu's strategists, a repeat of the Iraqi experience in another Middle East country would represent a direct threat to China's delicate economic and energy security (Chinese sources, September 2004).[11]

Unexpected difficulties in Russia and Kazakhstan

Naturally, one of Beijing's first – and most substantial – attempts to look beyond the Middle East is to secure oil and gas from nearby areas, namely Russia, Kazakhstan, and other Central Asian states, as well as resource-rich Asia-Pacific nations such as Indonesia and Australia (*The Australian*, 12 February 2005).[12] Deals with Jakarta and Canberra were concluded in a fairly straightforward manner. However, the unhappy saga of getting Moscow's permission to jointly build a 2,400 km pipeline to take oil from the Siberian town of Angarsk to the northeastern Daqing Oil field has illustrated the extent to which the intriguing triangular relationship between Beijing, Moscow, and Tokyo has complicated Beijing's petroleum diplomacy. After all, Beijing's "love–hate" relationship with both Moscow and Tokyo goes back centuries; and these convoluted relationships have played a role in China's energy-related dealings with the two powerful neighbours.

The pipeline was earlier billed as a landmark of the all-rounded strategic partnership as well as of the good neighbourliness forged between former presidents Jiang Zemin and Boris Yeltsin. Preliminary agreements on the Angarsk–Daqing link were reached in 2002 between Chinese state oil firms and Yukos, then Russia's second-largest oil producer. Yet another agreement on the petroleum lifeline for China was inked between Presidents Hu and Vladmir Putin in early 2003. Yet Moscow has been playing Beijing off against Tokyo. By late 2004, Moscow was tilting toward first satisfying the Japanese market via an Angarsk–Nakhodka line to the Pacific coast just opposite Japan. This was partly because Tokyo had offered a package exceeding $20 billion to cover both the construction of the pipeline and economic assistance to the Russian Far East. Moreover, while there are problems in Moscow–Tokyo ties – including the four disputed northern islands – the Putin leadership seems anxious to pursue some degree of equidistance in its relations with both the PRC and Japan. A number of Russian politicians, particularly those based in the Siberian and Far East regions, also harbour distrust of China. For instance, they fear that the construction of an Angarsk–Nakhodka line would increase the already sizeable Chinese population, mostly labourers, working in that relatively remote region (*Asia Times Online*, 25 October 2002).[13]

After a series of meetings in late 2004 between President Vladimir Putin, on the one hand, and Wen and Hu, on the other, Beijing was given an assurance of "ten years of supply" of Russian oil and gas. However, neither side has revealed the exact format in which this would come about. Obviously, oil would continue to be taken to China through the more expensive means of rail transport. Also, it is still possible that a branch line might peel off the Angarsk–Nakhodka link to satisfy the China market. In any case, the price tag for Beijing will be much higher (*Wall Street Journal*, 21 September 2004).[14]

Despite the Putin cabinet's apparent failure to honour an earlier pledge, Beijing has realized that because of energy and diplomatic reasons, it must continue to maintain a special relationship with its former socialist ally. For example, the party and government leadership has vowed to continue buying the bulk of its weapons from Russia even after the European Union has lifted its 15-year-old arms embargo on China. And the Hu team is believed to have made concessions to Moscow on the delineation of the Sino-Russian boundary, which was finalized during a Hu-Putin summit in Beijing in October 2004 (*People's Daily*, 15 October 2004).[15]

Beijing is also putting more efforts into resuscitating the Shanghai Cooperation Organization (SCO), which groups China, Russia, Kazakhstan, Tajikistan, Uzbekistan, and Kyrgyzstan. This is despite the fact that, particularly following the American invasion of Afghanistan, US presence in SCO members, especially Uzbekistan and Tajikistan, has become pronounced. These two countries, which provide bases for US troops, have become dependent on American economic aid (*Strategic Insights*, April 2002).[16] One consolation for Beijing is that work finally started on the much-delayed China–Kazakhstan oil pipeline in mid-2004. The 3,000-km link from Atasu to the Xinjiang Autonomous Region is set to provide western China with 20 million tonnes of Caspian Sea crude a year. Chinese authorities have claimed that owing to pressure from the US, Beijing had been unable to raise funds on the international financial market for this project. Moreover, central and regional authorities in Kazakhstan had demanded more money from Chinese state oil companies than had been stipulated in the relevant agreements and contracts (*International Herald Leader*, 2 February 2004).[17]

Exploring new sources in Africa and South America

One relatively successful initiative launched by the Hu-Wen team is making new friends and nailing down fresh sources of crude in myriad countries in Africa and Latin America. As Tan Zhuzhou, Chairman of China Petroleum and Chemical Industry Association, pointed out, China should "take its technologies and capital to Africa and South America and exploit oil there so as to diversify its sources" (*People's Daily*, 28 February 2004).[18] With foreign policy based increasingly on economic, *realpolitik* considerations, raising China's profile in these two relatively poor regions requires hefty investments. Fortunately for Beijing, China's foreign-exchange reserves have surpassed the $400 billion mark – and can, at least in the foreseeable future, afford to sink huge outlays in mines and oil fields in these far-off regions.

Boosting China's influence in Africa and Latin America also tallies with the PRC's long-cherished goal of being the leader of the developing world. Obviously, ex-President Jiang and, in particular, the Hu-Wen team, have shaken off Chairman Mao's romantic ideology of spearheading a "world Marxist revolution." However, African and Latin American support is deemed useful to Beijing's objective of building a "multi-polar world order" – and countering a Washington-led "anti-China containment policy." For example, China's clout in the United Nations will be strengthened. Then there is the Taiwan angle, particularly the fact that, out of the 27 countries that still recognize the island stronghold, eight are in Africa and 13 in Central and South America. Obviously, Beijing fast-growing influence in Africa and Latin America would help its longstanding goal of persuading more of these countries to switch diplomatic ties from Taipei to Beijing. For example, El Salvador already expressed the wish of forming formal ties with the PRC (APF, 28 October 2004).[19] These additional incentives have helped convince the Hu-Wen leadership that China's expensive, high-profile ventures in these two regions make good sense economically as well as politically.

Not surprisingly, Beijing's aggressive moves in Africa and Latin America have pitted it against a number of countries. Sino-Indian ties were strained in the second half of 2004 because Chinese state oil companies had edged out Indian ones in securing development rights to oil fields in Sudan and Angola. And during his visit to Beijing in mid-2006, Venezuelan President Hugo Chavez vowed to triple oil supplies to China to 500,000 bpd by 2010. Given hostile relations between Caracas and Washington – and the huge investments of US oil firms in Venezuela – China's "strategic partnership" with the Latin American country could hurt Sino-US ties (AFP, 16 October 2004; AFP, 25 August 2006).[20]

Forays into Africa

While Beijing started getting serious about African oil a decade ago, the historic visit by President Hu to Egypt, Algeria, and Gabon in early 2004 confirmed the country's determination to be a big player in this resource-rich continent. Other Politburo Standing Committee stalwarts, including Wu Bangguo and Zeng Qinghong, also toured the continent later that year. In 2003, China bought $4.85 billion worth of African oil, up 67.5 per cent from the year before and fully 24.3 per cent of total Chinese imports that year came from Africa. Beijing reckons that as much as 30 per cent of Chinese crude imports might be coming from Africa by the end of this decade. And, by late 2004, China had secured relatively reliable arrangements to ship oil from Angola, Sudan, the Republic of the Congo, Equatorial Guinea, Cameroon, Algeria, Lybia, Nigeria, and Egypt (*Twenty-first Century Economic Herald,* 2 February 2004).[21]

One advantage of African oil is its low sulphur content, which is good for China's budding automobile industry. The other advantage is unique African politics, which Beijing has adroitly exploited. Chinese-state oil companies have got away with doing business in countries with horrendous authoritarian traditions. A case in point is Sudan, which is shunned by many Western and Asian countries for genocidal atrocities committed by the Khartoum leadership. Beijing, however, has earned Sudanese support by defending the regime at the UN and other forums. In Gabon, the Chinese have maintained solid ties with the reportedly corrupt regime of patriarch Omar Bongo (VOA News, 21 July 2004).[22]

Beijing is also in a position to obtain special prices and mineral exploitation rights in Africa through non-conventional means such as selling relatively sophisticated weapons to countries that cannot buy them on the international market. For example, China is an important arms supplier of Sudan, Angola, and Zimbabwe. The New York-based Human Rights Watch has reported that the Khartoum government has purchased large quantities of Chinese arms, some of which have been used to quell anti-government rebels in Darfur. And in mid-2004, China agreed to sell Zimbabwe fighter jets as well as military vehicles worth an estimated $200 million. The PLA has also boosted defence ties with a number of African nations through visits by senior generals. Western PLA analysts say it is unusual that apart from members of the policy-setting Central Military Commission (CMC), generals at the regional-command level have also been calling on the continent. For example, CMC Vice-Chairman Guo Boxiong was in South Africa and Egypt in July 2004, and the commander of the Lanzhou Military Region (which oversees areas including the Xinjiang Autonomous Region), General Li Qianyuan, toured Angola at about the same time. Gen Li held extensive talks with the military brass there on a broad range of cooperation. (*International Herald Tribune*, 19 April 2006; Angola Press Agency (Luanda), 9 August 2004).[23] Until the the early 2000s, it was rare for PLA generals, let alone regional commanders, to visit this vast continent.

Forays into Latin America

Beijing is also harbouring great expectations about Latin American energy and other resources. President Hu's trip to South America in November 2004, which took in Brazil, Chile, Argentina, and Cuba, showed the weight that Beijing was attaching to tapping mineral resources, including petroleum, iron ore, agricultural produce, and other items in the backyard of the US. As far as oil and gas are concerned, state companies such as Sinopec have secured, or are close to nailing down, substantial deals in countries such as Brazil, Ecuador, Columbia, and Venezuela. Apart from its huge import market, Beijing is in a position to offer economic aid and high-quality but inexpensive technology ranging from mining to munitions (*Asian Wall Street Journal*, 22 November 2004).[24]

The "all weather strategic partnership" that Hu was able to cement with Brazilia was especially noteworthy. The Brazil-state oil firm, Petrobras, expected that China would in 2004 become the third-leading destination of Brazilian crude exports, with shipments of about 50,000 barrels per day. At the same time, Sinopec invested $1 billion in a joint venture with Petrobas for the construction of a gas pipeline from Vitoria in south Brazil to the northeastern state of Bahia. Other resources-based deals the Chinese have signed in the recent year or so have included iron-ore shipments from Companhia Vale do Rio Doce, one of the world's largest mining concerns, for Shanghai's famous Baoshan Steel Mill (Dow Jones Newswires, 26 May 2004).[25]

At the same time, the Hu leadership is willing to bring its enhanced global clout to bear in crafting a special Sino-Brazilian relationship. For example, Beijing has quietly lent support to Brazil's bid for a place in an expanded UNSC. Brazil's competitors include India and Japan, both of which may be able to garner the support of the US. More importantly, Beijing has made it clear that it is looking at expanding relations with the entire Portuguese world – and helping leading countries such as Brazil to gain their rightful places in the global community (NCNA, 17 November 2004).[26]

Moreover, the Beijing leadership is taking advantage of its reputation as a spokesman for the developing world to boost its influence in Latin America – and to increase its chances of winning good deals in the resources sector. In all four countries that Hu visited, the Chinese president stressed that China would, "forever stay on the side of developing countries." The Chinese supremo noted that China stood for a multi-polar world order, "a democratic international order as well as a multiple [approach] to development models" (NCNA, 12 November 2004).[27] Obviously, this is a reference to, and criticism of, the unilateralism, if not the "neo-imperialism," supposedly pursued by the Bush administration. Some analysts have even seen the sudden growth of Chinese influence as an indirect challenge to the 1823 Monroe Doctrine of the US, which says, in effect, that Central and South America are within Washington's "sphere of influence."

Exacerbation of territorial disputes

Locking horns with Japan

China's energy obsession has raised problems with countries and blocs such as Japan and ASEAN. The petroleum imperative has had a particularly detrimental impact on already shaky Sino-Japanese relations, which have been bedevilled by "the question of history" as well as by the perceived rise of xenophobic nationalism in China. Since early 2004, Beijing and Tokyo have been at loggerheads over rights to exploit natural gas under the East China Sea, which lies between the two countries. Tokyo has complained that the underwater Chunxiao Field, where Beijing had started large-scale prospecting, was close to the edge of Japan's special economic zone. And Beijing has responded that it has never recognized any "mid-point" line of demarcation in waters between the two countries. It was not until October of that year that both sides agreed to sit down to discuss the issue. However, by year's end, while Chinese and Japanese papers had speculated that the matter might be referred to the International Court at the Hague for arbitration, no solution was in sight (*Yazhou Zhoukan*, 18 July 2004).[28]

Moreover, disputes over the oil-rich Diaoyu Islands (known as the Senkakus in Japan) are also hotting up. This is despite the commitment made by the late patriarch Deng Xiaoping in the early 1970s – when both countries were negotiating Tokyo's official recognition of the PRC – that sovereignty-related conflicts over the Diaoyus should be "left for the next generation." From late 2003 onwards, however, nationalistic groups in China have organized high-profile protests over the Diaoyus, including sending boats to the islands to assert Chinese sovereignty. "Protect-the-Diaoyus" demonstrations outside the Japanese Embassy in Beijing – until recently stopped by Chinese police – have become fairly common (*Japan Times*, 27 March 2004).[29]

By late 2004, there were indications that quarrels over energy resources could lead to an arms race between the two countries, if not even to small-scale military confrontation. Tokyo launched a vehement protest to Beijing in November regarding the intrusion of a Chinese nuclear submarine into Japanese territory. The outspoken Trade Minister Shoichi Nakagawa linked the submarine incident to Sino-Japanese wrangling over the Chinese gas project. A widely read document released by the Japan Self-Defense Agency cited three hypothetical situations in which the country could be attacked by the PLA, one of the these scenarios concerned the East China Sea, the other two were sovereignty disputes over the Senkaku Islands. (*Ming Pao*, 9 November 2004).[30]

Flashpoints in the South China Seas

After a period of relative tranquility, disputes between China and ASEAN countries – mainly claimants to sovereignty over the Spratlys Islands, such as Vietnam, the Philippines, Malaysia, and Brunei – have flared anew. For instance, Beijing in early 2004 criticized Vietnam's announcement that it would organize tour groups to the Spratlys. Foreign Ministry spokesman Kong Quan said Hanoi's actions had "impinged upon China's territorial sovereignty." Chinese diplomats also decried efforts by unnamed countries to invite multinational companies to prospect for oil and gas in the Spratlys. As *Outlook Eastern Weekly*, a Communist Party-run current affairs magazine, put it, "Relevant countries have mounted offensives against China over sovereignty in the South China Sea – and they have strengthened their military grip over islands and sea lanes" (*Asian Wall Street Journal*, 2 April 2004).[31]

Beijing's decision to adopt a more assertive stance on the South China Sea seemed at variance with its previous, less confrontational position of shelving sovereignty disputes. In November 2002, ASEAN and China concluded a treaty that called on all claimants to avoid actions that might heighten tension in the flashpoint region. Furthermore, in 2003, China became the first country to accede to a Treaty of Amity and Cooperation with the major Asia grouping, meaning that disputes between the two should be settled by negotiation, not force (*People's Daily* (English edition), 29 April 2003).[32]

Moreover, the CCP leadership was criticized by some of its Asian neighbours for pursuing a Machiavellian, divide-and-conquer strategy regarding the

Spratlys. Sticking to its time-honoured policy of seeking bilateral – but not multilateral – agreements on disputes in the South China Sea, Beijing was in October 2004 able to come to a one-on-one agreement with Philippine President Gloria Arroyo on joint exploration of oil in waters with undetermined sovereignty. Beijing sweetened the deal with economic aid packages, including a $400 million loan for Manila's North Rail project (*Asia Times Online*, 4 September 2004). Beijing has also secured the backing of Indonesia, its "strategic partner" since 2005, in areas including energy-related diplomacy. This is partly due to China's vast aid to and investment in the populous Muslim country – and the fact that the latter enjoys a hefty trade surplus with the PRC (*China Daily*, 25 April 2005; NCNA, 10 May 2006).[33]

The "diplomacy of safe passage": tackling the Strait of Malacca imbroglio

Yet another major component of Beijing's multi-faceted "energy diplomacy" consists of efforts to ensure that its oil-supply routes would not be subject to attack by potentially hostile elements, including the American Navy and Air Force. Take the strategic Strait of Malacca. Some 80 per cent of the petroleum that China imports passes through this narrow strip of water. Oil tankers and other vessels plying this route are periodically attacked by pirates or intimidated by terrorists. Much more important, however, is the CCP leadership's fear that "hostile foreign powers" – meaning the US – could under certain circumstances strangle China's lifeline by dominating access to the Strait.

Many Western analysts might dismiss as far-fetched allegations that the US may use its unparalleled firepower to choke off oil supplies to China via the Malacca Strait. Yet this has become a national-security canon among Beijing's political and academic elite, who talk much about the Strait of Malacca imbroglio (SOMI). Hong Kong's Chinese-run *Wen Wei Po* newspaper cited Beijing experts as saying "some countries have continued to try to control and dominate navigation routes through the Strait," while the mass-circulation *China Youth Daily* quoted energy and security specialist Lu Guoxue as saying the Strait was "undoubtedly the key waterway where the US would want to consolidate its geopolitical superiority, prevent other big countries from rising, and dominate the flow of world energy supplies" (*Asian Wall Street Journal*, 30 July 2004).[34]

Hence the decision made by the Party and government leadership from mid-2003 to consider ways to circumvent SOMI. According to the official media, energy and military experts have proposed opening up new passageways via countries including Thailand, Myanmar, Pakistan, and even Bangladesh. Several of these scenarios envisage crude from tankers from the Middle East being unloaded at ports north of the Malacca Strait and then piped over to China's southwestern provinces such as Yunnan via secure land lines (*Wen Wei Po*, 15 July 2004).[35]

A more complicated but much talked-about possibility is dredging a conduit

– a so-called "Asian Panama Canal" – through the Kra Isthmus, a narrow strip of land stretching south of Bangkok and going as far as Phuket. This artificial channel, which was being vigorously promoted by the "pro-China" Thaksin Shinawatra government, will enable tankers bound for China and other Asian countries to go directly from the Andaman Sea to the Gulf of Thailand. According to Peking University international-relations professor Zhang Xizhen, China must seek a "faster, cheaper, and safer oil route than the Malacca Strait" – and the Thai canal was an "important option" (*Chinanewsweek*, 9 August 2004).[36]

The Thai solution, however, has major drawbacks. The estimated canal construction costs of $28 billion – much of it likely to be borne by China – are prohibitive. Yet a more crucial factor is strong US–Thai military links. The national media recently quoted Zhu Xingshan, an energy expert at the State Commission for Economic Development and Reform, as saying: "People are worried about SOMI because of fears of the US going for the jugular" (*New Capital Post*, 17 July 2004).[37]

By contrast, an overland connection via Myanmar had become more attractive by mid-2004. The proposed 1,000 km-odd pipeline, to stretch from Myanmar's deep-sea port of Sittwe to Kunming, capital of China's southwestern Yunnan province, is billed to solve the SOMI. The official *Orient Outlook* weekly magazine, a subsidiary of the state Xinhua News Agency, ran an article pushing the Chinese–Myanmar pipeline, which carries a $2 billion price-tag. *Orient Outlook* quoted Yunnan University world-affairs professor Li Chenyang as saying the provincial authorities had already submitted a blueprint to the State Council. Li said the Myanmar connection would cut the supply line of Middle East oil to China by up to 1,200 km – and that "it will be relatively much safer." Li and other Yunnan experts said the pipeline could be laid alongside a railway that Yangon was currently building from the Sittwe Port to the Yunnan boundary (*Orient Outlook Weekly*, 13 July 2004).[38]

Diplomatic sources in Beijing said the subject was raised between Premier Wen and then Myanmar premier Khin Nyunt, who spent one week in China in the summer. Given the size of the project and its global implications, the Hu-Wen leadership was unlikely to make a decision soon. The sources said, however, that in light of Beijing's perception that the US was boosting its forces in the Asia-Pacific region, the possibility of Beijing's opting for an unorthodox solution to SOMI, such as the Myanmar pipeline, had risen substantially.

Beijing's growing paranoia over oil – and over Washington and its allies' readiness to strangle China through whatever means – could worsen relations not only with the US but with American allies and quasi-allies in the region. For instance, Sino-Singapore ties had worsened well before then Deputy Prime Minister Lee Hsien Loong's "private" trip to Taiwan in early 2004. The gist of Beijing's unhappiness was that Singapore was providing base facilities to the US that could be used, among other things, to exacerbate China's SOMI. *China Youth Daily* commentator Shi Hongtao pointed out that Singapore backed the proposal that the US Navy be allowed to join forces with those of Singapore, Malaysia, and Indonesia, in patrolling the Malacca Strait. Fortunately for China,

Shi wrote, opposition from Kuala Lumpur and Jakarta had "smashed America's sweet dream" (*South China Morning Post*, 11 October 2004).[39]

The military dimension of China's petroleum diplomacy

Yet another factor contributing to the nervousness of China's neighbours about the PRC's petroleum diplomacy is the heavy military component of the country's effort to secure reliable supplies of oil and gas. As discussed above, Beijing is in a position to win over suppliers in the developing world by sweetening the petroleum deals with offers of cheap weapons. Moreover, much of China's special relationship with Myanmar and Thailand, both of which will play a sizeable role in ensuring safety of passage for Chinese oil imports, is based on military cooperation.

With Hu succeeding ex-President Jiang as CCP Central Military Commission Chairman in September 2004, it is possible that the Head of the LGFA will use China's fast-growing military muscle to push petroleum diplomacy. Hu underscored the inter-relationship between national defence and economic construction at a Politburo "study session" two weeks before he became Commander-in-Chief. "We must comprehensively implement the objective of the coordinated development of national defense and economic construction," Hu said. He added that there was no question that a strong military force was necessary to protect China's territorial integrity and ensure the success of China's economic take-off (*Wen Wei Po*, 4 February 2005).[40] Given the overriding importance of sufficient supplies of energy and other resources in economic growth, it is not surprising that the PLA will sub-serve the country's energy-related game plans. Indeed, since mid-2004, senior generals such as Cao Gangchuan have spoken about the need for civilian sectors such as infrastructure and transport to serve the goals of national defence.

Moreover, protecting China's territorial integrity has taken on a new meaning in the age of chronic energy shortages. For Beijing, this includes oil and gas that might lie below the South China and the East China Seas. It is conceivable that when the crunch comes, the prowess of the PLA Navy and Air Force will play a role in territorial disputes in the Spratlys or the East China Sea. Since disputes over the Diaoyus (or Senkakus) as well as over the East China Sea flared up in 2003, Beijing and Tokyo have traded numerous accusations about territorial intrusions by the other's naval or intelligence-gathering vessels. Given that China's energy supply lines have now been extended to pretty much all five continents, an important function of the PLA's blue-water fleet will be to safeguard the sea lanes through which China-bound oil tankers will pass. Indeed, an elite fleet demonstrated the prowess of the fast-expanding Chinese Navy in 2002 by circumnavigating the world for the first time. Four years later, two sophisticated PLA vessels visited American naval facilities in the US and Canada. A popular 2005 book entitled *The Battle in Protecting Key Oil Routes* even envisaged a sea engagement near the Strait of Malacca in which the Chinese Navy destroyed an entire US aircraft group (*China Brief*, 14 April 2006; NCNA, 19

September 2006).⁴¹ The generals are expected to spend more effort to secure military bases or other logistics facilities in different parts of the world.

Conclusion: benevolent elephant vs. hungry tiger

One of the more imaginative initiatives of the Hu-Wen administration has been that of the "peaceful rise of China," meaning that China's emergence as a major power would contribute to the prosperity of its neighbours instead of posing a threat to other countries. While, apparently for reasons of factional politics, the slogan was later changed to China pursuing "peace and development," the drift of Beijing's message has remained pretty much the same (www.YaleGlobal.org website, 22 June 2004).⁴²

As the foregoing sections have pointed out, however, China's aggressive search for oil and gas, while apparently justifiable, given the leadership's anxiety to make up for lost time in terms of economic development, has alarmed big as well as small countries in the Asia-Pacific and other regions. And Beijing's energy imperative has gone beyond petroleum to pretty much all types of minerals and resources.

For example, take water, the supply of which in sufficient quantity may in many respects be more difficult to ensure than oil or uranium. The per capita share of water resources in China is a mere 2,200 square metres, or one fourth that of the global average. Three hundred and sixty million Chinese, mostly peasants, have to drink contaminated water. Factories in the Pearl River Delta also experienced severe water shortage through 2004. The struggle over control of major waterways has pitted China against its neighbours. A case in point is Beijing's plan to build hydroelectric dams at the upper reaches of the Mekong and Nu Rivers – and to funnel more water from these waterways to irrigate China's arid western provinces. This has resulted in less – and poorer quality – water for countries reliant upon the downstream portions of these international rivers such as Thailand, Burma, Vietnam as well as Cambodia (Institute of Defence and Strategic Studies, Singapore, July 2004).⁴³ While countries such as Cambodia and Thailand that have become increasingly dependent on Chinese aid and imports are not in a position to noisily challenge Beijing, the latter's energy imperative is bound to hurt its much-ballyhooed "policy of good neighbourliness."

By 2004, many foreign governments and experts – and quite a few Chinese economists – have cast doubt on the wisdom and sustainability of the "China model" of development. While the country accounted for 4 per cent of global GDP growth in 2003, it consumed 40 per cent of the world's cement, 27 per cent of its steel, 19.7 per cent of copper, 18.6 per cent of aluminum, and 31 per cent of coal. "Our high-input, high-consumption, high-emission, crude method of growth remains unchanged," admitted Ma Kai, Chairman of the State Commission on Economic Development and Reform. The country's foremost environmental cadre, Pan Yue, also expressed alarm at how China's *cuguang* ("rough and quantity-based") approach to growth had led to gross wastage of resources and irrevocable environmental degradation (*Far Eastern Economic Review*, 1 April 2004).[44]

Against this background, it is perhaps not surprising that the image of the "benevolent elephant" that Beijing hopes to project via propaganda about China's "peaceful rise" has been replaced by that of the hungry tiger, an insatiable Leviathan or a King Kong, gobbling up everything in its way. For some, this has conjured up horror scenarios of another form of Yellow Peril. It is true that leaders such as Hu and Wen have reiterated that a strong China will never invade or harm other countries and peoples. Yet an energy-obsessed PRC could be seen as a predator bent on grabbing mines and oil fields around the world – as well as monopolizing oil and gas in territories and waters whose sovereignty is being disputed.

The bogey of China as tiger on the prowl has adversely affected Chinese energy- and resources-related diplomacy. Particularly in Western countries where the PRC's human rights and rule-of-law records are considered deficient, quite a few cases of Chinese acquisition of major foreign companies have been subject to embarrassing scrutiny. Take China Minmetals Corporation's $7 billion bid to acquire Noranda, deemed a "venerable Canadian mining firm" by the Toronto media. Noranda controls huge deposits of zinc, nickel, and copper. Critics of the deal, who include influential parliamentarians and newspaper editorialists, have zeroed in on Minmetals' alleged practice of employing prison labour in its Chinese plants. However, a more basic reason could be Western governments' perception of Beijing's take-no-prisoners approach to safeguarding its energy security (*Toronto Star*, 5 October 2004).[45]

The worldwide scramble for petroleum and other resources could also move forward what some analysts think is the inevitable showdown between the world's only superpower and its most potent would-be superpower. This is despite the fact that particularly in the wake of China's cooperation with the US in the global campaign against terrorism, Sino-American relations under Presidents Hu and Bush have been largely free from direct confrontation. Former US Secretary of State Colin Powell repeatedly characterized American–Chinese ties as "the best" since the early 1970s (*China Daily*, 14 November 2004).[46] However, it is also clear that since the US and its major allies such as Japan are also pursuing the same goal of oil sufficiency, China's assertive manoeuvres in areas where America has vested interests – Asia, Central Asia, and South America – would inevitably exacerbate Sino-American contradictions.

In large part because of the energy and raw-materials imperative, competition between China and other powers is likely to intensify in the Middle East, the Caspian Sea area, as well as in resource-rich Third World regions, such as Africa and Latin America. Because of China's long-standing image as a champion of developing countries, it has an edge over the US in quite a few of these nations. As US economist, David Hale, pointed out, "it is too soon to speak of a new era of Chinese imperialism in the Third World, but China will certainly play a more influential role in the affairs of many developing countries," including the exploitation of natural resources (author's interview).[47]

Compared with more developed countries in Asia, such as Japan and South Korea, China has had a relatively late start in thrashing out an energy sustainability programme. Despite is growing economic, diplomatic, and military clout, the Hu-Wen leadership realizes that it must balance the aggressive search for oil and gas with a policy of mollification. Not only China's immediate neighbours but powers in other continents have to be reassured that the PRC is after a win–win formula of co-prosperity and joint-development. Otherwise, the hungry tiger on the prowl might encounter problems in fueling its ambitious growth plans, problems which in turn will exacerbate potentially explosive domestic malaises such as unemployment. Clearly, not only the prestige and credibility of the Hu-Wen administration but the CCP authorities' Mandate of Heaven depends on the extent to which Beijing can conduct a successful energy diplomacy.

Notes

1 For a discussion of the oil-related rivalry between China and India see, for example, Keith Bradsher, "India joins China for a worldwide rush for oil and gas," *New York Times*, 19 February 2004.
2 Cited in Lin Tianhong, "Expert: China must have a strategic concept of 'petroleum diplomacy,'" China News Service (CNS) (an official news agency), 27 July 2004.
3 Brian Bremner and Dexter Roberts, "China and the great hunt for oil," *Businessweek*, 15 November 2004; "China: Surging oil demand changes energy scene," *Oxford Analytica*, 26 February 2004; Takio Murakami China becomes world-class oil buyer, *Asahi Shimbun* (Tokyo), 23 July 2003.
4 "Daqing to lower crude oil production," www.chinaview.cn website, 23 March 2004; "China petroleum strategy picks up speed," *Wen Wei Po* (a Chinese-run Hong Kong paper), 13 March 2004.
5 "China to build oil reserve in stages to limit effect on prices," Bloomberg news service, 14 December 2004.
6 Matthew Forney and Susan Jakes, "China's quest for oil," *Time* Asia edition, 25 October 2004.
7 Cited in "Hu Jintao makes major speech at the Politburo's Ninth Study Session," New China News Agency (NCNA) (an official Chinese news agency), 25 November 2003. Patriarch Deng Xiaoping first pointed out in the 1990s that the first two decades of the twenty-first century would be China's "major strategic period of opportunity" for developing its economy and overall strength. See Wang Lisheng, "Deng Xiaoping on how to take advantage of 'major strategic periods of opportunity'," reprinted in *People's Daily* website, 9 August 2006. Online. Available: www.cpc.people.com.cn/GB/68742/69115/69120/4684471.html.
8 For a discussion of Beijing's fears about America's containment policy, see "US army is encircling China from east, west and south," *Outlook Weekly* (an official Chinese newsweekly), 21 February 2005.
9 For a discussion of growing Chinese–Iranian ties, see Antoaneta Bezlova, "China–Iran tango threatens US leverage," *Asia Times Online* (Hong Kong-based Net-based news service), 30 November 2004.
10 Tang Zhichao, "China and Iran pursue normal cooperation as the US gets nervous," *International Herald Leader* (official Beijing news magazine), 12 November 2004; Robin Wright, "Iran's growing alliance with China could cost the US leverage," *Asian Wall Street Journal*, 18 November 2004.
11 Author's interviews with Chinese sources in Beijing, September 2004.

12 Beijing has encountered no major problems in securing oil and other resources from ASEAN countries as well as Australia. In fact, China's massive imports have resulted in a "pro-China tilt" in the foreign policy of these countries. For example, Canberra has embarrassed key ally, the US, by largely backing China's stance on the lifting of the EU's arms embargo. For a discussion, see Greg Sheridan, "PM defies Bush over China arms," *The Australian*, 12 February 2005.

13 For a discussion of Beijing's troubles in securing Russian oil, see, for example, John Helmer, "Dances with bears: oil to China is a race against time," *Asia Times Online*, 25 October 2002.

14 Charles Hutzler, "Halt of Yukos oil comes at bad time for Beijing," *Wall Street Journal*, 21 September 2004; Martin Sieff, "Russia calls oil shots with China," *United Press International*, 20 October 2004.

15 "Successful demarcation makes strong Russia ties," *People's Daily*, 15 October 2004; For a discussion of Sino-Russian relations in late 2004, see, for example, Willy Lam, "Beijing pushes for gains," *China Brief*, Jamestown Foundation (Washington), 11 November 2004.

16 For a discussion of US relations with Central Asian countries after September 11, see, for example, Elizabeth Skinner, "Enduring Freedom for Central Asia?" in *Strategic Insights*, Naval Postgraduate School, California, I, 2, April 2002.

17 For a discussion of Sino-Kazakhstan cooperation in oil exploration, see, for example, Staff reporter, "A turn-around in China's overseas petroleum strategy?," *International Herald Leader* (an official Beijing newsweekly), 2 February 2004.

18 Cited in "Experts: China have an eye on Africa, South American oil," *People's Daily*, 28 February 2004.

19 "El Salvador to study possibility of formal ties with China," AFP, 28 October 2004.

20 "China and India go toe to toe over West Africa's oil," AFP, 16 October 2004; "Chavez to triple oil sales to China," 25 August 2006.

21 For a discussion of the energy-related reasons behind the Beijing leadership's attention to Africa, see, for example, Xu Shengru, "Hu Jintao visits three African nations: Petroleum diplomacy has thrown into sharp relief China's energy gameplan," *21st Century Economic Herald* (a Guangzhou paper), 2 February 2004; "Sino-African petroleum cooperation." Online. Available: www.netease.com (Beijing), 14 July 2004; Howard French, "A resource-hungry China speeds trade with Africa," *New York Times*, 9 August 2004.

22 For a discussion between China's comradely relationship with Sudan, see, for example, Stephanie Ho, "China's oil imports from Sudan draw controversy," Voice of America news, 21 July 2004; Alexandra Polier, "A catalyst for peace: oil has played a major role in ending Sudan's civil war," *Newsweek* Asia edition, 21 February 2005.

23 Kenneth Roth, "China's silence boosts tyrants," *International Herald Tribune*, 19 April 2006; "Military cooperation between Angola and China under discussion," Angola Press Agency (Luanda), 9 August 2004.

24 Geraldo Samor and Alex Keto, "China cuts Latin American deals," *Asian Wall Street Journal*, 22 November 2004.

25 "Petrobas expects to boost crude oil experts to China," Dow Jones Newswires, May 26, 2004; Andrew Hay, "Brazil recognizes China as a 'market economy,'" *Reuters*, 12 November 2004.

26 "President Hu pledges stronger strategic partnership with Brazil," NCNA, 17 November 2004.

27 Hu Jintao address the Brazilian Parliament, NCNA, 12 November 2004. For a discussion of the significance of Hu's trip to Latin America, see, for example, Willy Lam, "China's encroachment on America's backyard," *China Brief*, Jamestown Foundation (Washington), 24 November 2004.

28 For a discussion of China–Japan disputes over the Chunxiao fields and related areas,

see, for example, Mao Feng, "More disputes between China and Japan over energy issues," *Yazhou Zhoukan* (a Hong Kong newsweekly), 18 July 2004; Liu Yameng, "China suggests 'joint exploration' to solve disputes over East China Sea oil fields," *Wen Wei Po*, 11 July 2004.
29 For a discussion over the Sino-Japanese conflict over the Diaoyu or Senkaku islands, see, for example, Reiji Yoshida, "Is the Senkaku row about nationalism–or oil," *Japan Times* (Tokyo), 27 March 2004. For a discussion of Deng Xiaoping's "pledge" about the Diaoyu islands, see Xu Yu, "Diaoyu islands can be solved by the next generation," *Wen Wei Po*, 6 November 2004.
30 "Japan envisages of three scenarios under which it may be attacked by China," *Ming Pao* (an independent Hong Kong newspaper), 9 November 2004.
31 Cited in Willy Lam, "China's energy obsession," *Asian Wall Street Journal*, 2 April 2004.
32 "China to join ASEAN Friendship Treaty," *People's Daily* (English edition), 29 April 2003.
33 Alan Boyd, "Oil worries lubricate South China Sea pact," *Asia Times* online, 4 September 2004; "Arroyo's China trip a tribute to Beijing clout," online. Available: www.news.1chinastar.com (Manila), 30 August 2004. For a discussion of the enhanced diplomatic ties between China and Indonesia, see "China, Indonesia forge strategic partnership," *China Daily*, 25 April 2005; "Substantiating China–Indonesia strategic partnership," NCNA, 10 May 2006.
34 Cited in Willy Lam, "China's energy paranoia," *Asian Wall Street Journal*, 30 July 2004.
35 Wen Min, "Ways to break through the Strait of Malacca imbroglio," *Wen Wei Po*, 15 July 2004.
36 Cited in Lin Xixing, "China must jump out of the Strait of Malacca imbroglio," *Chinanewsweek*, 9 August 2004; "17 vessels from Singapore, Malaysia and Indonesia to police the Strait of Malacca," Associated Press, 21 July 2004.
37 Hu Xiaoqun, "Will a Thai channel provide China with a new oil roadmap?" *New Capital Post* (Beijing), 17 July 2004.
38 Xu Ying, "China wishes to build pipeline in Myanmar to resolve the Strait of Malacca imbroglio," *Orient Outlook Weekly*, 13 July 2004; Tschang Chi-chu, "Build oil pipeline from Myanmar to China," *Straits Times* (Singapore), 16 July 2004.
39 For a discussion of Beijing's objection to Singapore's support for US naval patrol of the Strait of Malacca, see Eric Teo, "A counter to the US tilt," *South China Morning Post*, 11 October 2004; Willy Lam, "China's energy paranoia," op. cit.
40 For a discussion of new military chief Hu Jintao's instructions to the PLA, see, for example, "Hu Jintao's recent dictums on the PLA," *Wen Wei Po*, 4 February 2005; Ren Huiwen, "Hu Jintao's views on running the army," *Hong Kong Economic Journal*, 19 November 2004.
41 See Wenran Jiang, "China's 'new thinking' on energy security," *China Brief*, Jamestown Foundation, 14 April 2006; "Chinese fleet visits San Diego," NCNA, 19 September 2006.
42 For a discussion of the "peaceful rise" theory, see, for example, Evan S. Medeiros, "China debates its 'peaceful rise' strategy," oneline. Available: www.YaleGlobal.org, 22 June 2004.
43 For a study of the disputes between China and its neighbours over the use of Mekong River resources, see Evelyn Goh, "China in the Mekong River basin: the regional security implications of resource development on the Lacang Jiang," Working Paper, Institute of Defence and Strategic Studies, Singapore, July 2004.
44 Cited in Anthony Kuhn, "The death of 'growth at any cost,'" *Far Eastern Economic Review*, 1 April 2004.
45 "Editorial: China's disquieting bid for Noranda," *Toronto Star*, 5 October 2004;

Geoffrey York, "China set to buy Canada's resources," *The Globe and Mail*, 21 October 2004.
46 "Powell: US relations with China best in 30 years," *China Daily*, 14 November 2004.
47 David Hale, "Will China need a blue water navy to protect commodity imports," online publications of Hale Advisors LLC., 5 April 2004; Author's telephone interview with Hale, April 2004.

13 China's multilateralism and its impact on cross-strait relations
A view from Taipei*

Dong-Ching Day

Introduction

There are growing numbers of scholars in international relations, including experts in the People's Republic of China (PRC), who have put their research focus on China's multilateralism in order to better understand China's international behaviour after the Cold War and to explain why China would be in favour of multilateralism instead of bilaterlism, as it used to be. Those multilateral organizations, or mechanisms, which China joined as a full member, or in which it played an important role, could be simply be vehicles to facilitate its dealing with economic issues, such as the World Trade Organization (WTO), or managing security problems with other countries, in the case of the Six-Party Talks. However, economic and security issues are more and more difficult to clearly separate, since the concept of security has been expanded in recent decades.

The Taiwan issue is not only considered by Beijing as a core issue in the Sino-US relationship, but also as a very sensitive one in multilateral organizations in which both Taiwan and China are full members. Mainland China has always tried very hard to prevent Taiwan from exercising its membership in full capacity, in order not to create an image of the co-existence of two Chinas in the same organization. Because of its failure to bar Taiwan's joining international organizations, China, in order to trade with other countries, had to give up some benefits. Therefore, it may well be in China's interests to work out some kind of arrangement or formula with Taiwan to allow both to be functioning members of multilateral organizations, so that China can fully embrace multilateralism and get the most benefit from doing so.

In order to shed some light on China's shift of preference from bilateralism to multilateralism, this chapter first discusses the issue of what multilateralism actually means to China. The purpose of doing so is to understand the specifics of the doctrine and its implication for applying it in international relations. Second, the chapter examines under what circumstances China decided to go for multilateralism, what kind of opportunities and limitations it faces for so doing. Third, this chapter uses China's application for WTO membership as an example to explain its intention of embracing multilateralism. Lastly, the chapter looks into what has been the impact of the Taiwan issue on China's support of multilateralism, and how the issue likely could be settled in such a way that would benefit both China and Taiwan.

The essence of multilateralism

If we were to put unilateralism, bilateralism, and multilateralism together it would be very easy to find the differences between these three terms, for they represent one, two, and three or more actors, respectively, in game-playing or conducting business. However, if we put those concepts in the context of international relations, the meaning of the three terms is much more complicated. As Robert O. Keohane suggests, "multilateralism can be defined as the practice of co-ordinating national policies in groups of three or more states, through ad hoc arrangements or by means of institutions."[1] Besides, John Gerard Ruggie refers multilateralism to an institutional form that coordinates relations among three or more states on the basis of generalized principles of conduct.[2] Thus, the number of states does matter when we study multilateralism, as institutions and principles are more important than numbers in explaining why states choose to stick together instead of adopting unilateralism or bilateralism.[3]

Further questions will examine the conditions in which institutions and principles are created, and how those rules can be maintained. Keohane's answers are as follow: increase in issue density will lead to a demand for the creation of multilateral institutions, and reducing uncertainty will tend to create a demand for the maintenance of multilateral institutions.[4] Furthermore, as Lisa L. Martin proposes, states are self-interested and turn to multilateralism only if it serves their purposes, whatever these may be.[5] As a result, it is fair to say that comparative interest makes states create a multilateral institution to increase certainty in the relations with other states. If that were the case, institutions would remain unchanged no matter how international relations might change. However, the real world does not run that way.

In reality, it is in states' own interest to maintain the institution or follow the principle and it is also in states' own interest to change the institution or principle whenever states feel that a new rule would benefit them more than the original one. As both Lisa L. Martin and James A. Caporaso point out, states have strong temptations to defect from a cooperative outcome, since defection results in immediate pay-offs.[6] Therefore, mechanisms to promote cooperation must focus on the maintenance of agreements rather than on facilitation of bargaining prior to agreement.[7]

Another angle of a multilateral institution, which should not be ignored, is generally acknowledged to be a collective security system. What is distinct about a collective security scheme is that it comprises a permanent potential alliance "against the unknown enemy" on behalf of the unknown victim.[8] If a self-recognized potential enemy chooses and is permitted to join an organization, calculating that it is more beneficial to join than stay out, then other, antagonistic, members must be prepared to confront any challenges that state may face, in addition to their own.

Why does China join multilateral organizations?

China was a closed society until the Third Plenum of the Eleventh Congress of the Chinese Communist Party in 1978, when it decided to adopt a policy of opening up to the outside world. At that time, Minister of Foreign Trade Li Qiang announced that China would accept loans and economic aid from both bilateral and multilateral sources.[9] This was the very first time for China to use the term "multilateral." If China wished to accept loans from multilateral organizations, it would be easier if China were to join the organizations in question.[10] Furthermore, the establishment of formal diplomatic relations with the United States in January 1979 opened up a real possibility of greatly expanded Chinese involvement in the global economy.[11]

China's decision to join a given multilateral organization is based on careful cost–benefit analyses. Take China's application for the membership of the World Bank Group (WBG), as an example. A detailed assessment of the positive and negative consequences was done before it filed its application. In the assessment by leading officials in the Bank of China, etc. benefits would include: a major diplomatic victory for Beijing by expelling Taiwan; the reinforcing of bilateral relations with other important states; the acquisition of first-hand information about international economics and finance to assisting the development programme; eligibility for IMF loans at concessional interest rates.[12] Finally, China joined WBG because the positive factors outweighed the negative.

China's participation in the multilateral organization was partly the result of its support of a new multi-polar international order. As former Chinese Vice Foreign Minister Wang Yi argues, in a world of globalization, multilateralism is the sole solution to the world's problems and also the trend of our times; China maintains that the establishment of a new international order which is fair and rational, the realization of democracy and rule of law in international relations, and the promotion of multi-polarization represent the only way to facilitate the development of multilateralism.[13]

However, this does not mean that China was not troubled by whether to embrace bilateralism or multilateralism. As Xinbo Wu points out, Beijing favours bilateral rather than multilateral channels. One reason is that China lacks experience with multilateralism; the other reason is that China harbours a strong suspicion of international mechanisms and believes they mainly serve the interests of the dominant powers.[14] Because Wu finds that China still has significant reservations about multilateralism in diplomatic practices, he concludes that Beijing will stick to bilateralism as the major form of its interactions with other countries, and that its position on multilateralism will be selective and issue-specific, depending on how this may, in Beijing's calculation, affect China's interests.[15]

With regard to China's attitude toward multilateralism, what Xinbo Wu did not point out is that China does not want to be the target of a potential enemy within the multilateral organization, which is designed to be against the unknown enemy, especially in an atmosphere of "China's threat."[16] However, when China learned that joining the multilateral mechanism not only would dampen talk of a "China threat," but also could hinder containment by the US, it decided to embrace multilateralism.[17]

China began increasingly to uphold the idea of "multilateralism" in the late 1990s, and put the idea into practice in the twenty-first century, especially in the creation of the SCO in 2001, joining the Six Party Talks mechanism in 2003, and enhancing free-trade relations among the ASEAN Plus Three (APT) in 2002. The pivotal point of China's desire to embrace multilateralism is more that China wants to adjust the trend of hegemonism and unilateralism in the international politics. As Renwei Huang proposes, China regards this attitude as reflecting its proposal of international political democratization and reflecting the need to reform the international political and economic order by the majority of developing countries.[18] Furthermore, the rationale for China to do this is its comprehensive state capability.

Although Renwei Huang argues that the very first purpose of China's participation in multilateral mechanism is to accept and adapt to current international political and the economic order instead of changing it, he also suggests that we need to prepare for the new international political and economic order by accumulating experience and developing common interests with other countries through participation in an international mechanism.[19] His implication is quite clear that China would be trying to change the international political and economic order if the time were ripe, albeit possibly with a different emerging style.

China joins WTO as a case study

In March 1986 the fourth plenary session of the sixth National People's Congress (NPC) passed the working report submitted by State Council, in which multilateral diplomacy was raised for the very first time. It meant that China had decided to embrace multilateralism further.[20] In July of the same year China sent a delegation to Geneva to submit a formal request to join the GATT.[21] It is obvious that China chose the application for GATT membership as a proof to the world that it intended to embrace multilateralism.

As mentioned above, China joined multilateral organizations after careful calculation of cost and benefit. Therefore, it is meaningful to touch upon the issue of the cost and benefit of China's entry to GATT/WTO.[22] In China's assessment, benefits of entry to GATT/WTO would be: (1) China can expect to achieve a substantial increase in its foreign trade; (2) China can expect to gain a useful multilateral forum for ongoing consultation on trade matters, a more effective defense mechanism against trade discrimination and protectionism on the part of the industrialized countries; (3) China can make use of the arrangement both as a source of valuable information to affect its domestic policies and priorities and as a legitimizing device to support the decision of the reformist political leadership; (4) China will be able to participate in making the rules for the world trading system, and expand its role in the international economy; (5)

China can eliminate the annual review of Most-Favoured-Nation (MFN) trade status by the United States; (6) China can decrease corruption by reducing discretionary power and promoting transparency; (7) China would strengthen its case for access to the preferential arrangements that developed countries give to developing countries.[23]

Of course, China has to pay the cost of entry to the GATT/WTO. First, China will need to liberalize its trade policies by reducing tariffs and other restrictions on a wide range of goods. Second, China will need to practise non-discriminatory trade. Third, China will need to ensure transparency and openness for its trade regime by acquiescing to periodic GATT/WTO trade reviews and providing full disclosure of trade policies, pricing practices, trading organizations, data, and statistics.[24]

It is the consensus of China's political leaders that entry to the WTO could be more beneficial than otherwise, but the process of application for membership took too long for China to bear, making Chinese leaders reconsider whether the benefit of membership still outweighed the cost. In such a circumstance, some officials complained that China should not have to accede to rules that were created by a hegemon, and a "who-needs-WTO?" sentiment was growing within the government and the population.[25] The Chinese government had slowed the process of negotiation for membership of GATT/WTO since 1994, when it realized that it would not be admitted to GATT, and would not be able to become a founding member of the WTO afterwards.

The reasons for the delay of China's membership, as Nicholas R. Lardy contends, are as follows: first, most Western governments imposed economic sanctions on China because of the Tiananmen killings; second, Western governments implicitly adopted the strategy of bringing China in on relatively rigorous terms after the break-up of the Soviet Union; third, many members of the Working Party did not regard China as qualifying as a developing country for membership; fourth, the international economic community had increased the demands placed on China since the completion of the Uruguay Round trade talks in 1994; fifth, domestic interest groups in China mobilized against China's membership.[26]

The Chinese government argued that it should be offered a more generous timetable because its per-capita income figures cannot be compared with those of industrialized countries. However, the US argued that according to both the volume and the rate of growth of its exports, and its overall impact on the international trading system, China already is a developed country.[27] It is apparent that China and the US adopted different standards to judge whether China should be granted developing country status for membership. At last, both sides perceived that the sooner China gained admission to the WTO, the better it would be for the interests of both. Under that consensus, after a long march of 15 years, China acceded to the WTO as a full member in 2001.

The Taiwan factor in China's accession to the WTO and onward

Taiwan is regarded by China as a renegade province. In order to prevent Taiwan from becoming an independent country in the international community, or creating an image of an independent country, China put a lot of effort into prevention. If China could not stop Taiwan from getting membership in multilateral organizations, it would try to downgrade Taiwan's state status as an economic entity.

The Taiwan issue becomes a very sensitive factor in China's accession to multilateral organizations. As Margaret M. Pearson suggests, integration into international regimes and organizations would help legitimize the regime at home and abroad, particularly vis-à-vis Taiwan.[28] More important, Taiwan's application for the GATT/WTO membership in 1990 made Mainland China wish to be admitted to GATT/WTO ahead of Taiwan and also made the Taiwan issue intertwine with China's entry to the GATT/WTO.

With regard to Taiwan's application for membership in 1990, Chinese Premier Li Peng sent a letter to General Secretary of GATT to indicate China's position on Taiwan's case: (1) PRC is the sole legal government in representing the interest of all people of Mainland China; Taiwan is an inseparable part of China; (2) after Mainland China's assumption of membership, Taiwan would be considered to join GATT as a Separate Customs Territory; (3) Taiwan's entry to GATT has to be negotiated with, and approved by, Mainland China.[29] Because of the Taiwan factor, it seems that Mainland China's leader had to accept the potentially high short-term costs entailed in WTO membership in order to gain access to the WTO ahead of Taiwan.[30]

Even though both Taiwan and Mainland China have become full members in the WTO, China worried that Taiwan might take advantage of the membership to internationalize the Taiwan issue, and therefore tried very hard not to create the image of two co-existent Chinas in multilateral organizations. As Huang Jiashu and Lin Hong argue, the Taiwan authorities consider that the WTO framework should be used for promoting the economic interaction and settlement of disputes between the two sides, since both of them are members of WTO. But the Mainland insists on treating their economic relations within the context of the cross-strait relationship, considering that the mechanism of economic cooperation between them should be established to promote their economic communication and cooperation but the establishment of their equivalent relationship within WTO or APEC should be avoided, giving no chance for Taiwan to bargain with it.[31]

Take the anti-dumping case as an example, when China started to investigate whether Tawian's steel and PVC products were being dumped on China. She did not inform the related department of the Taiwan government directly but by way of private association. Also, when China sent documents to Japan, South Korea, Germany, EU, and Malaysia, to ask for bilateral negotiation on her safeguard measures to protect steel products in November 2002, once again she did not inform Taiwan.³² It is obvious that China did not want to negotiate with Taiwan under the structure of WTO to avoid the image of two Chinas.

Implication of China's multilateralism on cross-strait relations

To date, China's position has been uncompromising on its claim to sovereignty over Taiwan,³³ which makes the following assumption unworkable – China's entry into the WTO will lead to stronger trade and investment ties between China and Taiwan that may contribute to a gradual reduction of tensions between the two.³⁴ It is apparent that the tension between the two sides of Taiwan Strait has not been reduced even though the two joined the WTO nearly three years ago. On the contrary, the tension has been escalating to the brink of crisis at some future, undetermined, time.

China's strategy about Taiwan's membership is to bar Taiwan as far as possible from joining any multilateral organizations in order to press Taiwan to come to the negotiation table and accept a One-China principle, subject to its definition. The more powerful China becomes in the international community, the more likely it is that China will be able to block Taiwan's participation in multilateral organizations. In the WTO case, China successfully persuaded the WTO to delay approving Taiwan's accession until China was given the go-ahead to join.³⁵ Most importantly, as Gary J. Smith points out, the Chinese might not permit Taipei's participation if it were to have the opportunity to decide on membership all over again.³⁶

If China maintained a hawkish stance toward Taiwan's participation in multilateral organizations, it probably would encounter at least two consequences. First, Taiwan might drift even further away from the Mainland, instead of coming closer to the negotiation table. Needless to say, the interactions between two sides of the Taiwan Strait for the past decade made Taiwanese identity surge from 20 per cent in 1992 to 40 per cent in 2004 (see Figure 13.1). The double figure increase indicates that more and more Taiwanese people do not want to get closer to China. Beijing's Taiwan policy may not be the sole source causing the trend, but its policy definitely plays a significant role in it.

As a consequence today, the tension has become a vicious circle. The higher Taiwan's perception of identity rises, the more hostile the attitude taken by China toward Taiwan will be, and the more hostile China becomes, the higher Taiwan's identity will grow. However, to play hard ball or even to launch a war will not resolve the tension. On the contrary, it definitely would make things go from bad to worse. ROC is a democratic country, and its political leaders are elected by the general public through the "one-person-one-vote" system. At a certain point, any policies need the approval of the majority of Taiwan people.

It is appropriate for China to put its hopes on the Taiwanese people who decide what leaders China has to face. If Taiwan's leaders could not meet the demands of the people, they would be dumped by the people in the next elections. As a result, the key part of China's Taiwan policy is how to win the hearts

248 D.-C. Day

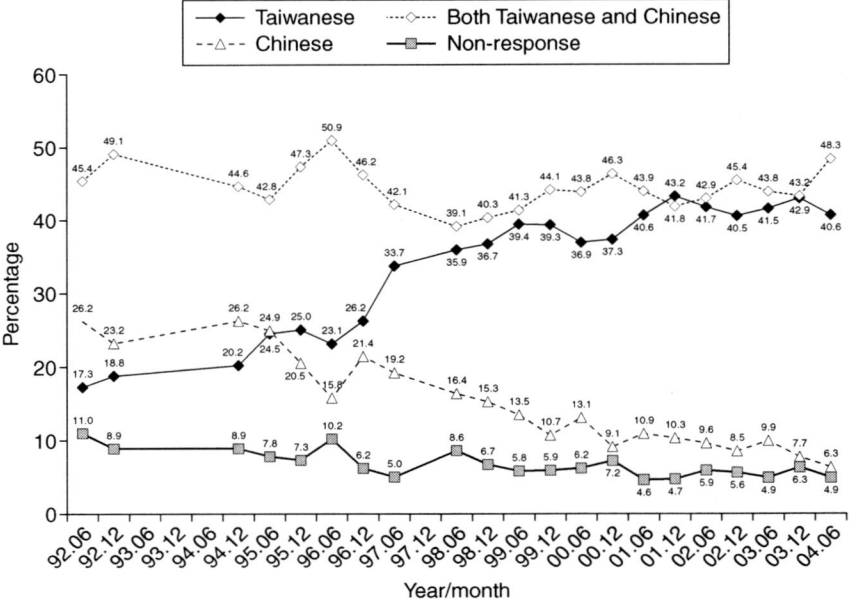

Figure 13.1 Changes in the Taiwanese/Chinese identity of Taiwanese as tracked in surveys by the Election Study Center, NCCU (1992–2004)

of the people. Once most people of Taiwan are in favour of China's Taiwan policy, their preference will directly reflect on the election. This might raise the question of whether Taiwanese people are rational enough to make a decision while facing emotional election campaigns. The election result of 2004 tells the whole story.

The ruling party, the Democratic Progress Party (DPP), won the presidency in March 2004, but pan-green (DPP plus Taiwan Solidarity Union) unexpectedly failed to win the majority of the Legislative Yuan in December 2004.[37] Two major issues in the Legislative Yuan election regarded as not in favour of the pan-green camp have troubled cross-strait relations and Taiwan–US relations.[38] Two different election results in the same year show how democratic systems operate. Parties could easily fail to win again, if they are not believed to have delivered better policies.

Second, there are worries remaining about whether China will turn its engagement in regional institutions into a lever for regional dominance if the "China threat" has not toned down.[39] Any temptation to use force against Taiwan will undo China's diplomatic gains, and reinforce the perception that China intends to dominate the East Asian region, which might spur ASEAN's opposition and Japanese counter-balancing. That would also make China's upholding of the ideas of "New Security Concept" and "Peaceful Rise" unworkable.[40]

Conclusion

Multilateralism is the practice of co-ordinating national policies in groups of three or more states, through ad hoc arrangements or by means of institutions on the basis of generalized principles of conduct. If one country decides to join or create the multilateral organization in the belief that multilateral interaction would be more beneficial than bilateral, it needs to play by the rules set by the other members.

China used to be in favour of bilateral relations. The central reason for China to embrace multilateralism more earnestly is that China wants to adjust the trend of hegemonism and unilateralism in international politics. China regards this attitude as reflecting its proposal of international political democratization and reflecting the need to reform the international political and economic order by the majority of developing countries.

In reviewing the case of China's accession to the WTO, it is easy to draw some conclusions to explain China's international behaviour toward multilateral organizations now and in the future. First, whether China joins or creates a multilateral organization very much depends on the cost–benefit analysis. Second, the cost and benefit of China's entry to a multilateral organization is dynamic, its entry depends on the final judgment of cost and benefit. Third, China has more and more capability to play the role of system-reformer rather than system-maintainer.[41] Fourth and last, it is really hard for other countries to exclude China from admission into the multilateral organization if China intends to join, because China's market and its strategic role cannot be ignored. The only factor which might obstruct China's playing of a more important role in multilateral organizations would be the Taiwan issue.

Both China and Taiwan have been full members of the WTO for quite some time. The tension between the two has not reduced, as some scholars suggested it would. The reason is that China is afraid of creating the image of two Chinas, so that the two sides of Taiwan Strait are not able to settle economic disputes under the structure of the WTO. China's strategy toward Taiwan's membership is to bar Taiwan as far as possible from joining any multilateral organizations in order to press Taiwan to come to the negotiation table and accept the one-China principle subject to its definition. If China's Taiwan policy aims to pull Taiwan closer to China, then the policy is a failure because Taiwanese identity increased from 20 per cent in 1992 to 40 per cent in 2004. The double-figure increase indicates that more and more Taiwan people do not want to get closer to China. China's Taiwan policy may not be the sole source causing the trend, but its policy definitely plays a significant role in that trend.

ROC is a democratic country, and its political leaders are elected by the general public through the "one-person-one-vote" system. It is understandable for China to rest hope on the Taiwan people who decide what leaders China has to face. If Taiwan's leaders cannot meet the demands of the people, they would definitely be dumped by the people in the next elections. The election results of 2004 prove that the Taiwan people are able to decide what benefits them most.

As a result, the key part of China's Taiwan policy is how to win the hearts of people. Once most people of Taiwan are in favour of China's Taiwan policy, their preference will have a direct reflection in the election. Under the circumstances, there is no need for China to pay an extra admission price in order to keep Taiwan away from multilateral organizations.

China has been proposing the ideas of "New Security Concept" and "Peaceful Rise" for quite some time. These two ideas seem incompatible with the use of force against Taiwan or other countries. The more powerful China is, the greater its influence is to keep Taiwan from joining multilateral organizations. However, if China continues to press Taiwan in this way, Taiwan may choose another way, such as independence, to break through the block set by China. If that were the case, we would probably see a disaster in the Cross-Strait area, and the whole region engulfed in instability. It is time for China to take appropriate action.

Notes

* For analytical convenience, in this article, China, PRC, Beijing, or the Mainland are used interchangeably to indicate the People's Republic of China. Likewise, Taiwan, ROC, Taipei are used to indicate the Republic of China. The usage of these terms does not reflect particular political positions held by the author. The author would like to thank Dr Alexander Chieh-cheng Huang for his contribution to the chapter.
1 Robert O. Keohane, "Multilateralism: An Agenda for Research," *International Journal* XLV, Autumn 1990, p. 731.
2 See John Gerard Ruggie, "Multilateralism: The Anatomy of an Institution," in John Gerard Ruggie (ed.) *Multilateralism Matters: The Theory and Praxis of An Institutional Form*, New York: Columbia University Press, 1993, p. 11.
3 As John Gerard Ruggie argues, "Norms and Institutions appear to be playing a significant role in the management of a broad array of regional and global changes in the world system today." See Ruggie, "Multilateralism", p. 3. Also Keohane says that institutions are significant in contemporary world politics; see Keohane, "Multilateralism," p. 733.
4 Keohane, "Multilateralism: An Agenda for Research," p. 744.
5 Lisa L. Martin, "The Rational State Choice of Multilateralism," in John Gerard Ruggie (ed.) *Multilateralism Matters: The Theory and Praxis of An Institutional Form*, New York: Columbia University Press, 1993, p.92.
6 Martin, "The Rational State Choice of Multilateralism," p. 96; James A. Caporaso, "International Relations Theory and Multilateralism: The Search for Foundation," in John Gerard Ruggie (ed.) *Multilateralism Matters: The Theory and Praxis of An Institutional Form*, New York: Columbia University Press, 1993, p. 64.
7 Lisa L. Martin, "The Rational State Choice of Multilateralism," p. 96.
8 Caporaso, "International Relations Theory and Multilateralism," p. 10.
9 William R. Feeney, "Chinese Policy Toward Multilateral Economic Institutions," in Samuel S. King (ed.) *China and the World: The New Directions in Chinese Foreign Relations*, Boulder, San Francisco: Westview Press, 1989, pp. 238–9.
10 As Samuel King argues, post-Mao foreign policy has become more complex, involved, multilateral, functional, institutionalized, self-serving, and adaptive. See Samuel King, "New Directions and Old Puzzles in Chinese Foreign Policy," in Samuel S. King (ed.) *China and the World: The New Directions in Chinese Foreign Relations*, Boulder, San Francisco: Westview Press, 1989, p. 25.
11 Ibid., p. 240.

Multilateralism and cross-strait relations 251

12 The negative side would be: to submit secret statistics on foreign-exchange reserves, gold production; to accommodate IMF visiting missions seeking information and developing reports; and to contribute financially to meet its significant monetary subscription quotas in the IMF. Ibid., p. 241.
13 Wang Yi, "Facilitating the Development of Multilateralism And Promoting World Multi-Polarization," speech at the XIV Ministerial Conference of the Non-Aligned Movement (19 August 2004, Durban, South Africa).
14 Xinbo Wu, "Four Contradictions Constraining China's Foreign Policy Behavior," *Journal of Contemporary China* 10 (27), 2001, pp. 293–301.
15 Ibid.
16 The basic argument of the China threat is that the disappearance of the Soviet Union has transformed Chinese military might from an asset to a long-term threat to Western and especially American interests. See Elizabeth Economy and Michel Oksenberg (eds) *China Joins the World: Progress and Prospects*, New York: Council on Foreign Relations Press, 1999, p. 7.
17 Amitav Acharya, "Seeking Security, the East Asian Way," *Straits Times*, 30 December 2003. Online. Available: www.taiwansecurity.org/ST/2003/ST-301203.htm (accessed 11 October 2004).
18 Renwei Huang, *Time and Space for China's Rising*, Shanghai: Shanghai Academy of Social Science Press, 2002, p. 70.
19 Ibid.
20 *People's Daily*, 14 April 1986, p. 1.
21 Mark A. Groombridge, "China's Accession to the World Trade Organization: Costs and Benefits," in Ted Galen Carpenter and James A. Dorn (eds) *China's Future: Constructive Partner or Emerging Threat?*, Washington, DC: Cato Institute, 2000.
22 GATT was succeeded by WTO in 1995.
23 William R. Feeney, "Chinese Policy toward Multilateral Economic Institutions," in Samuel S. King (ed.) *China and the World: The New Directions in Chinese Foreign Relations*, Boulder, San Francisco: Westview Press, 1989, pp. 255–6; Margaret M. Pearson, "China's Integration into the International Trade and Investment Regime," in Elizabeth Economy and Michel Oksenberg (eds) *China Join the World: Progress and Prospects*, New York: Council on Foreign Relations Press, 1999, pp. 161–205; Stuart Harris, "China's Role in the WTO and APEC," in David S.G. Goodman and Gerald Segal (eds) *China Rising: Nationalism and Interdependence*, London: Routledge, 1997, p. 138.
24 Feeney, "Chinese Policy toward Multilateral Economic Institutions," p. 256; Supachai Panitchpakdi and Mark L. Clifford, *China and the WTO: Changing China, Changing World Trade*, Singapore: John Wiley & Sons Pte Ltd., 2002, p. 36.
25 Margaret M. Pearson, "China's Integration into the International Trade and Investment Regime," in Elizabeth Economy and Michel Oksenberg (eds) *China Join the World: Progress and Prospects*, New York: Council on Foreign Relations Press, 1999, p. 183.
26 Nicholas R. Lardy, *Integrating China into the Global Economy*, Washington DC: The Brookings Institution, 2002, pp. 63–4.
27 For the arguments between China and US about the membership status, please see Margaret M. Pearson, "China's Integration into the International Trade and Investment Regime," p. 176.
28 Margaret M. Pearson, "China's Integration into the International Trade and Investment Regime," p. 165.
29 University of Guongdong Foreign Language and Trade (ed.), *China's Road to the WTO*, Guongzhou: Guongdong Economic Publisher, 1999, p. 28 (in Chinese).
30 Nicholas R. Lardy, *Integrating China into the Global Economy*, p. 16.
31 Huang Jiashu and Lin Hong, "An Analysis of Taiwan-related Diplomatic Problems of the People's Republic of China," paper presented at the conference 'Regional

252 *D.-C. Day*

      Integration, State-Building and Conflict Settlement in Europe and Asia' in Brussels on 11–12 October 2004.
32 Horng-ming Tsai, "The Trade Quarrels and Dispute Settlement Between Taiwan and China After Their WTO Accessions," *Review of Taiwan Economics*, 9(1), June 2003, pp. 24–61.
33 Supachai Panitchpakdi and Mark L. Clifford, *China and the WTO: Changing China, Changing World Trade*, p. 191.
34 This assumption is raised by Nicholas R. Lardy. See Nicholas R. Lardy, *Integrating China into the Global Economy*, p.165.
35 Supachai Panitchpakdi and Mark L. Clifford, *China and the WTO: Changing China, Changing World Trade*, p. 119.
36 Gary J. Smith, "Multilateralism and Regional Security in Asia: The ASEAN Regional Forum (ARF) and APEC's Geopolitical Value," The Weatherhead Center for International Affairs, Harvard University, Paper No. 97–2, February 1997. Online. Available: www.wcfia.harvard.edu/fellows/papers95–96/smg01.html.
37 Before LY elections, the pan-green camp was expected to win a majority. Please see John F. Copper, "Taiwan's Democracy Takes a New Step," *Far Eastern Economic Review* 168(1), December 2004, pp. 12–14.
38 Ibid.
39 Amitav Acharya, "Seeking Security, the East Asian Way," *Straits Times*, 30 December 2003. Online. AvailableP: www.taiwansecurity.org/ST/2003/ST-301203.htm (accessed 11 October 2004).
40 Renwei Huang, *Time and Space for China's Rising*, Shanghai: Shanghai Academy of Social Science Press, 2002; Marc Lanteigne, "Middlegames and Positional Sacrifices: China's 'New Security Concept's and Multilateral Cooperation." Online. Available: www.isppan.waw.pl/cbap/ww/lanteigne.htm (accessed 8 October 2004).
41 Supachai Panitchpakdi and Mark L. Clifford states that there are signs that China will play a more assertive role, at least economically, and that could have consequences for the WTO and other bodies. See Supachai Panitchpakdi and Mark L. Clifford, *China and the WTO: Changing China, Changing World Trade*, p. 191.

14 An exception to the growing emphasis on multilateralism
The case of China's policy towards Hong Kong

Jean-Philippe Béja

Since 11 September 2001, the People's Republic of China has increasingly emphasized the importance of multilateralism in international relations. This policy, which is not so new as it seems, can be regarded as an adaptation of the United Front tactics used by the Communist Party in its rise to power: it aims at rallying the largest possible number of countries around China, in order to fight the great powers which try to impose their hegemonism on the world scene. This tactic had already been used in foreign policy during the 1950s when China was quite active in the Afro-Asian movement. At the time of the Bandung conference, in 1955, the PRC endeavoured to rally most newly independent countries in a loose alliance against the United States. In this case, the Chinese leaders showed their ability to tone down revolutionary discourse in order to attain their goal. They helped set up the five principles of peaceful coexistence, and insisted on the right of under-developed countries, which represented the majority of the world population, to be exempt from intervention by great powers. At a certain point in the early sixties, they even went so far as to envisage the creation of an alternative United Nations. These developments show that the Chinese government has long been both aware of the value of multilateralism, and ready to collaborate with countries with different social systems.

In the recent past, however, this tactic has been pursued in the more general framework of the "new international order" and, as a member of the "international community," China has taken a more proactive role in the United Nations. In most of the crises that have shaken the world in the last 15 years, the PRC has insisted on the fact that only the United Nations had the legitimacy to intervene. This emphasis on multilateralism has been particularly marked in its relations with Southeast Asia, a region which has traditionally been wary of the growth of its giant neighbour. The Chinese Communist Party has gone to great lengths to convince the ASEAN countries that they should not regard China's development as a threat, be it in military terms – and China has considerably toned down its rhetoric on its claim on the Paracels and Spratly Islands – or in terms of economics, repeating that China's economic development, far from threatening its neighbours, represents an opportunity: the Chinese stress the fact that an intensification of relations will help Southeast Asian countries find new markets for their products, and will lead to an increase in Chinese investments on their soil, two positive factors for their development. Besides, the Chinese leadership has been careful not to offend the smaller countries of ASEAN, and has consulted them on most pressing issues, thanks to the ASEAN+3, and, more recently, ASEAN+one, meetings. Since the beginning of the twenty-first century, the Beijing government has been taking an active part in these regional organizations, and has agreed to tackle some problems in this setting rather than through bilateral relations. It is an active member of APEC, and has organized meetings of that forum on its soil. However, the Chinese authorities do not take part in the definition of norms of international relations, and are rather critical of the emphasis on categories such as human rights, or the rights of minorities.

Even if it has manifested an increasing interest in multilateralism, the Chinese government has consistently defended a rather traditional conception of national sovereignty. This was particularly clear during the debate on "human rights versus national sovereignty" which was raised at the time of the Kosovo conflict in 1999. The Chinese authorities then reiterated their position that sovereignty was more important than human rights, and that, as provided for by the United Nations Charter, the only possibility for an international force to intervene in an internal conflict, was when it was asked to by the legitimate government of the country concerned. This shows the limitations of China's commitment to multilateralism.

The Beijing government remains convinced of the overarching importance of sovereignty, and this is particularly clear with regard to Beijing's policy towards Taiwan and Hong Kong. Both cases are considered domestic affairs by the Chinese leadership which has constantly opposed "interference by foreign countries." In this chapter, I shall not treat the question of Beijing's relations with Taiwan, but it is worth noting that, despite the above-mentioned discourse, every time there has been a crisis in cross-strait relations, the Chinese government has tried to enlist foreign governments in support of its position. It was particularly clear in November 2003 when Taiwanese President Chen Shuibian announced his decision to organize a referendum on the China threat. At the time, Premier Wen Jiabao's was visiting the US, and he fought to obtain from President Bush a declaration condemning this initiative. A few months later, one of the main objectives of Chairman Hu Jintao's visit to France was to obtain a condemnation of the referendum by French President Jacques Chirac, which he did. This shows that the Chinese authorities are willing to tolerate (and even solicit) other countries' intervention when it suits their needs. Multilateralism is positive when it helps China attain its objectives.

In this chapter, I shall try to show that, all along, the Chinese government has tried to avoid practising multilateralism when dealing with the question of Hong Kong.

A question of sovereignty

In 1997, after 156 years as a colony of the Crown of England, Hong Kong returned to the fold of the motherland. A symbol of the humiliation of China for a century and a half, its peaceful recuperation by the People's Republic of China has been regarded as a success of Beijing's diplomacy. For, in order to regain sovereignty over the Territory, the Chinese Communists had negotiated with Great Britain for years, doing their best to gain the support of the international community. At the same time, all along the negotiation process, Chinese leaders have repeatedly warned against the "internationalization" of the Hong Kong question. This is undoubtedly a contradiction which has been going on for more than 25 years, as today Hu Jintao and Wen Jiabao still pledge to keep Hong Kong an international city, and even allow foreigners to take part in its political life, while insisting that relations between Beijing and the SAR are a purely domestic PRC matter. However, one should remember that the Sino-British Joint Declaration signed by the two governments in December 1984, although not an international treaty, has been registered with the United Nations, and therefore, to a certain extent, is guaranteed by the international community which holds some measure of responsibility in the survival of the "One Country, Two Systems" formula.

In fact, by involving the international community, the Chinese government has made it easier to strike a deal in its negotiations with Great Britain. The way China has solved the Hong Kong question in the early eighties can be seen as a first instance of its ability to innovate in the field of international relations. In a way, the PRC, which, until then, had always demonstrated a very strong commitment to the most traditional interpretation of the concept of sovereignty, has agreed to limit its power to act on the socio-political system of part of its territory in order to resume sovereignty over it. By pledging to keep Hong Kong capitalist for fifty years, and by writing this provision into an international declaration in order to reassure the international community, the Chinese government has accepted limitations to the exercise of its sovereignty over parts of its soil. Although this self-limitation of sovereignty is different from that which was required for the establishment of the European Union, it shows that Chinese diplomacy is able to show a lot of flexibility when it sees fit, in order to attain its objectives. Since China is increasingly open to new doctrines of foreign policy, and is revising its obsolete concept of sovereignty, the case of the relations between Beijing and Hong Kong could be an excellent opportunity to test this new openness.

However, while the new Chinese leadership has been speaking in favour of multilateralism and has been eager to practise it in East and Southeast Asia, it has kept insisting that no third party should interfere in its relations with the Hong Kong SAR. We shall see that in this field, the new leadership has been defending a wholly Westphalian and traditional conception of sovereignty.

A purely Sino-British question

When China was admitted into the United Nations in 1971, one of the first moves by the Beijing government was to have the question of Hong Kong and Macau removed from the agenda of the committee for decolonisation. The Chinese logic was as follows: the occupation of Hong Kong by the United

Kingdom was "a legacy of history" going back to the Unequal Treaties that were forced upon China by the great Powers in the middle of the nineteenth century. The problems of Hong Kong and Macau were therefore a question of reunification of the country that the Chinese government would resolve "when the time was ripe." It was out of the question to allow any foreign country or international organization to meddle in the affairs of China – even with the most idealistic motives in the world, and the ideas, such as anti-colonialism, were consistent with its own ideology. Beijing would never tolerate the "internationalisation" of this question. Therefore, under Mao Zedong, no step was ever taken to take back the Territory. And after the "Carnation revolution" broke out in 1974, when the new Portuguese leaders announced their desire to do away with their colonies, "[the Chinese government] tried all possible means to persuade the Portuguese government not to raise the issue of returning Macau to China" (Wong Man Fong, 8). Beijing was afraid that discussion about Macau would lead to the question of Hong Kong, which China did not want because it had a vested interest in the preservation of the status quo, as it needed Hong Kong to trade with the Western world. Even when, during Mao's reign, the People's Republic was virtually isolated from the West and did not allow foreign businessmen to settle on its soil, it never opposed the presence of the main international companies in Hong Kong. On the contrary, during the 1960s and the 1970s, it encouraged American, Japanese, and other Western companies to set their headquarters in the Territory.

Sources show that when Sir Murray MacLehose went to Beijing in 1979 to raise the question of sovereignty after 1997, the Chinese authorities were taken aback, as they had hoped to preserve the status quo (Wong Man Fong, 7). However, once it was put on the agenda, Deng Xiaoping was obliged to state that the Territory would "of course" reintegrate the fold of the motherland, but that foreign and Hong Kong businessmen could "put their minds at ease" as it would do so under the "One Country, Two Systems" formula. And, far from imposing this decision to the world, the Chinese Communist Party initiated negotiations with the British government. Therefore, although it did not recognize the legitimacy of the British presence on what it considered to be Chinese soil, Deng Xiaoping showed how pragmatic he could be, and refrained from imposing the re-establishment of Chinese control over the Territory by force. The Sino-British Joint Declaration, agreed upon on 26 September 1984, guaranteed that "the rights and freedoms, including those of the person, of speech, of the press, of assembly, of association, of travel, of movement, of correspondence, of strike, of choice of occupation, of academic research and of religious belief w[ould] be ensured by law." Such a pledge was, of course, meant to reassure the population of Hong Kong, but even more, the mostly Western foreign companies which had made the prosperity of the Territory. Through this text, the Chinese government was trying to reassure the international community.

However, during the negotiations as well as during the transition period which lasted more than 12 years, the PRC authorities were very careful not to allow the question to be, to use their term, "internationalized." For example, when in 1982 negotiations entered a difficult period, the Japanese government offered to act as a go-between, neither the Chinese nor the British accepted that proposal (Segal 1993: 165). Every time, when crises broke out in Sino-British relations – especially on the question of democratization – in 1989 and later, when Washington expressed its position, hoping to exert some moderating influence on Beijing, the Chinese government denounced the attempt at internationalizing the Hong Kong question. This did not keep the US government from adopting in the United States–Hong Kong Policy Act in 1992, whereby the US undertook to closely monitor the situation of Hong Kong's autonomy, and the administration is to determine whether the degree of autonomy enjoyed by the SAR is sufficient to allow it to enjoy a status different from the one granted to the PRC. The American authorities have, in fact, regularly commented on the political situation in the SAR. Recently, Deputy Assistant Secretary for East Asian and Pacific Affairs, Randall Schriver, warned: "It is important China understand our strong interest in the preservation of Hong Kong's current freedoms, as well as our interest in the continued democratisation of Hong Kong as called for in the Basic Law."

On 10 April 1997, the European Parliament asked the Commission to present an annual report on the developments in the economy, the politics, and the human-rights situation, before deciding which policy to adopt towards the HKSAR. The Chinese government has always regarded these decisions as an intrusion in its domestic affairs and has condemned them.

But, since 1979, the Beijing authorities have also shown their desire to maintain the specificity of Hong Kong. From the first day of the negotiations, Deng Xiaoping expressed his intention to keep the economic and some aspects of the political regime of the Territory after 1997. He clearly stated that the Chinese Communist Party would not impose socialist transformation of the city, which could maintain its system for 50 years after the reunification. To show his commitment, he added an article to the 1982 PRC Constitution (article 31) providing for the creation of an Hong Kong Special Administrative Region with a high degree of autonomy. According to the agreement between the UK and the PRC, Hong Kong was allowed to maintain (or gain) membership in many international organizations (concerned with economic, legal, cultural matters) under the name of Hong Kong, China. But in order to have this status recognized, China needed the approval of foreign countries. By seeking this recognition, Beijing was accepting, and even asking for, the internationalization of the Hong Kong question. "Since it has bilateral and multilateral treaties linking it to many foreign countries, its autonomy is subject to continual international oversight, which in turn enhances this status. Once an international network created by the HKSAR's bilateral and multilateral treaties has become well established, its autonomy will be fully guaranteed by international law" (Zeng Huaqin 2003: 323).

Actually, one of the objectives of the "One Country, Two Systems" formula was to maintain the international character of Hong Kong. The promotion campaign that the HKSAR government has been developing since the 2003 SARS crisis is based on the fact that Hong Kong should remain "Asia's world city." However, if "the government encourages foreigners to come and trade in Hong Kong to develop its economy, its culture, its educational system and to develop exchange and collaboration in all fields, ... [it] formally denies foreign governments the possibility to seize this opportunity to meddle in Hong Kong affairs... No 'world city' can exist without sovereignty" (Huang Qinghua 2004: 62)

This attitude shows that, as has been the case on the mainland since Deng Xiaoping's return to power in 1977, the CCP has adopted very different attitudes in the economic and the political fields: whereas it has always been careful to keep any foreign government from meddling in Hong Kong domestic politics, it has encouraged (and still does encourage) the greatest possible number of foreign companies to settle in the Territory. The Basic Law itself recognises the international character of the Region, and has inherited some characteristics of the colonial system. For instance, any person who has resided in the SAR for seven years becomes automatically a permanent resident and enjoys citizens' rights. According to Article 67, "permanent residents of the Region who are not of Chinese nationality or who have the right of abode in foreign countries may also be elected members of the Legislative Council of the Region, provided that the proportion of such members does not exceed 20 per cent of the total membership of the Council." It was later decided that they could be elected only as representatives of the functional constituencies. This article is very progressive, and can be regarded as a post-nation-state provision. It shows the ability of the Chinese authorities to experiment, not only in the economic field, but also in the realm of politics.

Democratization: a plot by foreign governments?

Even though China has become, in the last few years, more open than in the past to the new concepts of international relations and the renewed value of multilateralism – playing a more active role in the United nations, and accepting some measure of intervention by the UN to enforce peace after a civil war, as in the case of Haiti – it is still very punctilious on the question of sovereignty. In the case of Hong Kong, the Chinese government has repeatedly emphasized the necessity for the HKSAR to develop its relations with foreign countries, but it has tried by all the means at its disposal to prevent these countries (often dubbed "hostile forces") from meddling in the affairs of Hong Kong. And, since the early eighties, the CCP has been convinced that the policy of democratization was a plot by the British – acting as the vanguard of the Western world and especially of the United States – to make the return of the Territory to Chinese sovereignty devoid of meaning. Seen from Beijing, the late democratization started by the British after more than 120 years of presence in the colony was an attempt to "build up a pro-British force ahead of retrocession. In short, the British were trying to create a situation that would allow them to continue to run Hong Kong after their formal departure in 1997" (Xu Jiatun, 172). These attempts were regarded with even more suspicion after the repression of the pro-democracy movement in the People's Republic on 4 June 1989. After the demonstrations which mobilized one million participants – that is to say, one-fifth of the population of the territory – in May and June 1989, the Communist Party warned both the British authorities and the international community that it would never tolerate the transformation of Hong Kong into a basis for subversion of its rule. The fact that the Territory became a haven for some of the leaders of the 1989 pro-democracy movement in China was viewed with defiance by Beijing. For the PRC authorities, the Hong Kong democrats, who, for the most part, started their political career in the Hong Kong Alliance in Support of the Patriotic Democratic Movement in China, which organized the demonstrations, are manipulated by "hostile forces," i.e. Western intelligence agencies and Taiwanese organizations. An authoritative Beijing figure said: "the strategic plan of the US is to 'surround' China from north to south, a plan in which Taiwan and Hong Kong are two points. In this regard, some democrats have their own values and they can be the tools of the US" (Chan 2004). This is the reason why the CCP has refused discussion with them since 1989. The fact that, since the first direct Legco election in 1991, the pro-democracy camp has consistently obtained no less than 60 per cent of the popular vote at every election has not affected the Central authorities' attitude. They are all the more wary of the democrats' policies, as they consider them products of British education estranged from the Chinese political culture. And, according to the CCP, the British government did not hesitate to use them to reach its objectives: "The last governor has done everything he could to enforce a reform of the system designed to empty the Chinese sovereignty of its substance" (Huang 2004). The Democratic Party has shown that it was hostile to the Communist Party as its leaders have consistently asked for the rehabilitation of the 1989 pro-democracy movement, an attitude that deeply shocks the Central government.

The Article 23 controversy: an example of the fear of "internationalization"

In 2002, when Chief executive Tung Chee-hwa started his second mandate, the Chinese authorities insisted that one of his most pressing tasks was to pass Article 23 of the Basic Law, which provides for the fight against secession and subversion. One section of the draft proposal of the Article "prohibits foreign political organisations from conducting political activities in Hong Kong, as well as (…) SAR-based political organisations from establishing ties with foreign political bodies" (Loh and Ng 2002). These provisions show that a very narrow concept of sovereignty continues to shape the attitude of the Communist authorities. Besides, as the pro-democracy forces are viewed as closely linked to the international "hostile forces," the adoption of Article 23 could result in putting limitations on the political life of the HKSAR. Any person opposing the Communist Party could be considered unpatriotic, and to be working for sedition or subversion. Some observers have hinted that this radical stance was attributable to Jiang Zemin personally, and that the new leadership might adopt a more moderate policy towards the democrats. This was not the case in July

2003, as Hu Jintao himself warned the Chief Executive against "foreign powers and external forces" when he met him in Beijing in the wake of the demonstrations against article 23 (Loh and Ng 2002). The General Secretary of the CCP then set up a CP 18-member Central Group for Coordinating Hong Kong Affairs, headed by Vice-President and Politburo Standing Committee member Zeng Qinghong, an ally of Jiang's, with members from various departments. The Article 23 crisis has been so serious that the central government has decided to take a more direct responsibility in the affairs of Hong Kong. One of its first moves has been to send about 3,000 agents to the SAR to monitor the activities of Western intelligence agencies (Chan 2004). This decision might indicate that the Chinese authorities considered that the protests against Article 23 had been manipulated by Western governments wary of the limitations this article would put on the activities of their political allies. It seems that, despite their repeated statements that the Hong Kong question is an internal matter, the Chinese Communists consider that the Western governments tend to use it as a platform to meddle in China's internal affairs. It might be the reason why they are very careful not to let the question be "internationalized." This wariness does not prevent them from using united front tactics tactfully. When they realized that an important proportion of the population had been mobilized against the Article 23, and that a hardline attitude might seriously antagonize Hong Kong citizens and the Western partners of China, they made a tactical retreat, and agreed to postpone the adoption of the law. But this tactical retreat does not mean that they are ready to let any foreign or democratic force participate in the development of their policy towards the SAR.

Since the resumption of sovereignty over the Territory, any attempt by pro-democracy politicians to raise in international settings the question of the democratization of Hong Kong has been vehemently denounced by the authorities as an unpatriotic attitude. In the Chinese Communist political culture, the simple fact that an ordinary citizen discusses the evolution of the domestic political scene in a foreign assembly is considered a serious attack on sovereignty. Only official representatives, duly mandated by the Central government, can address these sensitive matters in public. So, when, in March 2004, the former President of the Democratic Party, Martin Lee Chu Ming, went to Washington to testify on the question of constitutional developments in Hong Kong at a hearing of the Senate Foreign Relations Committee, it was the State councillor in charge of Foreign Affairs himself, Tang Jiaxuan, who criticized the politician: "We shall believe that Chinese people, including Hong Kong patriots, completely have the ability and wisdom to properly handle the matter. There is no need at all to go worship at a foreign temple and invite a foreign Buddha to make irresponsible remarks. This is the biggest joke in the world [sic]."[1] Other Chinese leaders, such as Chen Zuo'er, Deputy Director of the Office of Hong Kong and Macau Affairs of the State Council, condemned this move by the democrats: "We do not want to see foreign countries interfere with this matter," he declared.[2] The Vice-Minister of Commerce, An Min, was even more aggressive and accused Martin Lee's family of having always been anti-communist.[3]

China's policy towards Hong Kong 261

The central authorities also criticized another leading figure of the pro-democracy camp, the leader of the Frontier, Emily Lau, when she went on a visit to Taiwan in August 2003. She was accused of being favourable to the independence of Taiwan. Both leaders have been deemed "unpatriotic" for trying to recruit international support for the democratization of Hong Kong.

The controversy over the pace of democratization

After the success of the demonstration against Article 23, the Hong Kong democrats asked for the election of the Chief executive and of all the members of Legco by universal suffrage. The Chinese Communist Party views these initiatives as an attempt to encroach upon Chinese sovereignty, since a totally fair and free election could lead to the victory of the pro-democracy camp that it regards as traitors to the motherland. The CCP leaders clearly stated – although this is in contradiction to some of Deng Xiaoping's statements in the early 1980s – that the "Hong Kong people ruling Hong Kong" must be patriots, which means that they must not oppose the Party's rule. Vice-Minister of Commerce, An Min, emphasized: "There are some who deliberately made confusing remarks, saying loving the country is not tantamount to loving the Communist Party. The Chinese Communist Party represents the Chinese people and it should also represent Hong Kong compatriots" (Ma and Cheung 2004). Some exponents of the Beijing line go even further and equate the democrats with proponents of Hong Kong independence. The Director of the Centre on Hong Kong and Macau, Zhu Yucheng, declared at a conference organized to celebrate the 14th anniversary of the adoption of the Basic Law:

> Some people do not appreciate the Centre's attitude, (…) challenge the authority of the Centre, and do not recognize the leading role of the Centre in the process of the constitutional review. This is absurd; they pretend to act for the so-called democratic future of Hong Kong, but in fact they really have only one goal: to make Hong Kong an independent or semi-independent entity, to transform its high degree of autonomy into complete autonomy, to serve the political and economic interests of certain interest groups, and to create a favourable atmosphere for the September [2004 Legco] elections in order to obtain more votes.[4]

These accusations are very serious as demanding independence is considered an attempt at "splitting the country," a crime which is punishable by the death penalty.

After months of agitation of the Hong Kong public for the instauration of universal suffrage,[5] the Standing Committee of the National People's Congress finally passed a resolution which excluded it for the 2007 and 2008 elections.[6] Any attempt to go against this decision was to be considered a breach of the Basic Law. By equating the adoption of universal suffrage to elect the Chief Executive to a plot for independence, and by denouncing the democrats who fight to obtain it as "unpatriotic," the Communist Party leadership has shown that it regards dissent as subversion. The NPC decision appears to be a serious restriction on the "high degree of autonomy" promised by the Joint Declaration and the Basic Law. According to these two documents, the Central government is responsible only for the foreign affairs and the defence of the HKSAR. To consider constitutional arrangements as concerning these two fields shows a very broad concept of national security, to say the least. It is nevertheless consistent with the idea that the democrats are manipulated by foreign government. If they obtained the majority at Legco, or if their candidate became the Chief Executive, the CCP would consider that the interests of the state could be jeopardized.

The Chinese leaders indeed believe in the existence of a foreign plot to devoid the PRC's sovereignty of its meaning. They are convinced that foreign intelligence agencies are still active in Hong Kong. In the spring of 2004, the former secretary-general of the Beijing Liaison Office in Hong Kong, Cai Xiaohong, was arrested in Guangzhou for selling state secrets to the British government for six million Hong Kong dollars. He received a 15-year jail sentence in November (Wang Xiangwei 2004).

Despite worries about the activities of foreign spies and their suspected relations with the democrats, the central government adopted a more moderate attitude after the September 2004 Legco elections which did not result in the expected overwhelming victory of the pro-democracy camp. Right after the election, representatives from Beijing sent signals showing that they were ready to mend relations to some Legco members of the pro-democracy camp. This could seem contradictory to the previous attitude, but if one considers this move in the framework of the United Front tactics, it is much easier to understand. Actually, the Communist Party tries to divide the pro-democracy camp by isolating the diehard "unpatriotic elements," such as Martin Lee, Emily Lau, and the members of the Alliance for the Support of the Patriotic Democratic Movement in China, and attracting the more moderate members, those who do not always raise the question of the rehabilitation of 4 June. The object is to split the pro-democracy movement and to reinforce the pro-Beijing camp. It remains to be seen whether this tactic will be successful.

Conclusion

Although the Chinese government keeps insisting that the Hong Kong question is an internal affair of the People's Republic, the real situation is much more complex. As we have seen, the HKSAR is a member of many international organizations, and its political system is different from the one on the mainland. Foreign organizations, whether political, religious, or concerned with human rights, are active in the Region. Because the Chinese leadership has committed itself in front of the international community to maintain the "One Country, Two Systems" formula for 50 years, and because it intends to keep Hong Kong an international city, its actions in the SAR have been closely monitored by foreign governments. Despite its lessened reticence towards multilateralism in recent years, Beijing has been careful not to let them intervene in the discussions about the pace of democratization and other issues concerning the political life of Hong Kong. The Chinese government is not ready to adopt all the aspects of multilateralism, especially the possibility for the international community to monitor the situation of democracy and human rights according to internationally accepted norms. Lately, Beijing has even proceeded to considerably restrain the autonomy of the Region. In dealing with the HKSAR, the Beijing government has shown that it is still attached to a traditional concept of sovereignty, in which monitoring of political evolution by international organizations is regarded as meddling in domestic affairs. However, it has also shown a remarkable degree of flexibility and pragmatism in order to maintain the special status of Hong Kong. It has made substantial concessions when submitted to pressure, and, using United Front tactics, has demonstrated an impressive ability to divide its adversaries. Therefore, although it has often changed its discourse on international relations, using the most modern concepts of modern diplomacy, the Chinese Communist Party has demonstrated a remarkable consistency, by using the magical weapon discovered by Mao Zedong: the United Front tactics.

Notes

1 *China Daily*, 03/05/2004.
2 *China Daily*, 03/05/2004.
3 *South China Morning Post*; 08/03/2004.
4 *Wen wei Po*, 05/16/2004.
5 On 1 January 2004, 100,000 persons took part in a demonstration to demand universal suffrage.
6 *Cf.* "NPC standing committee decision on issues concerning methods for slecting HK Chief Executive and forming Legislative Council," *Xinhua*, 26/04/2004.

References

Chan, Carrie (*Dong Zhoukan*) "July 1 made Beijing sit up," *Hong Kong Standard*, 31 May 2004.
Qinghua, Huang, *Yingdui Xianggang mianling de tiaozhan*, (How to reply to challenges facing Hong Kong), *Zhanlüe yu guanli*, 2004, no. 64, 3, pp. 58–67.
Loh, Christine and Margaret Ng, "Article 23: the debate begins," *South China Morning Post*, 25 September 2002.
Ma, Josephine and Gary Cheung, "Patriot games anger Beijing official – don't even think about jeopardizing stability – vice minister," *South China Morning Post*, 18 February 2004.
Segal, Gerald, *The Fate of Hong Kong*, London, Simon and Schuster, 1993.
Wang, Xiangwei, "Ex-liaison office man gets 15 years for spying," *South China Morning Post*, 8 November 2004.
Wong, Man Fong, *China's Resumption of Sovereignty over Hong Kong*, David C.Lam Institute for East-West Studies, 1997, Hong Kong Baptist University.
Xu, Jiatun, *Xianggang huiyilu*, (Hong Kong Memoirs), vol. 1, 1993.
Zeng, Huaqin, "Hong Kong's Autonomy: Concept, Development and Characteristics," *China: an International Journal*, vol. 1, no. 2, September 2003, pp. 313–25

Part V
Conclusion

15 Multiple levels of multilateralism
The rising China in the turbulent world

Guoguang Wu

This chapter aims to summarize the conclusions of individual chapters of this collaborative endeavour, and attempts to draw together these sometimes contending arguments under a coherent framework to understand recent Chinese multilateralism in regional and international affairs. Basically, we have found that there is a decreasing curve in China's new multilateral commitments, a curve coincident with the decreasing presence of Chinese power in different geographic regions and policy-issue areas. In other words, China's attitudes towards, and involvements in, multilateralistic practices of international politics vary depending on China's influence in different geopolitical scales. China is most committed to what this chapter calls 'core regions' close around China, where its multilateralistic commitment is strong, active, and even creative, often extending to arenas beyond economics, such as regional international security. The second layer of Chinese multilateral conduct lies in some general regionalist mechanisms in Asia, around which the economy, a domain in which multilateral cooperation is often relatively easy to achieve, takes command of Chinese multilateralism, while China's security cooperation under multilateralism often remains less persuasive and less institutionalized. What is even less substantive than such pan-regional multilateralism is China's global multilateral participation, where, in accordance with more symbolic, rather than substantial, status of China as a global power, Chinese diplomacy of multilateralism is accordingly more symbolic rather than substantial in non-economic matters. At the global level, furthermore, Chinese multilateralism changes according to its relative bargaining power vis-à-vis the single post-Cold War superpower, the United States, in different issues and geographic regions. Chinese multilateralism is, therefore, a foreign policy with multiple levels of seriousness, commitment, and involvements of the Central Kingdom to the international coordination of national conduct. That is to say, international multilateralism is not a linear, coherent, and committed principle for Chinese diplomacy, at least not in the recent past when Chinese diplomacy of multilateralism began to take its initial shape and as the authors of this volume observed in its practice.

This observation must be followed immediately by two caveats, however. First, the reference to China's power and its various degrees of geographical presence and, sometimes, its strengths in different issue-areas to evaluate

Chinese multilateralism doesn't imply that international realism is more proper than other contending approaches in international politics, say, liberalism or constructivism, to comprehend either principles of international multilateralism or the Chinese behaviour in that regard. Realism alone is not sufficient to explain why China turned to multilateralism in the recent decade, as the regime had been notoriously bound to unilateralism and bilateralism. Second, the increasing curve of Chinese multilateralism in accordance with China's increasing power takes a dramatic turn when China's power is almost absolute, without powerful checks, as some chapters in this volume have shown, on the issues of Taiwan and Hong Kong. Furthermore, to discuss Chinese domestic politics in a given context that connects with its foreign policy, the clear indication is that China tolerates less international coordination and intervention, as it is able to control the agenda. Domestic authoritarian politics and the leaders' perceptions of some key political concepts like "sovereignty" are often the factors sufficiently powerful to explain the excluding of international multilateralism from these realms. In a practical way, this is important in comprehending China's behaviour, as it helps avoid a false assumption that the growth of China's power and confidence in international affairs necessarily leads to its more open-minded embrace of multilateralism. It is even more significant for spelling out some theoretical implications, however, as it helps demonstrate that those elements traditionally ignored by international realism, such as domestic politics, often play vital roles in foreign policy and international conduct. Therefore, in this concluding chapter we also draw the readers' attention to China's domestic institutions. As informed by the literature concerning two-level games or domestic-foreign links, we know that the understanding of foreign policy without concern for domestic politics is incomplete.[1] China is unique in this regard in terms of its domestic political institutions and their connections with China's foreign relations, and this aspect deserves our attention, in order to work out a more accurate picture of Chinese international behaviour.

Having found that China's international multilateralism has multiple levels and multiple dimensions, this concluding chapter further argues that this multiple nature of multilateralism with Chinese characteristics can be theoretically informative to the general comprehension of the notion of international multilateralism, particularly on the questions like why a state turns to multilateralism in international politics and what strengths and limitations the practice of multilateralism can have on a country like China which adopts it. In the following pages, the conclusions will unfold, in the order with analyses of China's "core-region multilateralism," "pan-regional multilateralism," global symbolic multilateralism, and power-interactive multilateralism, as well as the domestic–foreign linkage in Chinese multilateralism before seeking the explanations of the questions.

Core-region multilateralism: security concerns with China's dominance

As a country with the greatest number of neighbours in the world and also being much concerned with its geographic integration around solid sovereignty and the maintenance of a peaceful environment favouring its ambitious economic modernization programme, China has never tried to conceal the primary emphasis in its foreign policy toward its surrounding regions.[2] This has been particularly true in the recent decade, with the stimulus of the changed international politics following the end of the Cold War, and is reflected in the newly invented official rhetoric of 'befriending, pacifying, and enriching neighbours' (*youlin, mulin, fulin*) in Chinese foreign-policy announcements, coincident with the Chinese turn toward multilateralism.

Not really coincidence. The recent Chinese multilateralism actually originated from its attitude adjustments toward neighbouring countries. As explicitly put by Yahuda in Chapter 5, "It was the experience of cultivating better relations with neighbouring states that led China towards the embrace of multilateral associations of states as vehicles within which to work with others on cooperative endeavours and within which it could also enhance its own interests." To a great extent, Chinese multilateralism is interwoven with China's new regionalism.

China's economic cooperation and even integration at a regional scale often draws much attention when Chinese regionalism and multilateralism come into discussion. The recent developments, however, have shown that China has even become active with initiatives to work with security multilateralism in managing neighbour relations. For the post-Cold War Chinese conduct of so-called "stabilizing the surroundings" (*wending zhoubian*) strategy in the early 1990s, security issues were on the agenda from the very beginning, particularly around China's various border disputes with its continental neighbours. The peaceful settlements of those long-standing disputes, except, so far, those with India, provided both confidence and, to a lesser degree, mutual trust between China and its neighbours, who hitherto had much feared China, due to its imperial and aggressive communist past and its ongoing rise. This was the first step toward multilateral cooperation on Chinese geographic peripheries – an ironic term, as they are actually "core-regions" for China's national security. The Shanghai Cooperation Organization (SCO), which Jianwei Wang has examined in Chapter 7, is the best example in this regard. In contrast to China's involvement in other regional multilateral mechanisms such as the ASEAN+1 or the APEC, the unique involving process and operational features of the SCO speak volumes about Chinese 'core-region' multilateralism. Wang has already subtly analysed these features, but I should like to highlight some of them for the purpose of linking this case to the broader framework in which China conducts its multilateralism.

First, China's dominance is obvious, almost without contention, within the SCO, though this role has unfolded gradually through the process and carefully conducted by China's skilful diplomacy to avoid any possible negative responses from other member states, particularly Russia. In many respects, the SCO has successfully demonstrated China's subtle management of the dilemma between enhancing China's regional dominance and, at the same time, delegitimizing the fear about the "China threat," for which multilateralism, rather than bilateralism, is of much help. As Wang puts it, "Beijing increasingly perceived multilateral diplomacy as a more effective and less alarming strategy to advance China's national interest and to project China's influence." In other words, multilateralism effectively helps China to present to its smaller neighbours a less threatening and more cooperative face of its power, while it enhances equally, if not more than bilateralism, Beijing's interest and influence and to resolve some real problems perplexing the states involved.

Second, the SCO is an organization scraped together from security issues. These were followed by the introduction of economic cooperation into the multilateral agenda, as the conventional path of an international cooperative mechanism evolving from economic cooperation to wider, and more sensitive, issue-areas. This is, in Wang's term, a path of "functionalism upside down." As a matter of fact, other member states of the SCO, particularly the four smaller Central Asian countries, are much interested in economic cooperation with China, and, as Wang observed, "In pursuing the economic function of the SCO, China obviously enjoys greater advantages vis-à-vis other member states, including Russia." As Chapter 7 documents, China pushed to expand the SCO's agenda from security cooperation to economic cooperation is a self-conscious effort to maintain what Beijing regarded as the group's flagging momentum.

In addition to organizational dominance and economic advantages, China's role in the regional organizations like the SCO also possesses a normative dimension, or the elements of "soft power." According to Wang, China is determined to have a say in formulating the new norms and principles in regional affairs, particularly through multilateral mechanisms. With the SCO, China advocates "new security concepts," and has tried to configure the so-called "Shanghai spirit." This "soft" dimension is also interwoven with the "hard" dimension, so to speak, of institutionalization in the case of the SCO, in contrast to China's generally reluctant approach of high institutionalization toward multilateralism. It seems that China has a clear realization that, as the SCO becomes more institutionalized and expands to comprehensive areas rather than remains single-issue-oriented, it even more meets China's need to handle the dilemma between actual leadership and a strategic low profile.

The Six-Party Talks sponsored by Beijing on the DPRK nuclear crisis is another example that, in many ways, although in much lesser degrees, mirrors the SCO, while it distinguishes itself by its involvement of the United States. As Yinhong Shi points out in Chapter 6, this multilateral institution highlights China's prestige in regional politics and its "almost uniquely effective working relations with the other five powers." In this mechanism, China is far from dominant, but it skilfully cultivates its connections with North Korea, which is what China indeed "uniquely" possesses in comparison with the US and other powers, to advance its own prominence and weight in regional international relations. Similarly to the SCO, this mechanism also started from zero, and focuses on security issues (in this case an urgent one) that involve China's national-security interests, and China has gradually gained confidence playing its role over time.

The Six-Party Talks is, of course, much less institutionalized and much less fruitful in comparison with the SCO, but this doesn't mean that China has gained little through its initiatives and sponsorship of this often extremely difficult-to-run mechanism. Besides highlighting China's leading position in regional international relations, the Six-Party Talks provided China with powerful leverage to increase its bargaining power with the United States, while gaining Washington's applause rather than its vigilance for the increasing weight of China in international affairs. Connected to this, the DPRK crisis and China's responses through the multilateral talks enable China to promote a new image as a "responsible power" in international society.

A refined concept of "relative power" should be mentioned here, as China enjoys the upper hand vis-à-vis the United States by sponsoring the Six-Party Talks, despite China's being generally a weaker power in comparison with the US. As Shi argues, the Six-Party Talks has promoted China's international prestige, diplomatic role, and strategic importance, as in this game China occupies a "vantage point as a leader and the indispensable middle-man between the United States and DPRK." This development is different from that of the SCO in which China's "comprehensive national power," a notion frequently emphasized in Chinese discussions of its national development, is stronger in comparison with all other member states, including Russia. Both the SCO and the Six-Party Talks have demonstrated China's behaviour adjustments following the principles and norms of international multilateralism, but they also vividly depict such international scenarios in which China feels more comfortable when it feels its own either absolute or relative strengths, particularly for utilizing multilateral mechanisms to address security issues concerning China's "core" national interests.

Pan-regional multilateralism: economic integration with the prosperous China

Southeast Asia is another critical "core-region" which engages China's close interest. But this region is different in many regards from Central Asia, where the SCO is operated with the leadership of China, hence the difference in China's multilateral practice of regional diplomacy. Institutionally, there had been already a series of regional multilateral organizations under the umbrella of the ASEAN before China extended its influence to the region in the post-Cold War era. The fact that both the United States and Japan have huge interests and powerful influence can also have its impact on China's attitudes towards this region, in comparison with Central Asia where the collapse of the Soviet Union left a power vacuum for the SCO before the region's geostrategic prominence came again into limelight after September 11. Furthermore, historical records show that Chinese diplomacy, particularly during Mao's radical years, was notorious for arousing local states' fear of Chinese expansion. In one sentence, many reasons exist to create an interstate political landscape in Southeast Asia that constrains China's multilateral strategy in the region, which one may find developing with some features different from those of Chinese "core-region" multilateralism.

The first difference lies in the selection of issues, where multilateral cooperation is developed among China and ASEAN states focusing on the economy rather than security. The economy is certainly the most important area in which China's and ASEAN's interests overlap, as Yongnian Zheng and Sow Keat Tok have observed in Chapter 10. "It is thus unsurprising that at the centre of these intensifying political engagements was the increasing interdependency between the two regional economies," in their words. China's economic rise seems to have been in favour of ASEAN's economic considerations. This complementarity in both ASEAN's and Beijing's interests has obviously prompted the China–ASEAN Free Trade Agreement (CAFTA), which is scheduled to come into effect in 2010, and is bound to be given greater emphasis in the years ahead.

China is cautious and often reluctant to join multilateral security arrangements in this region, in contrast with the Chinese priority of practising multilateralism through mechanisms like the SCO. For example, as Michael Yahuda (Chapter 5) and some other contributors have noticed, Beijing does not support the institutionalization of the ARF (the ASEAN Regional Forum, a security mechanism of the ASEAN), while such an institutionalizing process from the Shanghai Five to the SCO was quickly advanced with a push from Beijing. Yahuda finds that the Chinese effectively prevented the ARF from proceeding towards the stage of preventive diplomacy, which could have led to exposing China's territorial disputes with others in the South China Sea to external multilateral scrutiny, rather than leaving the disputes to be settled with different disputants individually at a later stage.

The Chinese preference for a lower degree of institutionalization of Southeast Asian regional organizations can be regarded as another major difference between China's "pan-region multilateralism" and its "core-region multilateralism." In the latter category, China is an advocate of regional multilateralism and an organizer of its practice, as reflected in the cases of the SCO and, to a less degree, the Six-Party Talks. In the former category, among which Southeast Asia stands prominent, China is at best more among equal members, less successful in leadership, though Beijing has been trying to make subtle, cautious, and active efforts to become an initiator of the multilateral agenda and operation in the region of Southeast Asia. Zheng and Tok have argued that this preference to an informal code of conduct has its cultural dimension and, further, well suits the "ASEAN Way," which emphasizes non-confrontational, sensitive, behind-the-door, elitist, politics and negotiations, and non-legalistic approaches, to help alleviate historical animosities and suspicions, which once prevailed among the states involved in regional politics. To Beijing, the "ASEAN Way" promotes more than just a simple multilateral approach. It enables Beijing to enjoy a certain level of anonymity and, hence, flexibility in its involvement. Yahuda further distinguishes "Asian multilateralism," from western multilateralism, based on the practices of the ASEAN, and has observed that China's approach to regionalism broadly follows the norms of ASEAN that stress consultative procedures based on consensus, voluntarism, and non-interference. Needless to say, behind China's feeling of being at home with the accommodation between the ASEAN ways and China's preferences of less institutionalized multilateralism, the security concerns are played down on the multilateral agenda.

Similarities exist, however, in the comparison of Chinese–ASEAN multilateralism with the SCO multilateralism. For example, both types of cooperation involve the elements of regime-type and ideology, or, at least and in a somewhat contradictory way, they don't care so much about regime-type or the political ideology of China. In the Southeast Asian story of Chinese foreign relations, the critical period emerged in the early 1990s, as Zheng and Tok have found, "through the ASEAN channel, China gained access to the international space that it was sorely denied after the Tiananmen Incident, and Beijing in turn rewarded ASEAN members with trade and investment opportunities in the largely untapped China market." Pressure exerted by the West on the issues of human rights and democracy precipitated a consensus between China and ASEAN, which bandwagoned against Western intervention in internal affairs, rallying around the notion of "Asian values." As Yahuda points out, "The multilateralism of the ASEAN kind has found favour with China precisely because it abjures interference in domestic affairs and because it does not impose rules of conduct." Unlike the multilateralism of Western institutions, such as those concerned with arms control, trade, or human rights, the regional institutions do not tie China down, nor do they demand changes in China's domestic arrangements. "In particular, the lack of transparency that is characteristic of CCP politics is not at all challenged by this," in Yahuda's words.

Both Yahuda and Lowell Dittmer (Chapter 2) also emphasize the Tiananmen crackdown in 1989 and the collapse of world communism as a turning point of Chinese relations with Asian countries under multilateralism. Dittmer pays more attention to the impact of the collapse of the strategic triangle at the end of the Cold War that seemed to reduce China's global leverage, hence China's increasing interest in Southeast Asian regional organizations for mutual opening without exclusion and with non-interference in internal affairs. Yahuda holds a more political rather than international structural arguments, maintains that Tiananmen made the Chinese regime soon come to appreciate its new significance as its Asian neighbours took a more forbearing attitude to the massacre, and, meanwhile, Beijing came to see how important the region was becoming to the growth and development of the Chinese economy, now the major source of the regime's seriously wounded political legitimacy.

Politics, therefore, is more primary than even the economy to China's multilateral efforts to integrate Southeast Asia with the prosperous Chinese economy. In Chapter 3, when sketching two contending yet complementary lines of reasoning of realism and liberalism on Chinese multilateralism, Thomas Moore has found that China's major purpose for promoting regional economic integration is less for extracting economic concessions from smaller partners such as ASEAN than for advancing its political objectives through stressing its status as a regional powerhouse of economic growth. "What China seems to value most is long-term political power rather than the short-term maximization of wealth." Economic functionalism in Southeast Asia or "functionalism upside-down" in Central Asia, both well serve China's regional strategies through multilateralism.

Global multilateralism: symbolism of a power that is arising

Moving to the global scale, China's commitment to multilateralism becomes even more complicated, echoing the multiple identities and subtle positions of China in world politics as a growing but still relatively weak power with political authoritarianism, economic transition, and unique cultural traditions. What has been much noticed in previous studies of China's participation in international organizations is the materialist point of view for pursuing both the favourite international environment for China's economic construction in general and the concrete benefits China might obtain from international society to help its modernization.[3] This works well in understanding Chinese multilateralism, marked particularly by China's participation in the WTO as well its behaviour in the United Nations and the UN-affiliated organizations. But new developments have since occurred, prominent among them being China's increasing involvements in multilateralism, both regionally and globally, of security and political-issue-oriented matters, such as human rights. Hence, the additional conceptual conclusions this chapter suggests, as elaborated below.

Like the two regional multilateralisms have been summarized in China's Asia strategies, a distinction between two levels, or facets, this concluding chapter also suggests, is useful for observing and comprehending China's complicated multilateralism conducted beyond China's neighbouring regions. First, the symbolic level, at which China is actively involved into global multilateral institutions for enhancing its image of a "responsible power" in world affairs, while cultivating some real interests of the nation and the regime. Second, the power interactive level, at which China carefully searches for the most possible cost-efficient ways to increase its status and bargaining power vis-à-vis other powers, particularly the single superpower of the post-Cold War world, the United States. Both are conducted around the niche carved by China as a rising global power facing a turbulent world.

To investigate this Janus-faced global multilateralism of China in world affairs, this chapter devotes two sections to each side. As the next section will focus on the second level, namely, the level at which China manages its relations with other powers in terms of multilateralism, here our attention is drawn to the symbolism of China's global multilateralism. As Zheng and Tok cite in Chapter 10, Lucian Pye uses the term 'symbolism' to describe such a practice in which "policy questions are often floated as part of the process of consolidating power." We may further add that symbolic elements in politics (rather than those interests that can be easily materialized), such as identity, culture, and image, are a part of China's global multilateralism and are unusually important in China's struggle to work out a global image of itself as a "responsible power" that is arising.

The first that comes to the point of symbolism is China's long-time emphasis on the role of The United Nations in world affairs. Dittmer (Chapter 2) notes that China has built a political base in the UN as the champion of the Third World and the only developing country with a permanent seat on the Security Council, one of the world's five acknowledged nuclear powers, an economic growth prodigy and potential future superpower. This unique identity among powers enhances China's positions vis-à-vis both the developing countries and, emphatically, with advanced industrial powers. According to him:

> China's voting record in the General Assembly has consistently favoured policies and causes deemed vital to the community of developing nations, at least on symbolic issues. This means it has also quite consistently voted against the United States. China's opposition to US-led sanctions for human rights violations is highly predictable as well as being popular among developing countries. Washington can contain its enthusiasm for China's voting record, but it is an effective constituency-building strategy and serves China's broader strategy of counterbalancing unipolar/unilateral tendencies in world politics.

In other words, China's cultivation of the UN pays much attention to its identity construction and image promotion.

More importantly, China's recent involvements in global regimes of arms control and nuclear nonproliferation can be best understood by this line of reasoning. As Jing-dong Yuan argues in Chapter 4, compared with its relatively more complete endorsement of multilateralism in the fields of international trade and investment, China's approaches to multilateral arms control and nonproliferation institutions and processes remain tentative, cautious, and selective. While it is more active and participatory in most international and multilateral institutions and processes, Beijing has yet to fully embrace the principles of multilateralism even as it becomes more active in both regional and global multilateral arenas. Yuan elaborates this by analysing how security concerns remain the guiding principle for Chinese arms control policies, while, at the same time, image consideration influences the degree and extent of Chinese participation in international nonproliferation arrangements. Electing to be constrained by regional arms-control measures may harm its military and security interests, but refusing to participate in the regional arms-control processes will tarnish China's image as a major force for global/regional peace and stability. A safe conclusion is that, in certain areas where China feels both its security interests and image can be boosted by multilateral diplomacy, it has been taking the initiative in promoting multilateralism and institutionalization of security cooperation. Cultivating its position as a weaker, particularly compared with the US, militarily inferior, and largely defensive, power, China likely will be the focus of any multilateral arms-control process.

On politically sensitive issues like human rights, China's multilateral commitments are also highly symbolic rather than substantive. According to Paltiel's study in Chapter 11, 'China has achieved considerable tactical success through acknowledging international human rights norms while vigorously rejecting their transnational implementation.' He has investigated in detail how China's domestic conduct of human-rights issues are not deeply constrained by international institutions, while China has since the 1990s become active in participating in UN human-rights organizations, for the purposes of legitimacy and anti-hegemonism. China's emphatic mobilization of traditional cultural values against international mainstream human-rights standards also highlights the fact that such multilateral participations are not designed to constrain China itself, as multilateralism is conceptually assumed, but mainly to prevent China's isolation from international society and, when possible, enhance China's voice on human-rights issues in front of the world. In this sense, Chinese symbolism in this regard is doubled: in terms of participation, it is a gesture for image considerations, rather than a commitment for practical implementations; in terms of the substantiation, it is with the emphasis on unilateral cultural particularism, rather than on international institutional constraints.

Power interactive multilateralism: sophistications of refusal and balance

In contrast to China's active yet symbolic involvements in some international multilateral regimes, China at the same time shows obvious reluctance to join those organizations it considers global power clubs which may show China's shortcomings as a weak and non-democratic power and, more importantly, may curb China's international influence. Furthermore, when other great powers with relative advantages in some regional, let alone global, multilateral mechanisms are present, China often inclines to refuse joining those mechanisms. At this level of multilateralism, China's focus moves from other attentions we have outlined in the previous sections to its own interactions with other powers, particularly the United States, and the increasing multilateral trend in Chinese foreign policy slows down, often becoming passive and defensive.

As a rising power, China's interactions with other powers, particularly the status quo powers, among which the United States stands out, are always a vital dimension through which one reads China's foreign policy and its implications for world politics.[4] In this volume, almost all individual chapters have discussed this subject with various empirical backgrounds. Opinions may be divided on China's intentions as a rising power to challenge or accommodate itself with status quo powers; a tentative consensus, however, has emerged suggesting that China's multilateral practices in different regions and on different issues are much affected by its interactions with the United States and other powers, particularly Russia, Japan, and sometimes India, in the given geopolitical contexts. Further, it is, to some extent, a shared view that China inclines to be not active in, or even to refuse joining, those multilateral mechanisms that the superpower or other powers tend to dominate. Instead, Chinese multilateralism becomes strong when other powers' influence is absent, weak, or seriously constrained.

China's attitude toward the Group 8 is a good example of such refusal. But this volume doesn't include any study of this topic, mainly because we are much more concerned with what has already happened rather than what has not happened. In the chapters included here, however, the temptation for China to be passive toward some regional multilateral arrangements already clearly reflects its consideration of the presence of global powers vis-à-vis China itself. For example, Yahuda has noticed China's negative responses to the idea of a multilateral Asian monetary mechanism, in which both the United States and Japan can be significant members with larger economies and stronger currencies, in comparison with China.

More detailed studies of such cases are presented in those chapters such as Chapter 9, where Keyuan Zou explains China's attitudes toward the South China Sea security mechanisms by China's concern with the American intervention in the Malacca Strait, and its fear of a military presence of the United States there. Although it realizes that regional cooperation is "indispensable" for maritime security, China prefers such a regional arrangement only without the shadow of the United States. Gaye Christoffersen, in Chapter 8, echoes this by stating that Beijing has acknowledged that it is dependent on US hegemony in the East Asian order, but is also aware that the US has the capacity to strategically deny these mechanisms to China in the event of a crisis. As stated, "China voiced concern over Malacca but let Malaysia take the lead in resisting US leadership."

Thus, we come to China's attitudes in regional multilateralism toward the United States. For this, Dittmer explicitly states that, "China's positions in world organizations have tended to be anti-American, while in regional organizations China has taken a 'East Asia for the East Asians' line precluding US participation." In general, China's participation in international organizations grows, "preferably (but not exclusively) in the absence of direct US involvement," citing Dittmer's words. Yahuda agrees that, "One distinctive feature of China's new regionalism was an emphasis on Asia as a principal organizing geographic theme," and that, "The United States has not been deliberately excluded as it has been invited' as a member of a series of regional institutions." America fits in only at the margins of China's new regionalism that is nurtured by, and interwoven with, multilateralism.

Moore goes further, to argue that, "The belief that globalization can be used to restrain US power is also reflected in the increasing emphasis Beijing places on multilateralism over multipolarity in official Chinese rhetoric," while in practice China seeks explicitly to balance against US power with the promotion of multipolarity and multilateralism. Moore's further analysis on Chinese strategic calculations convinces that China pursued institutionalized cooperation most enthusiastically either in global multilateral settings with a big number of members, where the superpower's dominance is less pronounced, than in venues with smaller memberships (e.g. WTO and UN) or regionally, with weaker partners, where China is the most powerful participant (e.g. SCO and ASEAN). In this perspective, China's multilateral engagements with ASEAN and SCO countries are also "a thinly-veiled effort to counter Washington's dominance in the region."

Not all contributors are in agreement on the last point. For example, Jianwei Wang downplays China's intention of promoting SCO to balance the US. The differing findings are partially attributed to China's subtle conducts of multilateralism. If there is balancing, it is "subtle or soft balancing," in Moore's terms. With multilateralism, China's tactics to refuse power dominance and its efforts to balance the United States are far more sophisticated than it once practiced before its multilateral turn in foreign policy. In Dittmer's observation, this "unusual sensitivity" includes that China has learned its lesson from the twentieth century's Germany and Japan, that a rising great power must not overtly offend stakeholders in the international status quo.

With respect to China's increasing use of sophisticated multilateralism, firstly, China does not embrace the denial of US prominence in world politics and US presence in Asian regional international relations. There was, though, a process for China to recognize such realities and develop its tactics to cope with them while turning to regional multilateralism. According to Yahuda, as late as 1998, Chinese leaders still continued to pressure their Southeast Asian neighbours to turn away from the American alliance system. China's embrace of multilateralism, however, involved, at a later stage, its acceptance of the American security presence in Asia as a positive factor, and came to two seemingly contradictory conclusions, which have nurtured China's subtle, rather than single-minded regional multilateral engagements: first, the United States was going to continue to be the world's pre-eminent power for some time to come, and China had better stabilize and improve its relationship with America bilaterally; and second, China should become more active in shaping its regional environment, multilateralism has largely been exploited as an effective way to do this. Together, these approaches paved the way for China's growing participation in ASEAN multilateral mechanisms, as both Yahuda's and Zheng/Tok's chapters have emphasized, as the ASEAN states regard their relations with the US and China as mutually reinforcing, and, furthermore, that an intensified Sino-US rivalry would pose great difficulties to the ASEAN states.

The acceptance of the American presence was also evident in China's revitalized approach to Central Asia, as Yahuda's chapter and other relevant chapters have noticed. The SCO dropped the alleged "common struggle against hegemony," as featured sometimes in key documents issued by the Shanghai Five, when it was established in June 2001, recognizing the transformed post-September 11 geopolitical reality of that region.

The second feature of the Chinese sophistication of balancing the United States through selective, strategic multilateralism is that potential antagonism is replaced by the effort to strengthen China's own bargaining power vs. the

United States, and regional multilateralism is often found by Beijing to be convenient and even advantageous for this purpose. The Six-Party Talks are a good example of this, as Shi has carefully examined. Through the sponsorship of this mechanism, despite how much (or little) achievement it has worked out, China has successfully improved its bilateral relations with Washington, its image in international society, and its profile as a "responsible" great power in regional affairs.

Third, China's strategy of multilateralism to balance the status quo superpower is enhanced with its special attention to "soft power." As Paltiel points out, China identifies with international society as a means of "soft" counter-hegemony, and this means identifying with secondary powers as a normative means of constraining US hegemony. This can be distinguished from balancing in a balance of power system by the absence of an overt power or security dimension. "Instead, China sees itself as a consensus power upholding traditional Westphalian concepts of sovereignty against a US power that threatens to undermine these concepts," according to Paltiel. "The irony in this posture is that for it to be effective China must identify with other multilateral actors, principally European, who promote a distinctively liberal version of multilateralism." For Beijing, a multilateral order offers the most effective means to counter hegemonism and secure China's sovereignty at the same time. This kind of "soft" counter-hegemonism through multilateralism does not contradict the maintenance of positive bilateral relations with the US.

Multilateralism in the lenses of domestic–foreign linkage: the primary of politics

It would be not accurate to conclude, based on the above discussions, that China is always more engaged in multilateralism when it becomes more confident about its own power, despite the form of power, either absolute or relative, material, coercive, or soft. The curve of the multilateral engagement, rising with the increasing power of China, takes a sudden turn when it meets those issues defined "internal" but actually with wide and deep international relevance. Hong Kong and Taiwan stand out prominently among such issues. As Hong Kong and, especially, Taiwan are doubtless among the significant problems on China's international agenda, Beijing never fails to repeat that all the issues concerning both belong to China's "internal affairs." Furthermore, as important to this volume, they become, in Dittmer's words, the "two most conspicuous flaws" in China's national image of a responsible and multilateral power. This logic, namely, that little or no multilateralism is allowed on the issues defined as "internal," also powerfully extends to the domain of Chinese domestic politics. For traditional international realism, this may go too far, as it comes beyond our coverage of Chinese foreign policy. It is meaningful, however, according to the rich literature on so-called "domestic–foreign linkage," for comprehending foreign policy through the lens of domestic politics of a given state. This section, therefore, moves the discussions of Chinese multilateral diplomacy closer to Hong Kong and Taiwan and, further, to China's domestic politics and their implications to the understanding of Chinese multilateralism.

For the Hong Kong case, as Dittmer has found, China's "one country, two systems" model has seen too much emphasis on "one country" and too little on "two systems," for the taste of many Hong Kong citizens. This imbalance between international sovereignty of China over Hong Kong (as crystallized in the "one country" framework) and popular sovereignty of Hong Kong (as demanded by Hong Kong people for local democracy under the SAR system) leaves little space for China to engage the issues concerning Hong Kong's fate on international multilateralism. Actually, in Chapter 14, which is exclusively devoted to examining Hong Kong, Jean-Philippe Béja explicitly concludes that the Chinese diplomatic practice concerning Hong Kong is "an exception" to multilateralism, and that Beijing has kept insisting that no third party should interfere in Beijing's relations with the Hong Kong Special Administrative Region. Despite the facts that the SAR is, paralleling with the PRC, a member of many international organizations, and that the political, religious, and human rights organizations, let alone foreign states, are much concerned with the Hong Kong issue, Beijing has been careful not to let them intervene even in the discussions about the pace of Hong Kong democratization and other issues concerning the political life there.

Taiwan is in an even more difficult and complicated situation in its relations with China vis-à-vis international society. Or, as Yahuda puts it, the way China tackles the Taiwan problem is perhaps "the most serious problem in China's approach to multilateralism." First of all, China claims its legitimate right, as Beijing finds necessary, to unilaterally seek military solutions of its dispute with Taiwan over the future of the new democracy of the island. Meanwhile, as there is concern throughout the Asia-Pacific region that a military conflict could break out with dire consequences for all the other states in the region, China, at least at the rhetoric level if not in diplomatic practice, denies other states' rights to utter this concern on either bilateral or multilateral occasions. As China has shown none of the multilateral tolerance it has displayed in its IGO diplomacy when dealing with Taiwan, a dilemma occurs with China's international multilateral participation, which is, in the words of Dong-ching Day, in Chapter 13, "The more powerful China becomes in the international community, the more likely it is that China could block Taiwan's participation in multilateral organizations." Because of this, as Yinhong Shi and some other contributors have pointed out, Taiwan is an obstacle to China's engagement with any possible East Asia multilateral security regime. Furthermore, as Zheng and Tok have noticed, as far as Beijing is concerned, Taiwan remains a domestic issue and is barred from all official discussions in international forums.

The Chinese regime's concept of sovereignty is a major problem identified by many contributors to this volume when comprehending Beijing's such attitudes. "State sovereignty" in the Chinese communist dictionary is exclusive not only to foreign interventions, but also to bottom-up citizen efforts to configure state authorities. Together, according to Béja's observation, "the simple fact that an ordinary citizen discusses the evolution of the domestic political scene in a foreign assembly is considered [by the Chinese regime] a serious attack on sovereignty." An issue defined as "internal" in China thus means that it will not be allowed to appear in the international public sphere where Beijing has influence.

In Chapter 11 Paltiel goes further to link this stubborn understanding of sovereignty with regime interests of Chinese authoritarianism, as elaborated with China's Janus-faced attitudes towards human-rights issues. He has found an obvious tension between China's growing international commitment to rules-based orders as part of its participation in trade and transnational flows, on the one hand, and China's fears about rule-driven multilateralism for the elective affinity between rules-based multilateralism and liberal governance under the rule of law, on the other. The central concern of the Chinese government here is political: China's Communist Party regime wishes to define itself and the rules under which it chooses to operate, rather than have the rules define the regime. Dittmer echoes this statement by saying that, for China, "multilateralism is meant to be relevant only to the international arena, not a Trojan Horse for domestic liberalism." Back to the understanding of sovereignty, Paltiel is right in saying that China's self-contradictory behaviour concerning the issues touching on sovereignty and the rule of law "stems from the problem of accounting for the peculiar system of sovereignty operating domestically – formal sovereignty of the people with de facto Party patrimonialism." In other words, politics not only occupies the primary place in China's considerations to conduct or not conduct international multilateralism, but politics, rather than norms or principles, is also primary to the comprehension of Chinese multilateralism.

Domestic political arrangements in China, therefore, are perhaps the ultimate liability of China's foreign relations in general and international multilateralism in particular. Or, in Yahuda's sentence, "it may be argued that the CCP itself is an obstacle to effecting the kind of intensive cooperation and coordination that China's leaders claim to seek in the region." For a regime that doesn't follow the constitution and other domestic laws made by itself, its compromises with, and promises about, international norms and laws can be deeply limited and handicapped.

Advantages of and adaptation to multilateralism: explaining the Chinese turn

Having analysed the multiple levels of Chinese multilateralism, we should advance further to seek explanations of the Chinese turn to multilateralism from its long-time adherence to unilateralism and bilateralism. This is a major question for all chapters of this volume. The authors have contributed their various answers to the question, and these answers emphasize respective dimensions of explanations with interactive and complementary lines of reasoning.

One attractive explanation of the Chinese change of approach, which many chapters in this volume have shared, is foreign-policy learning. Such learning can take place at the most superficial level, say, for acquisitions of new vocabularies of international conducts, though Dittmer thinks that rhetorical learning has also helped to encourage consonant behavioural change. Disagreements exist, of course. For example, Béja argues that China has often changed its discourse on international relations, using the most modern concepts of modern diplomacy, while the Chinese Communist Party has actually demonstrated a remarkable consistency in foreign policies. In this case, Béja argues, Chinese multilateralism is nothing more than a fashionable tactic of the United Front. In other words, rhetoric is simply rhetoric, and learning is about a game of wording.

Or, learning is about the number who are involved in the game, as Yuan has observed in Chapter 4. For him, when China refers to multilateralism, they are most likely talking about multilateral diplomacy, as differentiated from bilateral interactions. "There is a strong emphasis on the number of players and processes rather than the structural implications of multilateralism," such as nondiscrimination, indivisibility, and diffuse reciprocity. This implies that the Chinese have learnt a little bit more than wording: they now know the advantage to join group games, even though they do not want to be bound by rules of such games.

A number of chapters, nevertheless, emphasize the importance of political experience for deeper learning, which in this case, is China's past exposures to multilateral engagements. The economic opening of China is obviously among the most vital factors shaping this learning process favourably to later foreign policy adjustment to multilateralism, as many previous studies and some chapters in this volume have demonstrated. As multilateral involvements proved beneficial to China's economic modernization, China was encouraged to extend to other issue-areas such as international security. Moreover, as Day points out, economic and security issues are more and more difficult to clearly separate from each other, this spill-over effect of foreign-policy learning can be quite natural.

This argument raises some questions which, in turn, would reduce explanatory power of learning for the Chinese turn to multilateralism, however. Or, more accurately speaking, the questions can redefine the learning approach with the Chinese case. Apparently, this explanation emphasizes that it is the changing perception of national interest that causes policy learning, while the possible learning of international norms is downplayed in the Chinese learning process. This seems consistent to what most authors in this volume have observed from the Chinese case, but derivates from the literature of international relations on regime theory and norm compliance that, as Paltiel points out, postulates the significant functions of an "epistemic community" surrounding a given body of norms in foreign policy learning. Taking China's attitude towards human rights as an example, which views participation in international human-rights regimes as "struggle" more than accommodation, Patiel concludes that the role of epistemic communities in fostering intersubjective transnational discourse and normative conformity with international regimes cannot be overestimated.

Other contributors are more optimistic about China's capacity to learn about norms and principles. Wang thinks that, "From the very beginning the Shanghai Five-SCO reflected Beijing's interest in establishing a norm-based and new kind of post-Cold War security order in the region." Also, Moore, a propos the liberalism experiment, concludes that Beijing's promotion of ideas such as the New Security Concept and the "democratization of international relations" reflects the kind of genuine value change associated with foreign policy learning. For Moore, "What may begin as instrumental participation (adaptation) often leads to enmeshment (adaptive learning) as national interests are transformed over time through the experience of participating in multilateral cooperation." China's pursuit of institutionalized cooperation, therefore, in Moore's words, "signifies a growing commitment to a rules-based, norm-driven international order."

Although assessments are so divided, it seems all the contributors agree, more or less, that China's turn to multilateralism is based on its, also in Moore's words, "recognizing [of] the utility of institutions as tools of power politics." China's learning is, therefore, more adaptive learning than cognitive learning, and more instrumental than fundamental, as most authors of this volume have agreed in accordance with previous studies in this regard.[5] In other words, China has so far learnt more about how to calculate its national interests rather than how to accommodate international norms. Some authors in this volume, like Day and Moore, do assert that China's decision to join a given multilateral organization is based on careful cost–benefit analyses, while, at the same time, they recognize the importance of experience and the normative dimensions to bring about Chinese multilateralism (although Moore, meanwhile, argues that such instrumental initiations can lead to multilateralism transforming China's own national interest). Dittmer even retreats to the point where he thinks that China's long-term national interests have remained constant while Beijing keeps exploring better strategies to realize these interests, though he tries to show this is not necessarily contending with normative study. Perhaps we can say that normative learning is overshadowed by rational calculation, though it is safer to say that China chooses multilateral diplomacy when it enhances China's bargaining power in foreign relations.

So, what elements are significant in Chinese perceptions and calculations of its own national interests that lead to the turn to multilateralism? The above chapters have provided rich answers to this question. At bottom, China fears international exclusion and isolation. This was particularly true in the early 1990s when China experienced the 1989 Tiananmen crackdown and world communism was collapsing. Paltiel has found, for example, that China's concern over international human rights came out of its isolation following the Tiananmen repression, and the initial threat of exclusion had a substantial impact in promoting China's engagement with the multilateral human-rights system. The chapters by Dittmer, Yahuda, and Zheng and Tok also identify the Tiananmen tragedy as a turning point on China's relations with the world in general and, in particular, with Southeast Asia through multilateral involvements for avoiding isolation. As international space for Chinese communist authoritarianism greatly shrank during the period, China had to recognize the different value systems between itself and others in the world, and made an effort to work towards a consensus that accommodates the differences while allowing China the political space to survive and develop. To play the role of an antagonist to the existing order would not help China maintain legitimacy both abroad and at home. In this sense, regime interest stands prominent among what was defined by Beijing as China's national interests.

Equal to the regime's consideration in such circumstances is the problem of legitimacy. First of all, the Chinese Communist Party enjoys a historical resource of political legitimacy as it claims that it saved the Chinese nation and, further, made China proud of itself in international society. This logic worked again in the era after the worldwide collapse of communism. What is the Chinese status of a great power beyond overcoming isolation, which has been proved always effective to support the regime's domestic legitimacy through careful mobilization of nationalism.[6] Participation in international society serves as the benchmark of China's achievement of global status as a great power. Citing Paltiel, "To be a great power is to be a player in international society," we may add: to make China a great power in the world is to be legitimate to govern China.

The economic benefits, as already frequently mentioned in this volume and in many previous studies of Chinese foreign policy in the post-Mao era, are a significant factor in bolstering the CCP's domestic legitimacy and shaping China's international conduct. Of especial importance in this regard is China's embracing of globalization, a fundamental policy adopted by the Chinese state for stimulating its ambitious programs of economic modernization and, at the same time, sustaining the communist regime's legitimacy through good economic performance. At a minimum, as Moore interprets, China's leaders regard growing interdependence as a fundamental condition of international relations that cannot be resisted in conducting state-to-state relations. While promoting, rather than reducing, interdependence has become an end as well as a means in the conduct of Chinese foreign policy, and international organizational participation has had a substantial payoff for China "at relatively negligible cost," as pointed out by Dittmer, accelerating domestic economic development, China's turn towards multilateralism over the past decade owed much to its evolving understanding of globalization.

Having survived the collapse of world communism and having further achieved economic prosperity through the 1990s, China confronted a new challenge: the need to manage its rise as a great power while reducing the suspicion of international society and, in particular, of the status quo powers and neighbouring states on the negative impacts of China's rise over international and regional politics. In Yahuda's regionalism lens, this is to make China's growing weight in the region more acceptable to the resident states, while Moore identifies this challenge as finding "an efficient, internationally legitimate means of institutionalizing their country's ascendancy." Multilateralism has been found apt to serve this double-edged purpose. In the forefront of damage-control, China's engagement into multilateralism helped avoid the spread of the "China threat" perspective among neighbouring countries. As Yahuda explicitly puts it, "the multilateral approach is the best way to allay lingering suspicions about possible threats that China's rise may pose to the independence of its neighbours and fears about potential Chinese hegemonism," because the conduct of relations with smaller powers on a bilateral basis necessarily puts them at a disadvantage and raises suspicions that Beijing might seek to exploit divisions among them.

There is something more constructive, however, beyond this minimum and defensive function of multilateralism. The multilateral embracing has provided a further mechanism with which China can actively contribute to shaping both regional-global developments and China's own international image of a "responsible state." According to Yuan, China's acceptance of greater military transparency and the signing of the CTBT demonstrate that its participation in multilateral security and arms control affects how it defines its interests, including how it wants to be perceived. This is consistent with China's increasing appreciation of the importance of "soft power" in contemporary international relations, as many chapters note. Paltiel has also noticed that China even makes an effort to forge an international consensus favourable to China's views – not only China's image. For him, "China seeks to build an interpretive community in common with other developing countries designed to counter Western human rights criticisms. China sought to shape the international agenda and build a broader interpretive community around itself."

Thus comes the question about China's leadership. Multilateralism allows China to assert its leadership in regional organizations, as Moore states, "without unnecessarily exacerbating fears that Beijing harbours revisionist intentions." Along with the growing of China's "comprehensive national power," however, this has led to the point at which China began its efforts, as exemplified by the SCO and the Six-Party Talks, of "system-building" or "system-establishing," a new pattern of China's international organizational behaviour in addition to Samuel Kim's well-known concepts of "system-transforming," "system-reforming," and "system-maintaining/exploiting."[7] Without multilateralism, it is difficult to imagine that China could effectively play this new role.

The changing international environment and, in particular, the policies of other states also offer useful hints to understanding the Chinese adjustments of foreign policy. Christoffersen (Chapter 8) is correct in saying that "China's approach to multilateralism is interactive, and cannot be understood separately from US, Japan and ASEAN approaches to security multilateralism." According to her, Japan's pursuit of a regional multi-layered security architecture facilitates China's dual approach to both include and exclude the US in regional security multilateralism within the ASEAN institutional complex. The unilateral tendencies of the US following the September 11 tragedy, on the other hand, provided China with a powerful lever to stand with multilateralism. The assumption of multilateralism as anti-hegemonism works for China at two levels. At the level of norms, multilateralism weakens the "soft power" of the United States that inclines to unilateralism, and international mechanisms like the UN can more or less check Washington's unilateralism and interventionism. As Paltiel points out, "Soft counter-hegemonism requires China to adhere to a posture that aims at projecting greater respect for global institutions and regional sensitivities than the US, and indirectly more consistent support for rules-based orders and multilateral decision making than the US." At the level of power, China's active regional multilateral involvements do weaken Washington's bilateral alliance system in the region. This also offers a way to read China's incentives for some concrete moves with multilateral engagements. For example, Chrsitofferson finds that UNCLOS ratification gives China a stronger legal basis for participation in Malacca Strait security than has the US, and Yahuda has observed that China's 1995 agreement with the ASEAN states to collectively discuss issues of the South China Sea came as it did at a time of a Sino-American confrontation over Taiwan, and, therefore, showed the Chinese desire to cultivate neighbours for countering the United States.

In general, post-Cold War international politics and its new features nurtured an environment favourable to a turn to multilateralism. Many authors have noticed this, though they use different terms to express the point, as "international society," now that China has a new understanding, in Paltiel's observation, and a "global logic" suggested by Moore. The emergence of non-traditional security issues onto the international agenda is one of such features that define post-Cold War world politics while stimulates multilateral cooperation. China is no less than other states coming to encounter such issues. Partially because of this, there has also been growing inseparability between economic and security issues, which has obviously encouraged China to move from economic multilateralism to broader issue-areas. In Jianwei Wang's sentence, "Under the new international circumstances, and with a new understanding of international security dynamics, multilateralism has been increasingly regarded as a more effective means to address China's security concerns."

All of these features become particularly true in Asia, where China pays tremendous attention, and multilateralism has become strong in the region since the end of the Cold War. Such regional trends have tremendous impact on the Chinese attitude towards multilateralism, as many have emphasized in their respective chapters. As Keyuan Zou concludes based upon his maritime-security study:

> China has realized, though with some reluctance, that regionalization of the maritime security issues such as the South China Sea dispute is an inevitable trend, which China is unable to prevent but must adapt itself to, so that it still can play a significant role in dealing with regional maritime security issues.

Moreover, as Dittmer and Yahuda have analysed, regional characters of Asian multilateralism also provide larger space for China being engaged into "mutual learning," meaning that both China and the host IGOs have to modify their expectations and behaviours. Positive responses from international society for

China's multilateral adjustments, as Shi indicates in his chapter on the Six-Party Talks, further encourages China to go ahead along with the new path.

Conclusions

China has, since the beginning of the twenty-first century, accelerated its turn towards multilateralism in foreign relations, now going beyond economics to multilateral engagements of wider issue areas, including international security and with an emphasis on Asian regionalism. This is phenomenal for Chinese foreign policy from a historical perspective, but, from the perspective of principles, its essence of multilateralism is still limited and even handicapped, as Chinese multilateralism is often "flexible," to borrow Wang's term, "instrumental," as many contributors have concluded, "strategic" as adopted by Moore, more "nominal" than "qualitative," in Yuan's words, and even, for Dittmer, something that "conceals an underlying realism." In Yahuda's point of view, it suffers from many structural problems. It also suffers more, such as cognitive problems, as reflected in previous sections of this concluding chapter. One should not exaggerate this phenomenon of multilateralism, nor overstate its influence on overall Chinese foreign policy, though one also must pay close attention to its profound impacts, particularly on regional international relations with countries neighbouring China.

When practising multilateralism, China does not follow a unified model. As reflected in various chapters of this volume, and as Wang in Chapter 7 explicitly points out, it instead takes different modes of multilateralism to fit different geopolitical and geo-economic conditions. At the core, where China's tremendous security interests lie and China is able to dominate, China's incentives for making security multilateralism tend to be strong, as reflected in the SCO and the Six-Party Talks. The constraints that multilateralism implies to state behaviour, however, are comparatively weak for China. In the neighbouring regions where existing institutions already worked before China was involved in multilateralism, China has subtly handled its insertion into the context, mainly through economic integration in which the prosperous China is attractive to other states, rather than cultivating regional security issues, as it does in Central Asia. Only when the mechanisms on security issues are loosely organized, with voluntarism among non-powers, is China willing to join. China carefully calculates its relative strength in comparison with world and regional powers that are involved in regional and global multilateral organizations, and, when possible, practising "soft-balancing" against the superpower through regional multilateralism, or keeping its distance from those international regimes when China has to be closely attached to rules made, in China's perception, by other powers. Beijing seizes most opportunities, however, showing the world its rhetorical enthusiasm on multilateralism, which makes China, in comparison with the United States that increasingly inclines toward unilateralism, almost a standard-bearer of this discourse so popular in today's world.

With such a complicated and sophisticated series of different multilateralisms, China is searching for an effective way to manage the tensions between its rise as a global power and the various responses from the diverse yet turbulent world to this rise. China heartily embraces economic globalization, and even cultivates economic interdependence, for stimulating its ambitious economic growth. Its efforts to build an Asian community through multilateral arrangements are rewarding in many ways beyond economics, particularly in the sense of marginalizing other powers, including the single superpower of today's world politics, the United States. The utility of multilateralism has also been applied to various traditional and non-traditional security issues with quite remarkable substantial and symbolic achievements.

A gap remains with respect to China's use of multilateralism in its conduct of international relations. The multilateral approaches and institutions as applied by China have not been able to address the problems of Hong Kong and Taiwan, for example. The recent drastically increasing demands for energy and resource supplies, as veteran China watcher Willy Lam has powerfully demonstrated in Chapter 12, also have more to do with realist politics or turning multilateralism into realist arrangements of alliances than pushing China closer to a rule-bounded foreign conduct. Moreover, while China's behaviour in international society is, as Paltiel argues, more like resistance from within status quo arrangements of powers and norms, the Beijing leadership tends, as always, to violate Chinese laws while being quick to crack down on domestic trends towards political pluralization and liberalization. This, of course, has its implications for China's foreign relations, despite the Chinese authoritarian regime's struggle to separate domestic politics and foreign relations and to fend off external influences on China.

Finally, multilateralism is just one dimension of Chinese foreign policy, and it must be put into proper perspective and treated as one among a multitude of approaches to foreign relations, including security issues, as authors of this volume, particularly Moore, Yahuda, and Yuan have pointed out. Any assessment of the role of multilateralism in China's international conduct must take account of China's general foreign policies, and even domestic policies, of which multilateralism is only a part. The analyses presented in this collection do show that multilateralism has come to Chinese international behaviour, more or less, and that this trend will continue. Nevertheless, they are also reminding us multilateralism alone is not enough to account for Chinese foreign relations, and, if its understanding and embrace of multilateralism are to be successful, China still has a long way to go in the sense of norms, principles, and group consensus to constrain state behaviour.

Notes

1 For such literatures, see, for example, Robert D. Putnam, "Diplomacy and Domestic Politics: The Logic of Two-Level Games," *International Organizations* 42, Summer 1988, pp. 427–60; Peter B. Evans, Harold K. Jacobson, and Robert D. Putnam (eds), *Double-Edged Diplomacy: International Bargaining and Domestic Politics*, Berkeley:

University of California Press, 1993; Robert O. Keohane and Helen V. Milner (eds), *Internationalization and Domestic Politics*, New York: Cambridge University Press, 1996. For the attempts to understand Chinese foreign policy with the weight of domestic politics, see, for instance, Kenneth Lieberthal, "Domestic Politics and Foreign Policy," in Harry Harding (ed.), *China's Foreign Relations in the 1980s*, New Haven: Yale University Press, 1984, pp. 43–70; Carol Lee Hamrin, "Elite Politics and the Development of China's Foreign Relations," in Thomas W. Robinson and David Shambaugh (eds), *Chinese Foreign Policy: Theory and Practice*, Oxford: Clarendon Press, 1994, pp. 70–112; David M. Lampton (ed.), *The Making of Chinese Foreign and Security Policy in the Era of Reform*, Stanford: Stanford University Press, 2001; Guoguang Wu, "Passions, Politics, and Politicians: Beijing between Taipei and Washington," *The Pacific Review* 17, 2, 2004, pp. 179–98.
2 For China's neighbouring diplomacy in the post-Cold War era, see, for example, Harold C. Hinton, "China as an Asian Power," in Robinson and Shambaugh, *Chinese Foreign Policy*, pp. 348–72; David Shambaughed (ed.), *Power Shift: China and Asia's New Dynamics*, Berkeley: University of California Press, 2005. For an examination of it with a broader background, see Michael Yahuda, *The International Politics of the Asia-Pacific, 1945–1995*, London: Routledge, 1996.
3 Samuel S. Kim, "China's International Organizational Behaviour," in Robinson and Shambaugh, *Chinese Foreign Policy*, pp. 401–34. Also, Madelyn C. Ross, "China's International Economic Behaviour," in Robinson and Shambaugh, *Chinese Foreign Policy*, pp. 435–52; William R. Feeney, "China and the Multilateral Economic Institutions," in Samuel S. Kim (ed.), *China and the World: Chinese Foreign Policy Faces the New Millennium*, Boulder: Westview Press, 1998, 4th edn, pp. 239–63; Nicholas R. Lardy, *Integrating China into the Global Economy*, Washington, DC: Brookings Institution Press, 2002.
4 Alastair Iain Johnston and Robert S. Ross (eds), *Engaging China: The Management of an Emerging Power*, London: Routledge, 1999; Michael E. Brown, Owen R. Cote, Jr., Sean M. Lynn-Jones, and Steven E. Miller (eds), *The Rise of China*, Cambridge, MA: MIT Press, 2000; Shambaugh, *Power Shift*.
5 Particularly, Alastair Iain Johnston, "Learning versus Adaptation: Explaining Change in Chinese Arms Control Policy in the 1980s and the 1990s," *China Journal*, 35, January 1996, pp. 27–62.
6 Yongnan Zheng, *Discovering Chinese Nationalism in China: Modernization, Identity, and International Relations*, Cambridge: Cambridge University Press, 1999; Peter Hays Gries, *China's New Nationalism: Pride, Politics, and Diplomacy*, Berkeley: University of California Press, 2004; and Suisheng Zhao, *A Nation-State by Construction: Dynamics of Modern Chinese Nationalism*, Stanford: Stanford University Press, 2004.
7 Kim, "China's International Organizational Behaviour."

Index

9/11 terrorist attacks: Hong Kong 253; levels of multilateralism 3, 271, 278, 285; maritime security 147, 159; petroleum diplomacy 224; regional order 82, 84; RMSI 129, 133; SCO 108, 109, 110, 111, 114, 119; Sino-ASEAN relations 182, 191

Abe, Shinzo 86
ACFTA *see* ASEAN–China Free Trade Agreement
Achille Lauro incident 160
adaptive learning 47, 283
ADB *see* Asian Development Bank
Afghanistan 82, 108, 109, 119, 225, 227
Africa 187, 227, 228–9, 236
AG *see* Australia Group
aid: North Korea 94, 95; petroleum diplomacy 227, 229, 232, 235; Sino-ASEAN relations 188; Taiwan 243; United Nations 24
AIDS (acquired immune deficiency syndrome) 181
Angola 228, 229
An Min 260, 261
APEC *see* Asian Pacific Economic Cooperation
APT *see* ASEAN+3
ARF *see* ASEAN Regional Forum
ARF Security Policy Conference (ASPC) 31, 35, 131, 137–8
arms control 51–67; cooperative security 52–5; levels of multilateralism 6, 273, 275–6, 285; logic of policies 60–5; maritime security 162; multilateral arms control 55–60; new internationalism 29, 30, 33; overview 14, 51, 65–7; petroleum diplomacy 227, 229; regional order 76
Arroyo, Gloria 232

ASEAN (Association of Southeast Asian Nations): Hong Kong 253, 254; levels of multilateralism 8, 271–4, 278, 285, 286; liberalism and realism (globalization and regionalism 45, 46, 47; liberal internationalism 38, 39; overview 35, 37; realist internationalism 41, 42, 43); maritime security 15, 152, 153, 155, 162, 166; new internationalism 23, 28, 29, 30, 31; overview 14–15; "peaceful rise" and Sino-ASEAN relations 175–93 (ASEAN as test bed to "peaceful rise" 184–90; definition of "peaceful rise" 177–84; overview 16, 175–7, 192–3; US–China mutual accommodation 191–2); petroleum diplomacy 230, 231; regional order 14–15, 76, 78, 79, 81–3, 87; RMSI (American initiative 129, 130; ASEAN+3 131, 132; Chinese initiative 135, 136, 137, 139, 140; Malaysia and Indonesia 132, 134, 135; overview 127, 128, 142); SCO 107, 113
ASEAN–China Free Trade Agreement (ACFTA) 36–8, 41, 42, 44, 45
ASEAN+1 7, 13, 28, 79, 254, 269
ASEAN+3 (APT): Hong Kong 254; liberalism and realism 36; new internationalism 14, 28, 29, 31; regional order 79, 82, 84; RMSI 128, 129, 130–2, 134, 141; Sino-ASEAN relations 186, 191; Taiwan 244
ASEAN Regional Forum (ARF): arms control 61; levels of multilateralism 272; liberalism and realism 35, 38; maritime security 15, 161, 162; new internationalism 28, 29, 30; regional order 77, 78, 80, 83, 85, 88; RMSI 128, 131, 132, 135, 139, 140; Sino-ASEAN relations 186, 190, 191

ASEAN Way: pan-regional multilateralism 272; realist internationalism 43; regional order 85, 88; Sino-ASEAN relations 177, 189, 190, 192
ASEM *see* Asian European Meetings
Asian Bond Market Initiative 36
Asian Development Bank (ADB) 27, 31, 36
Asian European Meetings (ASEM) 28, 36
Asian financial crisis: liberalism and realism 40, 45; new internationalism 28, 29; regional order 84; Sino-ASEAN relations 188, 190, 193
Asian Pacific Economic Cooperation (APEC): core-region multilateralism 269; Hong Kong 254; liberalism and realism 36, 43, 44; new internationalism 14, 23, 28; regional order 77, 80; RMSI 129, 131; Sino-ASEAN relations 191; Taiwan 246
"Asian values" 29, 186, 204, 273
ASPC *see* ARF Security Policy Conference
Association of Southeast Asian Nations *see* ASEAN
Australia: liberalism and realism 36, 41; North Korea 103; petroleum diplomacy 225, 226; regional order 79; RMSI 130
Australia Group (AG) 58, 59

Bali bombing 133
ballistic missiles 54, 63, 65
Bandung Conference 179, 253
Bangkok Declaration 186, 204
Bangladesh 132, 157, 162, 232
Baoshan Steel Mill 230
bilateralism: arms control 66; levels of multilateralism 3, 8, 13, 268, 270, 281; liberalism and realism 48; SCO 105; Taiwan 241, 242, 243, 249
biological weapons 54, 59, 63
Bishkek 80, 109, 114
Boao Forum 83, 177
Bogor resolution 28
Bongo, Omar 229
"boomerang effect" 198, 217
border disputes: core-region multilateralism 269; petroleum diplomacy 227; regional order 76, 77, 81, 83; SCO 105–7, 110, 115, 116, 119; Sino-ASEAN relations 187

Brazil 157, 229, 230
Britain *see* Great Britain
Brunei 152, 186, 231
Bull, Hedley 201, 206
Bush Administration: Hong Kong 254; maritime security 132, 133, 159; North Korea 96, 97, 98, 101; petroleum diplomacy 225, 226, 230, 236; regional order 84; unilateralism 8; US–China mutual accommodation 191
Bush Doctrine 133
Bush, George W. 101, 132, 225, 226, 236, 254
Buzan, Barry 215

CAFTA *see* China–ASEAN Free Trade Agreement
Cai Xiao-hong 262
Cambodia 26, 187, 235
Cao Gangchuan 140, 183, 234
Caporaso, James A. 242
"Carnation revolution" 256
Caspian Sea 227, 236
CBMs *see* confidence-building measures
CCP *see* Chinese Communist Party
CD *see* Conference on Disarmament
Central Military Commission (CMC) 183, 229
Charter of the United Nations 155, 164, 254
Chavez, Hugo 228
chemical weapons 54, 57, 59, 63, 164
Chemical Weapons Convention (CWC) 31, 58, 59
Chen Qichen 78
Chen Shuibian 254
Chiang Mai Initiative 36
China Arms Control and Disarmament Association (CACDA) 62
China–ASEAN Free Trade Agreement (CAFTA) 28, 31, 79, 189, 190, 272
"China collapse" theories 178, 182
China Institute of Contemporary International Relations (CICIR) 130, 135, 137
China Minmetals Corporation 236
"China threat" theories: Hong Kong 254; levels of multilateralism 270, 284–5; Sino-ASEAN relations 175, 178, 183; Taiwan 244, 248
China Youth Daily 232, 233
Chinese Association for the Study of Human Rights 200, 201

Chinese Communist Party (CCP): Hong Kong 17, 253, 255, 256–8, 259–63; human rights 200, 208, 209, 212–14, 216, 217; levels of multilateralism 273, 281, 282, 284; maritime security 165; new internationalism 33; petroleum diplomacy 222, 225, 231, 232, 234, 237; regional order 84, 86, 87, 88; Sino-ASEAN relations 180, 181, 182; Taiwan 243
Chirac, Jacques 254
CICIR *see* China Institute of Contemporary International Relations
citizenship 205, 208, 211–16, 258
"Clash of Civilizations" hypothesis 206
Clinton, Bill 28, 212
CMC *see* Central Mililtary Commission
coal 224, 235
cognitive learning 22, 32, 47, 201, 283, 287
Cold War: arms control 52, 53, 54; human rights 206; levels of multilateralism 269, 273, 286; new internationalism 21, 27; regional order 78, 86; SCO 105, 117, 118, 119; Sino-ASEAN relations 180, 181, 185, 193
common security 40, 53, 116
communism: human rights 214; levels of multilateralism 4, 10, 273, 280, 283, 284; new internationalism 23, 33; regional order 81, 86, 87; Sino-ASEAN relations 181, 185, 186, 188; *see also* Chinese Communist Party
complete verifiable and irreversible de-nuclearization (CVID) 98, 99, 101
compliance theory 200–1, 202
comprehensive security 116
Comprehensive Test Ban Treaty (CTBT) 58, 59, 60, 62, 64, 285
Conference on Disarmament (CD) 24, 56–9, 64, 65
Conference on Security and Cooperation in Europe (CSCE) 53, 54
confidence-building measures (CBMs): regional order 76, 77, 78, 80, 81, 88; RMSI 134; SCO 104, 105, 107, 116
Confucian worldview 178, 180, 216
Constitution of Oceans *see* United Nations Convention on the Law of the Sea (UNCLOS)
"constructive engagement" 176, 186
contiguous zone 147, 148, 149
continental shelf 147, 148, 149, 157
cooperative security 5, 52–5, 77–8, 88, 116, 128

core-region multilateralism 269–71
Council for Security Cooperation in the Asian Pacific (CSCAP) 28, 134
CPC (Communist Party of China) *see* Chinese Communist Party (CCP)
Cranston, Maurice 205
crime 107, 108, 110, 135, 154
crude oil 223, 224, 225, 227, 228, 229
CSCAP *see* Council for Security Cooperation in the Asian Pacific
CSCE *see* Conference on Security and Cooperation in Europe
CTBT *see* Comprehensive Test Ban Treaty
culture 115, 275, 276
currency 32, 36, 84, 188, 190, 277
CVID *see* complete verifiable and irreversible de-nuclearization
CWC *see* Chemical Weapons Convention

Dai Bingguo 96
dams 235
Darfur 229
Datuk Sri Najib Tun 133
Declaration on the Conduct of the Parties in the South China Sea (2002): liberalism and realism 35; maritime security 152, 153, 154, 155, 162; regional order 79, 82; RMSI 135, 137
Declaration on the Territorial Sea (1958) 149
democracy: Hong Kong 257, 258–9, 260, 261–2, 263; human rights 200, 207, 208, 214, 216, 217; levels of multilateralism 273, 280; Sino-ASEAN relations 186, 192; Taiwan 243, 247, 248, 249
Democratic People's Republic of Korea (DPRK) *see* North Korea
Deng Xiaoping: Hong Kong 256, 257, 258, 261; human rights 206; liberalism and realism 48; new internationalism 21, 23, 32, 33; North Korea 93; petroleum diplomacy 224, 231; regional order 80; Sino-ASEAN relations 181, 182, 185
developing countries: global multilateralism 275; new internationalism 25, 27; petroleum diplomacy 230; Taiwan 244, 245, 249
Diaoyu Islands (Senkakus) 151, 231, 234
disarmament 30, 56, 57, 59–62
domestic–foreign linkage 279–81
DPRK (Democratic People's Republic of Korea) *see* North Korea

drug trafficking: liberal internationalism 39; maritime security 154, 162; regional order 82; SCO 107, 110, 117, 119
dual-use items 57, 59, 63

East Asian Seas Program 166
East Asian Summit (EAS) 7, 29, 36, 102
East China Sea: maritime security 148, 149, 151, 160, 161, 162; North Korea 102; petroleum diplomacy 230, 231, 234
economic development and growth: Hong Kong 253; human rights 204–5, 206, 207, 208, 209; levels of multilateralism 5, 267, 272–4, 284, 288; new internationalism 22, 24, 25, 31; North Korea 95; petroleum diplomacy 224, 234, 235, 237; regional impacts and global implications 11, 12, 13; regional order 75, 80, 82, 88; Sino-ASEAN relations 16, 181, 182, 187, 188, 190; size of economy 7; Taiwan 243, 245; why multilateralism? 9, 10
Economy, Elizabeth 61
EEZ see exclusive economic zone
Egypt 228, 229
elections 248, 249, 250, 261, 262
El Salvador 228
"embedded liberalism" 212, 213
energy diplomacy 223, 224, 232, 237
energy resources: levels of multilateralism 288; North Korea 102; petroleum diplomacy 16, 222–4, 226, 234–7; regional order 80, 83, 87; RMSI 135–6; SCO 115; Sino-ASEAN relations 183
"English School" 75, 88, 201, 206
enmeshment (adaptive learning) 47, 283
enriched uranium 99, 225
environment 6, 117, 166, 181, 236
EP-3E spy plane incident 155, 158
epistemic communities 201, 282
European Union (EU): Hong Kong 255, 257; human rights 76, 209, 212; new internationalism 28, 33; petroleum diplomacy 227; regional order 12, 76; SCO 106, 113; Sino-ASEAN relations 187, 190
Evans, Mark 215
exclusive economic zone (EEZ) 102, 142, 147–9, 155–8, 161
exports 28–9, 62, 63, 181
extremism 105, 108, 112
"Eyes in the Sky" initiative 139, 141

Fargo, Admiral Thomas B. 129, 133, 134, 140, 163
FDI see foreign direct investment
fishing 152, 157, 159
Five Principles of Peaceful Co-existence 16, 78, 166–7, 179, 184, 253
Foot, Rosemary 201
foreign direct investment (FDI): new internationalism 23, 27, 28, 29; regional order 80; Sino-ASEAN relations 188, 190
foreign-exchange reserves 181, 222, 227
"Four Modernizations" 181
Four Opinions of China 165
free trade agreements (FTAs) 36–8, 42–5, 77, 79, 82, 114

Gabon 228, 229
gas: maritime security 154, 161; petroleum diplomacy (Africa and South America 229, 230; military dimension 234; overview 16, 222, 235, 236. 237; securing long-term oil supplies 225, 226, 227; sudden urgency 223; territorial disputes 230, 231); regional order 80, 87; SCO 115
GATT see General Agreement on Tariffs and Trade
GDP (gross domestic product) 22, 27, 31, 235
G8 (Group 8) 6, 7, 277
General Agreement on Tariffs and Trade (GATT): arms control 53; new internationalism 24, 26, 27; Taiwan 244, 245, 246
Germany 32, 41, 44, 175, 278
Global Environment Facility 166
globalization: human rights 208; levels of multilateralism 277, 284, 286, 288; liberalism and realism 37, 39–40, 45, 47; regional order 79; SCO 116; Sino-ASEAN relations 179, 182, 190; Taiwan 243; why multilateralism? 9, 10
global multilateralism 274–6
Global Posture Review 129
Goh Chok Tong 140, 191
Gong, Gerrit 201
"good neighbor policy" 27
Gorbachev, Mikhail 53
Great Britain 225, 254–9
Group 8 (G8) 6, 7, 277
Group of 77 23
Guam Doctrine 185
Gulf of Tonkin 151

Hainan Triangle 160
Hale, David 236
Hamzah Haz 134
Han Dongfang 26
hegemonic power: Hegemonic Stability Theory 42; Hong Kong 253; human rights 206–9, 212–15; levels of multilateralism 7, 9–10, 276–9, 285; maritime security 134, 164; regional order 81, 82, 83, 87; Sino-ASEAN relations 176, 179, 180, 191; Taiwan 244, 245, 249
Hempson-Jones, Justin 38, 39
high seas 156, 159, 160, 161
Hirschman, Albert 41, 42, 44
Hong Kong (Special Administrative Region, HKSAR) 253–63; democratization 11, 258–9, 261–2; fear of internationalization 259–61; levels of multilateralism 268, 279, 280, 288; maritime security 160, 162; new internationalism 28, 32–3; overview 17, 253–4, 262–3; Sino-ASEAN relations 182, 188; Sino-British question 255–8; sovereignty 254–5
Huang Jishu 246
Hu Jintao: Hong Kong 254, 255, 260; liberalism and realism 48; North Korea 96; petroleum diplomacy 222, 223–4, 225–7, 228–30, 234, 236–7; regional order 86; SCO 111, 114, 115, 118; Sino-ASEAN relations 178, 179, 180, 181, 191
humanitarian intervention 209–10, 214, 215
human rights 198–217; advantages of multilateralism 282, 283, 285; domestic concerns 210–11; domestic–foreign linkage 280, 281; double resistance of Chinese state 202–10; global multilateralism 6, 274, 275, 276; Hong Kong 254, 257, 263; illiberal internationalism 199; inauspicious beginnings 199–202; international society and international citizenship 211–16; maritime security 165; new internationalism 23–6, 29, 30; overview 16, 198–9, 216–17; pan-regional multilateralism 12, 273; petroleum diplomacy 236; Sino-ASEAN relations 180, 186
Human Rights Commission 24, 25, 201, 204, 207, 212, 214
Human Rights Watch 229
Huntington, Samuel 206

hydroelectric power 224, 235

IAEA *see* International Atomic Energy Agency
ICCPR *see* International Covenant on Civil and Political Rights
ICESCR *see* International Covenant on Economic, Social and Cultural Rights
IGOs *see* intergovernmental organizations (IGOs)
Ikenberry, John 40
illiberal internationalism 199, 214
ILO *see* International Labour Organization
image of China: arms control 60, 61, 64, 65, 66; levels of multilateralism 275, 276, 279, 285; Sino-ASEAN relations 181, 183; why multilateralism? 10–11
IMB *see* International Maritime Bureau
IMF *see* International Monetary Fund
IMO *see* International Maritime Organization
imports 27, 223, 225, 228, 245
income 24, 181, 245
India: arms control 65; levels of multilateralism 269, 276; liberalism and realism 36; maritime security 131, 132, 140, 157, 162, 167; new internationalism 31; North Korea 103; petroleum diplomacy 16, 223, 230; regional order 79, 81, 85; SCO 113; Sino-ASEAN relations 187, 190
Indonesia: maritime security 159, 163, 164; North Korea 103; petroleum diplomacy 226, 232, 233; RMSI 128, 131–6, 140, 141; Sino-ASEAN relations 185, 186
Indonesia–United States Security Dialogue (IUSSD) 141
INGOs *see* nongovernmental international organizations
institutionalized cooperation 40, 42, 43, 44, 47, 48
instrumental learning 22, 32, 201, 283
intellectual property rights 6, 27, 31
intergovernmental organizations (IGOs): levels of multilateralism 280, 286; new internationalism 14, 21, 23, 29, 31–4
International Atomic Energy Agency (IAEA) 24, 57, 58, 59
"international citizenship" 211–16
International Conference of Women's Rights 206
International Covenant on Civil and Political Rights (ICCPR) 24, 210, 212

International Covenant on Economic, Social and Cultural Rights (ICESCR) 24, 210, 212
International Labour Organization (ILO) 11, 26
international law: human rights 203, 214; maritime security 147, 155–8, 160–1, 165, 166
International Maritime Bureau (IMB) 159, 163
International Maritime Organization (IMO): maritime security 158, 160, 166; RMSI 130, 138, 139, 141, 142
International Monetary Fund (IMF): liberalism and realism 36; new internationalism 24, 29, 31; regional order 84; Sino-ASEAN relations 188; Taiwan 243
international organizations (IOs): arms control 56; Hong Kong 257, 262, 263; levels of multilateralism 280, 284; multilateralism and multipolarism 5–6, 7, 8; new internationalism 21, 22; regional impacts and global implications 12, 13; SCO 113; Taiwan 241, 246, 247, 249, 250; why multilateralism? 9, 11
international relations (IR) 175, 203, 242
"international society": human rights 206, 207, 209, 210, 211–16; levels of multilateralism 286, 288
investment: arms control 56; Hong Kong 253; new internationalism 25; pan-regional multilateralism 273; petroleum diplomacy 222, 227; Sino-ASEAN relations 176, 188, 190; Taiwan 247
IOs *see* international organizations
Iran 31, 66, 113, 157, 164, 225
Iraq: human rights 215; maritime security 132; North Korea 96, 97, 100; petroleum diplomacy 224, 225, 226; regional order 84
iron 224, 229, 230
Islamic fundamentalism/terrorism 107, 108, 132, 133, 134
Israel 224
IUSSD *see* Indonesia–United States Security Dialogue

Jakarta Statement 139
Japan: arms control 65; Hong Kong 257; levels of multilateralism 6, 271, 276–8, 285; maritime security 151, 162, 163; new internationalism 28, 31, 32, 33;

North Korea 91, 94, 96, 98, 100, 102, 103; petroleum diplomacy 16, 223, 226, 230–1, 234, 236, 237; regional order 13, 75, 79, 82, 84, 85, 86–7; RMSI 15, 127–32, 134, 135, 137, 140–2; Sino-ASEAN relations 175, 188, 189, 190
Jemaah Islamiyah (JI) 132, 133, 134
Jiang Zemin: Hong Kong 259; human rights 200, 207, 212; liberalism and realism 48; new internationalism 24, 28; petroleum diplomacy 223, 226, 228; regional order 78, 79; SCO 106, 109, 111, 117, 120; Sino-ASEAN relations 181
Johnston, A. I. 31, 33, 60

Kant, Immanuel 205
Kazakhstan: new internationalism 30; petroleum diplomacy 226, 227; regional order 76, 80; SCO 104, 107, 110, 114
Kent, Anne 201
Keohane, Robert O. 242
Khin Nyunt 233
Kim Jong-il 96
Kim, Samuel 24, 25, 285
Koh, Tommy 137
Koizumi, Junichiro 130, 131
Korea *see* North Korea; South Korea
Kosovo 25, 254
Kra Isthmus 233
Kuala Lumpur Statement 141
Kyrgyzstan: new internationalism 30; petroleum diplomacy 227; regional order 76, 80; SCO 104, 107, 108, 109

labour standards 11, 26
Lardy, Nicholas R. 245
Latin America 187, 227, 228, 229–30, 236
Lau, Emily 261, 262
law: arms control 63; human rights 202–3, 205, 207, 209–10, 214, 216–17; levels of multilateralism 281; maritime security 147–50, 155–8, 160–1, 165–7; new internationalism 25, 27; petroleum diplomacy 236; Taiwan 243
Law of the Sea (UNCLOS) *see* United Nations Convention on the Law of the Sea
Leading Group on Foreign Affairs (LGFA) 223–4, 225, 226, 234
learning: arms control 67; human rights 201, 202; levels of multilateralism 281–2, 283, 286; liberalism and realism 47–8; new internationalism 22, 23, 32

Lebanon 26, 66
Lee Chu Ming, Martin 260, 262
Lee Hsien Loong 85, 233
Lee Kuan Yew 85
Legco elections 259, 261, 262
Leninism 33, 216
LGFA *see* Leading Group on Foreign Affairs
liberal internationalism 37, 38–41, 213
liberalism: levels of multilateralism 268; liberalist and realist interpretations 36, 47, 48; new internationalism 21, 22, 31, 33
Li Buyun 210–11
Limburg tanker attack 159
Lin Hong 246
Li Peng 24, 28, 201, 246
Li Qiang 243
Li Zhaoxing 36, 139, 225
loans 24, 27, 31, 114, 243
LOS Convention *see* United Nations Convention on the Law of the Sea (UNCLOS)
Lu Guoxue 232
Lu Shilun 211

Macau 255, 256
Macclesfield Bank 151
MacLehose, Sir Murray 256
Malacca Straits: levels of multilateralism 277, 286; maritime security 163, 164; petroleum diplomacy 232–4; RMSI (American initiative 129; ASEAN+3 131, 132; Chinese initiative 136–42; Malaysia and Indonesia 133, 134, 135; overview 15, 127, 128, 142, 143)
Malaysia: levels of multilateralism 277; maritime security 152, 157, 163; new internationalism 29; petroleum diplomacy 231, 233; RMSI (ASEAN+3 131; Chinese initiative 136, 138–42; Malaysia and Indonesia 132–5; overview 127, 128); Sino-ASEAN relations 185
MALSINDO 135, 141, 164
Manila Declaration 30
Mao Zedong: Hong Kong 256, 263; human rights 216; levels of multilateralism 272; new internationalism 24, 33; petroleum diplomacy 228; Sino-ASEAN relations 180–1, 185
Maritime Domain Awareness (MDA) 138
maritime security 147–67; China's response to RMSI 163–5; levels of multilateralism 277, 286; military activities in the EEZ 155–8; North Korea 102; overview 13, 15–16, 147–51, 165–7; piracy and maritime terrorism 158–63; Sino-ASEAN relations 187; South China Sea dispute 151–5; *see also* Regional Maritime Security Initiative
Martin, Lisa L. 242
Marxism 33, 200, 211, 216, 228
MDA *see* Maritime Domain Awareness
Middle East: petroleum diplomacy 224–6, 232, 233, 236; Sino-ASEAN relations 182, 183
military activities: arms control 53, 62, 64; human rights 215; maritime security 132, 133, 134, 155–8; multilateralism and multipolarism 8, 10; new internationalism 29; North Korea 93, 94, 95, 96, 98; petroleum diplomacy 234–5; SCO 107, 108, 109–10, 116, 120
military strikes: human rights 215; North Korea 93, 94, 95, 96; RMSI 133, 134
Milky Way (yinhe) freighter 164, 165
Mischief Reef 30, 78, 152
missiles: arms control 54, 58, 59, 63, 65; new internationalism 31; North Korea 103
Missile Technology Control Regime (MTCR) 31, 58, 59
Mohammed, Mahathir 79
Mongolia 31, 113
Monroe Doctrine 175, 230
Mori, Yoshiro 130, 131
MTCR *see* Missile Technology Control Regime
multilateral diplomacy: arms control 55–8, 60, 61, 65; human rights 215; levels of multilateralism 270, 282, 283; SCO 104; Taiwan 244
multilateralism: arms control 52–4, 55–60, 61–7; Hong Kong 253, 254, 255, 258, 262, 263; human rights 199, 212–13, 214, 215; levels of multilateralism 267–88 (advantages of multilateralism 281–7; core-region multilateralism 269–71; domestic–foreign linkage 279–81; global multilateralism 274–6; overview 267–8, 287–8; pan-regional multilateralism 271–4; power interactive multilateralism 276–9); liberalism and realism 35–48 (globalization and regionalism 45–7; is China learning?

47–8; liberal internationalism 38–41; overview 35–7, 48; realist internationalism 41–5); North Korea 101–3; overview (multilateral diplomacy 3–5; multilateralism and multipolarism 5–8; regional impacts and global implications 11–13; structure of book 14–17; why multilateralism? 9–11); regional order 75–88 (China's contribution 80–4; China's new multilateralism 76–80; limitations 84–7; overview 75–6, 87–8); SCO 105, 106, 117, 119, 120; Sino-ASEAN relations 189; Taiwan 241, 242, 243–4, 247–8, 249

multipolarism: definitions 7, 8; human rights 215; liberal internationalism 41; petroleum diplomacy 228, 230; power interactive multilateralism 277; SCO 116; Taiwan 243; why multilateralism? 9, 10

Muni, S. D. 189

Muslims 83, 107, 108, 132, 133–4

Myanmar: maritime security 135, 164; petroleum diplomacy 16, 223, 232, 233, 234; regional order 84; Sino-ASEAN relations 186, 187

Nakagawa, Shoichi 231

NAM *see* Non-Aligned Movement

Narine, Shaun 187

national interests: levels of multilateralism 282, 283, 284, 285; North Korea 91, 92, 93

nationalism: human rights 217; levels of multilateralism 284; North Korea 99; petroleum diplomacy 231; regional order 86; Sino-ASEAN relations 176, 179, 182

National People's Congress (NPC) 24, 244, 261, 262

NATO (North Atlantic Treaty Organization) 28, 118

Nazarbayev, Nursultan 111, 114

negative security assurance (NSE) 64

neoliberal institutionalism 22, 39

"new diplomacy" 4, 8, 13, 67

new internationalism 21–34; China and the UN 24–7; overview 21–3, 32–4; regional organizations 27–31

"new security concept" (NSC): levels of multilateralism 270, 283; maritime security 128, 161; regional order 78; SCO 116–17, 119; Taiwan 248, 250

"New Three Principles of People" 181

New Zealand 36, 41, 79, 103

Nixon, Richard 185

Non-Aligned Movement (NAM) 23, 61

nongovernmental international organizations (INGOs) 21, 56, 83

nonproliferation: arms control (cooperative security 54; disarmament 57, 58; logic of policies 60, 61, 62; overview 51, 66, 67); global multilateralism 275; new internationalism 24, 31

Non-Proliferation Treaty (NPT) 24, 31, 58, 59, 61

Noranda 236

normative learning 200, 201, 202, 282, 283, 285

North Korea (Democratic People's Republic of Korea, DPRK): arms control 60, 65, 66; core-region multilateralism 270, 271; maritime security 130; new internationalism 31, 33; nuclear problem 90–103 (aftermath of talks 97–9; background 91–3; diplomatic initiative 95–7; dynamic situation 93–5; future predictions 100–1; limitations on China 99–100; overview 15, 90–1; security multilateralism 101–3); petroleum diplomacy 223; regional order 4, 13, 84; Sino-ASEAN relations 192

NPC *see* National People's Congress

NPT *see* Non-Proliferation Treaty

NSC *see* "new security concept"

nuclear power 224, 225

Nuclear Suppliers Group (NSG) 58, 59

nuclear-weapon-free-zones (NWFZs) 57, 61

nuclear weapons: arms control (cooperative security 52, 54; logic of policies 60, 61, 63, 64, 65; multilateral arms control 56, 57, 58, 59, 60; overview 66); levels of multilateralism 270, 275; new internationalism 25, 31; North Korea 90–103 (aftermath of talks 97–9; background 91–3; diplomatic initiative 95–7; dynamic situation 93–5; future predictions 100–1; limitations on China 99–100; overview 13, 15, 31, 60, 90–1; security multilateralism 101–3); petroleum diplomacy 223; Sino-ASEAN relations 192

nuclear weapons states (NWS) 56, 60, 61, 64

NWFZs *see* nuclear-weapon-free-zones

298 Index

Nye, Joseph 40, 183

oil: maritime security 154, 161, 164; petroleum diplomacy 222–37 (Africa and South America 227–30; Malacca Straits 232–4; military dimension 234–5; overview 16, 222–3, 235–7; securing long-term oil supplies 224–7; sudden urgency 223–4; territorial disputes 230–2); regional order 80, 87; RMSI 128, 135, 136, 138; SCO 115; Sino-ASEAN relations 183
Operation MALSINDO 135, 141, 164
Opium War 55
order 75–6, 187, 188
OSCE (Organization for Security and Co-operation in Europe) 54, 113
Outer Mongolia 31, 113

Pacific Command (PACOM) 129, 140
Pakistan 31, 41, 113, 119, 157, 232
Palestine 224
pan-regional multilateralism 271–4
Paracel Islands 30, 152, 253
PAROS (Prevention of an Arms Race in Outer Space) 58–9
Partial Test Ban Treaty (PTBT) 54, 56
patrimonialism 214, 216, 217, 281
peace: human rights 203, 207; North Korea 92, 93, 100; SCO 118
peaceful nuclear explosions (PNEs) 64, 65
"peaceful rise": human rights 198–217 (domestic concerns 210–11; double resistance of Chinese state 202–10; illiberal internationalism 199; inauspicious beginnings 199–202; international society and international citizenship 211–16; overview 198–9, 216–17); new internationalism 32; petroleum diplomacy 235, 236; Sino-ASEAN relations 175–93 (ASEAN as test bed to "peaceful rise" 184–90; definition 177–84; overview 16, 175–7, 192–3; US–China mutual accommodation 191–2); Taiwan 248, 250
peacekeeping operations (PKOs) 26, 39, 66, 82, 157, 258
Pearl River Delta 235
Pearson, Margaret M. 246
People's Liberation Army see PLA
People's Republic of China (PRC): arms control 56; Hong Kong 253–9, 262; human rights 215; levels of multilateralism 280; maritime security 166; multilateral diplomacy 3, 4; new internationalism 21, 26, 27, 33; petroleum diplomacy 222–4, 226, 228, 236, 237; Sino-ASEAN relations 185; Taiwan 241, 246
Petrobras 229
petroleum diplomacy 222–37; Africa and South America 227–30; Malacca Straits 232–4; military dimension 234–5; overview 222–3, 235–7; securing long-term oil supplies 224–7; sudden urgency 223–4; territorial disputes 230–2
Philippines: maritime security 151, 152, 153, 154, 155, 162; petroleum diplomacy 231, 232; RMSI 129, 131; Sino-ASEAN relations 185
pipelines: maritime security 135, 164; petroleum diplomacy 226, 227, 230, 232, 233; regional order 80; SCO 115
piracy: maritime security 154, 158–63; RMSI 129–32, 135, 137, 138, 142
PKOs see peacekeeping operations
PLA (People's Liberation Army) 62, 64–5, 110, 229, 231, 234
PNEs see peaceful nuclear explosions
politics 12, 273–4, 279–81
population 177, 178
Potter, Pitman 216
Powell, Colin 81, 191, 236
power 8, 178, 274
power interactive multilateralism 276–9
Pratas Islands 151
PRC see People's Republic of China
pre-emptive strikes 133, 134, 215
preventive diplomacy 77, 78, 85, 88, 272
Proliferation Security Initiative (PSI): maritime security 163; North Korea 96; RMSI 129–30, 132, 134–5, 139–40, 142
PTBT see Partial Test Ban Treaty
Putin, Vladimir 112, 226, 227
Pye, Lucian 181, 184, 274

Qian Qichen 30
qualitative multilateralism 52, 56, 66, 67, 287

RATS see Regional Anti-Terrorism Structure
realism: arms control 54; levels of multilateralism 268, 287, 288; liberalist and realist interpretations 37, 38, 39, 41–5, 47–8; new internationalism 21–2, 31; "peaceful rise" 178; SCO 118

ReCAAP *see* Regional Cooperation Agreement on Combating Piracy and Armed Robbery Against Ships in Asia
regime change 97, 100, 214
regime theory 200, 282
Regional Anti-Terrorism Structure (RATS) 111, 112
Regional Cooperation Agreement on Combating Piracy and Armed Robbery Against Ships in Asia (ReCAAP) 131, 132, 138, 141
Regional Maritime Security Initiative (RMSI) 127–42; American initiative 128–30; ASEAN+3 130–2; Chinese initiative 135–42; Malaysia and Indonesia 132–5; China's response 163–5; overview 15, 127–8, 142–3
regional multilateralism: globalization and regionalism 45–7, 48; levels of multilateralism 278, 279, 287; multilateralism and multipolarism 7; regional impacts and global implications 11–12, 13
regional order 75–88; China's contribution 80–4; China's new multilateralism 76–80; limitations and problems 84–7; new internationalism 27–31, 32; overview 75–6, 87–8; Sino-ASEAN relations 187, 191, 192
Regional Seas Program 166
regional security 8, 9, 11, 13, 14, 101–3
Renwei Huang 244
Republic of China (ROC) *see* Taiwan
Republic of Korea (ROK) *see* South Korea
resources: human rights 208; levels of multilateralism 288; maritime security 148, 149; water 223, 235; *see also* energy resources
Rice, Condoleeza 139
rights *see* human rights
Risse, Thomas 198, 217
RMSI *see* Regional Maritime Security Initiative
Robinson, Mary 212
ROC (Republic of China) *see* Taiwan
ROK (Republic of Korea) *see* South Korea
Roosevelt, Franklin 213
Ruggie, John Gerard 52, 242
rule of law: human rights 202, 207, 209, 210, 214, 217; levels of multilateralism 281; maritime security 165, 167; petroleum diplomacy 236; Taiwan 243
Rumsfeld, Donald 129
Russia: arms control 54, 58; levels of multilateralism 6, 270, 271, 276; maritime security 133; new internationalism 30, 31; petroleum diplomacy 226, 227; regional order 76, 81, 83; SCO 104–8, 110, 112, 114; Sino-ASEAN relations 180, 187, 190

sanctions 25, 33, 186, 245, 275
SAR *see* Hong Kong
SARS (Severe Acute Respiratory Syndrome) 40, 257–8
Scarborough Shoal (Reef) 30, 151
Scheweller, Randell 191
Schriver, Randall 257
SCO *see* Shanghai Cooperation Organization
security: arms control (cooperative security 52–5; logic of policies 60, 61, 62, 65; multilateral arms control 56, 57, 58; overview 66, 67); human rights 213, 215; levels of multilateralism (advantages of multilateralism 282, 283, 285, 286; core-region multilateralism 269–71; domestic–foreign linkage 280; global multilateralism 275; overview 267, 287, 288); pan-regional multilateralism 272, 273); liberalism and realism 35, 37, 38, 44; multilateral diplomacy 4, 5; multilateralism and multipolarism 6, 8; new internationalism 22, 29, 31, 32; North Korea 90, 98, 101–3; regional impacts and global implications 13; regional order 82, 83; RMSI 130, 131; SCO 106, 107–10, 113, 115–18, 119; Sino-ASEAN relations 187, 188; structure of book 14, 15; Taiwan 241, 242; why multilateralism? 9, 11; *see also* maritime security
Security Council *see* UN Security Council (UNSC)
Senkaku (Diaoyu) Islands 151, 231, 234
separatism: regional order 82, 83; RMSI 133, 134; SCO 105, 106, 108, 112; Sino-ASEAN relations 182, 183
September 11 *see* 9/11 terrorist attacks
Severino, Rodolfo 189
Shambaugh, David 37, 39
Shanghai Communiqué 185
Shanghai Cooperation Organization (SCO) 104–20; arms control 61; building normative international order 115–18; expansion of security mandate 107–10; functionalism upside down 104–7; institutionalizing "Shanghai Five"

300 Index

Shanghai Cooperation Organization – *contd.*
110–13; levels of multilateralism (advantages of multilateralism 282, 285; core-region multilateralism 269, 270, 271; overview 7, 13, 15, 287; pan-regional multilateralism 272, 273; power interactive multilateralism 278); liberalism and realism 36, 38, 41, 43, 46–7; new internationalism 30–1; overview 104, 119–20; petroleum diplomacy 227; regional order 79–80, 82, 83; Taiwan 244; two-track strategy 113–15

Shanghai Five: levels of multilateralism 272, 278, 282; regional order 77, 79, 82; SCO (building normative international order 116, 117; expansion of security mandate 107, 108, 109; functionalism upside down 105, 106; institutionalizing 110–13; overview 119, 120; two-track strategy 113)

"Shanghai Spirit" 43, 117, 118, 119, 270

Shangri-La Dialogue 133, 137, 138, 139

Sha Zukang 59, 64

Shen Jiru 223

Shi Hongtao 233, 234

Shinawatra, Thaksin 233

Sikkink, Kathryn 198, 217

Simon, Sheldon 35

Singapore: maritime security 163, 164; new internationalism 29; North Korea 103; petroleum diplomacy 233; regional order 79, 85; RMSI (American initiative 129; ASEAN+3 131; Chinese initiative 138, 139, 140, 141; Malaysia and Indonesia 132, 134, 135; overview 128); Sino-ASEAN relations 186

Sino-British Joint Declaration (1984) 255, 256, 262

Sinopec 225, 229

Six-Party Talks: arms control 60, 66; levels of multilateralism 270–2, 279, 285, 287; new internationalism 30, 31; North Korea 13, 15, 92, 94–9, 101–3; Sino-ASEAN relations 191; Taiwan 241, 244

SLOCs (sea lines of communication) 128, 130, 135, 136, 138, 140

Smith, Gary J. 247

smuggling 60, 110, 162

socialism 179, 185, 200, 205

"soft power": arms control 67; human rights 212, 213, 215; levels of multilateralism 270, 279, 285–7; liberalism and realism 44; Sino-ASEAN relations 180, 183

SOMI *see* Strait of Malacca imbroglio

South Africa 229

South America *see* Latin America

South China Sea: levels of multilateralism 4, 13, 272, 277, 286; maritime security (China's response to RMSI 164; overview 15–16, 148, 151, 165; piracy and maritime terrorism 159, 160, 161, 162; territorial dispute 151–5); new internationalism 30; North Korea 102; petroleum diplomacy 231–2, 234; regional order 78, 79, 81, 85; Sino-ASEAN relations 187

Southeast Asia 12, 184–5, 189, 253, 271, 272, 283

South Korea (Republic of Korea, ROK): liberalism and realism 36, 41, 46; maritime security 162, 163; new internationalism 28, 31; North Korea 90, 91, 96, 97, 100–3; petroleum diplomacy 237; regional order 79, 82; RMSI 130, 131, 142

sovereignty: arms control 55; Hong Kong 254–6, 258, 259, 261–3; human rights (domestic concerns 211; double resistance of Chinese state 202–4, 206–9; international society and international citizenship 212–16); overview 16, 216); levels of multilateralism 268, 269, 279, 280–1; maritime security 134, 147, 148, 152, 163, 166, 167; petroleum diplomacy 222, 231, 232, 236; realist internationalism 43; regional order 76, 84, 85; Taiwan 247

Soviet Union: arms control 52, 54, 56, 57, 64; levels of multilateralism 10, 271; new internationalism 30, 31; regional order 76, 77; SCO 105, 107, 119; Sino-ASEAN relations 185, 186, 192

space weapons 57, 58, 59

Spratly Islands: Hong Kong 253; maritime security 151, 152, 166; new internationalism 30; petroleum diplomacy 231, 232, 234; regional order 78, 85

spying 155, 158, 262

Sri Lanka 132, 162

state sovereignty: human rights 202–8, 210, 211, 216; levels of multilateralism 280–1

steel 183, 235, 246

Strait of Malacca imbroglio (SOMI) 232, 233; *see also* Malacca Straits
SUA Convention (Convention on the Suppression of Unlawful Acts against the Safety of Maritime Navigation) 160, 161, 162
SUA Protocol (Protocol for the Suppression of Unlawful Acts against the Safety of Fixed Platforms Located on the Continental Shelf) 161
Sudan 16, 223, 228, 229
superpowers: arms control 53, 54, 56, 57, 60, 64, 65; human rights 214; levels of multilateralism 274, 275, 277, 278, 287, 288; petroleum diplomacy 236; Sino-ASEAN relations 191
"symbolism" (Pye) 181, 274, 275, 276

TAC *see* Treaty of Amity and Cooperation
Taiwan (Republic of China, ROC) 241–50; China joins WTO 244–5; essence of multilateralism 242; Hong Kong 254, 259, 261; implications of multilateralism 247–8; levels of multilateralism 268, 279, 280, 286, 288; maritime security 149, 151–3, 155, 164; multilateral diplomacy 4, 13; multilateral organizations 243–4; new internationalism 21, 27, 28, 30, 32, 33; North Korea 91, 94, 98, 100; overview 16–17, 241–2, 249–50; petroleum diplomacy 228, 233; realist internationalism 43; regional order 78, 84, 85–6; Sino-ASEAN relations 175–6, 182, 183, 188, 190, 192, 193; WTO and onward 246–7
Tajikistan: new internationalism 31; petroleum diplomacy 227; regional order 76; SCO 104, 107, 108, 110, 119
Tang Jiaxuan 81, 109, 260
Tan Zhuzhou 227
tariffs 27, 28, 31, 245
Tashkent summit 112, 113, 114
territorial disputes: human rights 209; levels of multilateralism 13, 272; maritime security 135, 147, 148, 149, 160; new internationalism 30; North Korea 102; petroleum diplomacy 230–2, 234, 236; regional order 76–8; SCO 106
territorial sea 135, 147, 148, 149, 160
terrorism: human rights 215; liberal internationalism 39, 40; maritime security 147, 158–63; new internationalism 31; North Korea 100;

petroleum diplomacy 225, 232, 236; regional order 80, 82, 83, 84; RMSI (American initiative 129, 130; ASEAN+3 131; Chinese initiative 135–9; Malaysia and Indonesia 132, 133, 134; overview 128, 142); SCO 105, 106, 108–9, 110–12, 117, 119, 120; Sino-ASEAN relations 182; *see also* 9/11 terrorist attacks
Thailand: new internationalism 29; petroleum diplomacy 223, 232, 233, 234, 235; RMSI 129, 131, 134; Sino-ASEAN relations 185, 188
Three-Party Talks 96, 99
Three Worldism 181, 184
Thucydides 175
Tiananmen crackdown (1989): Hong Kong 258, 262; human rights 199, 200; levels of multilateralism 273, 283; new internationalism 23, 25, 26, 29; regional order 80; Sino-ASEAN relations 176, 181, 186, 189, 192; Taiwan 245
Tiaoyu Islands *see* Diaoyu Islands (Senkakus)
Tibet 30, 167
"Tokyo Appeal" 162
trade: arms control 56, 62; human rights 213; levels of multilateralism 273, 281; liberalism and realism 36, 42, 43, 44; new internationalism 22–3, 27, 28, 29; petroleum diplomacy 232; regional order 81; SCO 113, 114, 115; Sino-ASEAN relations 176, 184–5, 188, 189, 190; Taiwan 241, 244, 245, 247
trafficking *see* drug trafficking
Treaty of Amity and Cooperation (TAC): liberalism and realism 35, 42; new internationalism 30; petroleum diplomacy 231; regional order 79, 82; RMSI 131–2, 137
Tung Chee-hwa 259

UN *see* United Nations
UNCLOS *see* United Nations Convention on the Law of the Sea
UN Covenant on Civil and Political Rights (UNCCPR) 212
UN Covenant on Economic and Social and Cultural Rights (UNESCR) 212
unemployment 27, 237
Unequal Treaties 256
unilateralism: human rights 214; levels of multilateralism 3, 8, 10, 13, 268, 281, 285–7; liberalism and realism 43;

unilateralism – *contd.*
  petroleum diplomacy 230; Taiwan 242, 244, 249
unipolarity 7, 46, 116
United Front: Hong Kong 253, 260, 262, 263; levels of multilateralism 282; Sino-ASEAN relations 180, 184
United Nations (UN): arms control 56, 57, 58, 61, 65; Hong Kong 253, 254, 255, 258; human rights 16, 201, 204–7, 212, 214; levels of multilateralism 6, 274–6, 278, 285; maritime security 151, 155, 157, 159, 160, 164, 165; new internationalism 14, 21, 23, 24–7; petroleum diplomacy 228, 229; regional order 82; RMSI 130, 138; SCO 113
United Nations Convention on the Law of the Sea (UNCLOS, LOS Convention): maritime security (military activities in the EEZ 155–8; overview 147–9, 165, 166; piracy and maritime terrorism 159–61; South China Sea dispute 151, 153); new internationalism 24, 30; RMSI 135–9, 141, 143
United States (US): arms control 52, 54, 56–8, 60, 64, 65; Hong Kong 257, 258; human rights 204, 207, 212–15; levels of multilateralism (advantages of multilateralism 285, 286; core-region multilateralism 270, 271; global multilateralism 274, 275; overview 3, 13, 267, 287, 288; pan-regional multilateralism 271; power interactive multilateralism 276, 277, 278, 279); liberalism and realism 35, 43, 44, 46; maritime security 156–8, 163–5; multilateralism and multipolarism 7, 8; new internationalism 21, 25, 31, 32, 33; North Korea 15, 90, 91, 93–9, 100–3; petroleum diplomacy 224–8, 230, 232–4, 236; regional order 75, 78, 79, 81–6, 88; RMSI (American initiative 128–30; ASEAN+3 132; Chinese initiative 136, 138, 140, 141, 142; Malaysia and Indonesia 132, 133, 134, 135; overview 127, 128, 142); SCO 108, 109, 115, 116, 118, 119; Sino-ASEAN relations 16, 175–6, 179–80, 182–3, 185–6, 189–93; Taiwan 243, 244, 245, 248; why multilateralism? 10
United States–Hong Kong Policy Act 257
Universal Declaration on Human Rights 16, 204, 205

UN Security Council (UNSC): arms control 56; levels of multilateralism 275; multilateralism and multipolarism 6, 7; new internationalism 21, 24, 25; petroleum diplomacy 225, 230; Sino-ASEAN relations 190
uranium 99, 225, 235
US *see* United States
US–Japan Defense Treaty 128, 132
USSR *see* Soviet Union
Uzbekistan 31, 83, 105, 108, 119, 227

Venezuela 16, 223, 228, 229
veto power 6, 25, 118
Vienna Declaration 206, 207
Vienna International Conference on Human Rights 204, 206
Vietnam: maritime security 129, 151, 152, 154, 155; new internationalism 30; petroleum diplomacy 223, 231, 235; Sino-ASEAN relations 185, 187

Wallerstein, Immanuel 198–9
Wang Yi 243
Wang Zhongchun 136, 137
war: Hong Kong 258; new internationalism 22, 32, 33; North Korea 91, 92, 93, 96, 100; realist internationalism 42; regional order 84, 86; Sino-ASEAN relations 176; Taiwan 247
war on terror (WOT): regional order 84; RMSI 129, 132, 133, 134; SCO 108, 109; Sino-ASEAN relations 191
Wassenaar Arrangement (WA) 58, 59
water resources 223, 235
WBG *see* World Bank Group
weapons: maritime security 164; petroleum diplomacy 227, 229, 234; SCO 110, 117
weapons of mass destruction (WMD) 54, 55, 60, 130, 225
Wen Jiabao: Hong Kong 254, 255; liberalism and realism 48; petroleum diplomacy 222, 223, 227, 228, 233, 236, 237; RMSI 131; SCO 114; Sino-ASEAN relations 178, 179, 180, 181
Westphalia international order 118, 212, 215, 255, 279
Wilson, Woodrow 175, 213
WMD *see* weapons of mass destruction
women's rights 206
World Bank Group (WBG) 24, 31, 36, 243
World Maritime Day 127

World Trade Organization (WTO): arms control 53; human rights 214; levels of multilateralism 274, 278; liberalism and realism 36, 39, 43, 44, 45, 46; new internationalism 14, 24, 26, 27, 31, 32; regional order 76, 78–9; Sino-ASEAN relations 186; Taiwan 17, 241, 244–7, 249
WOT *see* war on terror
WTO *see* World Trade Organization
Wu Bangguo 228

Xinbo Wu 243
Xisha Islands 149
Xu Jian 209

Yasukuni shrine 32
Yellow Sea 148, 151
Yeltsin, Boris 226

Yukos 226
Yunnan province 232, 233

Zanganeh, Bijan 225
Zangger Committee 58, 59
Zeng Qinghong 228, 260
Zhang Deguang 112, 118
Zhang Wenmu 208
Zhao Ziyang 186
Zheng Bijian 177, 178, 208, 209
Zheng He 127, 142, 159
Zhou Enlai 179
Zhu Feng 214
Zhu Muzhi 200
Zhu Rongji 48, 79, 111, 130, 131
Zhu Yucheng 261
Zoellick, Robert 140
Zou Yunhua 64

Lightning Source UK Ltd.
Milton Keynes UK
UKOW030610200911

178951UK00003B/73/P

9 780415 666466